Mental Institutions in America: Social Policy to 1875

MENTAL
INSTITUTIONS

THE FREE PRESS
New York
COLLIER MACMILLAN PUBLISHERS
London

IN AMERICA

Social Policy to 1875

Gerald N. Grob

The Free Press
A Division of Macmillan Publishing Co., Inc.
866 Third Avenue, New York, New York 10022

Collier-Macmillan Canada Ltd.

Library of Congress Catalog Card Number: 72–92868

        printing number
1 2 3 4 5 6 7 8 9 10

For
GEORGE A. BILLIAS

Contents

List of Illustrations

Preface

Nearly a decade and a half ago I became interested in the manner in which American society viewed the problems associated with mental illness and the ways in which it provided for mentally ill persons, particularly those without the financial resources to care for themselves. The initial result was the publication of several studies dealing with the growth of the mental hospital and the evolution of public policy toward mental illness in the Commonwealth of Massachusetts, the state that pioneered in providing facilities for the insane in the United States during the nineteenth century.

While engaged in an intensive analysis of a single state, I began to wonder if Massachusetts was a "typical" example. Subsequently, I decided to extend the scope of my inquiry to the national level. In this volume (the first of two), I have attempted to analyze how American society responded to the complex problems arising out of mental illness before 1875. All societies, after all, have had to confront sickness, disease, and dependency, and all have developed their own ways of dealing with these phenomena. In American society the mental hospital became the characteristic institution that was charged with the responsibility of providing care and treatment for individuals seemingly incapable of caring for themselves during protracted periods of incapacitation. The services rendered by the hospital were of benefit not merely to the afflicted individual but to the community as well. Moreover, such an institution embodied a series of moral imperatives by providing humane and scientific treatment of disabled individuals, many of whose families were unable to care for them at home or to pay the high costs of private institutional care.

Yet the mental hospital has always been more than simply an

institution that offered care and treatment for the sick and disabled. Its structure and functions have usually been linked with a variety of external economic, political, social, and intellectual forces, if only because the way in which a society handled problems of disease and dependency was partly governed by its social structure and values. The definition of disease, the criteria for institutionalization, the financial and administrative structures governing hospitals, the nature of the decision-making process, differential care and treatment of various socio-economic groups—all were issues that transcended strictly medical and scientific considerations. In this work, therefore, I have attempted to interpret the mental hospital as a social as well as a medical institution and to illuminate the evolution of social policy toward dependent groups such as the mentally ill. In a certain sense, then, this study falls somewhere between traditional medical history and contemporary social history.

One of the major problems encountered during the research and writing was the sheer magnitude and wealth of source material. It quickly became clear that it would be virtually impossible to provide a detailed history of developments in individual states or to trace the evolution of individual hospitals. Consequently, I decided to write an analytical and interpretive history. Many of my data, therefore, simply represent illustrative case studies and in no sense are comprehensive in scope. For a detailed listing of the sources upon which this work is based, the reader can consult the extensive bibliography at the end. I hope too that my study will contribute to the growing body of scholarship concerned with the history of social welfare in America—a subject that has just barely been touched.

One word about my basic approach and my underlying assumptions about the nature of history and the role of the historian. I have deliberately refrained from writing didactic history, partly because didactic history is primarily a commentary upon the present and often results in a distortion of the past, and partly because I am not at all certain that I am necessarily wiser and more knowledgeable than earlier generations of individuals whose achievements fell far short of their hopes and aspirations. Nor am I able to subscribe to the prevailing conventional wisdom that argues that Americans have traditionally penalized poor and dependent groups by imposing a welfare system whose basic objectives were to ensure social stability and control the behavior of lower-class groups and ethnic and racial minorities. Such arguments are invariably based upon an oversimplified and emotional view of the subtle ways in which complex social processes operate. What I have attempted instead is to study and understand the past on its own terms and avoid the imposition of a presentist framework upon the subject. I have therefore emphasized process as much as result, for too many historians have simply dismissed the former as trivial and emphasized only the latter. Sophisticated scholarship—at least in my eyes—requires an understanding of those incredibly obscure processes that often give rise to results that diametrically contradicted starting intentions and objectives.

No book, of course, is the result of the labor of one individual, and mine is surely no exception. I have drawn upon the work of many past scholars, and if I have disagreed with them, it has only been after lengthy and serious thought. A number of very good friends have taken time from their own busy schedules to read successive drafts and to offer me the benefits of their own insights. In particular I should like to thank Barbara G. Rosenkrantz, George A. Billias, Jacques M. Quen, Otto M. Marx, Richard P. McCormick, Peter N. Stearns, and Tilden G. Edelstein for their help. This work would have been much the worse had it not been for their penetrating and insightful comments.

All scholars benefit from the many librarians who collect and make available those materials without which no history could be written. A complete listing would be impossible, for my research has taken me to libraries in more than a dozen states. I would, however, like to single out Richard J. Wolfe of the Countway Library of Medicine at the Harvard Medical School. Over a period of years he aided me in ways that only habitual frequenters of libraries would appreciate; he also located the illustrations that I have used in this volume. I am indebted to the National Institute of Mental Health, Department of Health, Education, and Welfare, which supported my work with generous research grants (MH 12743 and MH 17859) without in any way seeking to influence the direction I took, and the National Endowment for the Humanities, which made possible a leave of absence from teaching during the final stage of this project.

Above all, I should like to thank my wife—Lila K. Grob—and my three sons—Bradford, Evan, and Seth—who put up with the capricious behavior that often marks the life of the would-be scholar and yet encouraged me to persevere. Without their love, understanding, and patience, this book would have never been completed.

G.N.G.

Abbreviations

AAS   American Antiquarian Society, Worcester, Mass.
AJI   *American Journal of Insanity*
AMSAII   Association of Medical Superintendents of American
                 Institutions for the Insane
AR   *Annual Report*
BR   *Biennial Report*
CLMHMS   Countway Library of Medicine, Harvard Medical
                 School, Boston, Mass.
HLHU   Houghton Library, Harvard University, Cambridge,
                 Mass.
IPH   Institute of the Pennsylvania Hospital, Philadelphia,
                 Pa.
MHS   Massachusetts Historical Society, Boston, Mass.

NOTE: The year listed for an annual or biennial report in the footnotes represents the period covered by the report, not the date of publication. Thus a report published in 1871, for example, may be cited as 1870 or 1870/1871, signifying the period actually covered.

Mental Institutions in America: Social Policy to 1875

Chapter I

The Mentally Ill
in Colonial America

I

"It is fair to say," a distinguished American neurologist declared in 1880, "that in the present state of psychiatry in America, to be pronounced insane by physicians, by a judge, or by a jury, means imprisonment for months, for years, or for life. To put it another way, there is a disease which reduces its victims to a level with persons accused of crime, and exposes them to loss of liberty, property and [to] unhappiness."[1] The moral was clear; the mental hospital was nothing more than a prison for insane persons.

Such a judgment would have come as a shock to many early nineteenth-century social activists and reformers who had condemned in no uncertain terms the manner in which their colonial predecessors had cared for dependent insane persons. During the seventeenth and eighteenth centuries the care of the mentally ill was subsumed under the existing poor law system. In the absence of specific therapies, mental disease during the colonial period was viewed as more of an economic and social problem than a medical one, for it often disrupted family relationships by undermining means of support. Nineteenth-century reform-

1. E. C. Seguin, "The Right of the Insane to Liberty," in Conference of Charities and Correction, *Proceedings*, VII (1880), 166.

ers, on the other hand, tended to see mental illness as a predominantly medical problem to be dealt with by confinement in mental hospitals. In their view these institutions combined the latest and best medical knowledge and practice with a humanitarian and philanthropic philosophy that emphasized the responsibility of the state toward the dependent insane. Mental hospitals, properly structured and administered, could not help but benefit both the individual and society; such institutions would contribute toward the recovery of the insane and thereby minimize the burden of support that fell on the shoulders of the community.

In retrospect it is clear that the disparity between the goals and achievements of most mental hospitals increased sharply during the nineteenth century. Established for therapeutic purposes, these institutions reflected the growing faith that medicine was a science rather than an art or a branch of speculative philosophy, and that the key to social and individual improvement was through greater application of scientific knowledge and techniques to existing problems. Although their supporters conceived of these hospitals as "scientific" institutions, they were never able to separate in any precise or meaningful manner mental illness as a purely "medical" abstraction from its social and economic ramifications. In view of the virtual impossibility of dealing with mentally ill persons in strictly medical terms, it was not surprising that mental hospitals proved vulnerable to a variety of external pressures which contributed toward their transformation into custodial institutions that provided cheap care for a variety of distressed persons coming from predominantly impoverished backgrounds.

Why did the character of mental hospitals deviate so sharply from their stated goals? It would be easy, of course, to answer this question in any number of ways: to say that hospitals were the product of an age that lacked a "scientific psychiatry" or a body of theory and empirical data that might serve as the basis for an enlightened social policy; that nineteenth-century Americans tended to see distressed groups in terms of their moral shortcomings or character deficiencies; or that the materialistic nature of American culture precluded substantial investments in health, education, and welfare. Yet these explanations—all of which contain an element of truth—suffer from an oversimplification of complex social processes and an inability to account for problems without fixing responsibility upon the shoulders of some malevolent agent.

More than a century ago Dr. Oliver Wendell Holmes observed that "medicine, professedly founded on observation, is as sensitive to outside influence, political, religious, philosophical, imaginative, as is the barometer to the changes of atmospheric density. Theoretically it ought to go on its own straightforward inductive path, without regard to changes of government or to fluctuations of public opinion. But . . . [actually there is] a closer relation between the Medical Sciences and the conditions of Society and the general thought of the time, than would at first be suspected."[2] Nowhere was the accuracy of Dr. Holmes's perceptive statement better illustrated than in the development of psychiatry and the mental hospital in America. Far from merely reflecting certain scientific and medical currents, both emerged out of the interaction of complex social, intellectual, and economic forces, and reflected to a large extent the unique characteristics of their indigenous environment.

Public mental hospitals, for example, performed a variety of functions, some of which were thrust on them by a society that lacked effective means of accomplishing certain ends. Mental hospitals not only were entrusted with the function of caring for sick individuals, but often they accepted old age and indigent groups as well as cases whose behavior was deemed socially disruptive by the community. Moreover, care and treatment was frequently a function of individual and group values not directly related to scientific or medical considerations. Above all, the fate of the mentally ill was bound up with social and economic considerations, in part because of the high cost of protracted institutionalization and in part because such a high proportion of patients came from lower-class and minority ethnic backgrounds. Neither the mental hospital nor American psychiatry, then, can be studied in medical and scientific terms alone; both must be viewed within an institutional framework related to the broader problems of dependent groups generally.

2. Oliver Wendell Holmes, *Medical Essays 1842–1882* (Boston, 1891), 177.

II

When the American colonies were first founded in the New World in the seventeenth century, the mentally ill presented no particular problem. Population density tended to be low, and most communities were predominantly rural and agricultural. Those cases of mental illness that appeared from time to time were handled on an ad hoc and informal basis by either the family or the community. Institutionalization was uncommon, if only because there was an insufficient number of insane persons to justify the establishment of special facilities or institutions. Reliance on familial and community traditions and practices, moreover, made it unnecessary to consider alternative approaches to the problem. Consequently, the very concept of social policy —which involved the conscious creation of new public structures or procedures on a regional or national basis to replace traditional means of dealing with distress—was largely absent for most of the seventeenth and eighteenth centuries.

During the colonial period the family was primarily responsible for the welfare of any of its members who became insane. Yet the local community was never able to remain completely aloof from the problems arising out of mental disease. The behavior of some "lunatics" or "distracted persons"—to use the terminology of that era—seemed to threaten public safety and security, and therefore dictated the adoption of certain protective measures. In other cases mental illness resulted in a loss of work and income, thereby making the individual a public charge. If the family possessed inadequate financial resources, the community was legally bound to intercede because of its obligations to care for indigent dependent persons. Finally, the issue of guardianship often involved the community, for the afflicted individual might be declared legally incompetent to manage property.

Throughout the seventeenth and much of the eighteenth century most cases involving the insane arose as a result of the application of the poor laws. Illness and ensuing idleness over an extended period of time often had a disastrous effect upon a mentally ill person and the immediate family. In such circumstances the community was forced to make some provisions for caring for the sick and insane as well as for their dependents because there were few, if any, institutions for this purpose in America.

Colonial laws and practices regarding indigency, generally speaking, were modeled after those of England. For several centuries prior to the settlement of the colonies, the mother country had been groping its way toward the adoption of a comprehensive policy regarding poverty. The kind of poverty existing during the fifteenth and sixteenth centuries, however, differed sharply from that experienced during the medieval period. Poverty during the Middle Ages had been endemic. Although various ecclesiastical institutions—especially monasteries and hospitals—and craft guilds had provided a form of social insurance, the absence of any strong and effective central authority and the intense regionalism of that era hindered the adoption of a cohesive and effective national policy. Many persons died of hunger, including serfs and lords, but there was little outcry or protest; death under such circumstances was not considered as anything unusual. Economic developments in England after the beginning of the fourteenth century, however—the introduction of a money economy, the appearance of towns, and growing commerce—gave rise to a new kind of rural and urban poor who were particularly vulnerable to changes in the economy. The disintegration of medieval society, the devastating plagues, and foreign and internal wars all tended to aggravate still further the problems arising out of poverty and unemployment.

During the sixteenth century the Tudor monarchy became deeply concerned with social problems—a concern that grew out of a conviction that poverty threatened the entire social order. England, like most other western European nations undergoing rapid economic changes, was experiencing a phenomenal increase in vagrancy and vagabondage. This situation resulted in the creation of a self-perpetuating social class. This new class probably drew many of its recruits from the agricultural displacement that occurred in the early sixteenth century and from the large numbers of persons who migrated from rural areas into rising urban centers in search of employment. Living by alms and engaging in activities that bordered on or actually involved what society judged criminal, they constituted a seeming menace to public order and morality. The result was the passage of a series of laws designed to suppress vagrancy. To many Englishmen the gravity of the problem was such as to require intervention by the state.

Much of the early sixteenth-century legislation dealing with poverty was relatively rudimentary in nature. A significant statute enacted in 1531, for example, provided that vagrants be whipped and returned to their homes, while the helpless poor were licensed to beg. Five years later another law required local authorities to assume full responsibility for the latter so that this group would not be compelled to wander as beggars. During the reign of Elizabeth England began to move toward a more comprehensive system of poor relief. This system took into account the fact that there were deserving poor who were neither helpless nor vagrant beggars or thieves. The recognition that poverty was a complex problem involving a number of different categories eventually culminated in the passage of a series of laws beginning in 1597 and culminating in 1601 with "An Act for the Relief of the Poor." Viewed in their entirety, these acts gathered together the legislative and administrative experience of nearly a century and served as the basis for a system that lasted for over two hundred years.

Under this legislation, all local communities were given fiscal and supervisory responsibility for poor persons within their jurisdiction. Every parish was required to appoint overseers of the poor whose duty it was to provide for all dependent destitute classes—able-bodied or helpless, young or old, lame or blind, or anyone without visible means of support. Those persons refusing to work could be committed to a house of correction or a jail. The law made parents legally liable to maintain their children and grandchildren, who, in turn, were made responsible for parents and grandparents unable to work. This legislation also included a codification of the law of charitable trusts in order to encourage the growth of such trusts as instruments of social betterment. The entire system assumed that public order required the establishment of appropriate mechanisms to ensure relief from poverty. It did not exclude or minimize private philanthropy; indeed, it rested on the premise that public responsibility, supplementing private charity, could mitigate if not prevent widespread poverty.[3]

The English principle that society had a corporate responsibility for the poor and dependent was reflected in early colonial legislation. As in England, most of the colonies required local communities to make provision for a wider variety of different groups of dependents. Virtually every colony passed settlement laws, which stipulated that all individuals eligible for relief had to prove that they were legal residents in the community in which they lived. The minimum period necessary to gain a legal residence tended to vary from colony to colony; in most it ranged from three months to one year. Those persons unable to establish legal residence could, under certain conditions, be compelled to leave. New England, for example, practiced the custom of "warning out" persons who were likely to become public charges. The reason for this procedure was to absolve the town from all obligation to aid individuals who required help and assistance but did not meet residency requirements.[4] In theory, dependent persons having no legal settlement had to look to the colony rather than the local community for aid.

While such legislation appeared harsh by modern standards, it

3. This discussion of the English poor law system is largely based on W. K. Jordan's *Philanthropy in England 1480–1660: A Study of the Changing Pattern of English Social Aspirations* (London, 1959), 54–125. Also useful were E. M. Leonard, *The Early History of English Poor Relief* (Cambridge, England, 1900), Chaps. I–VIII, and Sidney and Beatrice Webb, *English Poor Law History: Part I. The Old Poor Law* (London, 1927), Chap. II.

In 1662 Parliament enacted legislation that subsequently became known as the Law of Settlement and Removal. This law rapidly took its place as a second pillar stone of the poor law system. It made about nine-tenths of the population of England liable to be deported to their place of legal settlement unless they could give sufficient security that they would never become chargeable to the parish for support. Although the act was never consistently enforced, it (and later amendments) stimulated localities to avoid welfare expenditures by removing all nonresident paupers. In their study of the poor laws, the Webbs could not determine with any degree of precision the relationship between the settlement laws and the difficulties that plagued the poor law system through the nineteenth century. See Sidney and Beatrice Webb, *English Poor Law History*, 314–349.

4. See Josiah H. Benton, *Warning Out in New England* (Boston, 1911), for a detailed examination of this phenomenon.

reflected the social situation that prevailed in many communities in seventeenth- and eighteenth-century America. In a society facing threats to its very existence from natural catastrophes such as famine or disease and Indian warfare, there was little regard for persons—especially strangers—who did not contribute to the well-being and survival of society. Consequently, much of the colonial legislation was directed toward suppressing idleness and vagrancy. On the other hand, all of the colonies recognized their moral and legal obligations toward the helpless, the aged, and the infirm, and all made some provision for their welfare.

Since illness and dependency were intimately related, the care of the mentally ill usually came under the jurisdiction of the local community as a result of the poor laws. Various codes and laws enacted in Massachusetts, to cite one example which was quite typical, touched upon insanity in one form or another. The province's first legal code, adopted in 1641, contained several references to "distracted" persons and idiots. One section authorized a "generall Court" to validate the transfer of property made by such persons. Another provision stipulated that "Children, Idiots, Distracted persons, and all that are strangers, or new commers to our plantation, shall have such allowances and dispensations in any Cause whether Criminall or other as religion and reason require." By 1676 the General Court, noting the rise in the number of "distracted persons" and the problems stemming from their behavior, ordered town selectmen to care for such persons so that "they doe not Damnify others." Selectmen were also empowered to manage the estates of such individuals and to pay all expenses incurred from the property owned by them. If the afflicted individual possessed no property, the town was to assume fiscal responsibility. In 1694 the legislature enacted an even more comprehensive statute entitled "An Act for the Relief of Ideots and Distracted Persons." Under its provisions, all persons falling into a state of "distraction" and becoming "*non compos mentis*" and having no relatives to care for them became the legal responsibility of the community. The selectmen or overseers of the poor were empowered and enjoined "to take effectual care and make necessary provision for the relief, support and safety of such impotent or distracted person, at the charge of the town or place whereto he or she of right belongs, if the party has not estate of his or her own the incomes whereof may be sufficient to defray the same." The justices of the peace were granted authority to dispose of the estate of such individuals to pay for the costs of maintenance or could bind the person out to work. By the end of the eighteenth century another law authorized commitment to a house of correction of any person "Lunatic & so furiously mad as to render it dangerous to the peace or the safety of the good people, for such lunatic person to go at large."[5]

The other American colonies enacted statutes on this issue quite similar to those of Massachusetts. Connecticut, for example, virtually copied intact the Bay State law of 1694 when enacting in 1699 "An Act for the Relieving of Idiots and Distracted Persons." In New York an amendment to the Duke's Laws in 1665 provided for joint responsibility by communities for the care of "distracted persons" who were "both very chargeable and troublesome" and who proved to be too onerous for one town to bear. A century later the same colony authorized the confinement of dangerous insane persons by local officials. Rhode Island vested its town councils with authority to care for all persons and their estates who were "delirious, distracted, or non compos mentis" or those individuals likely to become a public charge. Two years after the adoption of its Constitution in 1777, Vermont mandated local responsibility for the care of its insane persons. A few colonies, on the other hand, enacted relatively little legislation bearing on insanity in any way. Prior to 1770 the only laws passed by the Virginia legislature were those dealing with the property and status of the insane. Nevertheless, the fact that Virginia followed in practice the English poor law system meant that it cared for dependent groups in much the same manner as other colonies. In terms of formal law, then, the pattern during the seventeenth and eighteenth centuries was clear.

5. Legislation pertaining to the mentally ill in Massachusetts can be found in the following collections: *The Colonial Laws of Massachusetts. Reprinted from the Edition of 1660, with the Supplements to 1672, Containing also, The Body of Liberties of 1641* (Boston, 1889), 35, 45; *The Colonial Laws of Massachusetts. Reprinted from the Edition of 1672, with Supplements through 1686* (Boston, 1887), 248; *The Acts and Resolves, Public and Private, of the Province of the Massachusetts Bay*, 21 vols. (Boston, 1869–1922), I, 151–152, II, 622–624, V, 594–595; *Acts and Laws of the Commonwealth of Massachusetts, 1796–97* (Boston, 1896), 451.

Provision was made for guardianship, for the support of the indigent insane, and, somewhat later, for the confinement of those regarded as a threat to the well-being of the community.[6]

Virtually none of the legislation enacted by colonial legislatures referred to the medical treatment of the insane; it emphasized mainly the social and economic side of mental illness. Such an omission was not surprising, nor did it reflect insensitivity to the needs of the insane. While an extensive literature dealing with mental disease was already in existence, much of it dealt with the nature of insanity rather than its treatment. Consequently, relatively few specific therapies were available during the seventeenth and eighteenth centuries. While bleeding and purging were sometimes employed as therapeutic agents, their use reflected largely the Galenic philosophy that there were no specific diseases, but only specific disorders of the humors that could be treated by such traditional remedies. Had legislatures desired to provide therapeutic facilities, therefore, they could have drawn upon neither precedent nor experience as a guide. Equally significant was the lack of medical personnel and facilities in the colonies. Many areas had no physicians at all. Medical men, moreover, were more concerned with common illnesses and epidemics that affected a far larger proportion of the population than they were with mental illness. Until the middle of the eighteenth century there were no hospitals in any of the colonies that could provide either therapy or custodial care for the insane persons. The best that such individuals received, therefore, was kind and humane care by those who loved and cared for them. Finally,

6. Edward W. Capen, *The Historical Development of the Poor Law of Connecticut* (New York, 1905), 47–49; David M. Schneider, *The History of Public Welfare in New York State 1609–1866* (Chicago, 1938), 81, 197; Margaret Creech, *Three Centuries of Poor Law Administration: A Study of Legislation in Rhode Island* (Chicago, 1936), 85; Lorenzo D'Agostino, *The History of Public Welfare in Vermont* (Washington, D.C., 1948), 95–96, 198; William W. Hening, ed., *The Statutes at Large: Being a Collection of All the Laws of Virginia from the First Session of the Legislature in the Year 1619*, 13 vols. (Richmond, 1809–1823), II, 39, 97–98, III, 381–384, 401–402, 517–535, IV, 12–20, 397–402, V, 220–225, 454–467, 513–515; Marcus W. Jernegan, *Laboring and Dependent Classes in Colonial America, 1607–1783* (Chicago, 1931), 175–188; Howard Mackey, "The Operation of the English Old Poor Law in Colonial Virginia," *Virginia Magazine of History and Biography*, LXXIII (January, 1965), 29–40.

there is little evidence that mental illness was widespread in colonial America.[7] Thus there was little need to formulate comprehensive policies to deal with a problem that only later became classified as being preeminently medical in nature.

Generally speaking, the care of the mentally ill prior to the nineteenth century did not reflect widespread public concern with the problems growing out of insanity; the community became involved only when an individual seemed to threaten public safety or else had no means of support. When the behavior or condition of an insane individual came within the sphere of public authority, officials employed a variety of methods to care for their charges. Communities sometimes authorized the construction of a building to confine a particularly troublesome individual. Since the family was widely regarded as the single most significant social institution, most localities attempted to maintain its integrity in times of distress. Thus it was not uncommon to provide families with supplementary funds to enable them to care for their afflicted relatives at home. Even the practice of boarding out mentally ill persons in unrelated households reflected the trust and esteem in which the family was held. Finally, there is little doubt that local officials from time to time attempted to rid their communities of insane indigent persons who had not established legal residency.[8] Although most colonies had settlement laws and provided severe penalties if they were violated, it is not certain whether such laws were rigidly enforced. Within most colonies, as a matter of fact, there were significant differences between the letter of the law and its actual operations on most issues.

7. Cf. Henry R. Viets, "Some Features of the History of Medicine in Massachusetts during the Colonial Period (1620–1770)," *Isis*, XXIII (September, 1935), 395, and Richard H. Shryock, "The Beginnings: From Colonial Days to the Foundation of the American Psychiatric Association," in *One Hundred Years of American Psychiatry*, ed. by J. K. Hall et al. (New York, 1944), 1–3.

8. Cf. Schneider, *History of Public Welfare in New York State*, 82; Albert Deutsch, *The Mentally Ill in America: A History of Their Care and Treatment from Colonial Times* (Garden City, New York, 1937), 42–50; Dora M. E. Blackmon, "The Care of the Mentally Ill in America, 1604–1812 in the Thirteen Original Colonies" (unpubl. Ph.D. dissertation, University of Washington, 1964), 102–107; Creech, *Three Centuries of Poor Law Administration*, 86–88.

Although relatively little is known about the manner in which local communities cared for their insane, it is clear that the low density of population obviated the development of formal institutional mechanisms. To most colonials mental illness was of concern mainly because of its economic and social ramifications and potential threat to public safety; its medical aspects were of minor significance. There is little evidence, moreover, to substantiate the oft-repeated allegation that the insane were singled out for harsh and inhumane treatment. Given the living standards in the colonial period, the limited resources, and the lack of medical knowledge and facilities, there is no reason for believing that the condition of the insane was appreciably worse than that of other dependent groups within colonial society.[9]

9. Albert Deutsch's *The Mentally Ill in America* had several chapters dealing with the mentally ill in colonial America. A more recent, but hardly satisfactory, study was written by Dora M. E. Blackmon ("Care of the Mentally Ill in America"). It is interesting to note that virtually all historians, in discussing particular instances of care and treatment, have referred to the same specific illustrations. The widest sample can be found in Deutsch's classic study. Yet to "prove" his point, Deutsch cited fewer than two dozen examples; from these he proceeded to generalize about the cruel and barbaric manner in which the insane were cared for during the colonial period. In an important sense he implicitly misread his own findings because of his preconceived belief that past generations feared or hated the mentally ill. He also treated the history of psychiatry in terms of a progression from a dark past to a somewhat more knowledgeable and enlightened present (even when he condemned present conditions he attributed them to society's disinclination to allocate sufficient resources to deal with this problem). The available evidence, however, is of such a varied nature that it is impossible to generalize with any degree of precision on this subject; about all that can be said is that each community, depending on the circumstances, improvised or attempted to do the best that it could under prevailing conditions. Even the few examples cited by Deutsch hardly substantiate his strong words of condemnation. What he and other historians have done is to project into the past the knowledge and values of the present—a technique that hardly lends itself to historical understanding.

Nearly every account of the history of the mentally ill also deals with the Salem witchcraft trials in Massachusetts in the late seventeenth century. While witchcraft obviously was important in early colonial society, there is no compelling reason why it should be treated as though it were an integral part of the history of mental illness. Here historians have subsumed witchcraft under mental illness because of their own assumptions about the cruelty, ignorance, and irrationalities of their ancestors (as contrasted with a more enlightened present).

III

Not until the late seventeenth and eighteenth century did institutionalization of the mentally ill become somewhat more common. When the confinement of insane persons did come about, it occurred because demographic changes slowly forced an alteration in the pattern of welfare rather than as a result of changes in medicine or hospital practice. The growth of population in a number of areas, accompanied by a corresponding increase in the number of sick and dependent persons, complicated the informal manner in which predominantly rural communities had cared for such persons. Many of the more populous towns found that nonresident and transient individuals were unable to support themselves because of disease and age and had nowhere to turn except to the community. Some insane persons (including even residents) were so severely incapacitated that boarding out was not feasible. To care for these individuals a few of the larger towns began to establish general welfare institutions such as almshouses. Such institutions were intended to fulfill the town's humanitarian and moral obligations while simultaneously effecting economies by virtue of their scale and efficiency. Eclectic in their admission policies, they accepted the very young, the aged, the infirm, and the mentally ill, among others.

While the almshouse movement in the United States did not assume major proportions until after 1800, most of the larger urban areas had established such institutions well before that date. In Boston the first almshouse was built with private bequests in 1662, although the selectmen did not admit its first inmates for several years. For over half a century this institution did not distinguish between its inmates; it accepted a variety of dependent and helpless individuals. In 1739 Boston also opened a workhouse. This institution, however, remained small and peripheral in its importance; the majority of poor persons continued to receive outdoor (outside of an institution) rather than indoor (within an institution) relief. Under these circumstances dependent persons who could not be cared for at home received aid in the almshouse.

By the end of the eighteenth century, the heterogeneous population of the almshouse had become a source of considerable difficulty. "The almshouse in Boston," observed a committee in 1790, "is, perhaps, the only instance known where persons of every description and disease are lodged under the same roof and in some instances in the same contagious apartments, by which means the sick are disturbed by the noises of the healthy, and the infirm rendered liable to the vices and diseases of the diseased, and profligate." It was not until 1821 that a House of Industry was established for the employment of the able-bodied poor. Even then the institution continued to serve as a receptacle for large numbers of insane and other dependent persons.[10] "Of the 500 inmates here," the superintendent reported in 1832, "50 are more or less insane and about one half may be described as 'furiously mad' requiring almost constant confinement in close dormitories. Others are periodically or occasionally violent or extremely irrational—all require much anxious attention."[11]

In most other colonial urban areas, including New York, Philadelphia, and Charleston, the pattern was basically the same. When the number of sick and dependent persons reached a critical size, the community moved toward the adoption of a more organized system. In the initial stage specialized institutions were not characteristic; most urban welfare institutions remained undifferentiated in both structure and function. Under these circumstances they seemed logical places to confine dependent and "dangerous" insane persons along with others.[12] The undifferentiated character of almshouses and similar welfare institutions reflected a deep undercurrent of public ambivalence. On the one hand, there was sympathy and compassion for the plight of orphans, widows, the aged, and the sick. On the other, there was hostility and distrust toward able-bodied inmates who

10. Robert W. Kelso, *The History of Public Poor Relief in Massachusetts 1620–1920* (Boston, 1922), 113–117; David J. Rothman, *The Discovery of the Asylum: Social Order and Disorder in the New Republic* (Boston, 1971), 39–42; Carl Bridenbaugh, *Cities in the Wilderness: The First Century of Urban Life in America 1625–1742* (New York, 1938), 81, 234, 393; Carl Bridenbaugh, *Cities in Revolt: Urban Life in America, 1743–1776* (New York, 1955), 125–126.

11. Artemas Simonds to Horace Mann, August 17, 1832, Mann Papers, MHS.

12. See Schneider, *History of Public Welfare in New York State*, *passim*, and Bridenbaugh's two books, *Cities in the Wilderness*, 78–85, 231–238, 391–398, and *Cities in Revolt*, 122–128.

were confined because of their seeming improvidence and laziness and toward dangerous mentally ill persons whose behavior represented an apparent threat to the safety of the community.

Colonial charity, however, was by no means confined exclusively to the public sphere. As in England, most colonies developed a mixed system in which public welfare and private charity mutually reinforced and complemented each other. Indeed, many of the early philanthropic undertakings were mixed in character, for private charities sought and often received funds from local communities or colonial legislatures. Before the Civil War the line of demarcation between the public and private sector was at best blurred. In many instances the public-private distinction simply did not exist in the minds of most Americans or within the framework of existing practices.

Out of this mixed system emerged the first urban hospitals beginning in the mid-eighteenth century and accelerating sharply in the nineteenth. In this respect the experiences of the American colonies were similar to those of England and other European countries. In England, prior to 1700, there were only a handful of special institutions. Between 1719 and 1750, however, five new hospitals were founded in London alone, and nine others came into being elsewhere in the country. By the end of the eighteenth century similar institutions had sprung into existence in most of the cities and larger towns of Britain. In France existing hospitals—especially those in Paris—had begun to undergo a series of profound changes that were to make that nation an acknowledged leader in medicine during the first half of the nineteenth century.[13]

It must be emphasized, however, that the growth in the number of hospitals did not immediately affect the quality of medical care (with the possible exceptions of a few specialities, including surgery). The thrust of medical theory during the early nineteenth century was to demonstrate the ineffectiveness of many traditional therapies rather than to introduce new approaches. Medical theory, moreover, was still speculative and

13. David Owen, *English Philanthropy 1660–1960* (Cambridge, 1964), 36–61; George Rosen, "The Hospital: Historical Sociology of a Community Institution," in *The Hospital in Modern Society*, ed. by Eliot Freidson (New York, 1963), 19–23; Erwin H. Ackerknecht, *Medicine at the Paris Hospital 1794–1848* (Baltimore, 1967), 15–22.

general in nature, and therapeutic nihilism or eclecticism remained dominant. Consequently, the spread of hospitals reflected to a considerable degree the growing social concern with the problems of disease and poverty and their relationship to the well-being of the nation as a whole. In a significant sense their founding was related to the growing heterogeneity of welfare rather than to changes in medical theory and practice, although eventually hospital experiences provided a body of clinical data that would contribute to the radical transformation of medicine in the late nineteenth and twentieth centuries.

These generalizations were as true for the American colonies as they were for England and Europe. The colonies lagged behind the mother country in founding hospitals for several reasons. Urban areas in America were smaller and fewer; the density of population was much lower; and the colonies lacked medical facilities and traditions. Nevertheless, there was already evidence of rising interest in hospitals during the eighteenth century. In 1709 a group of Philadelphia Quakers attempted to set up a hospital, but nothing came out of their endeavors. Some time later Philadelphia established a Pest House to confine its sick immigrants and thereby to prevent epidemics. This institution, however, did not serve native citizens. Indigent persons who became ill or insane and could not care for themselves were usually confined in the local almshouse. This practice had been authorized by the provincial Assembly after its members received a memorial from the Overseers of the Poor of Philadelphia. Although some rudimentary care was provided for its inmates, the Philadelphia Almshouse (out of which later evolved the Philadelphia Hospital) remained essentially a charitable and custodial institution for much of the eighteenth century.[14]

The Pennsylvania Hospital in Philadelphia was the first institution founded specifically for the care and treatment of the sick and the mentally ill. That Philadelphia, of all the American cities, should lead the way was not too surprising. By the middle of the eighteenth century it was the largest colonial city, and its population included individuals and groups who were disposed

14. Thomas G. Morton, *The History of the Pennsylvania Hospital 1751–1895* (Philadelphia, 1895), 3–5; Charles Lawrence, comp., *History of the Philadelphia Almshouses and Hospitals from the Beginning of the Eighteenth to the Ending of the Nineteenth Centuries* (n.p., 1905), 19–20.

to assume the financial and moral leadership of community projects. The city, moreover, was beginning to experience some of the consequences of urban growth and immigration.[15]

The founding of the Pennsylvania Hospital, however, was not simply a product of disinterested benevolence; it represented a clash of existing sectarian animosities and rivalries as well. By the mid-eighteenth century the Quakers no longer enjoyed unquestioned political dominance within the colony. Their refusal in 1750 to vote appropriations for frontier defense caused considerable bitterness. After relinquishing political leadership, the Quakers centered their energies on philanthropic work. In place of political power, they sought to influence society at large through private, voluntary, and nonsectarian organizations that embodied positive social purposes ordinarily within the responsibility of government. Although they had surrendered formal power and public office the Quakers attempted to retain moral leadership through example, remonstrance, and persuasion. The creation of a new hospital, therefore, admirably suited the changing role of Pennsylvania Quakers.[16]

The idea for the Pennsylvania Hospital originated with Dr. Thomas Bond, a man who had beeen disowned by the Friends in 1742 for taking an oath. Having visited England some years later, he was impressed with the care provided the mentally ill at Bethlehem Hospital. Not until he enlisted the aid and support of Benjamin Franklin, however, did the idea begin to move toward fruition. According to Franklin, it was difficult in Philadelphia at that time to provide suitable accommodations to care for the sick, particularly those who were poor and could not afford the expense of private care. In addition, there were inhabitants "who unhappily became disorder'd in their Senses, wander'd about, to the Terror of their Neighbours, there being no Place (except the House of Correction) in which they might be confined, and subjected to proper Management for their Recovery, and that House was by no Means fitted for such

15. The Quaker leadership of Philadelphia has been admirably described by Frederick B. Tolles in his *Meeting House and Counting House: The Quaker Merchants of Colonial Philadelphia 1682–1763* (Chapel Hill, 1948).

16. Sydney V. James, *A People among Peoples: Quaker Benevolence in Eighteenth-Century America* (Cambridge, 1963), 193–215.

Purposes." Recognizing that the cost of erecting such a hospital would be great, Franklin suggested that fundraising should be conducted on a colony-wide basis and that assistance should be requested from the provincial Assembly. Accordingly, a petition was presented to the Assembly in January, 1751.[17]

The petition itself is of more than antiquarian interest, for it reflected the existing concern with problems arising out of the combination of mental illness and poverty. The document opened with the following observations:

> THAT with the Numbers of People the Number of Lunaticks, or Persons distemper'd in Mind, and deprived of their rational Faculties, hath greatly encreased in this Province.
>
> THAT some of them going at large, are a Terror to their Neighbours, who are daily apprehensive of the Violences they may commit; and others are continually wasting their Substance, to the great Injury of themselves and Families, ill disposed Persons wickedly taking Advantage of their unhappy Condition, and drawing them into unreasonable Bargains, &c.

Yet proper treatment—as had been demonstrated at Bethlehem Hospital in England—could restore a large proportion of the insane to health. Although the province had already made substantial provision for the relief of the poor, it still required facilities for the care of needy people whose plight had been worsened by various diseases. Such facilities would be of benefit not only to the sick and poor, but ultimately to the entire community, since they would enable those individuals who had been restored to health to provide for themselves and their families.[18]

Although there was some opposition from rural members of the Assembly who feared that funds would be exhausted by the fees of attending physicians, the legislation eventually passed. Under its provisions the hospital was granted a charter as well as a matching subsidy of £2,000 when private donations reached that amount. The goals of the hospital, according to the act,

17. Benjamin Franklin, *Some Account of the Pennsylvania Hospital; From its First Rise, to . . . May, 1754* (Philadelphia, 1754), 3–4. See also Franklin's account in his autobiography, reprinted in *The Writings of Benjamin Franklin*, ed. by Albert H. Smyth, 10 vols. (New York, 1910), I, 376–379.

18. Franklin, *Some Account of the Pennsylvania Hospital*, 4.

included the public service of "saving and restoring useful and laborious Members," the humanitarian and "religious Duty" of providing "Relief for the Sick Poor," and the care of the insane. Controlled largely by Quakers (seven of the twelve managers and the treasurer were Friends), the hospital was immersed in provincial politics in its early years, since there was suspicion that the project was being used by the Friends to enhance the reputation of their sect. The institution eventually shed itself of its sectarian and political involvement and became primarily a benevolent and philanthropic institution serving the entire community.[19]

In January, 1752, the managers adopted a set of regulations for the hospital. While specifying that only curable cases were to be admitted, they exempted mentally ill persons from this particular requirement. They also agreed that precedence would be given to the sick poor up to the institution's ability to support them. Thereafter private paying patients would be accepted, and these patients were to be permitted to employ any physicians they so desired. The first two patients were admitted in February, 1752, one of whom was a "lunatick" recommended by the Visitors of the Poor of Philadelphia. The following month the first mentally ill private patient was admitted after a member of the family agreed to pay £20 per year for her board and support. As the idea of hospitalizing private mentally ill persons grew, a number of black insane slaves were committed by their owners, who assumed the costs of institutionalization.[20]

For the first four years of its existence the Pennsylvania Hospital was housed in temporary quarters. The cells for the insane, located below the wards, were damp and unhealthy, and a number of patients died of pulmonary disease. In 1756 the hospital moved to new quarters, but conditions in the insane wing remained poor. Dampness and lack of heat were perennial problems. But more significant was the fact that patients were continually escaping. Consequently, the managers authorized the erection of

19. Morton, *History of the Pennsylvania Hospital*, 7–11; James, *A People among Peoples*, 206–215; Blackmon, "Care of the Mentally Ill in America," 144–146.

20. Franklin, *Some Account of the Pennsylvania Hospital*, 25–27; Morton, *History of the Pennsylvania Hospital*, 113, 127; Blackmon, "Care of the Mentally Ill in America," 149, 151, 153.

restraining barriers and the strengthening of bars in the cells in which the insane were housed. The insane wing was such an object of public curiosity that in 1762 the managers decided to charge an admission fee. This policy was later abandoned when it became evident that such a practice had a decidedly adverse impact upon patients.[21] All patients remained under the care of a visiting physician, though day-to-day responsibility for their welfare was in the hands of male and female attendants.

While surviving records are somewhat vague on the nature of care and treatment during the eighteenth century, it is clear that restraint in one form or another was common. Benjamin Rush, who was associated with the Pennsylvania Hospital for nearly thirty years, became distressed at the use of the "mad shirt," or "straight waistcoat," because of its adverse physiological and psychological consequences. In its place he substituted his "tranquilizer"—a restraining chair designed to replace the older means of restraint. Medical therapy tended to be heroic in nature, and included extensive bleeding and blistering, the employment of emetics and restricted diets, and warm and cold baths. There were also sporadic attempts to provide occupational therapy, but inadequate facilities hampered significant progress along such lines.[22]

Throughout the eighteenth century the hospital continued to care for mentally ill patients, but the number was never large. Between 1752 and 1754, 18 out of 117 persons admitted were classified as insane. During this same period 15 of these insane

21. Morton, *History of the Pennsylvania Hospital*, 113–114, 127–132. Morton's volume is actually a primary source that reprints most of the manuscript material pertaining to the Pennsylvania Hospital. The originals are in the Archives of the Pennsylvania Hospital in Philadelphia. The American Philosophical Society has microfilmed most of these records, and keeps the film in its library in Philadelphia. See also Benjamin Rush to the managers of the Pennsylvania Hospital, November 11, 1789, in *Letters of Benjamin Rush*, ed. by Lyman H. Butterfield, 2 vols. (Princeton, 1951), I, 528–529.

22. Rush to Samuel Coates, April 30, 1798, Rush to John Redman Coxe, September 5, 1810, in *Letters of Benjamin Rush*, II, 799, 1058–1060; Morton, *History of the Pennsylvania Hospital*, 125–126. On the basis of his experience at the Pennsylvania Hospital, Rush wrote his famous *Medical Inquiries and Observations Upon the Diseases of the Mind* (Philadelphia, 1812).

1. House of Employment, Alms-House and Pennsylvania Hospital. The first hospital founded in the American colonies (c. mid-1760s). The undifferentiated functions of eighteenth-century hospitals were graphically illustrated by the placement of the hospital alongside welfare institutions. Source: Thomas G. Morton, The History of the Pennsylvania Hospital 1751–1895 (Philadelphia, 1895).

persons were discharged, including 2 as cured, 3 as relieved, and 6 who were removed by their friends. In 1787 Rush reported that there were 34 mentally ill patients in residence. Even in the five years prior to the opening of a separate and new hospital for the insane in 1841, the average annual number of admissions of insane patients was 66 (meaning that the number in residence at any given moment was considerably less).[23]

Prior to 1800 the patient body remained mixed in composition; some of the patients were committed by the overseers of the poor with the local community assuming financial liability, while others were affluent individuals who paid for their upkeep and in some instances had private attendants.[24] Private patients presumably received superior care because poor and indigent inmates were unable to pay equal sums. The hospital, however, never formally adopted or pursued such a differential policy consciously; the practice was largely a function of the nature of social and class relationships that existed between staff and patients.

The Pennsylvania Hospital undoubtedly provided an alternative to the custodial care given in undifferentiated welfare institutions such as almshouses. Yet the differences in care and treatment should not be exaggerated. Not all hospital care was kind and humane, and not all almshouse care was cruel and thoughtless. From time to time throughout the first century after the founding of the hospital there were proposals for sweeping reforms, but it was not until the new hospital for the insane opened in 1841 that significant changes were introduced in the conditions of the patient body.[25] The Pennsylvania Hospital,

23. Franklin, *Some Account of the Pennsylvania Hospital*, 36; Rush to John C. Lettsom, September 28, 1787, *Letters of Benjamin Rush*, I, 443; Morton, *History of the Pennsylvania Hospital*, 167.

24. Morton, *History of the Pennsylvania Hospital*, 132–134, 138.

25. Rush was especially active in pushing for certain reforms. See his letter to the managers of the Pennsylvania Hospital, September 24, 1810, in *Letters of Benjamin Rush*, II, 1063–1066, and Morton, *History of the Pennsylvania Hospital*, 143–151.

There are also a number of descriptions of the insane at the Pennsylvania Hospital in the late eighteenth century by visitors. See Morton, *History of the Pennsylvania Hospital*, 162–163, 448–449, for two such accounts (by the Rev. Manasseh Cutler and M. de Warville). While his-

then, remained a private (though state-aided) institution that was of more importance locally than nationally, at least insofar as the mentally ill were concerned. It never became a model institution which significantly altered public policy by providing an example for the care and treatment of the insane.

In the major town in the New England colonies—Boston— the inhabitants were less successful in their initial efforts to found a similar institution. As early as 1729 Boston selectmen had considered the possibility of building an addition to the almshouse in order to keep "Distracted Persons Separate from the Poor," but nothing came of the idea. Sixteen years later the overseers of the poor suggested that Boston might purchase the "Bridewell House" for use as a "mad house." The only result was the establishment of a committee in 1746 to study the subject. Shortly thereafter another committee was formed and empowered to raise subscriptions for building or purchasing a structure for the care of "Distracted persons." Although nothing came of all of these endeavors, they did indicate some concern for the interrelated problems of insanity and poverty. Indeed, the overseers of the poor reported in 1751 that the workhouse was not self-supporting simply because it contained a "number of distracted, helpless & infirm people" whose support would ordinarily have been chargeable to the town.[26]

The idea of some sort of institution specifically for the care of the mentally ill was again revived in 1764 after the death of Thomas Hancock, a wealthy and prominent Boston merchant and uncle of John Hancock. In his will Hancock left Boston a legacy of £600 to be used for the establishment of an institution for insane persons. When it became clear that this sum was in-

---

torians have often cited such travel accounts, I have in general found them to be so superficial as to be frequently misleading. In many instances the visitors were given "guided tours" intended to reveal only the best features of a hospital; in other instances the visitors were so lacking in rudimentary knowledge that they missed the implications of their own observations; and occasionally their accounts were simply wrong (a comparison with other primary sources can substantiate this generalization). Too much of American social history has been written from travel accounts.

26. *Report of the Record Commissioners of the City of Boston*, 39 vols. (Boston, 1876–1909), XIII, 194, XIV, 77, 89, 101, 198, XVII, 133. These volumes contain the town records of colonial Boston.

sufficient for such a project, an effort was made to raise additional funds, first by private subscriptions and then by petitioning the General Assembly for a subsidy. Neither of these efforts proved successful, and the bequest, which had a three-year limitation, was never used for the purpose intended by the donor.[27] Thereafter, no effort was made in Boston to establish a hospital for nearly half a century.

Although the reasons for Boston's backwardness (as compared with Philadelphia) are obscure, it is possible that its more homogeneous population, lack of strong sectarian rivalries, and low rate of immigration all played a role in making its social and economic problems less pressing. Certainly the leadership that existed in Philadelphia was either absent or ineffective in Boston.[28] Finally, it should be noted that Hancock's bequest came during a period of political crisis, since Boston became one of the major centers of opposition to British policy following 1763. Faced with larger problems and fearful of economic difficulties, Boston residents may very well have been reluctant to commit resources to projects unrelated to the developing imperial controversy.

In one of the major seaports in the Southern colonies—Charleston, South Carolina—a similar situation prevailed. As in Boston, local officials in 1754 requested that quarters for insane persons be established separate from the workhouse. The following year the Assembly considered a proposal for establishing an institution "for confining Persons disordered in their Senses, Fugitive Slaves, etc.," but no decision was reached. One decade later a grand jury investigation deplored the lack of a general hospital or poorhouse for individuals who flocked to Charleston. The existing quarters, the grand jury concluded, were "insufficient, and . . . a very improper receptacle for the poor, being crowded with criminals, vagrants, sailors, and negroes." During the 1760's and 1770's there were several other attempts to establish some type of hospital for the mentally ill, but surviving records about the actual creation of such an institution are vague. Whatever the case may have been, it is evident that although

27. *Ibid.,* XVI, 126, 139–140, 179–180, 184, 207, 215, XX, 98.
28. See Leonard K. Eaton, *New England Hospitals 1790–1833* (Ann Arbor, 1957), 19–21.

the citizens of Charleston were concerned with the problems arising out of mental illness, their efforts did not result in any significant institutional changes.[29]

At about the same time that Boston and Charleston were failing in their efforts to provide separate facilities for the insane, Virginia was establishing the first hospital devoted exclusively to the care and treatment of the mentally ill in the United States. Although Virginia was predominantly rural and agricultural in character and possessed no large urban center, British tradition in this most English of the English colonies seems to have provided much of the impulse. Having adopted the English poor law system, the colony probably cared for its relatively small number of insane persons within the framework of the poor laws. Prior to 1770 little legislation dealing with the care and confinement of the insane was enacted (although there were numerous laws dealing with the property of persons who were non compos mentis). Nevertheless, Virginia possessed a governing elite with a sense of noblesse oblige and knowledge of developments both in other colonies and abroad.

The initial call for a hospital came not from a Virginian, but from an Englishman, Governor Francis Fauquier. Sophisticated, urbane, and well-informed, Fauquier had a concern for the mentally ill that probably arose out of his humanitarian convictions as well as political considerations. Following his appointment to the governorship in 1758, he became embroiled in a number of divisive political struggles with the Assembly. When calling for the establishment of a new mental hospital in 1766, therefore, he could offer a proposal on which all factions could unite. "Every civilized Country," he told the legislators, "has an Hospital for these People, where they are confined, maintained and attended by able Physicians, to endeavor to restore to them their lost Reason." Unlike the group responsible for founding the Pennsylvania Hospital, Fauquier made no reference to the dimensions of the problem (there were, after all, only four insane persons in Virginia jails). In a later message he remarked that

29. Bridenbaugh, *Cities in Revolt*, 126; Henry M. Hurd, ed., *The Institutional Care of the Insane in the United States and Canada*, 4 vols. (Baltimore, 1916–1917), III, 583–584; Blackmon, "Care of the Mentally Ill in America," 168–170.

his proposal "could offend no party" but rather would unite all in its favor. The Burgesses failed to pass the necessary legislation until the mid-1770's, by which time Fauquier had died. It is interesting to note that no public campaign was organized in favor of the hospital; it was largely an undertaking carried out by a governing elite who conceived of the project as a fulfilment of their obligations toward less fortunate persons.[30]

The legislation passed by the Burgesses and ratified by the governor and Council justified the establishment of a hospital on the grounds that it would cure those insane persons whose cases were not "quite desperate" and restrain others who were "dangerous to society." The act provided for a self-perpetuating court of directors, who were authorized to purchase land, erect a building, provide "a proper keeper and matron . . . with necessary nurses and guards," to call upon a physician when his services were required, and to make all other necessary regulations. In addition, the Burgesses appropriated £1,200 for the land and building and the sum of £25 per annum for the maintenance and support of each patient. All mentally ill persons with sufficient resources were required to pay for their support.[31]

The first governing board, named in the act, consisted of fifteen laymen, all of whom were leading figures in Virginia. Within a short time they had purchased land in Williamsburg where the new institution was to be located. Construction of the building took longer than originally anticipated and an additional appropriation from the legislature was required. It was not until the end of the summer of 1773 that the structure was completed. Shortly thereafter James Galt was appointed keeper and his wife matron. Thus began the long association of the Galt family with the hospital, an association that was to last for no less than eighty-nine years. The first patient was admitted in September, 1773, and America's first hospital devoted exclusively to the mentally ill had become a reality.

30. This account of the origins and early history of the Virginia institution is based on Norman Dain's *Disordered Minds: The First Century of Eastern State Hospital in Williamsburg, Virginia 1766–1866* (Williamsburg, 1971).

31. The statute establishing the new hospital can be found in Hening, ed., *Statutes at Large*, VIII, 378–381.

2. The Virginia Eastern Lunatic Asylum, located in Williamsburg, was the first hospital devoted exclusively to the care and treatment of the mentally ill. Founded in 1770, it received its first patients three years later. Source: Virginia Eastern Asylum, Annual Report, 1884).

Although the keeper of the Virginia Eastern Asylum (to use its later name) was a layman, the wishes of the visiting physician were usually deferred to in providing medical treatment. Such an arrangement was common in the eighteenth and early nineteenth centuries. The role of the lay administrator (or keeper) was to oversee and to supervise the institutional regimen in order to provide humane care for the patient and security for the community. The physician, on the other hand, had responsibility for providing whatever medical treatment was deemed appropriate. At that time medical treatment of insanity did not differ appreciably from that of other diseases; therapy tended to be largely medicinal and heroic. Before 1800 the newer concepts of insanity developed in Europe that included considerable emphasis on psychological factors were as yet unknown to the Williamsburg institution. Philippe Pinel did not undertake his famous reforms until the 1790's, and his classic work—*A Treatise on Insanity*—was first published in French in 1801, while the English translation did not appear until 1806. The initial detailed description of the newer psychologically oriented therapy employed by the English Quakers at the York Retreat, founded in the 1790's by individuals unaware of Pinel's reforms, did not become available until 1813. Nor was Benjamin Rush's book on insanity published until 1812. Consequently, the treatment at the Williamsburg hospital was traditional and involved a liberal use of drugs, including cathartics, emetics, and sedatives.

Despite its novel character, the Williamsburg institution never emerged as a possible model for a systematic network of publicly supported mental hospitals. In the first place, its scope was severely limited by the fact that the physical plant was capable of caring for only twenty-four to thirty patients, while the average number at any given time was considerably less. In the four years following November 1, 1786, for example, the hospital received only 36 patients; of these 9 died, one escaped, 3 were removed by friends, and 8 were discharged. Secondly, major political events such as the American Revolution had a disastrous impact upon the newly opened facility, forcing it to close down entirely for a four-year period beginning in 1782. Being in its beginning stage, the hospital was not sufficiently strong or mature to resist the depredations of turmoil and conflict. Thirdly, the governing authorities never publicized the work of the hospital, and thereby reinforced its essentially local character. Finally, the social and economic milieu in which the hospital movement of the next century originated was quite different, and it made the example of the Williamsburg institution somewhat irrelevant to future developments. For all these reasons, then, the Old Dominion did not play a significant role in the development of public policy toward mental illness.

The only other colony to establish a hospital that accepted mentally ill patients was New York. By the mid-eighteenth century New York City was one of the three largest ports of entry for immigrants, a major center of colonial commerce, and an important metropolis. The city was already experiencing some of the problems affecting other growing urban areas in Europe and America. Despite its large population and pressing health problems, it lacked adequate hospital facilities for either the rich or poor. The almshouse had a small infirmary for sick inmates, and the strong room located in the cellar was probably used to confine cases of mental illness. Those who could afford to pay medical expenses were usually treated in their homes by private physicians. Like most large urban areas, New York City had attracted a number of prominent medical men by the mid-eighteenth century.

The first suggestion for a hospital came from one of these men—Dr. Samuel Bard, whose father (also a physician) had been intimately acquainted with Benjamin Franklin and the Pennsylvania Hospital. Aware of the need for both a medical school and a hospital, young Bard (who had just returned from abroad after completing his medical education at Edinburgh University) persuaded five other physicians to join him in an effort to found a medical school. Their efforts were successful, and in 1767 the governors of King's College (later Columbia University) agreed to establish such an institution. At the first commencement of the medical school two years later, Bard took the occasion to comment on the absence of a hospital in the city. Such an institution, he pointed out, would be of benefit to the entire community, rich and poor alike. Moreover, it would permit proper instruction of medical students and thereby raise standards of medical practice in the metropolis. Bard noted also that the city possessed sufficient resources and benefactors to support such an ambitious venture.[32]

His suggestion gained the immediate support of Sir Henry Moore, the royal governor of the colony. Moore immediately launched a subscription in order to secure the necessary funds. The governor no doubt saw the project as a benevolent and worthy undertaking and also one that might conceivably help to counteract the political developments that were dividing the colony from the mother country. In spite of the tense political atmosphere the hospital proposal received widespread support among New York's prominent citizens. On June 3, 1771, a royal charter was granted to the "Society of the Hospital in the city of New-York in America" for the purpose of "erecting an Hospital for the reception and relief of sick and diseased persons." The document provided that the hospital be under the authority of twenty-six governors, who would draw up regulations, select the physicians, and generally manage all fiscal matters.[33] Although the charter made no specific mention of insane persons, it is reasonable to assume that the individuals connected with the project were acquainted with the example of the Pennsylvania Hospital and probably expected that part of the new institution would be devoted to the care and treatment of such patients. Indeed, while the hospital was under construction, the committee charged with its supervision was instructed by the board of governors in October, 1774, "to appropriate the cellar part of the North Wing or such part of it as they may judge necessary into wards or cells for the reception of Lunatics."[34]

32. Samuel Bard, *A Discourse Upon the Duties of a Physician, with Some Sentiments, on the Usefulness and Necessity of a Public Hospital* (New York, 1769), 15–18. See also John B. Langstaff, *Doctor Bard of Hyde Park* (New York, 1942).

33. *Charter of the Society of the New-York Hospital, and the laws Relating Thereto . . . and Those of the Bloomingdale Asylum for the Insane* (New York, 1856), 3–14.

34. William L. Russell, *The New York Hospital: A History of the Psychiatric Service 1771–1936* (New York, 1945), 35. In a public announcement in 1794, the governors referred to their disappointment following the loss of their first building in 1775, which "was so far completed, as to afford hope that, in a few weeks, an asylum would be opened for the poor sick, and maimed, languishing under the various diseases of body and mind." *Ibid.*, 45.

Through the influence of two eminent English physicians, Dr. John Fothergill (an individual with widespread contacts in the colonies who attempted to reconcile Britain and America during the Revolution) and Sir William Duncan, the newly formed society received considerable financial support in London and elsewhere in England. In 1772 the New York legislature granted it an annual allowance of £800 for twenty years. With financial support assured, the society acquired land and commenced construction in mid-1773. When the hospital was nearly completed in early 1775, a disastrous fire destroyed the structure. Although the legislature came to the aid of the society with a supplementary appropriation to aid in the task of rebuilding, the Revolutionary War and the consequent use of the facility by British troops prevented the hospital from opening. Concern with other problems during the war and the general social and political disarray that followed the end of hostilities hindered any resumption of the project. Indeed, in October, 1790, the Medical Society of the State of New York suggested that the "empty and useless" hospital be converted into an almshouse with cells provided for lunatics and that the existing almshouse be turned into a dispensary. The following month the Common Council of New York City echoed this proposal. The governors of the New York Hospital naturally disapproved both requests as "foreign to the object of their charter," and they continued to implement their own plans. The institution was finally opened at the beginning of 1791.[35]

Until the establishment of a separate insane department of the New York Hospital in 1808, all cases of mental illness were treated by the general medical service. From the very beginning the institution accepted insane persons, although apparently with the stipulation that chronic cases be refused admission. The actual number of mentally ill persons in the hospital, however, remained relatively small. Between 1792 and 1794 fewer than ten cases of insanity seem to have been admitted; by 1800 the total was probably less than one hundred. After the turn of the century the number of insane cases at the hospital began to in-

35. *Ibid.,* 35–36. See also Pliny Earle's *History, Description and Statistics of the Bloomingdale Asylum for the Insane* (New York, 1848), and his "Historical and Descriptive Account of the Bloomingdale Asylum for the Insane," *AJI,* II (July, 1845), 1–13.

crease at a fairly rapid rate, leading eventually to two internal reorganizations. Out of the second of these reorganizations emerged the Bloomingdale Asylum for the Insane in 1821—a process similar to the structural changes at the Pennsylvania Hospital that led in 1841 to the establishment of a separate institution for the mentally ill.[36]

The care and treatment of the insane during the first decade of the hospital's operations followed much the same pattern as elsewhere. Restraint was common and corporal punishment seems to have been employed on occasion. The only quarters available for inmates prior to 1803 were basement cells. Upon observing them one medical student commented that the "sight affected me with very dismal reflections." In 1805 Dr. David Hosack, one of the most distinguished American physicians of the early nineteenth century, reported to the governors that the "lower apartments at present occupied by the Maniacs are in a state that renders them very unfit for their accommodations—in consequence of having never been painted the Cells have become so imbued with filth that they are extremely offensive and unwholesome." Conditions improved somewhat after additional quarters were constructed with the aid of an appropriation by the state legislature after 1803, but the overall situation was less than ideal.[37]

Like the Pennsylvania and Virginia institutions, the establishment of the New York Hospital did not significantly alter public policy toward mental illness. Beset with a variety of internal and external problems, the new facility did not accept a single patient in the twenty years following the receipt of its charter. After 1791 it functioned as a general hospital, and the care of mentally ill patients remained largely a peripheral activity. Although the hospital would have a greater impact in the future, it remained only of local significance in the early years of the nineteenth century and contributed no fundamental changes in the manner in which American society cared for its insane. As late as 1830 a committee appointed by the New York legislature to study the New York Hospital and Bloomingdale Asylum and its relationship to the people reported that while the institution had

36. Russell, *New York Hospital*, 50–51.
37. *Ibid.*, 46–47, 52–53.

done commendable work, its existence was no substitute for a rational and comprehensive public policy on the subject of mental illness. The legislature in 1807 authorized local officials to contract with the governors of the New York Hospital for the care and maintenance of pauper lunatics, but admission of such patients remained entirely optional at the discretion of the governors. Consequently, relatively few such persons were admitted to the hospital; most were cared for in jails or poor houses, were boarded with private families, or else roamed at large. "Although the State has displayed its liberality to the Bloomingdale Asylum, and has made provision for the safe keeping of the insane," the committee noted, "yet it is evident, that this falls far short of the necessities of the case. The whole system as to pauper lunatics and idiots, is radically defective."[38]

IV

During the seventeenth and eighteenth centuries, then, mental illness was not recognized as being a major medical problem or a matter of pressing social concern. American society was still predominantly rural, making it possible to provide for individual insane persons in an informal manner. The mentally ill, for the most part, were cared for under the aegis of the poor laws or private charity. Only in a few of the more urban areas did informal modes of care prove more difficult or impracticable. In these areas, local citizens, often with the aid of the legislature, attempted to found hospitals to deal with problems related in one way or another to disease. Such early efforts, however, were isolated and not part of a more general or systematic effort to provide medical care and treatment within a comprehensive hospital system. The few institutions founded before 1800, therefore, did not reflect the application of new medical knowledge, the energies of informed medical reformers, or the efforts of organized campaigns to improve health conditions or medical treatment. The Pennsylvania Hospital was nearly two decades old before a second institution was established, and the New York Hospital remained a proposal rather than a reality for no less than twenty years. Even the Williamsburg institution—the

38. New York *Assembly Document No. 263* (March 10, 1831), 29.

first to be devoted solely to the care and treatment of the mentally ill—was only of local importance in the half century following its establishment, and it never became a model followed by other states.

The lack of hospital facilities in colonial America was not the result of a callousness toward or ignorance of health-related problems. Most Americans were well aware of the threats that disease, particularly in the form of epidemics, posed to their very existence. Smallpox, yellow fever, diphtheria, malaria, dysentery—to cite some of the outstanding examples—not only resulted in high mortality rates but also incapacitated and debilitated great numbers of people. Devastating as were deaths and complications from these and other diseases (as compared with modern standards), Americans were much better off than their compatriots in England and Europe. Across the Atlantic a far higher population density made epidemics a greater danger. With the exception of a few urban areas, population in the American colonies was still widely dispersed, thereby mitigating the ravages of disease and lessening somewhat the need for institutional care.[39] The absence of a firm body of theory and clinical data also militated against the adoption of a clear and comprehensive social policy toward mental disease. Responsibility for providing care or assistance, therefore, remained in the hands of the family or the local community in which the individual resided. The role of institutions such as almshouses and hospitals was simply to provide auxiliary backup in the event that the family was unable (or unwilling) to care for its afflicted members.

39. For a discussion of health problems in seventeenth- and eighteenth-century America see John Duffy, *Epidemics in Colonial America* (Baton Rouge, 1953). Detailed longevity statistics for one New England community are provided in Philip J. Greven, Jr., *Four Generations: Population, Land, and Family in Colonial Andover, Massachusetts* (Ithaca, 1970).

Chapter II

Philanthropy and Hospitals

I

BY THE EARLY NINETEENTH CENTURY the factors that had obviated the need for hospitals had begun to diminish in strength and intensity. Demographic changes, a growing sensitivity to social and medical problems, a surge of philanthropic giving by elite groups, and knowledge of significant medical and psychiatric developments in France and England all combined to give rise to a movement to establish both general and mental hospitals. Originating in the more populous Northeast, the movement within a few decades had become national in scope; eventually it transformed sharply the manner in which American society defined and responded to health-related problems.

The hospital movement in its initial phase during the early nineteenth century was a product of private philanthropy. With the financial aid of affluent, elitist groups, psychiatric hospitals were founded in a number of urban areas. Although privately supported, these institutions were nevertheless intended to serve the entire community, including those persons unable to pay for the costs of care and treatment. The relative absence of government involvement—especially at the state level—reflected the prevailing localism of American society and the general tendency to deal with social problems in informal ways at the community level. Before 1830 those individuals and groups who played a major role in founding hospitals assumed that private beneficence would prove adequate for existing needs. Therefore, they devoted little or no thought to long-range issues concerning health and dependency. When it became evident that private philanthropy would prove inadequate to overcome the formidable difficulties that arose out of certain economic and social developments, those mental hospitals already in existence slowly began to redefine their responsibilities. They limited admissions to those individuals who could afford the high costs of protracted confinement. By so doing they created a serious problem for the overwhelming bulk of mentally ill persons who sought or required institutionalization.

II

The hospital movement of the early nineteenth century was not simply the creation of socially concerned and well-to-do individuals and groups. Nor was the movement simply a derivation of the older English and European tradition out of which had come a widespread network of hospitals, although Americans knew of and profited from this example. The movement arose rather out of the interplay of those demographic, economic, religious, social, and intellectual forces that were transforming a relatively young nation by creating indigenous institutional forms, values, and patterns of thought in all aspects of human behavior.

Dramatic demographic changes in the half century following 1800 forced American society to reappraise many of its traditional institutional arrangements. One of the major demographic developments was the increase not only in the number but the size of urban areas. In 1790 there were only six cities having more than 8,000 residents; these contained 3.35 percent of the total population. By 1850 there were eighty-five such urban areas containing nearly 12.5 percent of the total population. In 1790 there was not a single city with a population in excess of 50,000, and only two with more than 25,000. By 1850 the largest American city had considerably in excess of half a million people, while five others had between 100,000 and 250,000 and twenty more ranged in size from 25,000 to 100,000.[1] The process of urbanization, however, was much more complex than these statistics indicate. In terms of geographic mobility, the actual turnover of population within a given city was far greater than the figures for its absolute growth. One historian has estimated that the turnover rate in Boston between 1830 and 1860 was about 30 percent per year. To put it another way, in each of the three decades at least two to six times as many families passed through Boston as lived in it at the beginning of the decade.[2] The situation in other urban areas during the same period probably was not very different.

Such demographic changes exercised a profound impact on the issue of mental illness. The care of the insane proved to be far more complex in an urban than a rural environment. Not only was there a far greater concentration in the number of cases of insanity, but more people were able to witness and feel threatened by the aberrant and seemingly bizarre behavior of insane persons. Consequently, the issue of security became much more significant. Moreover, the spontaneous and informal manner in which most rural communities handled problems of sickness and dependency did not operate as well or efficiently in urban areas, where an extraordinarily high rate of geographic mobility tended to limit social cohesion and the efficacy of informal and traditional means of dealing with distress. All these considerations militated against the use of informal mechanisms and favored more systematic and institutionalized patterns for dealing with the mentally ill. In its origins, then, the mental hospital—irrespective of its specific medical role—was primarily an institution that was intended to serve more densely populated areas.

Urbanization was by no means the only demographic phenomenon that influenced the care of the mentally ill. Equally significant was the beginnings of immigration to the United States of large numbers of lower-class immigrants, a trend that

1. Adna F. Weber, *The Growth of Cities in the Nineteenth Century* (New York, 1899), 22; U. S. Bureau of the Census, *Historical Statistics of the United States: Colonial Times to 1957* (Washington, D.C., 1960), 14.

2. Peter R. Knights, *The Plain People of Boston, 1830–1860: A Study in City Growth* (New York, 1971), 60, 121.

markedly intensified problems arising out of disease and dependency. Between 1830 and 1850 total population increased from 12,901,000 to 23,261,000. During this same period over two and a third million immigrants landed on American shores, of whom nearly a million were from Ireland. Many immigrants were destitute upon their arrival. Being unskilled for the most part, they could only find work in low-paid, dangerous, and often unhealthy occupations. Living in crowded urban slums, they were particularly susceptible to diseases of all varieties; their mortality and disease rates were far higher than the comparable rates for native groups. An important contemporary study of mental illness in Massachusetts in the 1850's, for example, revealed a far higher incidence among Irish than among natives. This same study demonstrated too that foreign-born mentally ill persons were entering hospitals at a far higher rate than their proportion in the general population.[3] Because of their impoverished state and the fact that most members of the family had to work, they were often unable to care for their own sick.

As a result of the presence of large numbers of immigrants and other lower-class groups who could not care for their sick and mentally ill, many major urban areas were faced with a desperate need for additional institutional facilities. Although it was true that more affluent groups required care and treatment, they were able to pay for care at home by employing private physicians and nurses. Thus the dependency of middle- and upper-class groups on hospitals was less than that of immigrants and lower-class elements of the native population.

Changes in the size and character of population, important though they were, did not by themselves necessarily lead to the establishment of mental hospitals. What was required also was an awareness of an alternative to the usual informal methods

3. *Report on Insanity and Idiocy in Massachusetts, by the Commission on Lunacy, Under Resolve of the Legislature of 1854,* Massachusetts *House Document No. 144* (1855), 57ff. This pioneering investigation was the work of Dr. Edward Jarvis, a significant nineteenth-century psychiatrist and statistician. See also Oscar Handlin, *Boston's Immigrants: A Study in Acculturation,* rev. ed. (Cambridge, 1959), 114–115, 243; Robert Ernst, *Immigrant Life in New York City 1825–1863* (New York, 1949), 13–14, 22–23, 52–55, 200; Robert S. Pickett, *House of Refuge: Origins of Juvenile Reform in New York State, 1815–1857* (Syracuse, 1969), Chap. I.

of caring for the mentally ill within the existing framework of welfare and dependency. Such an awareness was already emerging in the early nineteenth century. In the late eighteenth century scientific and intellectual changes had given rise to a firm conviction that the problems of mankind were by no means beyond human capabilities. The new outlook stressed the desirability of innovation, condemned stagnation, and sought a greater application of human intelligence to social problems. The result was a widespread conviction not only that the conquest of disease was merely ·a matter of time, but that many of the perennial dilemmas of humanity—including poverty, vice, and ignorance —could be minimized if not abolished altogether. Such convictions sooner or later were translated into specific policy proposals that were intended to change sharply existing practices and institutions.

The general current of optimism and faith in reason slowly began to influence some of the prevailing practices and theories regarding mental illness. By the eighteenth century insanity was defined largely in traditional medical terms and resembled in many respects the naturalistic interpretation of the ancient Greeks and Romans. Yet theory had little relationship to practice, for the Galenic tradition persisted well into the nineteenth century. Consequently, there was no rationale for the establishment of therapeutic institutions.

Although a number of individuals played important roles in changing psychiatric theory and practice, the name of Philippe Pinel is usually accorded the most honored position. Born in 1745 in southern France, young Pinel studied mathematics and medicine at Toulouse and Montpellier. In 1778 he moved to Paris, where he came under the influence of a group of notable thinkers who developed what became known as the philosophy of "Ideology." Based on the epistemological theory advanced by the Abbé Étienne de Condillac, this philosophy was further developed by Destutt de Tracy, Helvétius, Condorcet, and Cabanis, among others. Condillac was an ardent disciple of John Locke; in many respects he was more Lockean than the master in that he only admitted sensory data as the basis of knowledge. All ideas and all the faculties of human understanding, furthermore, were simply compounds of sensations that could be resolved by an analytical method into their component parts. Ideas, in other words, rested upon experience; nothing could be present in the mind except that which entered through the senses. To Condillac's disciples, this method of radical empiricism was crucial. Not only would it enable man to learn and understand human nature, but he would then be able to undertake political, social, economic, and moral measures to better and improve his condition.[4]

Pinel was closely associated with many of the Ideologues. Influenced by their ideas, he undertook to redefine medical theory by applying to it an analytically empirical method. The result was the publication in 1798 of his major work, *Nosographie philosophique ou méthode de l'analyse appliquée à la médicine.* Pinel emphasized that medicine should employ the same methods "commonly used in all other branches of natural history." Psychological concepts could be broken down into original sensations; clinical data could be studied in a similar manner; and changes in human organs could be further investigated in order to analyze the entire pathological picture.[5] Thus Pinel rejected theorizing about the ultimate nature of disease; he confined himself to the accumulation and analysis of abundant data. "The time, perhaps, is at length arrived," he proclaimed, "when medicine in France, now liberated from the fetters imposed upon it, by the prejudices of custom, by interested ambition, by its association with religious institutions, and by the discredit in which it has been held in the public estimation, will be able to assume its proper dignity, to establish its theories on facts alone, to generalize these facts, and to maintain its level with other departments of natural history."[6]

4. George Rosen, "The Philosophy of Ideology and the Emergence of Modern Medicine in France," *Bulletin of the History of Medicine*, XX (July, 1946), 328–331.

5. *Ibid.,* 332–333; Richard H. Shryock, *The Development of Modern Medicine: An Interpretation of the Social and Scientific Factors Involved,* rev. ed. (New York, 1947), 151–153; Walther Riese, *The Legacy of Philippe Pinel: An Inquiry into Thought on Mental Alienation* (New York, 1969), 85ff.; Erwin H. Ackerknecht, *Medicine at the Paris Hospital 1794–1848* (Baltimore, 1967), 47–51, 168–169.

6. Philippe Pinel, *A Treatise on Insanity,* trans. by D. D. Davis (Sheffield, England, 1806), 2, 45. This book was originally published in French under the title *Traite médico-philosophique sur L'aliénation mentale, ou la manie* (Paris, 1801).

Because of his dislike of theorizing and hypothesizing, Pinel was reluctant to discuss abstract questions, such as the nature of mental disease or the operation of the mind and its relation to the body. He insisted instead that his primary task was to gather all the results of clinical observations and to bring order into therapy by means of critical and statistical investigations.[7] Concentrating upon the external characteristics of insanity, he observed and analyzed patients and kept extensive case histories in the hopes of ultimately uncovering the component parts of insanity. Pinel's own classification of mental disease was not particularly original, for his four major categories (melancholia, mania, dementia, and idiotism) had been used earlier. Similarly, his discussion of the causes of insanity contributed little that was novel. Believing in multiple causation, he included such factors as heredity, the social and physical environment, excessive passions, alcoholism, and even violent blows on the head as possible causes of mental illness.

If Pinel's contributions to psychiatric theory were modest, his therapeutic innovations were destined to play a major role in the development of institutional care and treatment of the mentally ill. Not only did Pinel insist upon a humanitarian approach; he also proposed a mode of care that made an institutional setting a sine qua non. As a result, the mental hospital became the foundation upon which psychiatry would develop for much of the nineteenth century. This was especially true in the United States, where private practice in psychiatry was virtually unknown before 1875. Yet Pinel's therapeutic innovations were less the product of changes in medical theory than they were a result of the social transformation that accompanied the French Revolution. His removal of the chains binding lunatics in 1793 was simply one aspect of the revolutionary attack on institutions that bound and repressed the individual. Pinel's psychiatric reforms, then, grew out of the prevailing faith in progress and the drive to liberate suffering humanity.

Being an empiricist, Pinel tended to judge therapies in terms of their results. Thus when he applied the pragmatic test to bleeding, corporal punishment, and other traditional practices, he found them wanting and therefore opposed their use. Because

7. *Ibid.*, 288.

he also rejected the idea that insanity could occur only in conjunction with physical lesions, he made room for a psychologically oriented therapy. Seeking to gain the patient's confidence and instill in him a sense of hope, he developed what became known as "moral treatment" or "moral management." Moral treatment involved the creation of a new environment. It assumed that insanity was a curable disease, given understanding, patience, kindness, guidance, and proper treatment. While moral treatment included all of the known nonmedical techniques, it more specifically referred to therapeutic efforts which affected the patient's psychology. "Moral treatment," one of Pinel's most famous students wrote, "is the application of the faculty of intelligence and of emotions in the treatment of mental alienation."[8]

But Pinel's approach was by no means libertarian or democratic. On the contrary, he saw the therapeutic relationship in authoritarian terms, with the physician clearly occupying a commanding and dominant position. Pinel could speak, therefore, about the "happy effects of intimidation, without severity; of oppression, without violence; and of triumph, without outrage." He advocated the recruitment of attendants from among convalescents who recognized the disadvantages of active cruelty but who had become "habituated to obedience, and easy to be drilled into any tactics which the nature of the service might require." The hospital, asylum, retreat—whatever the name given to the institution where mentally ill persons were confined—was indispensable, for only within its walls could an appreciation of normal behavior be instilled in patients.[9]

Although Pinel was undoubtedly the most famous and influential psychiatric reformer of his time, he was by no means the only one. The general humanitarian movements that had grown out of the Enlightenment, as well as the renewed interest in the relevancy of Christianity to social problems, produced other

8. Jean E. D. Esquirol, *Des Passions* (1805), cited in Eric T. Carlson and Norman Dain, "The Psychotherapy That Was Moral Treatment," *American Journal of Psychiatry*, CXVII (December, 1960), 519.

9. Pinel, *Treatise on Insanity*, 63, 91 (see also 59–60, 83, 99, 190, 215–216). Cf. Michel Foucault, *Madness and Civilization: A History of Insanity in the Age of Reason* (New York, 1965), 255ff.

figures who played significant roles in transforming the practice of psychiatry. In Italy Vincenzio Chiarugi introduced a series of sweeping reforms among the insane in Florence. In the United States the versatile Benjamin Rush, though still in the rationalistic system-building tradition of medicine, nevertheless fought for improvements in conditions among the insane at the Pennsylvania Hospital. His famous textbook on mental diseases, despite its mechanistic outlook, helped to spread at least some of the new psychologically oriented therapeutic concepts.[10]

More important than either Chiarugi or Rush in this regard was William Tuke, an English Quaker and merchant. Tuke was instrumental in founding the York Retreat in 1792, and established there the most famous family dynasty in the history of psychiatry. The founding of the York Retreat had an interesting and unusual history. In 1791 a female Quaker had been placed in an establishment for the insane. When some of her acquaintances came to visit her, however, they were denied permission because of her condition. After she died, a movement quickly got under way to establish an institution under the auspices of the Society of Friends to serve Quakers who were mentally ill. Within four years funds had been raised, a building had been erected, and the new institution had accepted its first patients.

The establishment of the York Retreat, however, was not solely a humanitarian and philanthropic act. The Society was concerned because its members had often been placed in institutions run by outsiders and then forced to mingle indiscriminately with other persons. "There has also been particular occasion to observe the great loss," remarked the managers of the Retreat in 1797, "which individuals of our Society have sustained, by being put under the care of those, who are not only strangers to our principles; but by whom they are frequently mixed with other patients, who may indulge themselves in ill language, and exceptionable practices. This often seems to leave an unprofitable effect upon the patients' minds, after they are restored to the use of their reason, alienating from those religious attachments

10. Benjamin Rush to the managers of Pennsylvania Hospital, November 11, 1789, in *Letters of Benjamin Rush*, ed. by Lyman H. Butterfield, 2 vols. (Princeton, 1951), I, 528–529; Rush, *Medical Inquiries and Observations Upon the Diseases of the Mind* (Philadelphia, 1812), *passim*.

which they had before experienced; and, sometimes, even corrupting them with vicious habits, to which they had been strangers."[11]

The therapeutic system developed at the Retreat was similar in some respects to the one advocated by Pinel, although the two were independently conceived since the managers did not learn of Pinel's work until a decade after their institution had received its first patients. Like Pinel, the leaders of the Retreat were distrustful of contemporary medical practice and tended to minimize the efficacy of medical treatment. The first physician there came to the painful conclusion that medicine possessed "very inadequate means to relieve the most grievous of human diseases," and that much more could be accomplished by moral treatment. The basic objective of the Retreat's regimen was to develop in patients internal means of self-restraint and self-control. In the past cruel and harsh treatment had been employed to achieve these goals. Such means, as Samuel Tuke (the son of William Tuke) emphasized, had often proved to be self-defeating. At the Retreat, on the other hand, it was made clear to inmates that their treatment was directly dependent on their personal conduct. While physical coercion and physical punishment were virtually eliminated, the "principle of fear" was judiciously applied and the "desire for esteem" encouraged. As Samuel Tuke put it:

> There cannot be a doubt that the principal of fear, in the human mind, when moderately and judiciously excited, as it is

11. Quoted in Samuel Tuke, *Description of the Retreat, an Institution Near York for Insane Persons of the Society of Friends* (York, England, 1813), 50. Samuel Tuke made much the same point (*ibid.*, 23), and in 1793 the society justified the establishment of the institution with the following statement: "For as the disorder is a mental one, and people of regular conduct, and even religiously disposed minds, are not exempt from it, their confinement amongst persons in all respects strangers, and their promiscuous exposure to such company as is mostly found in public Institutions of this kind, must be peculiarly disgusting, and consequently augment their disorder. Nor is this idea merely chimerical; for it is well known, that the situation of divers Members of our Society, hath, from this cause, been unspeakably distressing. A circumstance which, it needs no arguments to prove, must greatly retard, if not totally prevent their cure." Quoted in *Ibid.*, 37–38.

by the operation of just and equal laws, has a salutary effect upon society. It is a principle also of great use in the education of children, whose imperfect knowledge and judgment, occasion them to be less influenced by other motives. But where fear is too much excited, and where it becomes the chief motive of action, it certainly tends to contract the understanding, to weaken the benevolent affections, and to debase the mind. . . .

It is therefore wise to excite, as much as possible, the operation of superior motives; and fear ought only to be induced, when a *necessary* object cannot otherwise be obtained. If this is the true scale of estimating the degree in which this principle is, in general, to be employed, it is found, at the Retreat, equally applicable to the insane.[12]

There were, however, some significant differences between Pinel's definition of moral management and that of the managers of the Retreat. The former never emphasized to any great extent particular value structures, especially those having a religious basis. The authorities at the Retreat, on the other hand, were quite willing to enforce Christian morality. Thus they emphasized the important role of religion in moral management. In their eyes religion fulfilled two functions simultaneously. In the first place, it promoted self-restraint on the part of the patient; Quakers were convinced that their religious principles and values were conducive to and furthered social harmony and stability. Truly religious persons, they believed, did not behave in socially unacceptable or improper ways. The incorporation of religious beliefs and practices into the internal environment of the Retreat would prove to be beneficial for all patients. Secondly, religion reinforced in the mentally ill person "an attention to his accustomed modes of paying homage to his Maker." This was an obligation, Quakers believed, that no individual could or should avoid.[13]

12. *Ibid.*, 110–112, 141–143, 157–159. See also Daniel Hack Tuke, *Chapters in the History of the Insane in the British Isles* (London, 1882), 112–142.

13. Samuel Tuke, *Description of the Retreat*, 160–161. See also Kathleen Jones, "Moral Management and the Therapeutic Community," in Society for the Social History of Medicine, *Bulletin No. 5* (October, 1971), 6–10 (mimeographed).

The regimen at the Retreat (which included other features all aimed at achieving the same goal) was obviously designed to create an atmosphere in which internal self-restraint and discipline replaced external fetters. The underlying assumption, of course, was that insanity in some respects involved behavioral transgressions; a proper environment would demonstrate to a mentally ill person that he had to accept responsibility for his actions, and that rewards or punishment would follow accordingly. Thus while the management of the Retreat was benevolent in its operations, it was also somewhat authoritarian. "There is much analogy," wrote Samuel Tuke, "between the judicious treatment of children, and that of insane persons."[14]

The significance of psychiatric reformers such as Pinel and William Tuke was that they provided—at least in theory—an alternative to the confinement of mentally ill persons in undifferentiated welfare institutions that were serving a largely custodial function. Thomas S. Kirkbride, a Quaker and one of the most important American psychiatrists of the nineteenth century, noted in 1846 how the world was indebted to these men. Both of them, wrote Kirkbride, "by a singular coincidence, without any knowledge of each others movement, were at the same time, in different kingdoms, engaged in the same noble work of discarding time honoured prejudices and abuses, and from actual practice, giving to the world a code of principles for the moral treatment of Insanity, which even now can hardly be improved."[15] Their work led inescapably to the conclusion that if society wished to invest sufficient resources, the ravages of mental disease could be contained within certain limits, and even might be eliminated in a large percentage of cases. This point of view had major implications for public policy. While its im-

14. Samuel Tuke, *Description of the Retreat*, 150. A visitor to the Retreat in 1798 made much the same comment. The insane, he wrote, were regarded "as children who have an overabundance of strength and make dangerous use of it. They must be given immediate punishments and rewards; whatever is remote has no effect on them. A new system of education must be applied, a new direction given to their ideas; they must first be subjugated, then encouraged, then applied to work, and this work made agreeable by attractive means." Quoted in Foucault, *Madness and Civilization*, 252.

15. Thomas S. Kirkbride to the Superintendent and Managers of the Utica Asylum, March 28, 1846, Kirkbride Papers, IPH.

mediate impact was not great, the long-range influence of this notion was to be of major importance.

It must be noted, however, that "moral management" was more a reflection of social and intellectual currents than changes in medical theory. Though many historians and psychiatrists have attempted to interpret this therapeutic system in modern psychological terms and to relate it to "milieu therapy," figures like Pinel and Tuke were not thinking along such lines. Moral management was essentially a kind and humane (though strict) way of caring for insane persons. Precisely because it was a loose and ill-defined therapy, it was capable of being interpreted and applied in a variety of ways. Its vague theoretical foundations, moreover, left the mental hospital especially vulnerable to the influence of internal and external social, economic, and intellectual forces. In the long run, therefore, the development of the mental hospital was much more than merely the product of changes in psychiatric theory.

These newer views concerning the treatment of mental disorders did not remain solely those of a small group; they soon found a wide audience throughout much of the western world. Educated and upper-class laymen, physicians, intellectuals, and others demonstrated considerable interest in the findings of these early pioneers. The existence of a trans-Atlantic intellectual and scientific community facilitated the rapid exchange and dissemination of such views. Some Americans were educated abroad and brought back first-hand knowledge of European and English practices. Others were influenced by their reading, since most of the important English and European books were quickly imported into the United States. Language proved to be no barrier, for Pinel's famous treatise on mental illness was translated into English by 1806. The work of the York Retreat was widely publicized with the publication of Samuel Tuke's *Description of the Retreat* in 1813. Benjamin Rush's book on insanity in 1812 showed a complete familiarity with Pinel's ideas. In fact, a physician reviewing Rush's contribution noted that within a few short years "an entire revolution has been effected in the moral management" of the insane. The reviewer attributed the new-found attitude to "the pure and enlightened humanity of the Quakers in Great Britain, who first illustrated the good effects of a mild system, at their asylum at York, in England; and more, perhaps, to that active benevolence, which forms one of the striking characteristics of the age."[16]

The exchange of ideas was further facilitated by the contacts maintained by various religious and benevolent groups. American Quakers, to cite an outstanding example, were influenced by the work of their English brethren in treating the insane. Not only did they establish the Friends' Asylum in Pennsylvania in 1813, but individual Quakers also played significant roles in helping to found other nonsectarian hospitals. In New York Thomas Eddy, the famous Quaker philanthropist and reformer who had been active in the affairs of the New York Hospital for two decades, played a major role in reorganizing the care of the insane at that institution. His efforts resulted eventually in the opening of the Bloomingdale Asylum as a separate department in 1821. For many of his ideas Eddy was indebted to his fellow Quaker Samuel Tuke, a debt that he was quick to acknowledge.[17] Indeed, at least half of the mental hospitals established in the United States prior to 1824 drew heavily upon the experiences of the Quakers.

Knowledge about reforms in the care of the mentally ill, however, was only one ingredient in the transformation of public policy that took place during the first half of the nineteenth century. What was also required was support for concrete proposals that embodied some of the newer therapeutic approaches. Such support became available during the two decades following 1800 as a result of the combined impact of the Second Great Awakening and a sharp increase in the philanthropic activities of certain wealthy urban elites.

The Second Great Awakening—a movement that attempted

16. Rush, *Medical Inquiries and Observations*, 18, 46, 55–56, 109, 131, 133, 241; George Hayward, "*Some Observations on Dr. Rush's work, on 'the Diseases of the Mind.'* With remarks on the Nature and Treatment of Insanity," *New England Journal of Medicine and Surgery*, VII (January, 1818), 28. For a good general treatment of the spread of psychiatric ideas in the nineteenth century see Norman Dain, *Concepts of Insanity in the United States, 1789–1865* (New Brunswick, 1964).

17. See Thomas Eddy, *Hints for Introducing an Improved Mode of Treating the Insane in the Asylum; Read before the Governors of the New-York Hospital, on the 4th of Fourth-month, 1815* (New York, 1815), 4–5; Samuel Tuke, *A Letter on Pauper Lunatic Asylums* (New York, 1815); Samuel L. Knapp, *The Life of Thomas Eddy* (New York, 1834), 95–98.

to redefine the theory and practice of American Christianity in order to make it more relevant to the existing society—undoubtedly helped to create a climate that was more conducive to institutional reform. Beginning about 1800, the Awakening had the immediate effect of further weakening the Calvinistic emphasis on the essential depravity of human nature and the inability of men to save themselves. In place of such pessimistic tenets, some Protestant leaders substituted the idea of a loving and beneficent God, whose first concern was the happiness of His creatures. The central theme of their liberalized theology was the doctrine of the free individual and a belief in a moral universe. Good behavior, they argued, was dependent not so much on external restraints, but on the inner check of conscience and self-control. Thus individual conversion and regeneration were essential to the establishment and maintenance of the good society, for a truly converted person not only would be free from the temptations of evil but would voluntarily undertake the work of God in building a better world.

The individualistic philosophy that came in part out of the Great Awakening was not necessarily conducive to the spirit of *social* reform. When this belief in the free individual was fused with the millenial vision of a society performing a divine mission by eradicating all evidences of evil, however, one strain of evangelical Protestantism was transformed into an activistic social force seeking the abolition of those restraints that bound the individual and hindered his self-development. Ministers and laymen alike began to work actively to destroy the evil institutional restraints that presumably imprisoned the individual. All persons, they maintained, were under a moral law that gave them a responsibility for the welfare of their fellow man. As a result, a wide spectrum of individuals were drawn into reform activities, while others became more receptive to some of the goals of the movement. Nor was reform by any means confined to evangelical sects. Even the Unitarians, who opposed many of the tenets of evangelical Christianity, justified their more rational and intellectual approach to religion by emphasizing their concern with the well-being of the individual and of society.[18] Thus

18. See Octavius B. Frothingham, *Boston Unitarianism 1820–1850: A Study of the Life and Work of Nathaniel Langdon Frothingham* (New York, 1890), 127.

many Americans of different denominational affiliations accepted as an article of faith the belief that their institutions could be improved, if not perfected, and their national destiny fulfilled.

The second of the developments that aided the cause of reform was the growing financial support provided by relatively wealthy elites in certain communities. Philadelphia and New York, of course, had already benefited from the moral and financial support given to their new hospitals during the second half of the eighteenth century by such groups. Even Virginia's hospital had been established by an indigenous elite without having to appeal for broad public support. Being relatively small and homogeneous, possessing a sense of noblesse oblige, and taking their social responsibilities seriously, these older elite groups played an important role in the initial stages of the movement to found mental hospitals.

By the early nineteenth century, however, the older and more established elites found themselves increasingly challenged by newer groups that had arisen out of economic and occupational changes. This rivalry, when combined with the religious divisions that accompanied the growing sectarian tendencies within Protestantism, stimulated philanthropic giving. Each group seemed determined to demonstrate that its prominence and wealth had not been amassed solely for personal gain and satisfaction, but would be used as well to support socially desirable community projects.

Most of these elites developed an ideology and value structure. While holding virtues like ambition, thrift, hard work, personal responsibility, and honesty in high esteem, they rejected the idea that wealth and material possessions were good in themselves. Wealth, on the contrary, endowed its owner with a special and demanding responsibility to see that it was used properly. Regarding themselves as the harbingers of social progress, many members of these elites emphasized the concept of stewardship. The rich and fortunate, they argued, had a clear moral responsibility to the less fortunate groups in society as well as to the community as a whole. Money was not to be squandered indiscriminately, but was to be used instead for the benefit of all. The founding and support of socially desirable institutions such as hospitals, educational institutions, museums, and other philanthropic enterprises was especially worthy. Tied together by both business and family relationships, individual members of elite groups were to play prominent roles in the founding of the first corporate hospitals in the United States.[19]

The first indications of the shift away from reliance on traditional and informal modes of care for the mentally ill was a short-lived spurt in the founding of private hospitals in the Northeast. Supported largely by contributions from wealthy benefactors—although additional subsidies were sought from state legislatures in several instances—these new institutions were intended, in theory, to serve the entire community. Those who could afford to pay for their upkeep were to do so, while those with insufficient resources were to be supported by a combination of private philanthropy and higher charges paid by relatively well-to-do patients. Between 1811 and 1822 three new mental hospitals (the McLean Asylum, the Friends' Asylum, and the Hartford Retreat) were founded. During this same period the Bloomingdale Asylum was separated from the parent New York Hospital and given an autonomous identity. These early institutions, however, did not come into existence as a result of careful study and planning. There was no attempt to identify the incidence of various diseases, the potential need for hospital facilities, or the ability of individuals and groups to pay for the costs of institutionalization. The establishment of these hospitals rather arose out of indigenous local conditions; broad issues of public policy were never seriously considered, even though those active on behalf of these institutions assumed that their efforts could not help but further the welfare of the community and the mentally ill.

The first of these new hospitals was established in Boston, where an earlier attempt to found such an institution in the 1760's had failed. By 1800, however, the problems arising out of mental illness had become more intense because the city's population had mounted to 25,000. The emergence of a new business elite, religious divisions between Congregationalists and Unitarians, and the rapid growth of an intellectual and medical community, moreover, had all combined to stimulate more philanthropic undertakings. The first suggestion for a "Hospital for Lunatics"

19. Cf. Paul Goodman, "Ethics and Enterprise: The Values of a Boston Elite, 1800–1860," *American Quarterly*, XVIII (Fall, 1966), 437–451, and Leonard K. Eaton, *New England Hospitals 1790–1833* (Ann Arbor, 1957), 37ff.

was made in 1801 by the Reverend Jedidiah Morse, a conservative Congregationalist minister who gained fame as a geographer. While some financial support was forthcoming, nothing further came of his original proposal.[20] For almost a decade the establishment of such a hospital was raised from time to time, but to no avail.

In 1810, however, the Reverend John Bartlett, a Harvard graduate and chaplain of the city almshouse, called for the establishment of a general hospital in Boston similar to those already existing in New York and Philadelphia. Distressed by the indiscriminate mixing of paupers, pregnant women, and lunatics in the almshouse, he sought support for better facilities. Bartlett quickly interested some of the leading Bostonians in his proposal, and among those who joined a committee organized by him were John Collins Warren and James Jackson. These two men were among the city's leading physicians, and both had studied abroad and were well acquainted with the medical facilities of other nations. The two doctors issued a circular on August 20, 1810, which called for the establishment of a general hospital. Assisting the sick poor, they claimed, was a Christian duty. While the poor could provide for most illnesses, protracted sickness proved disastrous even to the most industrious. Both physicians found cases of insanity particularly distressing. When such cases went without proper care and treatment, the disease tended to become incurable. Most insane persons, they argued, were simply unable to provide for themselves, and their families often faced financial ruin. The ideal solution was a hospital that would accept all mentally ill persons, including those unable to pay for the costs of confinement. The two men were also confident that the General Court would appropriate public funds to supplement private donations. Finally, they pointed out, a hospital would serve to improve medical training within the state, which lacked adequate facilities.[21]

When the General Court met in Boston the following winter,

20. M. A. DeWolfe Howe, *The Humane Society of the Commonwealth of Massachusetts: An Historical Review 1785–1916* (Boston, 1918), 199–201.

21. Nathaniel I. Bowditch, *A History of the Massachusetts General Hospital*, 2d ed. (Boston, 1872), 3–9; Massachusetts Board of State Charities, *AR*, VIII (1871), xl; Eaton, *New England Hospitals*, 29–30.

the supporters of the hospital had prepared an eloquent appeal. Their petition emphasized the perplexing problems posed by illness within an urban environment. If the legislature admitted "that the necessities of the sick poor and unfortunate are in a certain degree one of the proper burdens of the public Treasury, it will be more generally acknowledged that in a certain other degree they are properly the burden of more fortunate individuals." As a result of a well-planned campaign by the petitioners, most of whom were leaders in the community, the General Court passed an act of incorporation in February, 1811. The act gave the state the authority to appoint four of the twelve trustees. It also granted the Province House estate in Boston (then valued at about $20,000) as an endowment with the stipulation that the corporation raise within five years an additional sum of $100,000 from private sources. The charter further stated that thirty sick or lunatic persons chargeable to the Commonwealth were to be supported at the hospital. In 1813, however, the legislature modified this requirement by making the number of poor and insane persons admitted to the new institution dependent upon the income derived from the Province House estate, and in 1816 repealed the clause altogether.[22]

After the charter had been granted, a money-raising campaign was launched by the sponsors. Delayed by the War of 1812, the effort got under way at the end of 1816, and in less than a year the required sum had been collected. Although 1,047 individuals contributed to the project, the bulk of the money came from a relatively small group. Of the total number of gifts, 245 were in excess of $100. The single largest gift of $20,000 was contributed by William Phillips (who also endowed the Andover and Exeter academies), while other merchants and businessmen also gave generous amounts. The thirteen largest gifts came to $56,000— well over half the total required by the legislature. The entire

22. Eaton, *New England Hospitals*, 30–34; Henry M. Hurd, ed., *The Institutional Care of the Insane in the United States and Canada*, 4 vols. (Baltimore, 1916–1917), II, 599–600; Massachusetts Board of State Charities, *AR*, VIII (1871), xl–xli. In 1814 George Parkman announced his intention of opening a retreat for the insane, but nothing further came of his proposal. See his *Proposals for Establishing a Retreat for the Insane, to be Conducted by George Parkman, M.D.* (Boston, 1814).

project, by and large, was conceived and executed by members of the Boston elite.[23] They were assisted by Congregational clergymen, whose ties with both the elite and the public enabled them to achieve a united community response to the project. In their own public appeals, the clergy explicitly exploited denominational rivalries in order to gain moral and financial support. They pointed out that the Roman Catholic, Greek, Lutheran, Calvinist, Presbyterian, and Quaker churches had all manifested Christian obligations and duties in regard to charity. "Shall the Congregational scion alone be barren of the sweetest fruits which the tree of Christianity had produced?" they asked. "Shall this metropolis give a colour to the aspersions which have been cast upon its religious principles, and afford reason to believe that its inhabitants are deficient in vital piety, that their religion is that of the lips and not of the heart? . . . It is not a gift which we ask, we demand the payment of a debt. We are all stewards of God's bounty, and we are bound and directed to distribute it." The local press, with only an occasional exception, threw its weight behind the fund-raising drive, and by 1817 over $100,000 had been pledged.[24]

Well before the hospital had commenced operations, the trustees decided to separate insane from regular patients. As a result, they located the Massachusetts General Hospital in Boston, and placed the asylum for the insane in nearby Charlestown. After receiving its first patients in 1818, the facility was officially renamed McLean Asylum for the Insane in 1826 in honor of John McLean, the prominent Boston merchant who not only had given the hospital corporation $25,000 but had designated it as his residual legatee. Eventually the corporation received nearly $120,000 from his estate—a huge bequest by early nineteenth-century standards.[25]

Although the state, at least according to the act of incorporation, played a role in the governance of the institution, actual

23. *Address of the Trustees of the Massachusetts General Hospital to the Subscribers and to the Public* (n.p., n.d. [c. 1822]), 4–5; Eaton, *New England Hospitals*, 45–48, 54–55; Bowditch, *History of the Massachusetts General Hospital*, 423–431.

24. Eaton, *New England Hospitals*, 48–54.

25. Hurd, *Institutional Care of the Insane*, II, 601; Bowditch, *History of the Massachusetts General Hospital*, 64–65.

power resided in the hands of the trustees. The parent corporation was large and met annually, but its members rarely raised substantive questions about the competency of the trustees, who from the very beginning were drawn from among the wealthiest and most respected members of the community. Even the financing of the institution reflected the dominance of a particular group. Besides the large bequests that the hospital received from time to time, it was also the beneficiary of an arrangement with the Massachusetts Hospital Life Insurance Company made in 1824. By its terms the company agreed to give to the hospital one-third of all profits that exceeded 6 percent. This agreement was facilitated by the fact that power within the hospital and company tended to be concentrated in much the same hands.[26]

While the Boston elite was establishing the Massachusetts General Hospital and McLean Asylum, Philadelphia Quakers were in the process of founding an institution modeled along the lines of the York Retreat in England. In 1811 proposals were made from several Quarterly Meetings to the Yearly Meeting of the Society of Friends that some provision be made "for such of our members as may be deprived of the use of their reason." A committee quickly reported back in favor of the plan. Like their English brethren, the American Quakers conceived of the new institution in sectarian terms; admission would be limited to members of the Society. Ability to pay, however, was explicitly excluded as a requirement for admission. By 1813 a constitution had been adopted and a fund-raising drive launched. Shortly thereafter the society purchased a 52-acre tract near Frankford, Pennsylvania, and began construction of a physical plant designed to accommodate about fifty patients.[27]

There can be no doubt that the new institution had received its inspiration from the example of William Tuke and the York Retreat. Aside from the contacts between American and English Quakers that kept the Philadelphia group well informed of developments abroad, one of the moving figures behind the project was Thomas Scattergood. A well-known Philadelphia figure,

26. Eaton, *New England Hospitals*, 33–37, 108–109.

27. *Account of the Rise and Progress of The Asylum, Proposed to be Established, near Philadelphia, for the Relief of Persons Deprived of the Use of Their Reason, With an Abridged Account of the Retreat, A Similar Institution near York, in England* (Philadelphia, 1814), 3–11.

3. McLean Asylum for the Insane. McLean, a division of the Massachusetts General Hospital, opened in 1818, and was perhaps the most exclusive mental hospital in nineteenth-century America. Source: Massachusetts General Hospital, Annual Report, 1844.

Scattergood had spent six years in England and Ireland in religious endeavors for the Society of Friends and had become acquainted with William Tuke.[28] At the same time that the asylum was being founded, Samuel Tuke's *Description of the Retreat* also appeared in an American edition shortly after its publication in England in 1813. An abridged version of the book was published the following year which was intended to keep members of the Society appraised of the project's progress and to help in fund-raising activities. Like the York Retreat, the new institution was intended to serve only members of the Society; others were excluded until a change of regulations in 1834 modified this policy.

The governing structure of the Friends' Asylum differed from that of McLean in certain important respects. Its charter, for example, specified that any Monthly Meeting belonging to the Yearly Meeting and contributing at least $200 or any individual subscribing $10 per annum or $50 at one time could appoint an agent to appear and to act on its or his behalf at the meetings of the governing association. The association, in turn, selected from among the contributors twenty managers, in whom control of the institution was vested.[29] For many years the asylum was directed by a lay superintendent (responsible to the board of managers) who administered the internal routine and treatment of patients. Strictly medical problems, however, were handled by a resident physician. Such an administrative structure reflected the basically religious rather than medical character of the undertaking. By the middle of 1817 the asylum had received its first patients. It remained small in size and sectarian in character, and its establishment had little influence over public policy.

The third corporate hospital for the insane to be established during the early nineteenth century was the Hartford Retreat in Connecticut. Unlike originators of the institutions in Boston and Philadelphia, the leaders in Connecticut were from the young medical profession. Between 1812 and 1816 the Connecticut

28. *Journal of the Life and Religious Labors of Thomas Scattergood, A Minister of the Gospel in the Society of Friends* (Philadelphia, n.d.), 202; *Memoirs of Thomas Scattergood*, compiled by William and Thomas Evans, (London, 1845), 382.

29. *Account of the Rise and Progress of The Asylum . . . near Philadelphia*, 7.

Medical Society at its annual meeting had discussed the possibility of establishing an asylum and even appointed a committee to take a census of the insane in the state. Although some statistics were compiled (largely by polling the state's clergy), they were not especially accurate. Between 1816 and 1821 the project lay dormant and nothing further was heard about the subject.[30]

The idea of an asylum was resurrected again in the spring of 1821 at the annual meeting of the State Medical Society, which appointed a committee to investigate the number of insane persons in the state. Composed of five distinguished medical figures, including Eli Todd and Samuel B. Woodward, the committee reported its findings in the autumn. The figures it compiled, together with future projections, indicated that there were nearly 1,000 mentally ill persons in the state. Most of them were suffering under wretched conditions. Pointing out that several other states already had "public asylums," the committee deplored the lack of similar facilities in Connecticut. Many maniacs had become incurable, it noted, since it was impossible to treat mental illness within the framework of private practice. In asking for contributions, the five men argued that a hospital in the long run would help to contain mental disease by assisting persons who might have become chronic to recover. It was also far more economical to care for mentally ill persons within a single hospital than to provide separate facilities either in welfare institutions or in private households. To implement its recommendations, the committee urged that a "Society for the Relief of the Insane" be established. Its draft of a constitution for such an organization was quickly adopted by the full convention.[31]

This plan, which became the basis for the act of incorporation approved by the legislature in 1822, provided for a hierarchical and somewhat complicated class of subscribers. One class

30. *Reprint of the Proceedings of the Connecticut Medical Society from 1792 to 1829 Inclusive* (Hartford, 1884), 172, 178, 184; *Society for the Relief of the Insane. . . . Annual Meeting at Hartford, 2d Wednesday of May* (Hartford, 1823), 11.

31. *Report of a Committee of the Connecticut Medical Society, Respecting an Asylum for the Insane, With the Constitution of the Society for Their Relief. Accepted by the Medical Convention, October 3, 1821* (Hartford, 1821). The report is reprinted in Hurd, *Institutional Care of the Insane*, II, 93–102 (which mistakenly gives the date of the report as 1842).

4. *Connecticut Retreat for the Insane at Hartford. Like most private hospitals, the Hartford Retreat (opened in 1824) remained small in scope, although it accepted some indigent groups in return for state subsidies. Source: Connecticut Retreat for the Insane, Report of the Medical Visitors, May 14, 1830.*

of directors was elected by the Society for the Relief of the Insane; another held office by virtue of its large contributions. Both groups were required to meet annually and elect officers. The first consisted of six physicians, of whom at least two visited the hospital monthly. The second was responsible for recruiting staff, deciding terms of admission, and regulating the finances of the institution. The superintendent had to be nominated by a committee of the State Medical Society and approved by the directors.[32] Such a system of governance in the long run was to weaken the authority of the superintendent, thus involving the institution in a series of internal controversies and dissension that lasted for well over half a century.[33]

Immediately following the passage of the act of incorporation, a state-wide fund-raising drive was launched. The lead was again taken by the five physicians who had written the original report in 1821. They were also assisted by a number of eminent clergymen. Support by the latter was natural, since the religious scene in the state for the previous two decades had been marked by a series of revivals. These revivals—a part of the Second Great Awakening—not only transformed many of the state's churches but also resulted in a heightened sensitivity toward the merits and importance of organized benevolence. Although not possessing the financial resources of Massachusetts, Connecticut citizens between 1800 and 1830 proved themselves willing and able to support a variety of charitable endeavors, including the Connecticut Asylum for the Education and Instruction of the Deaf and Dumb, the first of its kind in the nation.[34] Indeed, the involvement of a number of the physicians active in the establish-

32. Eaton, *New England Hospitals*, 66–67.

33. For evidence of internal problems at the Retreat see James H. Denny to Kirkbride, December 30, 1872, Kirkbride Papers, IPH; *Letters on the Construction of the By-Laws of the Retreat for the Insane* (Hartford, 1873); *On the Revision of the By-Laws of the Retreat for the Insane with Letters on Hospital Organization and Government* (Hartford, 1873); *Reasons for Considering the Expediency of a Revision of the By-Laws of the Retreat for the Insane* (Hartford, 1873); *Final Action on the Question of Government of the Retreat for the Insane at Hartford, Conn., with Letters of Endorsement* (Hartford, 1873); Connecticut Retreat for the Insane, *AR*, L (1874), 6–7.

34. Charles R. Keller, *The Second Great Awakening in Connecticut* (New Haven, 1942), is an excellent study of this subject.

ment of the new insane asylum was partly a product of their own religious convictions.[35]

By the spring of 1822 about $12,000 had been raised for the new asylum—a sum clearly insufficient for the undertaking. Because Connecticut did not have as broad an elite with the resources to underwrite its institution as had been the case in Massachusetts, the drive had to rely on a large number of relatively small contributions. The legislature also voted in 1822 a subsidy of $5,000, and later gave the Society for the Relief of the Insane the power to operate a lottery. In addition, the society employed both town and country agents and professional solicitors to raise funds for the asylum. The former "but illy served the interests" of the project. The latter, on the other hand, were far more successful, and the directors recommended that this method be used in the future.[36]

Financial problems, nevertheless, remained an obstacle during the Retreat's early years. It did not, as had the Bloomingdale Asylum, receive a significant amount of state aid, nor could it rely on wealthy benefactors. Indeed, even before the institution opened Woodward bitterly condemned the directors for their seeming refusal to pay a decent salary for a superintendent. "But when I find a board of directors limiting the salary of the superintendent to the paltry sum of 600 [dollars] and that obtained by a lean majority," he wrote to Todd, "my heart sickens at the prospect and I am almost ready to exclaim with the enemies of the Retreat, Citizens of Hartford, your object is aggrandizement."[37] Despite these problems, the Hartford Retreat following

35. The influence of religion on Samuel B. Woodward, for example, was evident even in his early student days. See his two essays written at the Morris Academy on "Benevolence" (Essay No. VII, January 19, 1807) and "Gaming, Drinking, etc." (Essay No. VIII, January 25, 1807), in Woodward, "Collected Writings," vol. III, typescript copy in the Library of Worcester State Hospital, Worcester, Mass., and "Errors of Education" (undated), Woodward Papers, AAS. The relationship between religion and the founding of the Retreat is also evident in Thomas Robbins, *An Address Delivered at the Retreat for the Insane, in Hartford, at the Dedication of that Institution . . . April 1, 1824* (Hartford, 1824).

36. *Society for the Relief of the Insane. . . . Annual Meeting at Hartford, 2d Wednesday of May,* 12–14; Eaton, *New England Hospitals,* 71–76.

37. Woodward to Eli Todd, August, 1823, Institute of Living Collection, Library, Institute of Living, Hartford, Conn.

its opening in 1824 remained for over four decades the only such facility serving the people of Connecticut.

At the same time that these new institutions were being established in Boston, Philadelphia, and Hartford, the insane department of the New York Hospital was undergoing a series of reorganizations that by 1821 had given it a largely autonomous character. The department in its administrative form emerged with a status similar to that enjoyed by the McLean Asylum of the Massachusetts General Hospital. For over a decade following the reception of its first patients in 1791, the New York Hospital had not possessed a separate building for mentally ill patients. Inadequate quarters had hindered therapeutic care, and the fact that insane persons were placed in the same building as patients with general diseases appears to have been a source of discontent to all concerned. Shortly after 1800, therefore, the governors of the hospital decided to erect a new and separate structure exclusively for the care of the insane. Intended to accommodate about eighty patients, the new facility was begun in 1806 and completed in 1808 at a cost slightly in excess of $50,000. Along with a separate building went an administrative reorganization. The governors authorized the appointment of a physician to the asylum (this position being in addition to a lay caretaker who exercised the powers of a superintendent); they also established an "Asylum Committee" that for all intents and purposes was responsible for issues of governance and financial management (although it reported to the ruling body of the hospital).[38]

Though the new building resulted in greater material comforts for the patients, it did not to any significant degree alter the hospital's internal regimen in accordance with some of the newer views regarding the treatment of mental disease. In the spring of 1815, therefore, Thomas Eddy presented to the governors of the New York Hospital a series of far-reaching recommendations that were intended to transform the character of the asylum. Influenced particularly by the York Retreat, Eddy summarized in lucid terms Samuel Tuke's *Description of the Retreat*.

38. "The New Lunatic Asylum in New-York," *Medical Repository*, n.s. V (February–April, 1808), 416–418; Pliny Earle, *History, Description and Statistics of the Bloomingdale Asylum for the Insane* (New York, 1848), 8–9; William L. Russell, *The New York Hospital: A History of the Psychiatric Service 1771–1936* (New York, 1945), 67–86.

He emphasized the moderate and judicious use of the "principle of fear," the necessity of treating the patient as a rational being, and the importance of promoting self-restraint by utilizing the precepts of religion. After offering eleven specific recommendations, Eddy then proposed that the hospital purchase a lot within a few miles of the city and erect a "Rural Retreat." This facility, he noted, would "afford an ample opportunity of ascertaining how far that disease may be removed by moral management alone, which it is believed, will, in many instances, be more effectual in controlling the maniac, than medical treatment, especially, in those cases where the disease has proceeded from causes operating directly on the mind."[39]

Eddy's communication was referred to a committee which quickly issued a favorable report. Present quarters, its members stated, were overcrowded; lack of land prevented further expansion; and an urban environment was ill suited for an insane hospital. The governors concurred and immediately authorized the purchase of 38 acres of rural land on Manhattan's upper west side, then known as Bloomingdale. They also presented a memorial to the state legislature, citing the large numbers of applications for admission, the lack of facilities, the difficulties of providing proper treatment in existing quarters, and the "indiscriminate mixture . . . of persons of different character, of various and opposite religious sentiments, the serious and profane, the profligate and virtuous." Prodded by Eddy's skillful lobbying, the legislature granted the hospital an annual subsidy of $10,000 until 1857. By July, 1821, the new hospital had been completed and the patients transferred from the older building.[40]

The Bloomingdale Asylum in a few significant respects differed from other corporate institutions. It was a mixed-type corporation, since it received public subsidies far greater than similar grants given other private hospitals. As early as 1772 the New York legislature provided the New York Hospital with an annual

39. Eddy, *Hints for Introducing an Improved Mode of Treating the Insane*, 4–16. See also Samuel Tuke to Eddy, July 17, 1815, in Samuel Tuke, *A Letter on Pauper Lunatic Asylums*, 4–11. Knapp's *Life of Thomas Eddy*, published in 1834, is an important source, although a complete study of Eddy is sorely needed.

40. Russell, *New York Hospital*, 123–127; Knapp, *Life of Thomas Eddy*, 97–98.

allowance of $2,000 for twenty years, and three years later it voted $10,000 to help defray the costs of rebuilding after a disastrous fire. After independence had been declared, this support continued. Between 1783 and 1801 the New York Hospital received at least five additional subsidies. In 1806 the legislature voted an annual annuity of $12,500 to be paid until 1857, and this practice was continued in future legislation. When the governors decided to build a separate asylum, the legislature granted an additional annual subsidy of $10,000 until 1857 to be used exclusively for the care of the insane. Such aid vested the institution with a quasi-public character, leading to the suggestion (which was not adopted) that the physician of the Bloomingdale Asylum be appointed by the governor of New York and the Senate rather than the board of governors.[41] Paradoxically, the close relationship between the hospital and the state may have inhibited the founding of similar state-supported institutions for a time, because New York—given its population and wealth—lagged slightly behind other states in establishing public hospitals during the 1830's.

Like several other institutions, the Bloomingdale Asylum functioned under a system of divided authority. General responsibility for the institution's affairs was vested in six governors, who reported to the full board of the New York Hospital. The governors, in turn, appointed a lay superintendent (or warden) who was in charge of the establishment, and a matron. The medical department, on the other hand, was conducted by a resident physician and by an attending physician who was required to visit the asylum at least once a week, or more often if circumstances warranted.[42] For many years this system of administration, despite occasional modifications, led to continuous internal strife between the warden, physician, and governors. The Bloomingdale Asylum found that its effectiveness was seriously impaired for more than three decades because of such friction.

41. New York *Assembly Document No. 263* (March 10, 1831), 7–10; *Charter of the Society of the New-York Hospital, and the Laws Relating Thereto . . . and Those of the Bloomingdale Asylum for the Insane* (New York, 1856), 15–17.

42. New York Hospital and Bloomingdale Asylum, *AR*, 1821, in New York *Assembly Journal*, 1822, 677; Earle, *History, Description and Statistics of the Bloomingdale Asylum*, 11–13; Russell, *New York Hospital*, 147ff.

III

ALTHOUGH all of these early corporate hospitals enjoyed considerable popularity in their respective communities, they failed to become the forerunners of a large and geographically dispersed system of institutions capable of caring for a considerable proportion of the nation's mentally ill population. It is true that they were instrumental in spreading and popularizing some of the newer concepts of mental disease with its hopeful prognosis (given early and proper treatment), and thus made possible future expansion of hospital facilities. It is also true that they served as training centers out of which would emerge a self-conscious and confident psychiatric profession. Yet their structure, financial base, and goals were such as to prevent them from emerging as the foundation of a comprehensive system of hospitals serving the entire community.

Consider, for example, the goals and practices of these corporate institutions. Essentially they were intended to serve a therapeutic rather than a custodial function. Though medical treatment remained an important element, far greater emphasis was placed on moral management, which involved the creation of a new environment to counteract earlier influences that had brought on the disease in the patient. Since the physician (i.e., medical superintendent) clearly played a dominant role in this therapeutic process, it was assumed that the institution would remain small in order to maximize his influence over the patient body. Consequently, the scale of these early corporate hospitals was never large.

Considerable evidence exists that early corporate hospitals succeeded in providing an internal atmosphere conducive to therapeutic goals. Because these institutions remained small in size, it was relatively easy for the superintendent to maintain close personal relationships with patients. Generally speaking, patients were encouraged to develop internal means of restraint, and a system of rewards and punishments usually reinforced this objective. Superintendents insisted that patients be treated as rational individuals capable of modifying their own behavior. Idleness was looked upon with disfavor, and most hospitals made determined efforts to provide some sort of occupation for their patients. Along with labor went amusements for recreation and relaxation, including games, riding, parties, lectures, and reading. Many patients received progressively greater freedom and liberty as they adjusted their behavioral patterns. Virtually every one of these early hospitals made religious worship and instruction one of the central pillars of its therapeutic regimen, an understandable practice given the strong religious convictions of both founders and superintendents. (In Europe, by way of contrast, anticlericalism and hostility toward established churches tended to minimize the role of religion.) Although the use of restraints was not encouraged, most superintendents found that it was impossible to dispense with their use entirely. Consequently, a number of techniques were employed, including isolation and the use of various confining devices.[43]

Reliance on moral treatment by no means implied abandonment of medical treatment. But medical treatment of insanity during the first three or four decades of the nineteenth century declined somewhat, if only because physicians were not at all clear as to its precise advantages. "My experience long since convinced me," wrote the second superintendent of McLean in words that echoed Pinel, "that the curative and custodial treatment of the insane was essentially moral treatment; that while constant regard was to be had to physical symptoms and medical agents now of use in assisting nature to restore the mind by regulating the body, there was no specific treatment for insanity *per*

43. See New York Hospital and Bloomingdale Asylum, *AR*, 1821, in New York *Assembly Journal*, 1822, 677; Friends' Asylum for the Insane, *AR*, IX (1826), 10–16; McLean Asylum for the Insane, *AR*, XXIV (1841), in Massachusetts General Hospital, *AR*, 1841, 22–32; R. R. Porter, "Reports of Cases of Insanity Treated at Friends' Asylum, near Frankford," *American Journal of the Medical Sciences*, XX (August, 1837), 350–369; Pliny Earle, "Researches in Reference to the Causes, Duration, Termination, and Moral Treatment of Insanity," *American Journal of the Medical Sciences*, XXII (August, 1838), 339–356.

There are some accounts of care (but less on treatment) at early corporate mental hospitals. See Eaton, *New England Hospitals*, 133–160, and "Eli Todd and the Hartford Retreat," *New England Quarterly*, XXVI (December, 1953), 435–453; Russell, *New York Hospital*, Chap. XV; Norman Dain and Eric T. Carlson, "Milieu Therapy in the Nineteenth Century: Patient Care at the Friends' Asylum, Frankford, Pennsylvania, 1817–1861," *Journal of Nervous and Mental Disease*, CXXXI (October, 1960), 277–290.

se; that the corporeal derangements, were as numerous as those of which pain or loss of appetite is a symptom; that a state of mind capable of reacting favorably on the physical cause was attained mainly by moral influences."[44] His predecessor, Dr. Rufus Wyman—who was given much of the credit for McLean's early successes—took essentially the same position. "The treatment of insanity," he told the Massachusetts Medical Society in 1830,

> chiefly depends upon the connexion between the mind and body. If there be inflammation of the brain, or its membranes, it is to be treated as inflammation of those parts. If there be other organic disease, whether of structure or of function, in any part of the body, medical treatment will be required. But in mental disorders, without symptoms of organic disease, a judicious moral management is more successful. . . . It requires, however, constant attention and vigilance, with the greatest kindness and attention in the attendants upon a lunatic. Moral treatment is indispensable, even in cases arising from organic disease.
>
> In regard to medical treatment, I believe, that purging, bleeding, low diet, &c. have been adopted with little discrimination. They are to be resorted to only when there is organic disease, which requires the *"reducing plan."* But these remedies, especially in debilitated subjects, are seldom useful in relieving mental disease. They are usually injurious, and frequently fatal. It is undoubtedly true, that impressions upon the alimentary canal by purging or vomiting, and upon the skin of the extremities by blistering, are useful in chronic cases of mental disorders. But these remedies must be suited to the strength and general health of the patient.[45]

One factor that permitted early corporate hospitals to implement moral treatment was their small size. Since they were not compelled to accept patients, they were selective in their admission policies. Throughout the 1820's and 1830's, therefore, patient populations at these institutions were extraordinarily low. McLean, for example, accepted an average of slightly over

44. Luther V. Bell to Dorothea L. Dix, February 14, 1843, Dix Papers, HLHU.

45. Rufus Wyman, "A Discourse on Mental Philosophy as Connected with Mental Disease, Delivered before the Massachusetts Medical Society, in June, 1830," in *Medical Communications of the Massachusetts Medical Society*, V, part I (Boston, 1830), 23–24.

61 patients a year between 1818 and 1830. During that same period it discharged an average of slightly over 55 per year, and at the end of each year the average number of patients in residence was less than 50. Bloomingdale was the largest of the corporate hospitals; its corresponding figures were nearly double those of McLean. Comparably, it usually had fewer than 100 patients during these years. The Hartford Retreat and Friends' Asylum were much smaller institutions. The former between 1824 and 1830 admitted an average of 41.2 patients annually, and the number in residence at any given time was considerably lower. The latter was even smaller; between 1820 and 1830 its annual admissions were half those of the Hartford Retreat.[46]

During their formative years corporate hospitals claimed that they had achieved striking successes. McLean, for example, discharged 666 patients between 1818 and 1830. Of these, 247 were listed as having recovered, 96 as much improved, and 91 as improved. These claims were by no means atypical. Of 1,841 patients admitted at Bloomingdale between 1821 and 1844, 1,762 were discharged, including 672 as cured, 104 as much improved, and 318 as improved.[47] While these claims may seem exaggerated (especially in the light of later nineteenth- and twentieth-century experiences), there is every reason for taking them seriously. The criteria for recovery, after all, were by no means unrealistic or vague. When discharging a patient who had recovered, early nineteenth-century psychiatrists were simply stating that in their judgment the individual concerned was able to function at a minimally acceptable level in an average familial and societal setting. While a number of individuals discharged as recovered

46. McLean Asylum for the Insane, *AR*, XXV (1842), in Massachusetts General Hospital, *AR*, 1842, 26; Connecticut Retreat for the Insane, *AR*, XVI (1840), 14; New York Hospital and Bloomingdale Asylum, *AR*, 1875, n.p.; Illinois Board of State Commissioners of Public Charities, *BR*, I (1869/1870), tables between 288 and 289.

47. McLean Asylum for the Insane, *AR*, XXV (1842), in Massachusetts General Hospital, *AR*, 1842, 26; Earle, *History, Description and Statistics of the Bloomingdale Asylum*, 108. See also Connecticut Retreat for the Insane, *AR*, VI (1830), 3–5. During its first two or three decades, Bloomingdale accepted a much larger proportion of cases of delerium tremens than other hospitals, partly because New York, with its large population, had no other facilities for such persons. This made Bloomingdale somewhat unique among the mental hospitals of this period.

were later recommitted to a hospital, a far larger proportion never reentered a mental institution.

Oddly enough, the striking success of the corporate hospitals in their early years was destined to have unforeseen consequences. At the time of their founding, virtually all of these institutions attempted to make some provision for patients who could not under any circumstances afford the protracted costs of hospitalization. Such a policy was defended on philanthropic, humanitarian, and religious grounds; it demonstrated that corporate hospitals served the entire community and thereby met their obligations to society. Since there was neither experience nor precedent to serve as a guide, little thought was given to long-range financial and economic issues that would face these institutions. At the outset the major emphasis was placed upon securing the necessary funds to open, the construction of the physical plant, and the problem of making the institution operational as quickly as possible.

Once opened, however, these institutions faced serious financial problems. What would be their source of operating funds, as contrasted with capital expenditures? This issue was complicated by the fact that institutionalization in a mental hospital usually was for a protracted period of time and involved far greater costs than those encountered by patients in a general hospital. If a patient and his family could not pay the charges involved, should they be denied admission? Should the state or local community subsidize such individuals? Or should trustees attempt to raise money from private sources to support such persons? While these may seem like mundane questions in the twentieth century, they were novel to nineteenth-century Americans, who had little or no experience with such economic matters.

In the beginning most corporate hospitals sought to admit a heterogeneous patient body. Yet the economic realities of the situation were such that ability to pay soon became a major factor in admission policies. McLean Asylum is a case in point. Under the terms of its original charter in 1811, the Massachusetts General Hospital was obliged to support thirty sick and lunatic poor ordinarily chargeable to the state. In 1813 this stipulation was modified and their support was made dependent on the income received from the Province House estate, which had been granted by the state as an endowment to the hospital. By 1816 this provision had been repealed altogether. Consequently, McLean—from the very moment it opened in 1818—accepted patients willing and able to pay its high charges. As early as 1822 the trustees regretted their inability to take in free patients; they noted also that several patients had been dropped because of the costs involved. As a result of several bequests totaling $20,000 by the Appleton family during the 1840's, the superintendent of the institution had at his disposal income to subsidize patients. Yet this money was not necessarily distributed on the basis of need. "Its manner of distribution," noted Luther V. Bell in 1856, "was well calculated to effect this best end [recovery from insanity], as friends from pride or other similar reasons, often would remove a half or two thirds restored patient, when a simple suggestion '*leave this patient till we send you word and there will be no more bills*', secured eventual recovery. Even the question of ability does not enter necessarily into its distribution, as it unfortunately is true, that selfishness of responsible relatives might sacrifice a most valuable and interesting patient."[48] McLean on the whole served a well-to-do clientele. Only on rare occasions did it accept individuals who were unable to pay the full costs of confinement. Considering its high charges, even those patients who received subsidies were hardly poor. By the 1840's it was undoubtedly the most exclusive mental hospital in the United States, and served groups in and around Boston and elsewhere who could afford its high charges.[49]

Much the same state of affairs existed at the Bloomingdale

48. Luther V. Bell to Robert H. Ives, February 14, 1856, Butler Hospital Papers, John Carter Brown Library, Brown University, Providence, R.I.

49. Eaton, *New England Hospitals*, 33–34; *Address of the Trustees of the Massachusetts General Hospital*, 23; McLean Asylum for the Insane, *AR*, XVI (1833), in Massachusetts General Hospital, *AR*, 1833, 2–3, XXII (1839), in *ibid.*, 1839, 16–17, XXIII (1840), in *ibid.*, 1840, 19–26, XXIV (1841), in *ibid.*, 1841, 20–21, LI (1868), in *ibid.*, 1868, 34–37; Luther V. Bell to Robert M. Ives, February 14, 1856, Butler Hospital Papers, John Carter Brown Library, Brown University, Providence, R. I. See also the description of the McLean Asylum in the "Account of a visit to 9 institutions in 1845 by Dr. Thomas S. Kirkbride and Mr. Jacob Morris," ms. in the Kirkbride Papers, IPH.

Asylum and Hartford Retreat. Both of these institutions, however, accepted a significantly larger number of persons unable to pay for their upkeep than did McLean. In 1807, well before the opening of Bloomingdale as an autonomous institution in 1821, the New York legislature had passed a law authorizing the governors of the New York Hospital to accept pauper insane persons if the local community assumed financial responsibility. The governors decided to levy a charge of $2 per week for their maintenance (a figure slightly below the actual average cost). The fact that admission of poor persons was entirely at the discretion of the governors, together with the reluctance of towns to send their poor insane to the hospital, eventually resulted in a diminished number of dependent patients. Nevertheless, Bloomingdale, for the first two decades of its existence, continued to care for a substantial number of poor patients, since the state subsidized its operations with liberal grants. In 1828 the cost of 17 percent of the patient body was being paid from public or charitable funds; by 1838 this figure had risen sharply to 40 percent. Dependent patients, however, did not receive the same care as private patients, whose quarters were distinctly superior. After New York City opened its own municipal institution in 1839 and the state followed suit a few years later, this figure dropped to an insignificant level. Thereafter, to quote its superintendent, Bloomingdale sought to serve "the wealthy" and "indigent persons of superior respectability and personal refinement." The latter group included the "families of clergymen, and other professional persons . . . teachers and business men who have experienced reverses . . . [and] dependent unmarried females." Both groups had lacked institutional facilities when they became mentally ill because they refused to enter the municipal asylum on Blackwell's Island (whose reputation was poor).[50]

At the Hartford Retreat the process of conversion into an exclusive private institution went along at a significantly slower pace than at McLean. This situation was due, in part, to its greater reliance on public subsidies and the fact that Connecticut did not, as did most other states, establish a public mental hos-

50. New York *Assembly Document No. 263* (March 10, 1831), 29; New York Hospital and Bloomingdale Asylum, *AR*, 1851, 15–16, 1856, 19–20, 1862, 11, 1866, 17–25; Russell, *New York Hospital*, 150–155.

5. *Bloomingdale Asylum was separated from the parent New York Hospital and given a separate identity in 1821. Although located in the nation's largest urban center, it remained small and relatively exclusive in nature. Source: New York Hospital and Bloomingdale Asylum, Annual Report, XXV (1845).*

pital until after the Civil War. In the decade following the opening of the Retreat in 1824, it became clear that Connecticut required both additional facilities and means for admitting patients unable to pay the costs of protracted illness. In 1837 the directors of the Retreat, after taking a brief census of the insane, presented a memorial to the legislature urging that a state hospital be established. A legislative investigating committee concurred, but the General Assembly took no further action. During succeeding years the same issue was unsuccessfully raised from time to time. In 1842 the Assembly finally voted an appropriation of $2,000 per year for five years for the support of the poor insane at the Retreat, and it later granted funds for a capital building program at that institution. The annual appropriation was also increased and the governor of the state was given authority to use the funds to pay for the care of needy insane persons. After the opening of Connecticut's first state hospital in 1868, however, the Retreat rapidly assumed a position as one of the nation's more eminent and expensive private institutions.[51]

Even the Friends' Asylum underwent a somewhat similar process. Prior to 1834, when its admissions were limited to members of the Society of Friends, the institution usually attempted to accommodate as many applicants as possible irrespective of their pecuniary status. Because the asylum could not attract enough self-supporting Quaker patients or subsidize a sufficient number who could not afford to pay regular charges—a fact that complicated efficient utilization of the physical plant and increased the difficulties of classification—its managers in 1834 opened their doors to all persons. The managers also attempted to make provision for those lacking sufficient resources by charging affluent patients higher rates and seeking endowment funds. Nevertheless, their efforts were not especially successful, and the asylum served a predominantly middle- and upper-class patient body—a fact that was noted by one visitor even before 1840. Although individuals connected with the institution made

51. *Report of the Committee on the Insane Poor in Connecticut, to the General Assembly, May Session, 1838* (New Haven, 1838), *passim;* Connecticut Retreat for the Insane, *AR*, VI (1830), 5, XXII (1846), 6–8, 28–30, XXIII (1847), 20–21, 27, XXVIII (1852), 19, XXXV (1859), 21–25, XXXVII (1861), 14–15, XLII (1866), 20–21.

sporadic attempts to change this situation, their efforts proved unavailing and the Friends' Asylum also assumed the status of an expensive private hospital.[52]

The growing exclusiveness of private mental hospitals, however, was not confined to corporate institutions established prior to 1830. On the contrary, it was a general phenomenon that was characteristic of most private institutions irrespective of the circumstances under which they had been founded. The Pennsylvania Hospital for the Insane (reorganized and given autonomy within the structure of the Pennsylvania Hospital in 1841), with the assistance of individual benefactors, spent substantial sums on patients who were admitted without charge or else paid an amount well below actual costs. Between 1841 and 1866, for example, it expended over a quarter of a million dollars on free patients, an annual average of $9,091. Yet the proportion of such patients was never large. In 1849 the hospital had 46 persons on the free list; in that year it admitted 171 and cared for a total of 401 individuals.[53] Similarly, the Butler Hospital in Providence, Rhode Island, which opened in 1847 as a result of a large bequest from Cyrus Butler, attempted to care for poor patients in its early years. Like the Hartford Retreat, it was for over two decades the only facility in the state. Consequently, a significant proportion of its patients were sent by local communities that assumed the costs of institutionalization. The state legislature, moreover, appropriated $1,000 in 1850 to be used for the support of the indigent insane and also provided a subsidy of $60 per year per person to each local community supporting an insane patient at the hospital. With the opening of the "State Farm" in 1870, most of the chronic paupers were removed from Butler, and this was followed by the adoption of more selective admission policies.[54] This transformation was approved privately by Dr. John

---

52. Friends' Asylum for the Insane, *AR*, XXIV (1841), 4–5, XXXII (1849), 5–6, XXXVIII (1855), 17–18, XLVIII (1865), 7–8, LI (1868), 4–5; George Combe, *Notes on the United States of North America during a Phrenological Visit in 1838–9–40*, 2 vols. (Philadelphia, 1841), I, 299; Dain and Carlson, "Milieu Therapy in the Nineteenth Century," 277–280, 285–286.

53. Pennsylvania Hospital for the Insane, *AR*, II (1842), 45–47, XIX (1859), 36, XXVI (1866), 40–43.

54. Butler Hospital for the Insane, *AR*, 1848, 8–10, 1850, 13–14, 1851, 15–16, 27–36, 1861, 3–6, 1870, 7–8.

W. Sawyer, superintendent of Butler. "I think," he informed Dorothea L. Dix, "it will result in increased usefulness and a firmer hold upon the interest and good will of the people." On the other hand, Sawyer noted in his published annual report that while "the establishment of separate institutions for the incurable insane is almost universally condemned, and can be justified only as a choice of evils, it is especially to be regretted that false ideas of economy should be allowed to deprive the most destitute sufferer, be he native or foreign born, of any advantages of treatment which might offer reasonable hope of cure."[55]

The fact that corporate institutions catered to a predominantly affluent clientele is not difficult to understand, given the fact that access to funds rested upon a relatively narrow base. Private philanthropy during the first half of the nineteenth century was limited in scope; the magnitude of personal fortunes did not come close to approximating comparable financial holdings of the succeeding century. Moreover, there were a variety of projects competing for available funds, including general hospitals as well as welfare, educational, and religious institutions. Even if a few private donors had had far greater resources to invest in such philanthropic ventures, it is doubtful that the establishment of mental hospitals would have taken precedence over other projects concerned with social reform.

Nor is it clear how privately built mental hospitals could have secured sufficient operating revenues to enable them to accept a heterogeneous rather than a homogeneous patient population. Endowment funds were not available in amounts sufficiently large enough to permit a change in exclusive admission policies. And if the hospital's charges were set on the basis of its costs, it then excluded most individuals because the protracted period of confinement made the total cost prohibitive for the overwhelming majority of families.[56] One solution, of course,

55. John W. Sawyer to Dix, September 16, 1870, Dix Papers, HLHU; Butler Hospital for the Insane, *AR*, 1870, 12. See also Isaac Ray to John W. Sawyer, March 10, 1872, Butler Hospital Library, Providence, R. I.

56. For the middle two quarters of the nineteenth century, in cases in which an individual recovered, the average stay in a mental hospital was between three and four months. Chronic cases remained for far longer periods of time.

was to have the local community in which an insane person resided assume responsibility for either part or all of the costs involved. Most communities, as we shall later see, were sharply opposed to such a policy. Thus local government financing of operating costs was never seriously considered, even though it was tried sporadically on a number of occasions. As early as the 1830's, therefore, it was becoming evident that private hospitals would be unable to serve as the nucleus of a hospital system in which ability to pay was not one of the prime considerations in setting admission policies.

Internal developments at most corporate hospitals further inhibited the possibility that they would serve all segments of the population in their respective communities. From the very beginning it was evident that paying patients would provide the bulk of the operating revenues. Theoretically, the income from affluent patients made it feasible to accept other patients at charges below actual costs. In practice, however, such was not the case, for well-to-do inmates received the type of care that necessitated large expenditures. As institutions moved to provide such care, their costs rose rapidly, thereby eliminating any potential surplus from the income received from payments by affluent families. Average patient costs at private hospitals were slightly higher than those at public hospitals by the 1830's; the gap widened steadily in succeeding decades, as the example in the following table indicates. By 1872 the average weekly expenditure per patient at McLean, Butler, Friends', Pennsylvania Hospital for the Insane, and the Hartford Retreat was $10.33; at twenty-eight public institutions the comparable expenditure was $4.13.[57] These figures also do not reflect the cost differential in capital expenditures, since private hospitals constructed physical plants that provided far greater privacy and comforts than those of their public counterparts.

The shift to a homogeneous and affluent patient body, nevertheless, was not solely a function of institutional economics. For the fact of the matter was that most individuals—given the nature of American pluralism—tended to move within the relatively narrow parameters of a cohesive and clearly defined group. This

57. New York State Board of Charities, *AR*, VII (1873), 19.

AVERAGE ANNUAL EXPENDITURE PER PATIENT

Year	McLean Asylum	Worcester State Lunatic Hospital	Utica State Lunatic Asylum
1837	$174.14	$159.64	
1843	169.90	114.40	$165.36*
1848	193.74	106.09	115.78
1853	213.21	103.14	143.52
1858	352.83	102.86	160.68
1863	362.83	166.03	177.84
1868	858.65	194.74	245.44

* The costs at Utica in 1843—its first year of operations—were abnormally high. In 1844 the average annual cost per patient had dropped to $134.68.

SOURCES: Figures compiled from the annual reports of the McLean, Worcester, and Utica hospitals; New York Board of State Commissioners of Public Charities, *AR*, II (1868), xix; and Illinois Board of Commissioners of Public Charities, *BR*, I (1869/1870), tables between 288 and 289.

tendency became even more pronounced with the arrival on American shores of minority ethnic groups, beginning with the Irish in the 1830's and continuing for nearly a century. Affluent families probably sent their mentally ill members to a hospital with the implicit belief that there would be no indiscriminate mixing with groups they had little in common with and often did not understand. In this respect mental hospitals were fairly typical of many other American institutions. Just as church membership (and membership in other types of organizations) correlated with class, status, and educational level, so corporate hospitals drew a remarkably homogeneous patient population in terms of class and status.

Although superintendents of corporate hospitals recognized the growing differentiation between the patient populations at private and at public institutions, they did not necessarily oppose this development. Most of them, after all, came from backgrounds similar to the private patients' and shared their views and outlook. Moreover, asylum psychiatrists had considerable difficulty in communicating with patients from backgrounds dissimilar from his own, making therapeutic successes (which often depended on verbal relationships) far more difficult. Under such circumstances these professionals were by no means adverse to a dual hospital system—one in which well-to-do and better-educated patients were placed in private institutions while the rest were sent to public hospitals. A dual system was compatible with the goal of homogeneous patient populations, which many psychiatrists believed to be conducive to both individual and institutional well-being and effectiveness.

The tendency of early corporate mental hospitals to become more exclusive was evident almost from the very beginning. When he considered returning to Connecticut as superintendent of the Hartford Retreat on two occasions, Samuel B. Woodward was tempted by the differences between the Worcester State Lunatic Hospital (which he headed) and the Retreat. "On many accounts," he noted in 1834, "the Retreat is pleasanter than this Hospital, the patients are more select, the duties are less arduous —and less of the responsibility rests upon the Superintendent." Six years later his views remained much the same. "The class of patients, you know, are of a higher order, and would afford, I should think, a larger sphere of operation for the exercise of skill and ingenuity, and for the accumulation of results which would benefit mankind."[58] Although he finally declined on both occasions—partly out of a sense of obligation to the Worcester hospital and partly because the governing structure at the Retreat was less than desirable—his comments were revealing about differences between private and public institutions in the formative years of their existence.

Nor were Woodward's views atypical of this period. "It is not unreasonable," argued Luther V. Bell, superintendent of McLean, in 1839, "that one Institution in New England should be designed for the reception of those whose pecuniary ability justifies their enjoying not only the necessaries and comforts, but the luxuries and superfluities of life to which they may have been accustomed. There surely would be nothing unjust in this.

58. Samuel B. Woodward to George Sumner, March 18, 1834, Woodward to Thomas H. Gallandet, February 21, 1840, Woodward Papers, AAS.

To the polished and cultivated it is due as much to separate them from the coarse and degraded, as to administer to them in other respects." Much the same sentiments were expressed by later superintendents of McLean.[59]

Such opinions were by no means confined to a few isolated individuals. On the contrary, they were typical of virtually all those associated with private mental hospitals. Many of the superintendents of public institutions expressed the same sentiments, as we shall see later, though in somewhat different terms. The managers of the Friends' Asylum noted with approval in 1841 that the location and limited size of their institution rendered it "a very desirable place of retreat for Patients of a better class, whose friends may desire to avoid the exposure incident to larger and more public establishments."[60] The superintendent of the Hartford Retreat echoed these views. "It is evident," declared John S. Butler in 1867,

> that different classes will require different styles of accommodation. The State should provide for its indigent insane, liberally and abundantly, all the needful means of treatment, but in a plain and rigidly economical way. Other classes of more abundant means will require, with an increased expenditure, a corresponding increase of conveniences and comforts, it may be of luxuries, that use has made essential. This common sense rule is adopted in other arrangements of our social life—our hotels, watering places, private dwellings and various personal expenditures.[61]

And John W. Sawyer of Butler maintained that the demands of the wealthy for "not only comfortable rooms, kind attendants, wholesome food, pure air and skillful treatment, but also . . . a degree of the elegance and luxury to which they were accus-

59. McLean Asylum for the Insane, *AR*, XXII (1839), in Massachusetts General Hospital, *AR*, 1839, 16. For other statements by Bell and his successors see the *AR* of McLean, XXIII (1840), in *ibid.*, 1840, 25–26, XXIV (1841), in *ibid.*, 1841, 20–21, XXXIV (1851), in *ibid.*, 1851, 21–22, and LI (1868), in *ibid.*, 1868, 34–37.

60. Friends' Asylum for the Insane, *AR*, XXIV (1841), 5.

61. Connecticut Retreat for the Insane, *AR*, XLIII (1867), 33. See also *ibid.*, XLV–XLVI (1869–1870), 21.

tomed in health" was a "natural and proper desire" that should be satisfied.[62]

IV

With the opening of the Hartford Retreat in 1824 the first phase of the movement to establish mental hospitals had come to a close. Although two more corporate institutions were founded in the 1840's (notably the Pennsylvania Hospital for the Insane and the Butler Hospital), the limited nature of private philanthropy, the high costs of extended institutionalization, and the growing exclusiveness of admission policies all but destroyed the hope that such institutions could serve the entire community rather than well-to-do groups alone. While corporate hospitals were not established with such an outcome in mind, their existence presaged the advent of a dual system of public and private institutions, each serving a separate clientele and providing differential care based on ability to pay.

Indeed, the success of corporate nonprofit hospitals inadvertently stimulated the establishment of asylums owned and operated by private physicians. One of the first such asylums was opened by Dr. Nehemiah Cutter in Pepperell, Massachusetts, in the mid-1820's. The venture proved so successful that he found it necessary to take in a partner in 1839. A similar institution was opened in Hingham, Massachusetts, during the 1830's.[63] After 1840 the number of these proprietary institutions increased sharply. Some were small and short-lived; others were more successful. Whatever the case, it was clear that their establishment was made possible by the reluctance of affluent families to commit relatives to public hospitals having large numbers of poor and indigent patients. Brigham Hall in Canandaigua, New York, for example, announced that it was "designed for the

62. Butler Hospital for the Insane, *AR*, 1868, 22. A similar statement by Kirkbride appeared in the Pennsylvania Hospital for the Insane, *AR*, VIII (1848), 19–20. See also Edward Jarvis, "On the Proper Functions of Private Institutions or Homes for the Insane," *AJI*, XVII (July, 1860), 19–31, 35–45.

63. *Boston Medical and Surgical Journal*, III (April 6, 1830), 131, XVI (February 8, 1837), 18–19, XXIII (January 6, 1841), 355–357.

accommodation of patients of the independent class."[64] The superintendent of the New Brighton Retreat for Insane Females made this point clear even in his first published report. Many people, he noted, were reluctant to commit friends and relatives to public hospitals. Existing institutions, moreover, lacked the capacity to meet demand. State institutions, he continued,

> fail to reach the vast majority of claimants; the acts establishing State asylums, either by letter or in spirit, give precedence to the indigent insane and recent cases; the *alien* pauper, before the independent *native*. The inevitable result is, the retention of the latter class at home, until they become incurable either from reluctance of their friends to commit them to the promiscuous associations of State hospitals, or from inability to meet the greater expense of maintenance at those institutions established for the wealthy classes. Finally, they are compelled to consign them to the tender mercies of the jail or alms-house. As foreign immigration, and various causes incident to the times, must rapidly increase pauperism and consequently insanity, we can look for no abatement of the demand upon the State charities in the future. The general plan of relief thus falling far short of what is required, compels a resort to special efforts to remedy the evil. . . .
> The principal design of the Retreat is to furnish to the so-called incurably insane females of the independent class of our citizens a comfortable home.[65]

By the 1870's private mental hospitals, often owned and operated by a single individual, were fairly common. New York State had at least six such institutions and Illinois three.[66] The

64. *Announcement of Brigham Hall, A Hospital for the Insane. . . . January 1860* (New York, 1860), 16; Brigham Hall, *AR*, 1862, 6, 1872, 6–7; *AJI*, XVI (April, 1860), 486–488.

65. New Brighton Retreat, An Asylum for Insane Females, *AR*, I (1864), 7–8.

66. See the following: New York State Commissioner in Lunacy, *AR*, I (1873), 38–41; *Report of the Trustees of the State Lunatic Asylum, with the Documents Accompanying the Same, Pursuant to the Act of the Legislature Passed May 26, 1841*, New York Senate Document No. 20 (January 12, 1842), 60–61; John M. Galt, *The Treatment of Insanity* (New York, 1846), 525–527; *Boston Medical and Surgical Journal*, XXXVII (October 13, 1847), 228; *AJI*, XII (July, 1855), 102–104; William W. Burke, "The Supervision of the Care of the Mentally Diseased by the

spread of these private ventures, nevertheless, was by no means a welcome development, for their proliferation often meant a noticeable diminution in the pressure to upgrade state and municipal hospitals. As early as 1854 Samuel Gridley Howe warned of the dangers of a dual hospital system, one catering to poor and indigent patients and the other to more affluent groups. "The multiplication of these private establishments," he pointed out, "would be a great evil. It is one that may be prevented by making public hospitals unobjectionable residences for patients of any class; but it will be difficult of cure, if once it obtains footing."[67] Moreover, unless regulated by some independent authority, there was no guarantee that private "madhouses"—as they were sometimes called—would remain free of the gross abuses that characterized such establishments in England. Indeed, Dorothea L. Dix devoted some of her own time investigating them and exposing what she regarded as inadequate and substandard conditions.[68]

Perhaps the only nonpublic hospitals that made a distinct attempt to maintain a heterogeneous patient body were those under religious control. Although organized more along proprietary than corporate lines, their founding was exclusively a function of religious benevolence rather than a desire for profits. The best known was the Mount Hope Institution, established about 1840 by the Sisters of Charity in Baltimore. Despite its Catholic affiliation, the hospital accepted patients of all denominations. Like the founders of the famous corporate hospitals of the Northeast, the Sisters of Charity hoped from the beginning to accept large numbers of poor and indigent patients in addition to those who could afford higher charges. Such an objective implied

---

Illinois State Board of Charities (1869–1909)" (unpubl. Ph.D. dissertation, University of Chicago, 1934), 186–187.

67. Worcester State Lunatic Hospital, *AR*, XXII (1854), 12. A decade earlier Kirkbride made the same point in his description of Sanford Hall in New York. See "Account of a Visit to 9 institutions in 1845 by Dr. Thomas S. Kirkbride and Mr. Jacob Morris," ms. in the Kirkbride Papers, IPH.

68. H. L. Buttolph to Kirkbride, March 8, 1855, Kirkbride Papers, IPH. See the discussion by Edward Jarvis in his article "On the Proper Functions of Private Institutions or Homes for the Insane," *AJI*, XVII (July, 1860), 19–31, 35–45.

substantial financial support. Yet Mount Hope was never the recipient of large contributions, even though Baltimore had an old and large Catholic population that was by no means lacking in resources. Nevertheless, the institution managed to retain a heterogeneous patient population by arranging to receive city and state payments for poor and indigent inmates. Much the same situation existed at the St. Vincent Insane Asylum opened by the Sisters of Charity in St. Louis in 1858.[69]

The policies pursued by the few religiously affiliated hospitals, however, were the exception rather than the rule. Most corporate hospitals, although conceived as broad-based community institutions, sooner or later limited their commitments by narrowing the groups from whom their patients were drawn. Yet the justification of institutional care and treatment of mental illness that accompanied the first surge in founding corporate hospitals during the second and third decade of the nineteenth century had begun the process of stimulating public consciousness of alternative means of handling distress other than by relying on traditional mechanisms located in the family, community, ethnic or religious group. When it became clear by the mid-1820's that corporate institutions would be unable to meet what were by now defined as legitimate needs that required concerted action, the thrust of the movement to establish hospitals was transferred from the private to the public sector.

69. Mount Saint Vincent's Hospital (original name of Mount Hope), *AR*, I (1843), 15; Mount Hope Institution, *AR*, III (1845), 40–41, VII (1849), 8–10, IX (1851), 6–12, XXI (1863), 28–29, XXII (1864), 24–26, XXIV (1866), 26, XXVII (1869), 3–4, XXXIII (1875), 26–29; St. Vincent Insane Asylum, *AR*, I (1859), 3–5, II (1860), 3–5, 1862/1863, 15–16.

Chapter III

The Growth of
Public Mental Hospitals

I

THE SURGE IN THE FOUNDING of corporate institutions by private philanthropy during the early nineteenth century, though short-lived in duration, had important consequences. Not the least of them was the stimulation of public awareness of the supposed humanitarian, medical, and economic benefits to both society and the individual of institutional care and treatment of mental illness. At the same time it was becoming increasingly evident that the private sector was unable to provide the resources required for establishing and maintaining a broad network of hospitals that served all groups irrespective of their ability to pay for care and treatment. During the second quarter of the nineteenth century, therefore, responsibility for dealing with the problems associated with mental disease slowly shifted away from traditional structures such as the family or hospitals supported by private philanthropy toward public hospitals under state authority and supported by funding from both state and local government sources.

The increasingly important role of the state in providing institutional facilities for the insane, however, did not come about solely because officials and socially minded individuals and groups recognized that corporate hospitals could not meet the challenges growing out of this malady. The movement to establish public hospitals was also an expression of a growing concern with problems arising out of and related to poverty, pauperism, disease, and crime, which in turn stimulated the emergence of distinct social policies and institutional structures intended to deal with these issues in the early decades of the nineteenth century. Formation of welfare policies inevitably involved the mentally ill precisely because of the devastating economic impact of insanity upon family structure and relationships. This impact was especially pronounced among lower-class and immigrant groups. The high incidence of insanity among such groups merely magnified the economic consequences of the disease. Public mental hospitals, therefore, had to deal with their patients within the context of welfare and dependency, a fact that was destined to play a major role in shaping both their internal structure and the external legal, administrative, and financial framework within which they functioned.

Although there was emulation, the founding of public hospitals did not follow a predetermined or regular pattern, for each state had its own indigenous circumstances and problems. In some states a hospital was established shortly after the issue was first raised; in others considerable time elapsed before action was taken. Nor did identical groups take the lead in founding institutions, although physicians, social activists, and political and conventional social leaders all generally played important roles in their respective areas. Moreover, the administrative structures and modes of support of hospitals were not always similar. Some were exclusively state institutions; others were mixed in character, receiving financial support from both public and private sources. But whatever the pattern, the drive to establish hospitals became national in scope; by 1860 most states had at least one hospital and some more than one caring for its mentally ill citizens. Moreover, in virtually every state the issue of the care and treatment of the insane was usually raised within the framework of welfare and dependency. The establishment of mental hospitals, therefore, was but one phase of the larger thrust toward the creation of public structures for dependent groups. As early as 1842 Charles Dickens noted with approval that in America mental hospitals were either supported or assisted by the state—

a fact that made government a merciful and benevolent protector of people in distress. In England, on the other hand, where public charity was minimal, the government offered "very little shelter or relief beyond that which is to be found in the workhouse and the jail, [and] has come, not unnaturally, to be looked upon by the poor rather as a stern master, quick to correct and punish, than a kind protector, merciful and vigilant in their hour of need."[1]

Although the circumstances of hospital-founding varied from state to state, there were also certain similarities. Interestingly enough, these similarities involved the manner in which issues were defined and policies formulated. In the early nineteenth century the legislative process did not rely as heavily as it did later upon professional expertise and bureaucratic personnel. Although legislatures were somewhat aware of the need for hard data that would serve as the basis for rational policy-making, the personnel, procedures, and even theories of social planning were simply not available. To cite one example, the censuses—both federal and state—were relatively simple and rudimentary compilations that did not always provide the type of information that lent itself readily to use in the legislative process. It is true that legislative committees attempted to collect pertinent material, but in general these data consisted largely of a simple enumeration of items (e.g., the number of mentally ill persons and where they were confined). The relatively unsophisticated nature of the information-gathering process was not simply a matter of the investigators being unable to amass the necessary data. It grew instead out of the lack of any broad theoretical constructs regarding mental illness, welfare and dependency, and social and class relationships, and an inability to understand how American society functioned. Since the absence of broad theoretical models relating to public policy made it difficult to gather or to use empirical data in a meaningful way, policy often reflected external factors such as unconscious class interests or similar social assumptions that were never questioned. This is not to imply that mid-nineteenth-century legislators and administra-

1. Charles Dickens, *American Notes and Pictures from Italy* (London, 1957; *American Notes* first published in 1842), 28.

tors were deficient in intelligence or malevolent in character. It is only to say that lack of theory and methodology often led to the adoption of policies that in the long run had results which were quite at variance with the intentions of those involved in their formulation.

The manner in which legislatures functioned during the first half of the nineteenth century reinforced the narrow dimensions of policy formulation. Most state legislatures were not yet institutionalized in their operations. The tenure of members was extraordinarily brief and a high proportion served only a single term. There was no internal division of labor within legislatures, and the complex structure of such bodies that exists in the twentieth century simply did not exist in the nineteenth. Precedents and rules were vague, and there was often little carryover of either personnel or deliberations from session to session. Bills were frequently introduced by petitions or memorials of private citizens and groups. Investigating committees (especially those that dealt with mental disease) were usually made up of public-spirited individuals who were recruited from outside of the legislature. Standing committees were not especially effective, and the inexperience of their membership and lack of a permanent staff limited their autonomy and importance. There was also very little in the way of supporting services; most legislatures had neither a legal staff nor a research or reference division. Consequently, the legislative process inhibited rather than promoted the formulation of comprehensive and rational policies toward dependent groups such as the mentally ill. The relative lack of institutionalization, in other words, gave rise to legislation concerned with immediate problems and issues, especially when it came to the establishment of individual hospitals.

The arguments employed by proponents of mental hospitals reinforced the narrow dimensions of public policy that grew out of the structure and modus operandi of state legislatures. Concern with building the necessary support for the establishment of hospitals led supporters to employ often utopian language about the potential benefits of such institutions and to slight or ignore long-range policy issues that arose out of the broad economic, demographic, and structural changes that were affecting American society. Mental hospitals, they argued, would sharply diminish the incidence of insanity and thereby contribute to the alleviation of other problems, including poverty and immorality. Such claims often avoided consideration of the many complex problems related to mental illness, and also contributed to the heightened public expectations about the potential achievements of institutionalization and the ensuing diminution in the importance of traditional modes of care.

Theories of disease during the first half of the nineteenth century also had a subtle though significant impact in shaping the framework within which mental hospitals were created. In the absence of demonstrable etiological concepts or a germ theory of disease, American physicians and laymen interpreted health as a consequence of a proper and orderly relationship between nature, society, and the individual. Disease followed the violation of the natural laws that governed human behavior and was indissolubly linked with filth, immorality, and improper living conditions. Health, on the other hand, was synonymous with virtue and order. While such concepts were suitable to sanitary reform and general preventive measures, they offered little guidance when it came to providing treatment for specific disease categories. The prevailing emphasis on health, therefore, reflected an inability to deal with disease per se. The resulting therapeutic nihilism was further strengthened by the impact of French medicine and the application of the numerical method of Pierre Louis, which demonstrated the ineffectiveness of most traditional remedies.

The specific definition of mental disease, as we shall see later, was similar in nature; insanity followed the violation of the natural laws that governed human behavior. Therapy involved the recreation of a healthy and moral environment. Yet the theory of moral treatment often tended to be vague and abstract; it meant different things to different psychiatrists. Under these circumstances the mental hospital—precisely because of the diffuse nature of medical theory and its inability to provide firm guidelines—was particularly susceptible to nonmedical influences, including dominant social values as well as changing attitudes toward and practices with dependent groups generally. The weakness of specific theoretical constructs of disease and etiology, in turn, reinforced the absence of long-range planning.

Consequently, the form that mental hospitals assumed during the 1850's and in succeeding decades was sharply at variance with the goals and intentions of their early founders and supporters.[2]

II

During the seventeenth and eighteenth centuries there was no widespread concern with poverty and pauperism in the American colonies. The number of paupers and dependent persons, at least by English and European standards, was relatively small. As late as 1814 Hezekiah Niles pointed out that the Philadelphia Almshouse, which sheltered an average of more than 700 paupers, would have had to care for 18,000 if pauperism had been as prevalent in that city as it was in England.[3] Much of the legislation enacted in the various colonies both before and after independence did not reflect a conviction that poverty and dependency constituted a problem of such magnitude as to require structural solutions. It was intended rather to reinforce and preserve traditional means of handling distress, including the maintenance of the family or the reliance upon social mechanisms located in the immediate community or the church.

By the early nineteenth century such complacency was less common. Population growth, urbanization, periodic economic depressions accompanied by unemployment, and immigration of minority ethnic groups all combined to undermine the reliance upon traditional and informal mechanisms to alleviate distress. Concern with maintaining a measure of social cohesion and a desire to contain some of the social problems arising out of poverty and dependency stimulated a far-ranging debate over these issues. While there was general agreement that social problems were increasing in magnitude, there was far less unanimity on the precise causes for this situation. The explanations that were offered by individuals and groups varied sharply in

2. For a discussion of nineteenth-century theories of disease and public policy, see Barbara G. Rosenkrantz, *Public Health and the State: Changing Views in Massachusetts, 1842–1936* (Cambridge, 1972).

3. Benjamin J. Klebaner, "Public Poor Relief in America 1790–1860" (unpubl. Ph.D. dissertation, Columbia University, 1952), 3.

nature. Most saw poverty in moral terms; the poor were poor because of their own improvidence, extravagance, lack of ambition, indolence, and intemperance. Yet even those who recognized the moral roots of poverty could on occasion see mitigating circumstances. Alcoholism, after all, could derive from the despair engendered by chronic misfortune, while unforeseen events such as illness and death could play havoc with family stability. Others were impressed more with the structural roots of poverty, including low wages, inequitable social and economic arrangements, and the unemployment that resulted from overproduction.[4]

By the 1820's—if not before—the debate over contemporary social problems had broadened to include an evaluation of existing poor laws and a consideration of alternative policies. In theory state governments presumably had played a major role in policy formulation by virtue of the fact that they had mandated the general legal and administrative framework for the alleviation of distress and then delegated operating authority to local officials. In practice, however, distress had generally been taken care of in an ad hoc and informal manner at the local level. The actual role of the state had tended to be nominal. In the reexamination that commenced in the 1820's, there was a clear trend away from the reliance on traditional mechanisms to deal with distress and a move toward the adoption of more formal structures by local and particularly state governments. Indeed, in

4. In recent years historians have turned their attention to the history of welfare as a significant field of study. Although a number of scholars have emphasized the fact that Americans saw poverty in terms of moral deficiencies, the available evidence indicates a far more complex picture. It was possible, for example, for the same individual to see poverty as the result of both character shortcomings *and* structural defects in society. In many ways the most balanced studies of poverty prior to the Civil War are Benjamin Klebaner's unpublished dissertation ("Public Poor Relief in America 1790–1860"), previously cited, and his article "Poverty and Its Relief in American Thought, 1815–61," *Social Service Review*, XXXVIII (December, 1964), 382–399. More recent—and in many ways too one-sided both in terms of interpretation and evidence—are David J. Rothman's *The Discovery of the Asylum: Social Order and Disorder in the New Republic* (Boston, 1971) and Raymond A. Mohl's *Poverty in New York 1783–1825* (New York, 1971).

the half century following 1820 the welfare role of most state governments expanded at a rapid pace.[5]

The growing responsibilities of states in the area of welfare were reflected in legislative deliberations of the nature, causes, and extent of pauperism. Although not entirely novel, these investigations went far beyond earlier studies. Comprehensive in scope and forceful in their recommendations, they provided clear evidence of widening state involvement in complex social problems. In Massachusetts the influential Josiah Quincy chaired a legislative study of pauperism in 1820 that proved to be only the first of many. The New York legislature followed the same procedure and in 1823 authorized a comprehensive study of the state's poor laws by Secretary of State John Yates. Concern with poverty was also evident among urban officials. The Philadelphia Guardians of the Poor, to cite one illustration, appointed a committee in 1827 to review welfare practices in other urban areas, including Baltimore, New York, Providence, Boston and Salem.[6]

All of these studies began with the assumption that a crisis existed in the dispensation of public welfare. The Quincy report, for example, emphasized that expenditures and the number of individuals on welfare were rising rapidly; that existing poor laws were actually perpetuating and fostering pauperism; and that it was becoming common for those receiving aid to regard such assistance as a right. Nor were existing provisions for de-

5. Cf. Oscar and Mary Handlin, *Commonwealth: A Study of the Role of Government in the American Economy: Massachusetts, 1774–1861*, rev. ed. (Cambridge, 1969); Louis Hartz, *Economic Policy and Democratic Thought: Pennsylvania, 1776–1860* (Cambridge, 1948); James N. Primm, *Economic Policy in the Development of a Western State: Missouri, 1820–1860* (Cambridge, 1954); Milton S. Heath, *Constructive Liberalism: The Role of the State in Economic Development in Georgia to 1860* (Cambridge, 1954).

6. [Josiah Quincy] *Report of Committee to Whom was Referred the Consideration of the Pauper Laws of the Commonwealth. Submitted to the Massachusetts Legislature, 1821* (Boston, 1821); report submitted by John V. N. Yates, in the New York State *Senate Journal*, 47th Sess., 1824; *Report of the Committee Appointed by the Board of Guardians of the Poor of the City and Districts of Philadelphia, to Visit the Cities of Baltimore, New-York, Providence, Boston, and Salem* (Philadelphia, 1827).

pendent persons either adequate or efficient. The practice of placing paupers, by public bidding, with families or under the charge of a single individual was practical only in very small communities. The practice was usually liable to abuse, the report warned, while support of paupers in their own homes would be wasteful and fostered perpetual dependency. The best remedy, Quincy argued, was institutional care of the poor in almshouses or houses of industry where they could be provided with useful employment. The state, he concluded, should foster and promote a system of town and district almshouses under its direct supervision. Much the same views were expressed twelve years later by another legislative commission, which urged the elimination of all laws requiring the support of the poor. The state, its members insisted, should permit local communities to determine their own policies. To protect the virtuous and industrious, local officials should have the authority to compel welfare recipients to work, while the state should encourage communities by providing generous subsidies for the construction of workhouses.[7]

In New York the Yates study was equally critical of the operations of the poor laws in that state. The system was costly and inefficient; the practice of farming out the poor often led to cruel and barbarous treatment; the education and morals of children of paupers were neglected; there was no provision for adequate employment and the ensuing idleness generated "vice, dissipation, disease and crime"; dependency was perpetuated; and the needs of the insane and idiotic were ignored. To overcome these defects, Yates urged significant structural changes in the state's poor laws, including the establishment of houses of employment in each county. Subsequently, the legislature ordered sixteen of the state's fifty-five counties to establish a poor house.[8]

The thrust of these investigations was to undermine still further the traditional and informal mechanisms employed by

7. [Quincy] *Report of Committee. . . . to the Massachusetts Legislature, 1821*, 1–11; *Report of the Commissioners Appointed by an Order of the House of Representatives, February 29, 1832, on the Subject of the Pauper System of the Commonwealth of Massachusetts*, Massachusetts *House Document No. 6* (1833), 30, 39–43, *et passim*.

8. New York State *Senate Journal*, 47th Sess., 1824, 100–108.

local communities to alleviate or ameliorate distress and to move toward a structured system in which institutionalization replaced outdoor relief. The new system, moreover, was far more comprehensive than its predecessor. The goal of men like Quincy, Yates, and others who were urging structural innovations in welfare was nothing less than the eradication of poverty and pauperism by positive state action. "The improved state of society," Yates informed the New York legislature, "the diffusion of useful knowledge, by means of common schools, and other seminaries, the vast tracts of territory yet to be reclaimed and cultivated, the spirit of enterprise and habits of industry which so generally pervade our country, the purity of our laws, the excellence of all our civil institutions, and our remote situation from European conflicts, oppression and slavery, offer strong inducements for believing that pauperism may, with proper care and attention, be almost wholly eradicated from our soil."[9]

The findings and recommendations of legislative inquiries—which mirrored comparable public discussions—were not without their effect, for they contributed to the growing movement to provide institutional care for dependent groups generally. Before 1800 only the larger urban areas provided for some type of institutional care for the poor and indigent. During the first half of the nineteenth century, on the other hand, the number of such institutions increased sharply. By 1824 Massachusetts had 83 almshouses; fifteen years later the number had increased to 180, and by 1860 the total had risen to 219. Nor was the Bay State unusual in this respect; most other states, in varying degrees, followed a similar pattern.[10]

The almshouse movement was by no means the only or even the most important element in the drive to provide institutional care. A comparable expansion in the number of penitentiaries, houses of refuge, and mental hospitals occurred at the same time. Indeed, the thrust in the direction of larger and more complex structures was a general one that transcended the specific problems posed by dependency. Moreover, the rationale and arguments employed by those active in different movements were remarkably similar. The rapid growth of educational institutions

9. *Ibid.,* 107–108.

10. Klebaner, "Public Poor Relief in America," 73–99.

during the second quarter of the nineteenth century, for example, was defended in equally enthusiastic language; education would produce the type of person who would be incapable of behaving in an immoral or antisocial manner and thereby contribute toward the creation of a better society.

In general, most of the institutions founded during the first half of the nineteenth century were neither narrow nor singular in their purpose. Almshouses, for example, were intended to provide work for the able-bodied as well as shelter and refuge for the aged and helpless poor. Houses of refuge, which cared for homeless orphans and other juveniles, were supposed to inculcate in young inmates proper behavioral attributes as well as a trade that would enable them to achieve self-sufficiency and independence by adulthood. Penitentiaries were intended both to punish and to reform convicted lawbreakers. And mental hospitals would serve both the community and the individual by providing care and treatment of mentally ill persons.

The rapid growth of institutions caring for dependent persons soon raised basic policy issues. Should these institutions accept all types of dependents, including the young, the aged, the sick, the infirm, and the mentally ill, as well as those guilty of criminal behavior?[11] Or should institutions begin to differentiate among their clientele? Such questions invariably involved considerations that transcended pauperism and poverty per se. By the beginning of the nineteenth century the work of Pinel and others had provided a theoretical justification for the care and treatment of mentally ill persons in specialized institutions. Even before Pinel, John Howard (the famous English penal reformer) had begun to question the wisdom or desirability of incarcerating criminals together with dependent groups. Such a

11. Many early and mid-nineteenth-century welfare institutions were undifferentiated in function; they cared for a variety of dependent groups. Philadelphia's Blockley Almshouse, which was by no means atypical, had 1,588 inmates in 1848. Of these, 111 were in the children's asylum, 718 in the hospital and lunatic asylum, 188 in the old men's infirmary and incurable section, 79 in the male working wards, 42 in the mechanics' ward, 256 in the old women's asylum and incurable section, 71 in the women's working ward, 21 in the nursery, and 23 children. The black population, housed separately, had 3 women and 10 children in the nursery, and 66 others in the colored working and incurable ward. The situation was much the same elsewhere. *Ibid.*, 206–216.

practice not only had detrimental effects on the latter, but in many cases inhibited rehabilitation of the former. The growth of institutional structures, in other words, was accompanied by a wide-ranging debate on their precise organizational form. Slowly but surely, therefore, the discussions about the care of dependent groups began to influence the manner in which American society provided for insane persons—especially those without the financial resources to pay for care and treatment.

III

By the early nineteenth century concern with the broader problems of dependency had begun to stimulate the creation of specialized institutional structures alongside undifferentiated ones. In some instances they were controlled and administered by the local community; in others the state assumed the major responsibility. Whatever the case, it was clear that the burden of providing for dependent groups would rest increasingly with formal organizational structures, while traditional means of alleviating distress would accordingly diminish in significance.

Yet the shift that occurred in the manner in which dependent groups were cared for did not reflect a sustained or systematic analysis of existing problems or the future ramification of particular programs. The debate over policy, on the contrary, was generally characterized by concern for immediate or short-range issues. Moreover, the values embedded in particular proposals usually remained hidden from view despite the fact that these values exercised a profound influence on the course of events and even helped to shape the interpretation of empirical data that served as the basis for policy-making. Because policy decisions tended to flow out of immediate circumstances, they were often made on an incremental basis. The result was that the broad framework of public policy was for the most part not the conscious choice of legislators and officials, but rather the sum total of incremental decisions. Since few of these decisions were consistent with those that came previously, overall policy remained vague and ill defined, a fact that inhibited serious consideration of alternative models.

Before 1830 a self-conscious movement to found public

mental hospitals was not yet in existence. A cohesive and determined leadership to act as a catalyst was still absent; knowledge of European and English psychiatric theory and practice had not yet been widely disseminated in many parts of the United States; and broad policy issues concerning the proper role of the state were first beginning to be discussed.

Certainly these generalizations held true for Kentucky, South Carolina, Maryland, and Virginia, the only four states to have public mental hospitals before 1830. The Kentucky and South Carolina institutions were little more than poor houses before 1840; the Maryland hospital came into existence more by accident than by design and before the 1840's functioned as both a general and a mental hospital; and the Virginia Eastern Asylum (the oldest public facility in the nation) and the Virginia Western Asylum both remained far removed from the mainstream of psychiatric practice before 1840. None of these hospitals signified any change in the framework of public policy. All were small, isolated, and parochial; they did not serve as a prototype for other hospitals. Their relative insignificance was reinforced by the fact that they remained somewhat anonymous. None published any lengthy annual reports or accounts of their activities during the 1820's, and the rural nature of the states in which they existed tended to preclude any influx of visitors to help publicize their existence. Even had they been innovative (which they were not), therefore, their example would have remained largely unknown.[12]

One of the earliest attempts to found a public institution in accordance with early nineteenth-century psychiatric thought came, not surprisingly, in Massachusetts. By then the Bay State was already the nation's acknowledged leader in cultural and intellectual activities—a position it would retain for decades to come. The multiplication of diverse interests within its borders and a conviction that government should actively promote the general welfare led its citizens to embark on a wide-ranging program of social reform that by 1850 gave the state a unique character and made it a model for other states.

Concern with the mentally ill in Massachusetts had mani-

12. A detailed study of the founding of state institutions before 1860 can be found in Appendix I.

fested itself on a number of occasions in the late eighteenth and early nineteenth century. The founding of McLean Asylum as part of the Massachusetts General Hospital was but one indication of such concern. Another indication was the proliferation of welfare and penal institutions, most of which were required under legislation enacted in 1797 and 1816 to accept "lunatics, and persons furiously mad" who either threatened the security of the community or were so impoverished as to require public assistance. The confinement of different categories of individuals within the same institution, however, raised a number of serious problems. This practice was particularly troubling to those active in penal reform, for it undermined efforts to rehabilitate criminals and simultaneously did a severe disservice to mentally ill persons.

The formation of the Boston Prison Discipline Society in 1825 under the energetic and sometimes authoritarian leadership of the Reverend Louis Dwight gave prison reformers a national organizational component with which to disseminate their views. While Dwight's philosophy of prison reform was not always acceptable to others, his insistence that mentally ill persons belonged in hospitals aroused a responsive chord, especially since his investigations demonstrated that large numbers of such persons were confined in degrading circumstances. Given the prestigious membership of the society and the fact that its reports had wide national circulation, it was not surprising that it emerged as a leading advocate of the establishment of mental hospitals—a position that it would retain until the early 1840's.[13]

A year after the founding of the Prison Discipline Society the Massachusetts legislature established a committee to investigate conditions in public jails and to recommend changes. Chaired by George Bliss—who was also the president of the Prison Discipline Society—the committee urged that the state make illegal the confinement of mentally ill persons in jails

13. For the activities of the Boston Prison Discipline Society in psychiatric reform see its *AR*, I–XXI (1826–1846). Samuel Gridley Howe, who with Charles Sumner and Horace Mann broke with Dwight over the proper role of prisons, argued that Dwight was "*de facto* the Society. He acts for it, speaks for it, and directs its whole policy." Howe, *An Essay on Separate and Congregate Systems of Prison Discipline; Being a Report Made to the Boston Prison Discipline Society* (Boston, 1846), 7.

and provide for alternative means of care. For two years the legislature failed to act. New life was breathed into the proposal when Horace Mann, who had just launched his public career, introduced a resolution urging the legislature to take some action. As a result of his efforts, the General Court in early 1830 overwhelmingly approved a bill providing for the erection of a state lunatic hospital for 120 patients and appropriated the sum of $30,000 for the project.[14]

Located in Worcester, the new hospital opened in 1833. Under the leadership of Samuel B. Woodward, the first superintendent, the hospital quickly gained a national reputation. Unlike existing hospitals, it cared for relatively large numbers of patients; between 1833 and 1846 its average daily census rose from 107 to 359. More important, the hospital was structured in such a way as to maximize the efficacy of moral and medical treatment, for Woodward was closely acquainted with contemporary psychiatric and medical theory. Above all, Woodward seemed to demonstrate that mental disease—given prompt care and treatment—was as curable as, if not more curable than, "any other acute disease of equal severity." Between 1833 and 1845 the number of recoveries of recent cases averaged between 82 and 91 per cent (based on the number of patients discharged). These claims about the curability of insanity received widespread attention and played an important role in setting in motion the hospital movement of the 1830's and 1840's.[15]

Given Massachusetts' preeminent role in mid-nineteenth-century America, it was no surprise that its example acted as a powerful stimulus in other states facing similar problems. For whatever can be said about Bay State activists, they could hardly be described as a retiring and introverted group with limited vision. On the contrary, their ideals and visions were broad and universal rather than narrow and parochial; they were concerned with all of suffering humanity; and they could

14. Massachusetts *House Report No. 50* (February 16, 1827); Massachusetts *House Report No. 28* (1828); *Reports and Other Documents Relating to the State Lunatic Hosptial at Worcester, Mass.* (Boston, 1837). A more detailed study of the origins and history of the Worcester hospital and the development of public policy in Massachusetts can be found in Gerald N. Grob, *The State and the Mentally Ill: A History of Worcester State Hospital in Massachusetts, 1830–1920* (Chapel Hill, 1966).

15. Grob, *The State and the Mentally Ill,* Chaps. II–III.

Engraved by J.C.buttre from a Daguerrotype

6. *Although best known for his activities as an educational reformer, Horace Mann (1796–1859) launched his career as a psychiatric reformer in 1829. He was directly responsible for the passage of legislation in 1830 that established the first state hospital in Massachusetts. Source: Massachusetts Historical Society.*

see no good reason why their work should be limited by artificial political boundaries that were largely the results of accident and history. Whether fighting for reforms on behalf of the mentally ill, criminals, slaves, illiterates, or women, they raised issues to a plane that transcended geographic areas.[16]

During the 1830's the example set by the citizens of Massachusetts became known in a number of states. Dwight and the Prison Discipline Society—whose activities were national in scope —often held up the Worcester hospital as a model worthy of emulation.[17] Cognizant of the common practice of confining dependent persons in jails, the society adopted a resolution introduced by Horace Mann in 1834 that condemned this practice on the grounds that it confused "calamity and guilt." The resolution urged other states to establish curative rather than penal institutions for the mentally ill.[18] Mann himself remained active in the hospital's affairs as a trustee and friend for more than a decade, and helped to secure legislative approval for an expansion of its facilities in 1835. In fact, his involvement in educational reform beginning in the mid-1830's was nothing but a logical extension of his concern for the mentally ill. For if the "calamities and sufferings of men" arose out of either ignorance or disbelief of the laws "impressed upon our being by our Creator," might not the most fundamental reform involve the education of human beings in their formative years so that they would know and follow the natural laws governing mankind and thereby avoid incurring the penalties of misbehavior?[19]

16. Though unyielding in their struggle against social and individual evils, many activists devoted considerable thought to the logic and philosophy of reform and the relationship between means and ends. In a number of cases individuals became active in more than one movement when they recognized that their fight on behalf of one oppressed group would be compromised by their unwillingness to help another group. Aileen S. Kraditor in *Means and Ends in American Abolitionism: Garrison and His Critics on Strategy and Tactics, 1834–1850* (New York, 1969), has a penetrating discussion of this problem.

17. Cf. Boston Prison Discipline Society, *AR*, IX (1834), 75–77.

18. *Ibid.*, 4.

19. For Mann's activities see Mann to Charles Sumner, April 29, 1837, in Mary Mann, *Life of Horace Mann By His Wife* (Boston, 1888), 56–57; Mann to Lydia B. Mann, March 18, 1833, Mann to Elizabeth P. Peabody, undated letter written in the spring of 1835, Mann to Lydia B. Mann,

When Mann was helping to launch the hospital movement in the early 1830's, he received strong support from Samuel B. Woodward, who became one of its first publicists. Woodward was a humanitarian and a perennial optimist, and his friend Thomas S. Kirkbride once described him as a man who "has the happy temperament, which believes whatever he has, is the best that can be had, and of course never seems very anxious for any improvement."[20] He constantly reiterated his conviction that mental illness was a curable malady, given early and proper treatment, and predicted that in the long run it would be cheaper for states to establish therapeutic hospitals than to care for the insane in other ways.[21] Unlike the superintendents of the Virginia, Kentucky, and South Carolina public institutions, who made little or no effort to publicize their activities, Woodward made certain that the example of the Worcester hospital was known nationally. His annual reports, which sometimes approached 100 pages in length (as compared with the brief reports of other hospitals), were printed in editions as high as three to four thousand copies and were circulated throughout the country. When individuals outside of Massachusetts attempted to induce their legislatures to found institutions, they often cited the Worcester hospital as a model to buttress their case.[22] Recog-

---

November 9, 1838, Mann to Woodward, February 16, 1842, June 26, November 20, 1843, Horace Mann Journal, entries of May 5, 9, 10, 23, June 27, 1837, September 5, 1838, Mann Papers, MHS.

20. "Account of a visit to 9 institutions in 1845 by Dr. Thomas S. Kirkbride and Mr. Jacob Morris," ms. in the Kirkbride Papers, IPH.

21. Woodward to Samuel Gridley Howe, March 4, 1843, Howe Papers, HLHU; Worcester State Lunatic Hospital, *AR*, VIII (1840), 68, XII (1844), 60.

22. *The Vermont Asylum for the Insane. Its Annals for Fifty Years* (Brattleboro, 1887), 14–15; *Report Made to the Legislature of New Hampshire on the Subject of the Insane. June Session, 1836* (Concord, 1836), 13, 18, 22; *Report of the Committee on the Insane Poor in Connecticut, to the General Assembly, May Session, 1838* (New Haven, 1838), 7–9; *Report of the Directors to Whom was Committed the Charge of Erecting a Lunatic Asylum for the State of Ohio December 24, 1838* (n.p., n.d.), 5; *Report of the Commissioners Appointed by the Governor of New Jersey, to Ascertain the Number of Lunatics and Idiots in the State* (Newark, 1840), 19–23; *A Second Appeal to the People of Pennsylvania on the Subject of an Asylum for the Insane Poor of the Commonwealth* (Philadelphia, 1840),

7. *Samuel B. Woodward (1787–1850). Superintendent of the Worcester State Lunatic Hospital from 1833 to 1846, he also served as the first president of the Association of Medical Superintendents of American Institutions for the Insane (now the American Psychiatric Association) and helped to promote the founding of public hospitals in the 1830's and 1840's. Source: John Curwen,* The Original Thirteen Members of the Association of Medical Superintendents of American Institutions for the Insane *(Warren, Pa., 1885).*

nizing the political value of the seemingly favorable therapeutic results in mental hospitals, Woodward urged others to publicize their findings. "I think the statistics of insanity have done great good," he wrote to a fellow superintendent, "and the extensive and enthusiastic movements in favor of the insane in the United States has been produced by comparing the results of institutions and looking at the success of the best as given in the published statistics."[23] Woodward's contribution was recognized by the infant psychiatric profession, for when the Association of Medical Superintendents of American Institutions for the Insane (AMSAII) was founded in 1844, he was elected as its first president. And Pliny Earle, who in his later career attempted to demonstrate the inaccuracy of the curability claims of early American psychiatrists, gave Woodward full credit for his role in promoting the hospital movement of the 1830's and 1840's. "His very elaborate reports," noted Earle, "abounding in statistics, as well as in other matter more attractive to the general reader, were widely circulated, and he soon became known, not only throughout the States, but likewise in Europe, and was generally regarded as the highest living American authority in the treatment of mental disorders. In the course of the ten years next following his removal to Worcester, no less than twelve hospitals for the insane were founded and opened within the States, and seven of them were State institutions."[24]

By the 1840's Mann had turned to educational reform and Woodward was growing older and less active. The seeming void in leadership, however, was immediately filled by Dorothea L. Dix, who without doubt became the most famous and influential psychiatric reformer of the nineteenth century. A woman whose

21, 27–28; Edward Jarvis, review article in the *Western Journal of Medicine and Surgery*, IV (December, 1841), 449–457.

23. Woodward to Pliny Earle, March 18, 1842, Earle Papers, AAS. See also William M. Awl to Woodward, April 18, 1842, Woodward Papers, AAS.

24. Pliny Earle, *The Curability of Insanity: A Series of Studies* (Philadelphia, 1887), 25–26. See also Earle, "A Glance at Insanity, and the Management of the Insane in the American States," Conference of Charities, *Proceedings*, VI (1879), 43–44, and Isaac Ray to Robert H. Ives, January 8, 1844, Butler Hospital Papers, John Carter Brown Library, Brown University, Providence, R. I.

most striking characteristic was her determination, Dix dedicated her life to proper care of the mentally ill. Born in Hampden, Maine, in 1802, she had an unhappy childhood because of an indifferent mother and an intemperate father. At the age of twelve her desire to leave home was to great that she traveled to Boston by herself to live with her wealthy grandparents. After an unhappy love affair, she followed her training as a teacher by heading a private school in Boston. When her grandmother died in 1837 Dix received a modest bequest which made it possible to support herself without an occupation and to devote all her energies to reform activities.

Like many other contemporary reformers, Dix was strongly motivated by religious considerations. Occasionally writing on religious subjects, she reflected, in the words of her biographer, "the finest flower of Unitarianism."[25] After a protracted illness in 1836, she traveled to England to convalesce and while there visited the York Retreat and possibly met Samuel Tuke. Upon returning home she began to search for a way to live a useful life. Her health was such that teaching appeared too strenuous, and her family may have compounded her uneasiness because of their suspicions that she was malingering. Therefore, when John T. G. Nichols, a young theology student at the Harvard Divinity School, asked Miss Dix if she knew someone who could teach a Sunday school class to women convicts in the East Cambridge Jail in March, 1841, she volunteered her services. After classes she walked through the jail and to her horror found a group of insane persons confined with hardened criminals and suffering from years of neglect.[26] Deeply touched by what she had seen, she decided to launch a crusade on behalf of the mentally ill.

After consulting with Samuel Gridley Howe and Charles Sumner, Dix undertook to make an exhaustive personal examination of conditions in Massachusetts—a task that took well over a

25. Helen E. Marshall, *Dorothea Dix: Forgotten Samaritan* (Chapel Hill, 1937), 39. Most of the biographical material on Dix has been taken from this source and from Francis Tiffany, *Life of Dorothea Lynde Dix* (Boston, 1890).

26. This state of affairs was well known to informed observers. See the *Abstract of Returns of Inspectors and Keepers of Jails and Houses of Correction*, Massachusetts *House Document No. 39* (February 7, 1840), *passim*.

year. Howe, meanwhile, had become involved in a struggle in the legislature over the expansion of the Worcester hospital. In the midst of the controversy Dix presented her famous "Memorial to the Legislature of Massachusetts," the first of many such documents on the subject. Combining passion and knowledge, she presented an extraordinarily detailed picture of conditions at virtually every jail, house of correction, and almshouse in the state. Insisting that the state had a moral, humanitarian, and legal obligation toward the mentally ill, she demanded that the legislature fulfil its duty by providing additional facilities at the overcrowded Worcester hospital.[27]

Successful in her first venture, Dix followed a similar path in other states for the next three decades. After arriving in a state, she spent considerable time and effort in surveying actual conditions and then presented her findings to the legislature, usually in the form of a lengthy memorial. Unconcerned with developing a mass following or arousing public opinion, she then turned with unerring political instinct to those leaders in a position to introduce changes.[28] Indeed, her singular devotion to her cause often resulted in consternation among her friends and allies, some of whom felt that she took unnecessary liberties with the truth. "I see Miss Dix has been over your state & *Memorialized* your legislature," Amariah Brigham wrote to Kirkbride. "I hope good will result from it—& trust that her experience in this state [New York] may make her more courteous in observing & publishing. In this state I am afraid she did hurt by *coloring* & by not accurately observing. She was often mistaken & this has thrown a doubt over all her statements with many."[29] Time and age, however, did not change Dix, for Isaac Ray, her friend for many years, observed in 1873 that she often censured "without good judgment, but has generally a basis for her censures."[30]

27. Dix, "Memorial to the Legislature of Massachusetts 1843," *Old South Leaflets*, VI, No. 148 (Boston, n.d.), *passim*, and Grob, *The State and the Mentally Ill*, 104–112. For Mann's comments on the memorial see Mann to Dix, January 27, 1843, Dix Papers, HLHU, and Dix to Mann, February 1, 1843, Mann Papers, MHS.

28. Tiffany, *Life of Dorothea Lynde Dix*, 92.

29. Amariah Brigham to Kirkbride, March 3, 1845, Kirkbride Papers, IPH.

30. Isaac Ray to John W. Sawyer, December 11, 1873, ms. in Butler

8. *Dorothea Lynde Dix (1802–1887). Her career as a psychiatric reformer spanned four decades, during which time her influence and activities were national and international in scope. Source: Houghton Library, Harvard University.*

Dorothea Dix's singular devotion to the cause—a devotion that was reflected in her extraordinarily close friendships with a small circle of individuals who constantly worried about the seemingly precarious state of her health and well-being[31]—gave her a key position in the history of American psychiatry and mental hospitals from the 1840's to the 1870's. Many superintendents owed their position to her influence, and it became a practice for younger men to consult with her about their future plans and aspirations.[32] Nor was her position as a powerful arbiter and leader honorific in nature, for often she was called upon to adjudicate or to pass judgment on internal institutional conflicts. Such was the case at the Bloomingdale Asylum in New York in the early 1850's, an institution noted for its unstable management and divided authority. In the fall of 1851 Dix visited the asylum and prepared a highly critical report. Although willing to modify a few aspects of Bloomingdale's operations, the governors were reluctant to increase the authority of the superintendent, who submitted his resignation the following year. Throughout the entire controversy Dix was closely involved with all concerned, for few individuals—whatever their views—could afford to ignore this remarkable woman.[33]

By the close of her career Dix had been responsible for founding or enlarging over thirty mental hospitals in the United States and abroad. Although in many cases the groundwork had been prepared by others, her role was to act as a catalyst and to bring

---

Hospital, Providence, R. I. A year later Ray observed that Dix "must have a grievance in some shape or another." Ray to Sawyer, December 9, 1874, *ibid.*

31. Cf. Ann E. Heath to Dix, November 4, 1853, and Millard Fillmore to Dix, December 20, 1853, Dix Papers, HLHU.

32. See, for example, John Curwen to Dix, June 19, 1850, Charles H. Nichols to Dix, September 11, 20, 1852, Millard Fillmore to Dix, October 1, 1852, Ray to Dix, November 3, 1852, Barnard D. Eastman to Dix, February 5, 1879, *ibid.*

33. Kirkbride to Francis T. Stribling, June 15, 1844, Charles H. Nichols to Kirkbride, November 11, 1851, March 3, 30, April 22, 1852, Kirkbride Papers, IPH; Ray to Dix, December 8, 1851, Luther V. Bell to Dix, December 20, 1851, James Donaldson to Dix, December 26, 1851, Charles H. Nichols to Dix, February 7, 23, May 4, 9, June 22, 1852, Dix Papers, HLHU; William L. Russell, *The New York Hospital: A History of the Psychiatric Service 1771-1936* (New York, 1945), 247-254, 516-521.

to fruition the specific project. Her strong personality and persistence made it difficult for legislators to ignore her efforts. Indeed, in many ways Dix's most important contribution was to stimulate the thrust toward broadening the role of government in providing institutional care and treatment of the mentally ill. Her influence, moreover, was national and international in scope precisely because she insisted on excluding virtually all extraneous issues (prison reform being the only exception). Thus she was one of the few New England social activists who received a warm welcome in the South, because she never coupled antislavery and psychiatric reform.

Dix's work, of course, would have been futile without some base of support. Such support existed, for most states already possessed influential groups that were committed to the amelioration of distress and social improvement through the expansion of governmental activities. However one may view American society during the first two-thirds of the nineteenth century, it is clear that the creation and strengthening of formal public institutions represented a major trend. In building schools, colleges, hospitals, prisons, houses of refuge—to mention only a few institutions—Americans manifested an awareness that traditional structures, whether formal or informal, were no longer appropriate to their society. Dix's insistence upon institutional care for the mentally ill, therefore, struck a responsive chord among those who were committed to the creation of a better society by diminishing the role of the family and other traditional institutions and increasing sharply the role of government.

The individuals who provided the support that was necessary for the creation of public structures to deal with distressed and dependent groups by no means came out of a common background or shared similar or identical interests. Indeed, it is difficult to abstract a set of characteristics that provide a clue to their common identity. They came from diverse backgrounds; some were Quakers, others belonged to the Congregational Church, and yet others were Unitarians. In terms of age the movement was not one of youth—although young people were involved in it. A large proportion had attended college, but their involvement in reform cannot be explained on the basis of their educational background alone; far more who had received college degrees showed no interest whatsoever in social reforms.

While New England produced proportionately more activists than other regions, most states had significant numbers of such persons. It is true that most reformers were, if not wealthy, quite economically secure; thus their economic standing allowed them the freedom to devote most of their time to agitating for social change. Nevertheless, it is difficult to interpret social involvement as a function of class alone.

From an ideological point of view it is equally difficult to categorize activists in any simple manner. Some saw social evils arising out of improvident and immoral behavior on the part of the individual. Others, however, recognized that an imperfect environment was at fault and that a meaningful solution involved structural changes as well. A few saw reform as a conservative phenomenon in that it would diminish class rivalries and antagonisms and thereby preserve a fundamentally sound and moral social order. But many more were primarily concerned with uplifting the mass of suffering humanity and were not particularly aware of political or economic considerations. In general, few activists distinguished between private and public action—if voluntary means failed they were prepared to advocate public subsidies and even state intervention on a massive scale.

Although reform was heterogeneous in nature, a few common themes were apparent. In the first place, most social activists were optimists. In their eyes no problem was too difficult to be solved; no evil was so extreme as to be ineradicable; no situation was so far gone as to be beyond human control; and no illness was so severe as to be incurable. Secondly, most reformers held strong religious convictions—even though they came from different sects. Disinterested in and even hostile toward fine points of doctrinal dispute, they were all motivated, however, by a sense of obligation and stewardship. All human beings, they argued, were under a moral law that gave them a responsibility for the welfare of their fellow man. No individual could afford to ignore this obligation. In the third place, most reformers believed that science and reason provided the means of fulfilling the moral and religious obligations that bound all men. Fourth, most reformers recognized the complexity and interdependence of society. Consequently, their concerns tended to be broad rather than narrow; more often than not they were involved in more than one crusade. Finally, activists tended to present their case in glowing rhetoric and with a firm conviction that it was indeed possible to eliminate social and individual evil and create the good society. Whether speaking about the virtues of mental hospitals, schools, penitentiaries, almshouses, or houses of refuge, they held out the hope that crime, disease, and poverty could be eradicated by these new public structures. Mental hospitals, they argued, would diminish or eliminate mental illness; schools and houses of refuge would train children to become moral and productive adults; penitentiaries would reform criminals; and almshouses would alleviate poverty.

The rhetoric and framework in which activists phrased their case was to have significant implications for the future. Although it is unclear whether their claims were intended primarily to secure legislative appropriations, there is little doubt that they contributed to the rising public expectations of the benefits accruing from public institutions. When it later became evident that the achievements of many of these institutions fell far short of their promise, a marked reaction set in that had important consequences for public policy. Moreover, the glowing rhetoric often precluded serious consideration of long-range financial and demographic projections as well as the internal problems faced by most institutions. Above all, social activists and reformers stimulated greater reliance upon public structures, which contributed to the diminishing role played by traditional institutions and modes of behavior—a process that tended to accelerate over a period of time.

IV

During the 1830's the movement to found public mental hospitals slowly began to accelerate. The example set by Massachusetts was followed in other states with similar problems. The significance of the Bay State was that it offered an alternative model in the form of a public institution devoted to therapy as well as custody. As long as custodial care had been the major objective, there was little incentive to establish special institutions; mentally ill persons could just as well be confined in general welfare institutions at lower cost. Therapeutic hospitals, on the other hand, held out the hope of recovery—a hope that would

9. State Lunatic Hospital, Worcester, Mass. The prototype of the modern state mental hospital, The Worcester institution opened in 1833 and served as a model for other states during the 1830's and 1840's. Its subsequent history mirrored most of the major trends in the care and treatment of the mentally ill in America. Source: Worcester State Lunatic Hospital, Annual Report, V (1837).

both satisfy humanitarian sentiments and reduce expenditures by removing people from welfare roles.

The process of emulation also had an important part in the role that public mental hospitals played in the country. During the nineteenth century structural innovations in one area were adopted elsewhere—often uncritically and without consideration of alternatives. The fragmented nature of the decision-making process merely reinforced the tendency to emulate rather than innovate. Indeed, the spread of mental hospitals in the decades following 1830 was like the ripples caused by a stone thrown into the center of a pond.

In few states did the drive to establish a public hospital succeed immediately. Characteristically, two to five years (and sometimes more) of agitation were required before the legislature would pass the necessary law and provide an appropriation. An additional three years were then necessary for planning purposes and construction of the physical plant. Consequently, a decade often elapsed from the time that the issue was first raised to the moment when the facility was actually opened for the reception of patients. The only states besides Massachusetts to have a hospital in operation before 1840 were Ohio and Vermont. Between 1840 and 1849, however, Maine, New Hampshire, New York, New Jersey, Indiana, Tennessee, Georgia, and Louisiana had opened public institutions, and in the succeeding decade sixteen new state, one federal, and four municipal institutions were opened. Even in states like Connecticut and Rhode Island—neither of which had public hospitals before the Civil War—alternative arrangements were made to have the Hartford Retreat and Butler Hospital accept indigent patients in return for public subsidies.

Generally speaking, mental hospitals received their greatest support from state governors and small groups of relatively well-to-do individuals both within and without public life (including the medical profession) who viewed such projects in terms of noblesse oblige and the moral obligation of society toward less fortunate groups. Some opposition, on the other hand, often came from local communities, whose citizens were concerned primarily with the potential impact on their tax rates, for in most states localities were financially liable for the support of their indigent insane at state hospitals. Most communities evinced

10. Utica State Lunatic Asylum. The first state institution in New York, it was also the home of the American Journal of Insanity. Its physical plant was a typical example of mid-nineteenth century American mental hospital architecture. Source: Utica State Lunatic Asylum, Annual Report, XIV (1856).

little enthusiasm at the prospect of spending larger sums to support indigent insane persons at hospitals when such cases could be cared for in a cheaper manner at local welfare institutions.

There were, of course, considerable variations from state to state and region to region. Some states established hospitals with the stipulation that part of the funds for construction had to be raised from private donors; others provided all capital funds but required the institution to be self-supporting; and everywhere modes of governance varied somewhat. There were also sharp differences between regions in terms of funding and the quality of care provided patients. Southern hospitals lagged far behind their Northern and Western counterparts in terms of institutional quality. A few states on occasion introduced some interesting innovations; one briefly experimented by abolishing all charges irrespective of the individual's ability to pay for the high costs of institutionalization and defended its action on the grounds that such procedures would eliminate all differentials in care and treatment.

The similarities between public hospitals, nevertheless, far outweighed the differences. In virtually every state the care of the mentally ill became of public concern because of the devastating economic impact of mental disease on both the individual and the family; the establishment of most hospitals inevitably occurred within the framework of dependency and welfare. The structure and functions of hospitals, as we shall see later, tended also to become more similar in time, a process that was hastened by the rapid development of professionalization among superintendents. Above all, the movement to found hospitals in virtually every state began with the belief that a single institution, centrally located and emphasizing therapeutic functions (thereby discharging cured persons and making room for new cases), could meet the needs of its citizens. When the pressure to admit patients became overwhelming as a result of increased population, some states—notably Ohio and Massachusetts—founded additional hospitals, a development that was widely emulated during the second half of the nineteenth century.

By the 1850's there was little disposition to question the growing role of the state in providing institutional care and treatment for persons unable to pay the high costs of extended confinement. On the contrary, the establishment of public hospitals was defended in positive rather than negative terms. Less than a decade after the opening of the Worcester hospital an influential Bay State journal anticipated the future when it observed that the "walls of the hospital should be made to grow till they can embrace every applicant. The State has done well; but this is no reason why it should not do better. . . . These public Charities should rather, we think, be termed public Duties. They are, rightly considered, the fulfilling of obligations; not the mere indulgence of benevolent sympathies. We like the doctrine, that the State is the parent of the people. It is a genuine part of republicanism. And it is only this,—that the people, in their collective capacity, will look after and protect themselves, so that the poorest brother of them all shall not want, for the reason that he *is* a brother, an equal, a man."[34]

V

The increase in the number of state hospitals between 1833 and 1860 did not, however, reflect a careful analysis of existing needs and future projections. Although there was a growing emphasis on the gathering of quantitative as well as qualitative materials, there was little effort to make certain that policy would follow the knowledge already at hand. Some of the empirical data, for example, demonstrated the inadequacy of those assumptions that underlay the founding of most public hospitals. Yet the institutional weakness of state governments and the lack of some type of mechanism that would ensure the efficient use of data heightened the incremental nature of public policy. Indeed, the inability to make use of the available data often gave rise to problems of considerable magnitude.

34. "Lunatic Hospital at Worcester," *Christian Examiner*, XXVI (May, 1839), 258. When Dix began her notable career as a psychiatric reformer in 1841 and a battle over expanding the Worcester hospital occurred in the state legislature, the argument that the state had a moral, humanitarian, and legal obligation toward the mentally ill was heard over and over again. See Samuel Gridley Howe, "Insanity in Massachusetts," *North American Review*, LVI (January, 1843), 171–185; Robert C. Waterston, "The Insane of Massachusetts," *Christian Examiner and General Review*, XXXIII (January, 1843), 338–352 (also widely circulated in pamphlet form under the title *The Condition of the Insane in Massachusetts*); and Dorothea L. Dix, "Memorial to the Legislature of Massachusetts 1843," *passim.*

A careful examination of the gap between data and policy substantiates such a generalization. By the 1830's and 1840's there was a determined effort by some individuals to collect quantitative materials. These materials, in turn, would presumably serve as the basis for a more enlightened and scientific formulation of policy and thereby overcome the disabilities that often followed the passage of legislation. Admittedly, some of the data were simple in nature. As early as the 1830's, to cite one illustration, superintendents were emphasizing that the accumulation of chronic cases within their hospitals was curtailing therapeutic functions. New hospitals in particular tended to receive large numbers of chronic persons. Many of these individuals had been confined in local welfare institutions for years, and their chances for recovery were statistically remote. When the Worcester hospital opened in 1833 more than half of the 164 patients received during that year came from jails, almshouses, and houses of correction. About one-third had been confined for periods of between ten and thirty-two years.[35] Since the average stay for a recent case in which the patient recovered was about three to four months, the retention of every chronic person meant that the hospital would be unable to accept two to three recent cases presumably amenable to therapy in any given year. Similarly, it was well known that the number of insane persons far exceeded existing spaces at institutional facilities. In a memorial to Congress in 1848 Dorothea Dix noted that there were about 22,000 mentally ill persons in the United States and less than 3,700 spaces.[36]

Some of the data, on the other hand, were relatively sophisticated and complex. In 1850 Edward Jarvis, the noted statistician

35. Worcester State Lunatic Hospital, AR, I (1833), 5, 25. This state of affairs was fairly typical. See the following: Maine Insane Hospital, AR, II (1841), 7; Utica State Lunatic Hospital, AR, I (1843), 6, II (1844), 6; Ohio Lunatic Asylum, AR, VII (1845), 39; New Jersey State Lunatic Asylum, AR, II (1848), 24; Indiana Hospital for the Insane, AR, I (1849), 13.

36. Memorial of D. L. Dix, Praying a Grant of Land for the Relief and Support of the Indigent, Curable and Incurable Insane in the United States. June 27, 1848, 30th Cong., 1st Sess., Senate Miscellaneous Document No. 150, 5. In gathering these estimates, Dix consulted with a number of leading psychiatrists. Luther V. Bell in particular warned that the statistical data represented guesses, and that the census of 1840 "was an aggregation of fraud and blunders." Bell to Dix, June 5, 1848, Dix Papers, HLHU.

and psychiatrist, pointed out that the assumption that a state institution would serve all citizens equally was an incorrect one. In a careful study that took into account nearly every mental hospital in the country, the place of residence of all patients, and the total population by county and state, he demonstrated conclusively that areas adjacent to hospitals used hospital facilities to a far greater extent than more distant areas. The proportion in some cases was at least four to one.[37] Jarvis, in another study, pointed out that the mere existence of mental hospitals tended to sensitize a community to the very concept of mental disease and thereby stimulated greater use. The opening of hospitals, he wrote,

> the spread of their reports, the extension of the knowledge of their character, power, and usefulness, by the means of the patients that they protect and cure, have created, and continue to create, more and more interest in the subject of insanity, and more confidence in its curability. Consequently, more and more persons and families, who, or such as who, formerly kept their insane friends and relations at home, or allowed them to stroll abroad about the streets or country, now believe, that they can be restored, or improved, or, at least made more comfortable in these public institutions, and, therefore, they send their patients to these asylums, and thus swell the lists of their inmates.[38]

Such findings were of major importance. They seemed to run counter to the widely held view that the establishment of one state hospital (or two), centrally located so as to be accessible to all, was an appropriate response by society to the problems posed by mental illness. Given the lack of effective decision-making mechanisms capable of digesting quantitative data, however, social policy instead continued to be formulated increment-

37. Edward Jarvis, "The Influence of Distance From and Proximity to an Insane Hospital, on Its Use by any People," *Boston Medical and Surgical Journal*, XLII (April 17, 1850), 209–222; *AJI*, VII (January, 1851), 281–285; Jarvis, "Influence of Distance from and Nearness to an Insane Hospital on Its Use by the People," *AJI*, XXII (January, 1866), 361–406. This situation was recognized by various hospital superintendents. See Ohio Lunatic Asylum, *AR*, XI (1849), 46–47, and Maine Insane Hospital, *AR*, X (1850), 36–37.

38. Edward Jarvis, "On the Supposed Increase of Insanity," *AJI*, VIII (April, 1852), 344.

ally. The result not only was a policy incompatible with its own stated goals, but one whose framework was determined largely by unforeseen events and developments rather than by the conscious choice of public officials. Over a period of time, therefore, the absence of firm policy guidelines gave rise to unwelcome consequences.

Consider, for example, the simultaneous growth of municipal hospitals in large urban areas. When the drive to establish state hospitals began, no thought was given to founding a dual system of public institutions. The placement of state hospitals, however, had an immediate impact upon larger urban areas. Centrally located, most state hospitals drew a disproportionate number of patients from adjacent areas. The larger cities, on the other hand, were usually located on the coast or navigable waterways at some distance from the geographic center. Consequently, cities found that the benefits of state institutions were distributed unequally, and that they were forced to assume greater responsibilities for mentally ill persons than was the case in less densely populated areas. The result was the simultaneous growth of municipal insane hospitals that arose in response to the inadvertant discrimination inherent in state policy. The problem was further complicated by the fact that urban populations included a high percentage of minority ethnic immigrant groups often so impoverished that they used welfare facilities at a far greater rate than other groups. Urban governments, therefore, were faced with the prospect of significantly higher welfare expenditures than rural areas.

A brief analysis of the problems of the major urban areas reveals not merely the incremental and haphazard nature of public policy but also the intimate relationship between mental illness and welfare. New York City is a case in point. By the early nineteenth century it was the largest urban area in the United States. The city had also a large number of impoverished immigrants. Its citizens thus confronted a variety of social problems at an earlier date than other cities. Before 1825 New York's insane poor were either kept at the almshouse or at Bloomingdale. In 1825 they were brought together in the basement and first story of the building erected as a general hospital on Blackwell's Island (later Welfare Island)—the location where most of the city's welfare and penal institutions were situated. For the next fourteen years New York maintained a "Lunatic Asylum" as part of its almshouse and prison complex. Conditions at that time were so depressing that the commissioners charged with responsibility for the institution described it in the following words:

[The Lunatic Asylum] yet remains, a witness of the blind infatuation of prejudice and miscalculation; affording to a class more deserving commisseration than any other among the afflicted catalogue of humanity, a miserable refuge in their trials, undeserving the *name* of an "Asylum," in these enlightened days. These apartments, under the best superintendence, cannot be made to afford proper accommodations for the inmates, much less can they be so, when (as your Commissioners first saw them,) the same neglect and want of cleanliness witnessed in other parts of the building, was visible here; and a portion of the rooms seemed more like those receptacles of *crime*, "to whose foul mouth no healthsome air breathes in," than tenements prepared for the recipients of an awful visitation of Divine Providence, justly considered the worst "of all the ills that flesh is heir to."[39]

The city on a number of occasions was urged to provide better facilities for its insane. In 1834 Dr. James McDonald sent to the aldermen a long communication in which he spelled out in detail the minimal requirements for such an institution. The council the following year authorized construction of a separate building on Blackwell's Island to serve as a mental hospital. Because of delays, however, the structure was not completed until 1839. At that time the lunatic asylum was separated from the other municipal welfare and penal institutions and given autonomy as a hospital. But the change in structure proved more apparent than real. Conditions at the lunatic asylum remained an open scandal for the next three or four decades. The number of patients increased from 278 in 1840 to about 1,300 in 1870, even though the physical plant was incapable of caring for anywhere near that number.

39. *Report of the Commissioners of the Alms House, Bridewell and Penitentiary* [*1837*], New York City Board of Aldermen *Document No. 32* (September 11, 1837), 208; New York City Lunatic Asylum, Blackwell's Island, *AR*, 1848, in New York City Alms House Commissioner, *AR*, 1848, in New York City Board of Aldermen *Document No. 44* (March 5, 1849), 112–113.

The asylum's size—which far exceeded even that of the largest state hospital—hindered its internal administration. Indeed, the problems of welfare and dependency in New York City appeared so overwhelming and costly that the institutional structures that it established did not come close to meeting minimal standards for that time. At the lunatic asylum, for example, convicts from the penitentiary on Blackwell's Island were used as attendants so as to save money; the patients' diet was substandard for a hospital; epidemics were not infrequent; and political considerations sometimes dictated hospital policy.[40] Charles Dickens and Thomas S. Kirkbride, both of whom visited the hospital in the 1840's, were extremely critical in their comments. "As an evidence of the kind of attendants employed," noted Kirkbride in his notes, "it may be stated, that a large red faced masculine looking woman, was pointed out, as an 'admirable hand'—her only fault being that she was a drunkard!"[41]

Generally speaking, the lunatic asylum on Blackwell's Island was used to provide cheap custodial care for impoverished mentally ill immigrants. In 1850, for example, 534 patients were immigrants (of whom virtually every one was destitute), while there were only 121 native-born inmates. These figures were disproportionate, when one remembers that the foreign-born

40. This paragraph and the previous one are based on the following sources: New York City Board of Assistant Aldermen *Document No. 101* (March 10, 1834), 813–833; Boston Prison Discipline Society, *AR*, XII (1837), 25–26; New York City Board of Aldermen *Document No. 30* (November 30, 1840), 383–386, *Document No. 28* (October 5, 1842), 211–217, *Document No. 119* (May 8, 1843), 1403–1409, *Document No. 11* (July 15, 1844), 155–168, *Document No. 40* (December 30, 1844), 397–403; *AJI*, II (October, 1845), 145, V (July, 1848), 89–95; James McDonald to Kirkbride, May 25, 1848, Kirkbride Papers, IPH; New York City Lunatic Asylum, Blackwell's Island, *AR*, 1848, in New York City Almshouse Commissioner, *AR*, 1848, in New York City Board of Aldermen *Document No. 44* (March 5, 1849), 119–120; New York City Lunatic Asylum, Blackwell's Island, *AR*, 1851, in New York City Governors of the Alms House, *AR*, III (1851), 98; New York City Lunatic Asylum, Blackwell's Island, *AR*, 1856, 5, 11–12, 1865, 3–15; New York State Commissioner in Lunacy, *AR*, II (1874), 22–24, III (1875), 10–16; James C. Hallock to Dix, July 21, 1870, Dix Papers, HLHU.

41. "Account of a visit to 9 institutions in 1845 by Dr. Thomas S. Kirkbride and Mr. Jacob Morris," ms. in the Kirkbride Papers, IPH; Dickens, *American Notes*, 92–94.

constituted slightly less than half of the city's total population. Admissions continued to reflect this pattern; 297 out of 366 patients admitted in 1856 were from abroad. Because the institution performed a largely welfare function, it made little pretense at providing therapy. "The feeling is quite too common," complained its superintendent in 1861, "that a lunatic asylum is a grand receptacle for all who are troublesome." For the next several decades the institution continued to face seemingly insoluble problems—many of which were clearly related to a low level of funding. In 1874 the average annual expense per patient was $84.58, as compared with an average of $246.90 for the early 1870's at thirty-six other public institutions. Indeed, a new superintendent noted as one of his major accomplishments that the institution had managed to stay out of the news during 1880 and 1881.[42]

Although more mental hospitals were established by the state in the 1860's and 1870's, the impact on New York City was negligible. Most of the new state institutions were located at some distance from the city. Recognizing this situation, the superintendent of the Blackwell asylum on a number of occasions in the 1850's urged state officials to provide financial aid on the grounds that it was very difficult for the city—given the magnitude of its problems—to assume responsibility for non-resident insane persons. Moreover, he pointed out that local citizens were already being taxed for the support of the state hospital at Utica, a facility that provided no benefits whatsoever to the city. The state, he concluded, should either assume financial responsibility for nonresidents (as in Massachusetts) or else establish a state facility in the city. Continued inaction by the state on any of these suggestions forced New York City to open another asylum on Ward's Island in 1871 similar in character to the one on Blackwell's Island. Within three years the new facility, though having space for 423 inmates, had slightly

42. New York City Lunatic Asylum, Blackwell's Island, *AR*, 1856, 6, 1858, 12, 1861, 18, 1870, 6–8, 1874, 13–14, 1875, 22–33; New York State Commissioner in Lunacy, *AR*, II (1874), 22–24, III (1875), 10–16; James C. Hallock to Dix, July 21, 1870, Dix Papers, HLHU; T. M. Franklin to Pliny Earle, May 15, 1881, Earle Papers, AAS. See also the description by a former inmate, "Blackwell's Island Lunatic Asylum," *Harper's New Monthly Magazine*, XXXII (February, 1866), 273–294.

11 and 11a. An outgrowth of the welfare complex in New York City, the Lunatic Asylum on Blackwell's Island enjoyed a notorious reputation for most of the nineteenth century. Catering predominantly to lower-class immigrants, the asylum was the object of numerous attacks by the young psychiatric profession. Source: "Blackwell's Island Lunatic Asylum," Harper's, XXXII (February 1866).

under 700 patients. Lacking adequate operating revenues, it too employed convicts as attendants and had difficulty in providing an adequate diet. Political and religious considerations also seem to have been responsible for a rapid turnover among its chief administrative officers.[43]

Much the same state of affairs existed in Kings County (Brooklyn), which did not officially become part of New York City until the end of the nineteenth century. By 1850 it was the third largest urban area in the country and faced the same problems of welfare and dependency as did other cities. In 1844, therefore, its authorities obtained permission to erect a lunatic asylum adjacent to the almshouse. Opened in 1852, the new facility grew rapidly. By the 1860's friction had arisen with New York City, since Kings County officials felt that the metropolis was deliberately dumping its insane paupers in Brooklyn in order to lighten its own burdens. Continued conflict led the superintendent to urge that the state found a mental hospital in the metropolitan area, thus relieving the county of the responsibility of having to provide facilities for nonresidents. Aside from such issues, the lunatic asylum itself was plagued with the same problems as its New York counterparts. During the 1870's several state and local investigations resulted in a condemnation of both the county administrative structure governing the asylum and the internal management of the institution. In 1877, for example, a county investigating committee concluded that the superintendent, his assistants, and the nursing staff were incompetent, and that the institution was "a reproach and disgrace to Kings County."[44]

The situation in Philadelphia, another major metropolitan

43. New York City Lunatic Asylum, Blackwell's Island, *AR*, 1855, 12–15, 1856, 11–12, 1858, 13–19; New York City Asylum for the Insane, Ward's Island, *AR*, III (1874), 13–20, IV (1875), 16–17, 21–25; New York Board of State Commissioners of Public Charities, *AR*, VI (1872), 64–71; James C. Hallock to Dix, December 25, 1871, November 7, 1872, January 22, December 30, 1873, Dix Papers, HLHU.

44. *AJI*, X (January, 1854), 284–285; Kings County Lunatic Asylum, *AR*, 1860, 7, 1866, 12–14, 1870, 9–11; New York State Commissioner in Lunacy, *AR*, II (1874), 28–44, III (1875), 25–64; *Report of the Investigation of the Board of Supervisors of Kings County, in the Matter of Alleged Abuses at the Lunatic Asylum, Together with the Evidence Taken by the Committee. Presented April 19th, 1877* (New York, 1877), 6.

area, was no different from that in New York or Kings County. Prior to 1859 there was no formal structure within the municipal almshouse specializing in the care of the pauper insane. Such persons were usually kept in the almshouse along with the indigent, the sick, and the aged. As early as 1845 there were suggestions that the existing undifferentiated structure be changed and that the insane department of the almshouse be given some measure of autonomy. Although a resident physician was appointed, partial autonomy did not come until 1859. Even then the superintendent lacked clear authority, and conditions at that time were described as "in the depths of degradation."[45]

The organizational change that occurred in 1859 did little to alter the character of the insane department. A large proportion of the inmates, as at other municipal institutions, were poor immigrants. In a typical year (1863) 501 out of 861 patients were foreign-born (immigrants at this time constituted slightly less than one-third of the city's total population). The continued growth in numbers (by 1875 the average daily population was 1,104) and the lack of adequate financing merely intensified existing problems. Neither the medical nor the supporting staff was noted for competency; the diet remained substandard; and the physical plant was notably deficient. The distinguished English psychiatrist John C. Bucknill—who was by no means an unfriendly critic—could find few good things to say about the institution when he visited it during his American tour in 1875. He thought the New York and Philadelphia asylums were among the poorest in the country.[46] Isaac Ray, who settled in Phila-

45. "The Insane Poor of Philadelphia," *Journal of Prison Discipline and Philanthropy,* I (April, 1845), 179–183, II (January, 1846), 61–66; *AJI,* II (October, 1845), 150; Kirkbride to Charles B. Trego, February 23, 1846, Samuel W. Butler to Kirkbride, March 5, 1859, Kirkbride Papers, IPH; N. D. Benedict to Dix, February 26, 1859, Dix Papers, HLHU.

46. Insane Department of the Philadelphia Almshouse, *AR,* XIII (1863), 10–11, XIV (1864), 48–49, XV (1865), 42–44; Pennsylvania Board of Commissioners of Public Charities, *AR,* III (1872), cclix, IV (1873), 364–365, 371, VI (1875), 378–380; S. W. Butler to Kirkbride, June 25, 1860, Kirkbride Papers, IPH; *AJI,* XXI (January, 1865), 419–420; John C. Bucknill, *Notes on Asylums for the Insane in America* (London, 1876), 40–53; Bucknill to Henry I. Bowditch, January 23, 1877, CLMHMS. For a general history see Charles Lawrence, comp., *History of the Philadelphia Almshouses and Hospitals from the Beginning of the Eighteenth to the Ending of the*

delphia after his retirement from Butler, expressed a similar view at the annual convention of the AMSAII in 1876 (to an audience that manifested little disagreement with his position). Philadelphia, he argued, needed a "strictly State Institution. The insane poor are the wards, not of the city, but of the Commonwealth. . . . As long as the Institution is under the charge of our municipal government, just as long will it be a field for jobbery and meanest parsimony."[47]

The municipal mental hospitals in New York, Brooklyn, and Philadelphia had grown out of undifferentiated welfare and penal institutions. Boston, on the other hand, established an entirely new and independent hospital to deal with its mentally ill. As elsewhere, the opening of the state hospital in Worcester in 1833 had not significantly alleviated the problems arising out of mental disease in Boston, which was 40 miles away. As Worcester officials began to face requests for admission that far exceeded their institution's capacity, they began to refuse admission to some and to discharge others deemed incurable and harmless. Boston in particular received a number of persons belonging in the latter category, taxing its welfare facilities still further. A committee of the city council, chaired by the mayor, urged in 1837 that Boston establish its own mental hospital. With relatively little opposition this suggestion became law, and at the end of 1839 the Boston Lunatic Hospital received its first patients.[48]

The history of the Boston institution, nevertheless, was essentially the same as that of its companion urban asylums. The hospital rapidly filled up with indigent and immigrant patients, and all pretenses at providing therapy were soon abandoned. By 1845 slightly more than half of the patients were foreign-

Nineteenth Centuries (n.p., 1905); Charles K. Mills, ed., *Philadelphia Hospital Reports*, Vol. I (1890) (Philadelphia, 1890); and John W. Croskey, comp., *History of Blockley: A History of the Philadelphia General Hospital from Its Inception, 1731–1928* (Philadelphia, 1929).

47. *AJI*, XXXIII (October, 1876), 262–266, 294–295, 300–307. Three years earlier Ray had published a devastating description of the Philadelphia Almshouse, "What Shall Philadelphia Do for its Paupers?," *Penn Monthly*, IV (April, 1873), 226–238.

48. Boston Lunatic Hospital, *AR*, I (1840), 9–11; *Memorial of the Board of Directors for Public Institutions in Relation to the Lunatic Hospital. 1863*, Boston *City Document No. 11* (1863), 21–23.

born, of which the largest number were from Ireland (foreign-born persons at that time constituted slightly less than one-third of the city's total population). In the decade following the opening of the asylum 450 out of 611 patients were foreign paupers. "Our inmates," observed the superintendent in 1850,

> are principally foreigners; and of this class a large majority are from Ireland. Many of these have been the subjects of treatment elsewhere—perhaps at the Asylum at Worcester, or in some of the neighboring Almshouses or Prisons. Nothing can be ascertained of the history of many of the cases. They are generally found to be uneducated, superstitious, and jealous; and, being unused to the manners and customs of our countrymen, they are very suspicious of us; and therefore it is quite difficult to win their confidence, and of course, to treat them satisfactorily.

More than twenty years later the secretary of the Massachusetts Board of State Charities condemned the institution as unfit for either therapy or custody. But despite a clear recognition by community leaders as early as the 1850's that drastic action was required, the hospital continued to serve as an undifferentiated welfare institution for lower-class and immigrant mentally ill persons.[49]

Government officials in Boston, like their counterparts elsewhere, consistently pointed out that the burden of welfare fell

49. Boston Lunatic Hospital, *AR*, III (1842), 21–22, IV (1843), 15–16, VI (1845), 13, VII (1846), 3–5, 10–12, IX (1848), 3–4, 13, X (1849), 10, XI (1850), 15; Massachusetts Board of State Charities, *AR*, X (1873), 12. For the heated controversy in Boston during the 1860's over the issue of a new hospital, see the following sources: Boston *City Document No. 11* (1863), *No. 97* (November 13, 1865), *No. 105* (1867), *No. 75* (1868), *No. 107* (1869); *Report of a Committee of the Board of Directors for Public Institutions in Relation to the Condition of the Lunatic Hospital, Made May 23, 1862* (Boston, 1862); Board of Directors for Public Institutions of the City of Boston, *AR*, VIII (1864), 84–87, 96–104; Samuel G. Howe, *Objections to the Proposed Plan for a City Hospital for Lunatics at Winthrop; with Answers to the Article by J. Putnam Bradlee, in the "Daily Advertiser," Nov. 6* (Boston, 1871); *Boston Medical and Surgical Journal*, n.s. IV (December 30, 1869), 398–399, n.s. VIII (October 19, 1871), 257–259. There is an interesting, though bland, comparison of the welfare system and institutions of Boston, New York, Philadelphia, and Baltimore by a visiting committee of the Public Institutions of St. Louis County, *AR*, 1875, 5–19.

to a disproportionate extent upon the cities. This was especially true of those urban areas serving as a port of entry, for they had the largest number of immigrant and indigent groups. With the establishment of the state almshouses in the 1850's and the acceptance by the Commonwealth of responsibility for state insane paupers (those persons having no legal residence), the pressure on the city was somewhat alleviated. The rapid expansion in the number of state hospitals, moreover, aided Boston, which was able to use state facilities at Taunton and elsewhere. While these developments partly mitigated the financial burden, they did create hardships for families having relatives in distant hospitals because they were unable to visit them on a regular basis. Moreover, the law that gave state hospitals the right to return surplus patients to the counties from which they were received worked to the detriment of larger urban areas.[50] Even in Massachusetts, where the state government accepted more responsibility for welfare than elsewhere, the problems of the cities (especially Boston) remained pressing. As long as large numbers of poorer groups (and particularly immigrants) lived in urban areas, such areas would find that the burden of welfare would fall on their shoulders to a disproportionate degree.

The difficulties of Boston, New York, and Philadelphia were by no means atypical. Other urban areas encountered similar problems, though on a smaller scale and at a somewhat later date. The smaller scale of the problems, nevertheless, did not result from anything that municipal authorities learned from the experiences of Northeastern cities. The differences were due mainly to the fact that the cities outside the Northeast were established at later dates and it was some time before population growth and immigration gave rise to comparable problems.

Cincinnati was a case in point. In 1795 it had but 500 inhabitants. Within twenty years its population had increased twelvefold. In terms of numbers, however, its significant phase of growth began after the end of the War of 1812. By 1820 the town had a population of 9,462; a decade later this figure had risen to nearly 25,000. With its growth, the city found that an

---

50. Boston Lunatic Hospital, *AR*, 1871 and 1875, in Boston Board of Directors for Public Institutions, *AR*, XV (1871), 29–30, XIX (1875), 47–48.

informal approach to disease and welfare was unsatisfactory. At the behest of Dr. Daniel Drake, therefore, the legislature in 1821 established the "Commercial Hospital and Lunatic Asylum for the State of Ohio." Located in Cincinnati, in Hamilton County, the new institution was intended to care for patients whose costs would be borne either by the state, the county, or the family, depending on economic status and place of residence. With a small subsidy from the state, the hospital was opened in 1824. More a welfare than a medical facility, it served also as a poor house and orphan asylum.[51]

When Ohio opened its first state hospital in 1838, the Commercial Hospital ceased to be a state-related institution. Yet it continued to serve Cincinnati and environs for incurable and dangerous cases, since the state facility at Columbus accepted relatively few individuals from Hamilton County. By 1853 conditions at the Cincinnati institution had so deteriorated that a meeting of physicians adopted a resolution condemning the lunatic department. The facility, they declared, was "totally unfit for the purposes for which it was intended, and that its continuance as an Asylum for the Insane is at variance with the dictates of a sound philanthropy, and disgraceful to the humanity of a civilized and christian community." The resolution urged, therefore, the establishment of a new institution. Crowded conditions at Commercial Hospital also led its directors to turn away all new mentally ill patients. An investigation by the county commissioners confirmed the rising chorus of criticism.[52]

To alleviate some problems, local authorities initially concluded an arrangement with a private retreat to accept patients. The high costs and inadequacy of the building quickly forced abandonment of this arrangement, and by late 1853 the county had founded a temporary asylum for its mentally ill. Conditions at the new asylum, however, were little better than those at the Commercial Hospital. Despite its problems, the Hamilton County Lunatic Asylum, as it was called, grew rapidly; the number of

51. Richard C. Wade, *The Urban Frontier: The Rise of Western Cities, 1790–1830* (Cambridge, 1959), 54, 195; Longview Asylum, *AR*, XXXIII (1892), 59–61.

52. Longview Asylum, *AR*, XXXIII (1892), 61–62; Hamilton County Lunatic Asylum, *AR*, I (1853/1854), 3–7; *AJI*, V (July, 1848), 83.

resident patients increased from 107 in mid-1854 to 273 in mid-1859. In arguing for a newer and more modern facility, the superintendent pointed out that many patients were immigrants who had left their country in a healthy and vigorous state. Misfortunes in a new environment (without friends and family as well) often led to mental collapse. To return such individuals to their country of origin was clearly impracticable. The only sensible solution, he argued, was to provide curative facilities, which would be cheaper in the long run and also fulfil society's humanitarian obligations. Although the county asylum had obvious defects, it continued to serve the city and county for seven years.[53]

Only with a change in state policy did conditions in Hamilton County begin to improve slightly. When Ohio opened two additional state hospitals in 1855, it divided the state into three districts, each to be served by one of the public institutions. One was located in Dayton. It was intended for the inhabitants of Hamilton County, since the county was within the area it serviced. Yet the small capacity of the Dayton hospital made realization of this objective an impossibility. In 1857, therefore, the legislature passed a somewhat novel act that made Hamilton County a separate district for insane asylum purposes. All taxes paid by the county for the support of the insane to the state were returned for the support of the county lunatic asylum. By 1860 a new hospital—the Longview Asylum—had been opened for the reception of patients in the county. Unique in its administrative and financial structure, the new institution was not exempt from the problems afflicting other urban areas. It soon was overcrowded and contained a large number of infirm and aged patients. By the late 1860's more than half of the inmates were immigrants, and by the mid-1870's the average patient population was nearly 600 even though the buildings were intended for about 450. In addition, the supposedly equitable financial arrangements with the state often worked poorly and led to constant friction. Though Ohio contributed to the support of Cincinnati's insane, the caliber of Longview—while superior to that

53. Hamilton County Lunatic Asylum, *AR*, I (1853/1854), 7–8, 20–25, II (1855), 3–7, 17–19, VII (1859), 10–13.

of comparable institutions in New York City and Philadelphia—remained below that of state institutions.[54]

Virtually every urban area in the nineteenth century faced seemingly insoluble problems insofar as the care of the insane was concerned. Some recognized their difficulties but—as in the case of Baltimore—took no action. Others established "temporary" asylums which remained in operation a long time. That of New Orleans, for example, was operated for nearly three decades despite the fact that it resembled, in the words of one observer, a "lock-up, calaboose or man-kennel." Still others—St. Louis, Newark, Chicago—founded municipal institutions in the face of a state policy that worked to their disadvantage.[55] Overall the record of cities in dealing with the mentally ill was not impressive. While state policy clearly did not favor urban interests, there is also little doubt that municipal authorities did not do as much as they could have done. Aside from the discriminatory aspects of state policy, the fact that the relationship between expenditures and tax rates was so clear and direct at the local level (as compared with the more indirect relationship at the state level) created resistance to welfare expenditures. Hostility between natives and immigrants reinforced the disinclination to appropriate funds for the alleviation of distress, since a disproportionate amount was spent for foreign-born persons.

VI

By the outbreak of the Civil War, the mental hospital had become a familar and accepted institution to Americans every-

54. Longview Asylum, AR, XII (1871), 7, XXXIII (1892), 61–68; AJI, XXXIII (October, 1876), 193; James C. Hallock to Dix, May 17, 1870, William L. Peck to Dix, March 18, 1872, Dix Papers, HLHU.

55. Report on Pauper Insanity; Presented to the City Council of Baltimore, on March 28th, 1845: by Dr. Stephen Collins (Baltimore, 1845), 7; Stanford Chaillé, A Memoir of the Insane Asylum of the State of Louisiana, at Jackson (New Orleans, 1858), 11–12; St. Louis County Insane Asylum, AR, III (1871/1872), 21–22, IV (1872/1873), 7–8, V (1873/1874), 3–5; "A Brief History of the Care of the Insane in Essex County, New Jersey" (typescript copy, Essex County Overbrook Hospital, Cedar Grove, N. J.), 1–3; Roswell Park, "The Medical Charities of Cook County, Illinois," Conference of Charities and Correction, Proceedings, VII (1880), li.

where. With a few exceptions, most states had at least one (and some had more than one) public institution. Larger urban areas had been impelled by circumstances to found their own hospitals. Alongside these hospitals existed a number of corporate and proprietary institutions that served affluent groups desiring high-cost quality care. Such institutions arose because many families were unwilling to use a public system that accepted large numbers of persons from poor and minority groups.

The manner in which public institutions had been founded, however, was to have a profound impact in future decades. The absence of systematic guidelines based on a careful analysis of empirical data meant that there had been no effort to engage in conscious social planning. Consequently, relatively little attention had been given to the financial and administrative structure governing hospitals; the relationship between therapeutic and custodial functions remained murky; the degree to which institutions should serve as a haven for aged persons as well as individuals apparently incapable of surviving the vicissitudes of life was undetermined; and the chronic tension between public responsibility and the professionalism of superintendent-psychiatrists was increasing rather than diminishing. While most officials recognized the close relationship between mental illness and welfare—if only because protracted institutionalization had a decided impact upon family structure—there was no conscious attempt to deal with the economic ramifications of the problem. Instead of facing some of these difficult and baffling issues, the supporters and promoters of hospitals simply argued that institutional care would satisfy both humanitarian and economic needs; hospitals would cure insane persons and thereby diminish public expenditures. When these expectations were not realized and when it became clear that the structure and functions of hospitals had strayed far from the ideal, a crisis of major proportions developed during the 1850's and 1860's that set the stage for a change in public policy governing the mentally ill.

Chapter IV

American Psychiatry:
Origins of a Profession

I

ONE OF THE BYPRODUCTS of the founding of mental hospitals was the beginning of the professionalization of psychiatry. This fact was of major importance; it meant that psychiatric thought and practice had not played a dominant part in shaping the structure and functions of these institutions. Instead the reverse was true. Psychiatry was, to a large extent, molded and shaped by the institutional setting within which it was born and grew to maturity. Many dominant characteristics of psychiatric ideology were but rationalizations of existing conditions within mental hospitals as well as popular attitudes. The mental hospital in its formative years was an institution created by society to cope with abnormal behavior and to provide care and treatment for a variety of dependent groups; the result was that psychiatry—despite its claims about its scientific and medical character—reflected the role assigned to it by society. This is not to imply that psychiatrists *consciously or deliberately* attempted to define their discipline within such a context, or to justify institutionalization on other than medical grounds. It is only to say that psychiatry, as was true of most professions and institutions, was influenced by its peculiar origins. Having developed within an institutional framework created by society in response to its perception of its needs, psychiatrists inevitably absorbed the validity of those needs into their view and understanding of their profession.

The newly emerging profession to a great extent reflected many of the dominant values of American society. Psychiatric theory and practice, for example, were not only derivatives of European experiences or the results of disinterested scientific knowledge. On the contrary, theory and practice evolved within a much broader social context. Although psychiatrists preferred to conceive of the mental hospital as a strictly medical institution, their analysis of the nature and etiology of mental illness and their modes of care and treatment were not far removed from the values of American society. Just as most states had founded mental hospitals as part of their general thrust toward the establishment of welfare institutions, so psychiatrists defined their profession in a manner that also encompassed problems of dependency and its alleviation as well as the treatment of disease.

The professionalization of psychiatry had profound implications for both the care and treatment of the mentally ill and the formulation of public policy. By the 1840's many of the complex problems associated with mental illness were increasingly being analyzed and defined by a small but influential group of superintendent-psychiatrists who were in the process of creating a confident and self-conscious profession that proclaimed its authority on the basis of its unique expertise. Oddly enough, the emergence of a profession did not imply an outright rejection of contemporary trends. Indeed, quite the opposite was true. Psychiatrists reaffirmed many of the dominant features of the developing institutional complex caring for the mentally ill largely because their own training and experiences had taken place within the existing structure. Professionalization, then, did little to impede and in some respects hastened the trend toward institutional care and the identification of mental illness within the more general framework of welfare and dependency.

II

At the beginning of the movement to found hospitals in the 1830's, a clearly defined group of psychiatrists possessing a body of specialized knowledge and expertise did not exist in America. Lay superintendents in some cases directed existing hospitals. Even where physicians were placed in charge of newly opened institutions, they were selected for qualities often having little to do with their experience and knowledge about mental illness. Yet by the 1840's the bare outlines of a profession were beginning to emerge. By that time superintendents had articulated a body of systematic theory about mental illness and mental hospitals; they had staked out a claim for their professional competency and authority in their particular domain; they had to some degree persuaded the community that their efforts should receive sanction; they had begun to develop a code of ethics that would govern themselves; and they had created the beginnings of a professional subculture. While internal disagreements existed, they were generally over the means by which certain goals would be reached; there was little disposition to challenge the fundamental assumptions governing the profession. Indeed, although licensing laws and certification were absent and training facilities nonexistent, the specialty had developed a series of informal procedures and controls that accomplished much the same ends.[1]

During the 1820's and 1830's those individuals drawn toward a career as a mental hospital superintendent tended to come from the ranks of socially concerned physicians. The activism and sense of responsibility especially characteristic of the first generation of superintendents often flowed from deep religious convictions that emphasized a sense of moral obligation to mankind in general. Not surprisingly, a disproportionately large number came from New England, a center of activism and

1. See Ernest Greenwood, "Attributes of a Profession," *Social Work,* II (July, 1957), 44–55, and Theodore Caplow, *The Sociology of Work* (Minneapolis, 1954), 139–140. The number of individuals who served as superintendents before 1875 was small (slightly more than eighty); the number of assistant physicians was twice as large. If size is included among the attributes of a profession, it is possible to argue that psychiatry was not professionalized until the twentieth century. If, on the other hand, a profession is defined in terms of functional specialization, role, and power, it is justifiable to study the evolution of psychiatry within such a framework even though the mature stage in the process of professionalization was obviously not reached until after 1900.

organized reform. Of the thirteen original founders of the Association of Medical Superintendents of American Institutions for the Insane (now the American Psychiatric Association), five had been born in Massachusetts and two each in Connecticut, New Hampshire, Pennsylvania, and Virginia. If their personalities were characterized by any general traits, these were their deep commitment to the cause of the mentally ill, their leadership abilities, and their charismatic aura. The fact that a hospital superintendency was not prestigious or lucrative (relative to other branches of medicine as well as other occupations) proved to be no barrier in recruiting able men.[2] If anything, low status, mediocre remuneration, and personal sacrifices simply reinforced the sense of mission common to this early group. Annual salaries of superintendents ranged from slightly less than $1,000 to $2,000 in the 1830's and 1840's, with assistant physicians being compensated at a lower level (although both groups received living quarters and allowances). When accepting the superintendency of the Worcester hospital, Samuel B. Woodward received an annual salary of $1,200, a sharp drop from his earning potential of $5,000 in private practice.[3] "It is abominable," noted the *Boston Medical and Surgical Journal* more than a decade later, "for legislatures to demand high moral, social, literary and scientific qualifications for the medical superintendents of such institutions, and yet pay them less than a grocer's clerk gets by the year for weighing out soap and candles."[4]

As the number of hospitals grew in the 1830's, common interests and problems tended to bring superintendents together. On many occasions a superintendent was employed as a consultant to out-of-state committees charged with the responsibility of

2. An English observer, on the other hand, argued that low status and poor remuneration discouraged competent people from entering the field. See "Dr. Burrows and Others on Insanity," *Monthly Review* (London), reprinted in *Museum of Foreign Literature and Science* (Philadelphia), XIV (April, 1829), 359.

3. Horace Porter to Samuel B. Woodward, October 5, 1832, Woodward Papers, AAS; *Boston Medical and Surgical Journal*, XII (March 11, 1835), 80.

4. *Boston Medical and Surgical Journal*, XXXIV (February 11, 1846), 45.

erecting a new hospital. It was common also for superintendents to recommend their assistants as candidates to head new institutions, thereby giving the infant profession a means of perpetuating its distinctive characteristics. Reinforcing the sense of group identity was the homogeneous social background of most superintendents. Before 1860 virtually all of them were from middle-class, Protestant backgrounds, college-educated, and medical school graduates. Minority ethnic and racial groups simply were not represented, nor were women ever employed as superintendents.

The personal and familial problems as well as the dangers of living on the grounds of a mental hospital likewise served to strengthen the ties of fellowship that bound these men together. When Thomas S. Kirkbride narrowly escaped death at the hands of a patient who had somehow secured a weapon, he received a sympathetic letter from a fellow superintendent who had faced similar dangers on several occasions. All superintendents, moreover, confronted inescapable responsibilities, and few were able to avoid considering the temptation of private practice with its higher income and greater leisure time. Their occupation also entailed sacrifices for their families as well as themselves. When the superintendent of the Western Pennsylvania Hospital for the Insane submitted his resignation (which he later withdrew upon urging by the board of trustees), he listed as his reasons the "want of social intercourse for his family; no Church advantages; distance from schools; his children growing up in seclusion"; and the fact that the older he grew the more difficult it became to return to private practice. Some individuals found their health impaired by the demands of the position; a few took leaves of absence and spent time as a patient elsewhere under the friendly care of a fellow superintendent. The criticisms of former patients who published "exposés" represented a recurring threat. The fact that most superintendents conceived of themselves as being under constant siege by politicians who saw hospitals in terms of patronage further contributed to the development of a professional self-identity.[5]

5. James Bates to Kirkbride, October 22, 1849, William M. Awl to

As superintendents developed a sense of self-identity, they naturally began to think of forming an organization. Such an organization would facilitate regular contacts and permit them to share experiences and discuss common problems. It might also serve as a vehicle for the formulation and enforcement of standards to govern their profession. In 1844, therefore, a group of thirteen of the most distinguished superintendents in the nation met in Philadelphia and organized the AMSAII. Meeting annually thereafter, the association began to lay down guidelines to govern the care and treatment of the mentally ill. These guidelines included the setting of architectural standards for the physical plant, size of institutions, modes of governance, and the personal and professional qualifications required of practitioners. They also promoted uniform reporting procedures in order to build up a body of data that would serve as the foundation for research that might result in the discovery of laws pertaining to mental disease. Above all, the new organization promoted close personal relationships and enabled its members to speak with a united voice to the society at large. "If our yearly conventions," noted Isaac Ray in 1854, "had accomplished nothing more than to make us acquainted with one another, and with other institutions besides our own, creating feelings of personal regard and mutual sympathy, I should think they had not been in vain."[6]

The AMSAII, fortunately, was provided also with a means of disseminating its views. Just prior to the first meeting of the association, Dr. Amariah Brigham, the renowned superintendent of the Utica State Lunatic Asylum in New York State, had established the *American Journal of Insanity*. Although published independently by the hospital, the new journal reported in

---

Kirkbride, May 27, 1847, October 25, December 24, 1849, Woodward to Kirkbride, December 31, 1845, D. T. Brown to Kirkbride, September 4, 1854, N. D. Benedict to Kirkbride, April 7, 1855, John R. Lee to Kirkbride, December 11, 1865, Kirkbride Papers, IPH; Isaac Ray to Dorothea L. Dix, May 24, 1852, John Harper to Dix, January 8, 13, 18, 22, 1868, Mark Ranney to Dix, August 29, 1874, H. M. Harlow to Dix, July 30, 1879, Dix Papers, HLHU. For the literature of exposé, see the bibliography at the close of this volume.

6. Ray to Kirkbride, May 18, 1854, Kirkbride Papers, IPH.

great detail the proceedings of the association; most of its articles came from the membership of the AMSAII.[7]

Along with the growth of the new organization went an increasing emphasis on the belief that the problems associated with mental disease should be solved by professionals possessing both competency and expertise. Mental illness, argued superintendents, was fundamentally no different from physical illness; it therefore required trained and experienced personnel. Many difficulties pertaining to commitment procedures and internal management of hospitals, they maintained, arose out of the fact that policies were all too often determined by individuals and organizations lacking the requisite knowledge and competency. Although superintendents did not move toward a licensing system and formal educational requirements—perhaps because most legislatures were distinctly hostile toward licensing in the decades before the Civil War—both their words and deeds clearly pointed in this direction.

One of the early indications of the growing awareness of professionalization was the cleavage that developed between prison reformers and hospital superintendents following the organization of the AMSAII in 1844. Since the 1820's prison reformers had been actively involved in psychiatric reform, if only because it was common for insane persons deemed dangerous to the community to be confined in jails. Thus Louis Dwight and the Boston Prison Discipline Society had been fighting for the establishment of mental hospitals since 1825. The loose coalition between prison and psychiatric reformers persisted throughout the 1830's without outward evidences of friction. Dorothea L. Dix and Samuel Gridley Howe, for example, thought it perfectly proper to be active in prison as well as psychiatric reform during and after the 1840's.[8]

7. For the founding of the AMSAII and the *American Journal of Insanity* see the following: Kirkbride to Francis T. Stribling, June 15, July 5, August 28, 1844, Kirkbride to Samuel B. Woodward, August 22, November 18, 1844, Woodward to Kirkbride, November 21, 1844, Kirkbride to Amariah Brigham, July 12, 1844, Brigham to Kirkbride, March 3, 1845, Kirkbride Papers, IPH; John S. Butler to Pliny Earle, April 16, 1844, Earle Papers, AAS; Woodward to George Chandler, July 28, 1844, Chandler Papers, AAS; *AJI*, I (January, 1845), 253–258.

8. See Samuel Gridley Howe, *An Essay on Separate and Congregate Systems of Prison Discipline; Being a Report Made to the Boston Prison*

By the time that the AMSAII was founded, on the other hand, superintendents were expressing distinct unhappiness at the involvement of prison reformers with mental hospitals. "I have ever felt that it is wrong," wrote Woodward to his friend Horace Mann after learning that the latter had been named to the committee to which had been referred Dwight's annual report, "for these reports to embrace an account of the Insane Hospitals, associating crime with misfortune. The insane poor in the prisons and houses of correction are proper subjects for the Report but the Institutions for the Insane have no more connection with Prison Discipline than colleges and other seminaries of learning. The respectable insane are very much disturbed by this notice of the institutions of which they are inmates."[9] Woodward and other superintendents, however, did not hesitate to express their own views on prison routine and discipline.[10]

The conflict between the two groups erupted into the open when the *Journal of Prison Discipline and Philanthropy* (the organ of a Philadelphia-based group opposing the Boston organization) began publication. In its first issue the new periodical had included a long article devoted to hospitals for the insane poor. The piece aroused the wrath of Amariah Brigham. "I cannot say," he wrote to Pliny Earle, "I like the *comingling* of the *insane* and the *criminal* and to be *catalogued* with Sing Sing and Auburn. . . . It tends to keep up a notion we strive to do away—that Asylums and Prisons are alike."[11] Within three months Brigham had published in his new *American Journal of Insanity* an article that was sharply critical of the practice of the *Journal of Prison Discipline and Philanthropy* and the annual reports of the Prison Discipline Society in discussing mental hos-

---

Discipline Society (Boston, 1846), and Dorothea L. Dix, *Remarks on Prisons and Prison Discipline in the United States* (Boston, 1845).

9. Woodward to Mann, June 5, 1845, Woodward Papers, AAS.

10. Woodward to Rev. Louis Dwight, February 26, March 5, 1846, Woodward to A. D. Foster, September 30, 1846, Woodward Papers, AAS; Kirkbride to Amariah Brigham, January 10, 1846, January 29, 1847, Kirkbride to John Evans, July 10, 1845, Kirkbride Papers, IPH.

11. Amariah Brigham to Pliny Earle, February 27, 1845, Earle Papers, AAS. See also Brigham to Kirkbride, March 3, 1845, and Kirkbride to Brigham, January 10, 1846, Kirkbride Papers, IPH.

pitals along with prisons. Brigham's contribution, in turn, drew a response from an unidentified but supposedly well-known jurist. This correspondent argued that insanity and crime were indeed "kindred subjects"; "the moral as well as the intellectual faculties can be deranged by accident or disease," he wrote, "and while the latter fills up the Asylums, the former crowds our Prisons." In commenting upon this communication, the *American Journal of Insanity* insisted that lumping prisons and hospitals reinforced fear of the latter. The rejoinder went on to discuss at length the origins of crime and treatment of criminals. Its words drew a long reply from the *Journal of Prison Discipline and Philanthropy*, which insisted that criminal and insane behavior were subsumed under the same general scientific laws. The needs of both groups, therefore, required the maintenance of the broad coalition of reformers and militated against any form of exclusiveness.[12]

In the long run the superintendents tended to have their way. The Prison Discipline Society sharply cut the space it devoted to hospitals. Yet the residual influence arsing out of the common origins of both movements was never completely overcome. Later in the century prisons and hospitals tended to come under the jurisdiction of unitary public regulatory agencies. While the affair that developed in the 1840's was seemingly a minor one, it revealed the concern of superintendents with their self-image and that of their institutions. The identification of crime and disease—at least in the context raised by penal reformers—was unacceptable, for it undermined the image of hospitals and lowered the status of psychiatrists. Nor was it coincidental that some leading superintendents—notably Kirkbride and Earle—sought to have the use of the term "asylum" discontinued in favor of "hospital."[13] At a time when psychiatric leaders were

12. *AJI*, I (April, 1845), 381–382; " 'Journal of Prison Discipline,' and Lunatic Asylums," *ibid.*, II (October, 1845), 175–183; " 'Journal of Prison Discipline' and Lunatic Asylums," *Journal of Prison Discipline and Philanthropy*, II (January, 1846), 49–57.

13. For typical examples see N. D. Benedict to Kirkbride, January 31, 1855, Kirkbride Papers, IPH; Pliny Earle, "Reports of American Hospitals for the Insane," *American Journal of the Medical Sciences*, n.s. XLVI (July, 1863), 173–175; Northampton State Lunatic Hospital, *AR*, XIX (1874), 39–42.

bent upon altering public and legislative attitudes toward hospitals and mental illness, it was natural for them to strive to enhance their authority and status. In this respect it should be noted that the effort to create a professional image was not directly related to financial considerations. Although underpaid as compared with other professions, superintendents were not inclined to press for higher salaries. Woodward actually discouraged the attempt by the trustees of his hospital to raise his salary, and Kirkbride once made an issue of it only after his managers had reduced his salary without consulting him, apparently breaking a previous arrangement.[14] Since superintendents defined their occupation within the context of benevolent, humanitarian, and scientific goals, they tended to minimize financial self-improvement for much of the nineteenth century. The fact that psychiatry was one of the few specialties that did *not* develop within the context of private practice also helped to dampen the association of professionalism and high levels of compensation.

The greatest obstacle to professional autonomy, however, came from legislatures and public officials charged with the responsibility of defining and administering public policy. State governments saw welfare and medical institutions as the embodiment of goals established by their constituents. It followed that such institutions could not be independent of the community, but instead were dependent upon it. Superintendents, on the other hand, saw policy in terms of their own professional expertise and knowledge; they often regarded legislative and executive leaders as politicians meddling with a subject about which they were ignorant.[15] The result was a chronic tension

14. Minutes of the trustees' meetings of January 9, February 11, 19, 1839, in "Trustees Records, 1832 to 1849," ms. volume, Worcester State Hospital, Worcester, Mass., and Woodward to Mann, January 15, 1839, Woodward Papers, AAS; Kirkbride to unidentified correspondent, February 22, 1845, Kirkbride to the Board of Managers of the Pennsylvania Hospital, May 20, 1845, Kirkbride Papers, IPH.

15. Ohio superintendents continuously charged that politics influenced the choice of a superintendent (or his dismissal). See S. Hanbury to Kirkbride, March 8, 1852, Kirkbride Papers, IPH; *AJI*, IX (October, 1852), 207; William L. Peck to Dix, October 30, 1873, April 23, 1874, Dix Papers, HLHU; Northern Ohio Hospital for the Insane, *AR*, XXI (1875), 17–18.

between the competing claims of the profession on the one hand and the elected representatives of the society on the other. This tension was frequently reflected in the relationships between superintendents and public officials. After returning from the annual meeting of the AMSAII in the spring of 1852, Isaac Ray noted that a "large share of the brethren are in great tribulation, and their troubles are not very creditable to the cause." Nearly half a dozen superintendents seemed on the verge of being forced from office. Ray, nevertheless, was unable to define precisely the ideal relationship between mental hospitals and the society that sanctioned and supported them. He suggested that hospitals be located as far as possible from state capitals in order to spare them from "the political vortex which is eternally boiling and seething there." Aside from this modest proposal, he offered no more definitive advice.[16]

Political considerations undoubtedly played some role in the difficulties confronting superintendents, for there is little question that certain men were removed from office when a new political party came into power. Yet the charge of political interference sometimes concealed important policy differences. Dr. John Curwen of the Pennsylvania State Lunatic Hospital at Harrisburg, for example, insisted in 1857 that he had "so strong a repugnance" to even the appearance of political involvement that he "would rather submit to very great inconvience than be suspected of a leaning in that direction." When discharged by the trustees some two decades later, he complained bitterly of attempts by the board to curtail his authority within the hospital. But one element in the controversy was his seeming refusal to accept a female physician whom the trustees had employed.[17]

In another episode Peter Bryce, superintendent of the Alabama Insane Hospital, indicated to Dix that he was in imminent danger of being removed from office by the Radical Reconstruction regime in the state. Bryce's own comments, on the other hand, revealed that more than politics alone was involved. "As the legislature is composed largely of negroes, and illiterate

16. Ray to Dix, May 24, 1852, Dix Papers, HLHU; Ray, "The Popular Feeling Towards Hospitals for the Insane," *AJI*, IX (July, 1852), 50–51.

17. John L. Atlee and Traill Green to John Curwen, November 24, 1880, Curwen to Dix, May 4, 1857, December 6, 31, 1880, S. S. Schultz to Dix, January 21, 1881, Dix Papers, HLHU.

white men of no intelligence or social standing," he wrote, "it is not likely that they will be influenced by high motives in bestowing office." Despite his fears, he was able to maintain his position. A similar situation prevailed in South Carolina, where the superintendent of the state lunatic asylum was forced from office after it became evident that the gulf between himself and some black regents was unbridgeable. Apparently neither the Alabama nor the South Carolina superintendent was disposed to deal with blacks, thereby ensuring conflict with public authorities.[18] Racial rather than political strife, then, was the issue.

The chronic tension between public authority and professional autonomy was reflected in a number of other substantive issues. Less than a decade after its founding, the AMSAII in 1851 and 1853 adopted a series of proposals delineating architectural standards and modes of governance. These proposals were representative of the young profession's quest for autonomy and authority, and included, for example, an insistence that no hospital should be built unless the plans were reviewed by experienced alienists. Architecture, members of the AMSAII insisted, had to reflect institutional function, and function could only be defined by competent authority. Kirkbride, who had already made a careful study of hospital architecture, published a classic volume on that subject just three years after the AMSAII had adopted its proposals. In his book he laid down general principles and specific details relating to mental hospitals. For most of the remainder of the century, the majority of institutions were constructed according to the "Kirkbride Plan."[19] Yet too many hospitals—at least in the eyes of alienists —were the work of inexperienced building committees whose members were completely ignorant of the needs and requirements of the mentally ill. Indeed, those superintendents having

18. Peter Bryce to Dix, April 23, May 8, August 28, 1868, J. W. Parker to Dix, May 5, 1868, January 22, 1869, Dix Papers, HLHU; Francis Tiffany, *Life of Dorothea Lynde Dix* (Boston, 1890), 350–352.

19. *AJI*, VIII (July, 1851), 79–81, X (July, 1853), 67–69; Kirkbride, "Remarks on the Construction and Arrangements of Hospitals for the Insane," *American Journal of the Medical Sciences*, n.s. XIII (January, 1847), 40–56, and *On the Construction, Organization, and General Arrangements of Hospitals for the Insane* (Philadelphia, 1854; second edition, Philadelphia, 1880).

12. *Thomas S. Kirkbride (1809–1883). Superintendent of the Pennsylvania Hospital for the Insane for four decades, his book* On the Construction, Organization, and General Arrangements of Hospitals for the Insane *(1854; 2nd ed., 1880) was the bible of the psychiatric profession for much of the nineteenth century. Source: John Curwen,* The Original Members of the Association of Medical Superintendents of American Institutions for the Insane *(Warren, Pa., 1885).*

some leeway tended to be the exception rather than the rule. "You are a most fortunate man," wrote Kirkbride in congratulating a fellow superintendent concerning a new verandah, "in having the power to arrange the detail of your hospital—few physicians in this country ever have such a privilege."[20]

Isaac Ray was particularly incensed at this state of affairs. Both his private correspondence and his public writings reflected his hostility toward contemporary construction procedures. The first step, he noted in a long article in the influential *North American Review* in 1854, was the appointment of a building committee. "Their most common qualification for the office," he wrote in bitter words, "is a little political notoriety; their least common, a practical acquaintance with these institutions, and a familiarity with the details of construction. In fact, most of them, had they been appointed to build a clipper-ship or to codify the laws of the State would have been as well fitted for the service by their previous habits or pursuits." Because of the inexperience and ignorance of such committees, a new superintendent often had to undertake drastic and extensive alterations in the physical plant, usually with unsatisfactory results. "All of this," Ray concluded, "arises from a fundamental mistake of the building-committee, in supposing that the proper discharge of their duty requires that they should make themselves acquainted with points of a strictly professional nature."[21]

The fact that superintendents usually presented a united front in the face of external challenges to their autonomy did not mean that internal friction and conflict were absent. On the contrary, they fought—sometimes bitterly—over issues and personalities. In general, such conflicts were confined within the profession; there was little disposition to appeal for outside support in these intragroup struggles. Even when there was general agreement that a superintendent was doing a poor job, there was little inclination to raise the issue in public. Upon acquiring information that the superintendent of the Vermont institution was "doing harm—and should be exposed," Amariah

20. Kirkbride to William M. Awl, June 27, 1843, Kirkbride Papers, IPH.

21. Isaac Ray, "American Hospitals for the Insane," *North American Review*, LXXIX (July, 1854), 88–90. See also Ray to Kirkbride, January 16, 1847, Kirkbride Papers, IPH; Ray to Dix, December 8, 1851, November 3, 1852, March 7, April 15, 1854, Dix Papers, HLHU.

13. *Isaac Ray (1807–1881). Probably the most influential nineteenth-century American psychiatrist, Ray served as superintendent of the Maine Insane Hospital and the Butler Hospital for the Insane in Providence. Possessing an acute and critical mind, his book* A Treatise on the Medical Jurisprudence of Insanity *(1st ed., 1838) became a classic in forensic psychiatry. Source: John Curwen,* The Original Thirteen Members of the Association of Medical Superintendents of the American Institutions for the Insane *(Warren, Pa., 1885).*

Brigham expressed the hope that the public would become aware of the situation. Yet he apparently never considered the possibility of so informing Vermont officials. Nor was criticism —either direct or implied—accepted in the spirit of scientific inquiry. After reading an article by Ray, Brigham wrote to Kirkbride that both Ray and Luther V. Bell were too "dictatorial" and prone to idealize their own institutions while denigrating all others by impugning the accuracy of their annual reports.[22]

The most acrimonious conflict, without doubt, revolved around the policies of the *American Journal of Insanity*. Although ostensibly the organ of the young specialty, the journal was actually and technically published by the managers of the Utica hospital. Frequently its policies represented the views of Utica's superintendent rather than the profession at large. The result was chronic bickering over the criteria employed for the acceptance or rejection of papers, and a number of prominent psychiatrists refused to publish in the journal. The situation was exacerbated still further when Dr. John P. Gray succeeded to the editorship, a position he attained in 1854 and held for more than three decades. Intolerant of dissent, he freely criticized all those who disagreed with him, and for much of his career attempted to dominate and control the AMSAII. In reaction, John Curwen unsuccessfully attempted to found a new journal only a few years after Gray assumed his new position.[23]

The most complex problem facing psychiatrists, generally speaking, was their relationship to the medical profession generally. By the time that the AMSAII was founded in 1844, virtually all superintendents were physicians who accepted without question the tenet that insanity was a disease within the conventional usage of that term. Yet when the American Medical

22. Amariah Brigham to Pliny Earle, October 25, 1845, Earle Papers, AAS; Brigham to Kirkbride, June 12, 1849, Kirkbride Papers, IPH.

23. D. T. Brown to Kirkbride, May 3, 1853, July 28, 1858, Pliny Earle to Kirkbride, August 4, 1858, John Curwen to Kirkbride, July 31, 1860, Kirkbride Papers, IPH; D. T. Brown to Kirkbride, November 4, 1861, in Clifford B. Farr, "The Civil War and its Aftermath: Based on Contemporary Letters," typescript in Kirkbride Papers, IPH; H. B. Wilbur to Pliny Earle, August 16, 1876, May 14, 1878, January 29, 1879, Earle Papers, AAS.

14. *John P. Gray (1825–1886). Head of the Utica State Lunatic
Asylum from 1854 to 1886 and editor of the* American Journal of
Insanity *during these same years, he aroused antagonism because of
his domineering personality and strong views. Source:* American
Journal of Psychiatry, C *(April 1944).*

Association was founded only three years later, there was considerable reluctance on the part of the AMSAII to affiliate with the new organization. Indeed, a motion to that effect was thoroughly defeated in 1853. The following year the AMA decided to establish its own standing committee to report on the subject of insanity; but it gave no report for over a decade. By the 1860's the AMA was urging a unification with the AMSAII, but it was all to no avail. The latter felt that its special interests would be subordinated to the broader concerns of the medical profession as a whole. All efforts at amalgamation, consequently, proved futile.[24]

While fear of having their power dissipated by affiliation with a far larger organization undoubtedly played a role in the reluctance of superintendents to surrender their independence, more substantive issues were also involved. By the time the AMA was founded, the status of the American medical profession had declined precipitously. A number of states had repealed all legal restrictions on the practice of medicine, and others had never enacted any legislation on the subject; the result was the proliferation of a variety of medical sects. The inability of physicians generally to deal with disease contributed to the decline of the profession, and the attack on monopolies and emphasis on equality characteristic of this age contributed to the widespread belief that learned and exclusive professions were unnecessary for the maintenance of social stability and cohesion. Under these circumstances hospital superintendents could see little virtue in identifying themselves with the medical profession.[25]

The character that American institutional psychiatry had assumed by the 1860's also contributed to the reluctance of superintendants to identify themselves with the larger profession. By this time psychiatry was largely (as we shall see

24. *AJl*, X (July, 1853), 85, XXVIII (October, 1871), 205–208, 212; American Medical Assciation, *Transactions*, XVII (1866), 121ff., XVIII (1867), 399ff., XIX (1868), 161ff., XXII (1871), 101–109.

25. For discussions of the medical profession in mid-nineteenth-century America see Charles E. Rosenberg, *The Cholera Years: The United States in 1832, 1849, and 1866* (Chicago, 1962), Chap. IX, and Joseph F. Kett, *The Formation of the American Medical Profession: The Role of Institutions, 1780–1860* (New Haven, 1968).

later) an administrative specialty; admission to the profession was less a function of specialized training than a matter of actual experience within mental hospitals. Indeed, the AMSAII did not even admit assistant physicians to membership. A psychiatric self-identity, to put it another way, was not a function of a common education; it arose rather out of the institutional affiliation of its members. Consequently, superintendents could exert some measure of control over their specialty by limiting admission only to those individuals who met the scientific and personal qualifications deemed important in the care and treatment of the mentally ill. The lack of concern with mental disease manifested by the numerous medical schools that flourished at this time confirmed the suspicions of superintendents that they had much to lose and little to gain by affiliation.[26] Moreover, psychiatry was an institutional specialty largely dependent upon public support; identification with a profession held in low esteem could only hinder the drive toward the establishment of additional hospitals caring for the insane. Its institutional base, therefore, imparted to psychiatry a character that differentiated it somewhat from other medical specialties. Most superintendents were also partly isolated from European psychiatry, and they seemed—at least to critics—to be overly sensitive to and dependent upon the values of the society that sanctioned and supported their existence. As late as 1875 American psychiatrists had not yet faced up to the baffling problems that had arisen out of their unique origins.

26. While there was some interest in psychiatric education as early as the 1840's, relatively little was done. For some evidence on this point see the following: Maine Insane Hospital, *AR*, VII (1846), 39; *AJI*, IV (October, 1847), 181; Pennsylvania Hospital for the Insane, *AR*, XXXI (1871), 44–49; R. P. Huger, "Psychological Medicine, Considered as a Specialty," *AJI*, XXI (October, 1874), 264–268.

A comment by Isaac Ray in 1870 is revealing. "You say the world moves," he wrote to an eminent jurist. "We have had some internation of that sort of motion here. One of the medical colleges in this high seat of medical learning [Philadelphia], having recognized the existence of such a disease as insanity, has requested me to give a course of lectures thereon, which I am now doing." Ray to Charles Doe, September 20, 1870, ms. in the Library of Butler Hospital, Providence, Rhode Island. The strongest case for the inclusion of psychiatry in general medical curriculums was made by Pliny Earle in his article "Psychologic Medicine: Its Importance as a Part of the Medical Curriculum," *AJI*, XXIV (January, 1868), 257–280.

III

The rise of a self-conscious psychiatric profession was accompanied by an extensive body of literature that attempted to provide clear definitions of the nature of mental disease, including its etiology and treatment, a rationalization for institutionalization, and a model of the ideal mental hospital. The articulation of such a coherent body of thought proved a significant element in the formulation of public policy. By the 1850's and 1860's public officials had absorbed on a selective basis some of the theoretical beliefs expressed by American psychiatrists. Few of the latter, of course, thought of their profession or their hospitals as part of a larger welfare complex. But many of their views—especially those that posited some relationship between mental illness, character defects, poverty, and crime—were attractive to public servants who were in the process of developing a rationalized and centralized welfare system and who were seeking scientific sanction for their policies. The psychiatric understanding of the etiology of mental illness, precisely because of its moral content, was useful, since it seemed to confirm the validity of many new policy proposals concerning welfare. The inadvertent result of the thrust of mid-nineteenth-century American psychiatric thought, therefore, was to strengthen rather than to weaken the development of the mental hospital within the framework of public welfare.

Not surprisingly, psychiatrists thought of their specialty in scientific and medical terms. Yet psychiatric theory had not developed in complete isolation. On the contrary, theory was especially vulnerable to certain influences external to psychiatry proper. The mental hospital, after all, had preceded the emergence of psychiatry as both a scientific discipline and a profession. Consequently, psychiatric thought partially reflected the institutional framework within which it developed as well as some of the values of society at large.

Superficially, the concepts of mental disease held by American psychiatrists seemed to be neutral and not at all a rationalization of hospital conditions or social ideology. Their theoretical views were derived from fairly conventional sources. These sources included, among others, classical medical thought, sensationalist and associationist psychology, phrenology, and Scottish Common Sense philosophy, as well as the ideas and values characteristic of Americans generally at this time. Most mid-nineteenth-century psychiatrists began with Lockean assumptions; they believed that knowledge came to the mind through sensory organs. If the senses (or the brain) became impaired, false impressions would be conveyed to the mind, leading in turn to faulty thinking and abnormal behavior. Phrenology—which gained a rapid foothold in America after being imported from Europe in the 1820's and 1830's—provided a means of connecting mind and matter. The mind, according to phrenological theorists, was not unitary, but was composed of independent and identifiable faculties, which were localized in different regions of the brain. To this theory phrenologists added the belief that individuals could deliberately and consciously cultivate different faculties by following the natural laws that governed physical development and human behavior. The popularity of phrenology seemed to confirm the psychiatric belief that all normal and abnormal functions of the mind were dependent on the physical condition of the brain.[27]

27. The best discussions by American psychiatrists of this period on the nature of mental illness are to be found in the annual reports of mental hospitals and in the *American Journal of Insanity*, although some alienists wrote for the general public as well. For some examples of concepts of mental illness see the following: Amariah Brigham, "Insanity and Insane Hospitals," *North American Review*, XLIV (January, 1837), 91–121; Worcester State Lunatic Hospital, *AR*, VII (1839), 65–66, X (1842), 64–65 (Samuel B. Woodward); John M. Galt, *The Treatment of Insanity* (New York, 1846); Edward Jarvis, "Causes of Insanity," *Boston Medical and Surgical Journal*, XLV (November 12, 1851), 289–305; New Jersey State Lunatic Asylum, *AR*, VI (1852), 22–28 (H. A. Buttolph); Butler Hospital for the Insane, *AR*, 1853, 11–29 (Isaac Ray); Isaac Ray, *A Treatise on the Medical Jurisprudence of Insanity* (Boston, 1838); Maine Insane Hospital, *AR*, XIV (1854), 25 (Henry M. Harlow); Northern Ohio Lunatic Asylum, *AR*, I (1855), 12 (L. Firestone); McLean Asylum for the Insane, *AR*, XLII (1859), in Massachusetts General Hospital, *AR*, 1859, 26–31 (John E. Tyler); Alabama Insane Hospital, *AR*, II (1862), 20–22 (Peter Bryce); Utica State Lunatic Asylum, *AR*, XXI (1863), 34–40, XXVII (1869), 16–23, XXIX (1871), 62–63, XXXII (1874), 23–24 (John P. Gray); H. A. Buttolph, "The Relation Between Phrenology and Insanity," *American Phrenological Journal*, XIV (November, 1851), 103–104; *AJI*, VI (July, 1849), 56–57 (October, 1849), 127–136.

Such reasoning provided psychiatrists with a model of mental illness that was especially compatible with a psychological and environmental etiology. Mental illness in their eyes was a somatic disease that involved lesions of the brain (the organ of the mind). Disease followed the violation of the natural laws that governed human behavior. In other words, mental illness (like organic illnesses), though somatic in nature, could have psychological, hereditary, or physical origins. Thus the abnormal behavior of the individual (who possessed free will) could be the primary cause of insanity, leading as it did to the impairment of the brain. Mental illness, therefore, was to some extent self-inflicted; by ignoring the laws governing human behavior the individual placed himself on the road to disease (a belief that went back to Hippocrates, if not farther).

The psychiatric model of mental illness was in most respects similar to the model of disease adhered to by other physicians and laymen. Before the 1870's American medicine lagged far behind European medicine in terms of theory, research, and institutions. There were, of course, innumerable debates in America over the nature and causes of disease, but the absence of demonstrable and specific etiological concepts together with the low status of the medical profession resulted in an emphasis on those broad mental and moral factors that caused disease. Such etiological concepts, however, offered little in the way of treatment of disease; Americans often faced a choice between the sectarian remedies of nonorthodox practitioners on the one hand and therapeutic nihilism on the other. Under these circumstances there was a distinct tendency to emphasize the maintenance of health and the prevention rather than the cure of disease. Disease —irrespective of its specific manifestations—was seen as a direct result of the violation of the natural laws governing behavior; it was identified with immorality, vice, and filth. Mid-nineteenth-

---

Norman Dain, *Concepts of Insanity in the United States, 1789–1865* (New Brunswick, 1964), is the most authoritative discussion of American psychiatric thought, while David J. Rothman, *The Discovery of the Asylum: Social Order and Disorder in the New Republic* (Boston, 1971), emphasizes the role of psychiatrists in terms of social control. John D. Davies, *Phrenology: Fad and Science: A 19th-Century American Crusade* (New Haven, 1955), is a superior study dealing with the relationship of phrenology to American society in the antebellum decades.

century medical theory in America, then, represented a curious fusion of morality, social attitudes and values, and "science."[28]

Most superintendents were by no means unaware of the problems that followed from their view of disease. The absence of empirical data to verify conclusively the somatic basis of mental illness was troubling. The concept of a lesion, moreover, was amorphous; its acceptance rested largely on faith rather than observation. Classification of mental diseases was also difficult, since it was impossible to correlate physiological changes with specific behavioral patterns. Indeed, it was not uncommon for psychiatrists to minimize the utility of existing nosologies, especially since the thrust of early nineteenth-century French clinical medicine went in this direction. No system of classification, observed Brigham in 1843, appeared to be of "much practical utility." All categories based on symptoms "must be defective, and perhaps none can be devised in which all cases can be arranged."[29] And when Pliny Earle at the end of his long career was approached on the possibility of developing a universally accepted classification of mental diseases, he took issue with the proposal. "In the present state of our knowledge," he noted, "no classification of insanity can be erected upon a pathological basis, for the simple reason that, with but slight exceptions, the pathology of the disease is unknown. . . . Hence, for the most apparent, the most clearly defined, and the best understood foundation for a nosological scheme for insanity, we are forced to fall back upon the symptomatology of the disease—*the apparent mental condition*, as judged from the outward manifestations." The oldest, simplest, and most practical classification systems (mania, monomania, melancholia, dementia, and idiocy), therefore, were still of considerable value.[30]

28. There are good discussions of the mid-nineteenth-century concept of disease in Rosenberg, *The Cholera Years, passim,* Barbara G. Rosenkrantz, *Public Health and the State: Changing Views in Massachusetts, 1842–1936* (Cambridge, 1972), Chaps. I–II, and Phyllis Allen, "Etiological Theory in America Prior to the Civil War," *Journal of the History of Medicine and Allied Sciences,* II (Autumn, 1947), 489–520.

29. Utica State Lunatic Asylum, *AR,* I (1843), 36. For similar comments see Worcester State Lunatic Hospital, *AR,* VI (1838), 45, VIII (1840), 41, and H. A. Buttolph, "Modern Asylums, and their Adaptation to the Treatment of the Insane," *AJI,* III (April, 1847), 376.

30. Pliny Earle to Clark Bell (copy), April 16, 1886, Earle Papers, AAS.

Identification of mental disease through observance of a person's outward behavioral symptoms, nevertheless, caused further difficulties. In some cases the criteria for diagnosing cases of mental disease seemed clear. Hallucinations, smearing of feces, and dramatic neurological symptoms associated with advanced cases of what was later diagnosed as syphilis—to cite only a few illustrations—seemed to place the individual clearly within a pathological category. Other types of abnormal behavior, however, were less clear and distinct. With respect to abnormal behavior, the normative standard applied by the psychiatrist at times became of considerable significance, if only because it entered into the relationship with the patient. This normative standard was not merely a physical one that involved proper organic functioning; in many respects it was culturally defined and often placed a premium on dominant social values. Such values were to play a significant internal role within mental institutions, particularly since these institutions catered to heterogeneous groups coming from quite different social, economic, and cultural backgrounds.

Few nineteenth-century American psychiatrists were willing to argue that their concepts of insanity grew out of their own personal ideology. But when they took up the problem of etiology, their own values and commitments became clearer. Outwardly, their categories seemed to be objective and scientific in nature; the causes of mental illness could be subsumed under two general headings—physical and moral. The physical causes, to quote Edward Jarvis, produced "their primary effect on the physical structure of the brain or some other organs, and disturbing the cerebral actions, produce their secondary effect on the mental operations; as a blow on the head, or epilepsy, or a disordered stomach." The moral causes acted "directly on the mind itself; as excessive study, disappointment, grief, trouble, &c."[31] While the two categories were not always clearly defined, most superintendents used them in reporting upon the problem.

Generally speaking, the physical causes of mental disease presented psychiatrists with formidable difficulties. In the first place, many were beyond control and were due to accident or chance. Insanity arising from various physical diseases (e.g., smallpox),

31. Edward Jarvis, "Causes of Insanity," *Boston Medical and Surgical Journal*, XLV (November 12, 1851), 294.

concussions, falls, and other accidents obviously could not be prevented by the patient or physician. In such cases treatment—not prevention—was the normal procedure. Secondly, superintendents possessed neither the techniques nor equipment that would enable them to explore the ways in which physical causes presumably led to organic lesions of the brain, thereby producing insanity. Virtually none were trained pathologists. Unlike their European counterparts, few performed post-mortem examinations. Moreover, their administrative functions and outlook left little time for research. Finally, most of them believed that physical causes did not account for the majority of the total number of cases. Consequently, superintendents tended simply to list the physical causes without any extended commentary.

Without question, superintendents were more interested in the moral (or intellectual) causes of insanity, partly because of their own commitment to prevention (and most preventable causes seemed psychological) and partly because such cases seemed to account for the largest proportion of cases. As firm believers in the tenets of organized religion, they also felt much freer in their discussions of morality than they did in their pathological observations. The moral causes of mental disease included —to cite only a few examples—intemperance, overwork, domestic difficulties, excessive ambitions, faulty education, personal disappointments, marital problems, jealousy, pride, and, above all, the pressures of an urban, industrial, and commercial civilization which was considered to be unnatural to the human organism. Psychiatrists, in other words, saw mental illness as the inevitable consequence of behavior that represented a departure from their own normative model.

Like many Americans during the first half of the nineteenth century, psychiatrists held a romantic and sentimental ideal of mankind, an ideal that seemed threatened by developments that augured ill for the future. Thus they extolled the agrarian way of life and denigrated the values of urbanization. "We find," wrote Kirkbride, "as was always believed, that no life is so generally conducive to health as one that, like agriculture, gives active exercise in the open air, that none is so likely to be troubled with nervous affections, and none so generally to be preferred for those who are constitutionally disposed to this class of infirmities." Psychiatrists, above all, saw a clear relationship between the advance of civilization and the incidence of mental illness. As Ray put it in 1852, mental illness was "the price we pay for civilization."[32] The beliefs of most midnineteenth-century psychiatrists in many ways were not fundamentally dissimilar from those of other critics of American society whose own values were hostile to social and economic change and who rejected the newly emerging urban-industrial order and romanticized the American past. A substantial part of psychiatric theory, therefore, was but a reflection of a particular social ideology, presented as empirical fact.

In dealing with the specific moral causes of insanity, superintendents ranged far afield. So broad was their analysis that few institutions remained exempt from their critique. Religious and political institutions in particular were singled out as causal elements in bringing on insanity. Superintendents were especially fond of emphasizing the defects of American education, which failed to provide children with a proper and healthful environment. Some condemned existing educational institutions as being too permissive; others attacked them as too rigid; still others argued that schools raised the expectations of children to unattainable levels and thereby led to inability in later life to deal with reality.[33] Nor was it unusual for psychiatrists to relate

32. Pennsylvania Hospital for the Insane, *AR*, XXII (1862), 15; Butler Hospital for the Insane, *AR*, 1852, 19. For similar statements see the following: Vermont Asylum for the Insane, *AR*, III (1839), 13, XXIV (1860), 11; Connecticut Retreat for the Insane, *AR*, XXII (1846), 24, XXIV (1848), 16–17; Edward Jarvis, "On the Supposed Increase of Insanity," *AJI*, VIII (April, 1852), 363–364; Butler Hospital for the Insane, *AR*, 1852, 19ff., 1858, 11ff.; Pennsylvania Hospital for the Insane, *AR*, XIII (1853), 25ff.; Indiana Hospital for the Insane, *AR*, I (1849), 15; South Carolina Lunatic Asylum, *AR*, 1853, 16; Virginia Eastern Asylum, *BR*, 1853–1854/1854–1855, 18–23; McLean Asylum for the Insane, *AR*, XXIX (1856), in Massachusetts General Hospital, *AR*, 1856, 18ff.; Kentucky Eastern Lunatic Asylum, *BR*, 1858/1859, 26–27; Taunton State Lunatic Hospital, *AR*, VIII (1861), 11–12, XIII (1866), 29; St. Vincent's Institution for the Insane, *Report*, 1862/1863, 24–27. See also the discussion of this issue at the sixteenth annual meeting of the AMSAII in *AJI*, XIX (July, 1862), 47–81.

33. See the following: Samuel B. Woodward to unidentified correspondent, February 25, 1834, Woodward Papers, AAS; *AJI*, I (January, 1845), 249–253, II (October, 1845), 148–149, IV (January, 1848), 207, VII (July, 1850), 71–72; Connecticut Retreat for the Insane, *AR*, XVIII (1842), 17; New Hampshire Asylum for the Insane, *AR*, IV (1844), 20; Friends' Asylum for the Insane, *AR*, XXVIII (1845), 23–25, XXXVII (1854), 19–20; Virginia Eastern Asylum, *AR*, 1846, 8; Northern Ohio Lunatic Asylum,

the vague and amorphous social structure to insanity. "In this country," noted Edward Jarvis,

> where no son is necessarily confined to the work or employment of his father, but all the fields of labor, of profit and of honor are open to whomsoever will put on the harness and enter therein, and all are invited to join the strife for that which may be gained in each, many are in a transition state, from the lower and less desirable to the higher and more desirable conditions. They are struggling for that which costs them mental labor and anxiety and pain. The mistake or the ambition of some leads them to aim at that which they cannot reach, to strive for more than they can grasp, and their mental powers are strained to their utmost tension; they labor in agitation; and they end in frequent disappointment.[34]

Although superintendents tended to place the greatest weight on social and environmental causes, they did not hesitate to view mental illness in terms of individual, inherited, or racial attributes. William M. Awl, for example, argued that the incidence of insanity was highest among those with the "highest refinement, and the greatest intellectual cultivation and activity." Thus no people were more affected by it than the *"Anglo-Saxon race."* Conversely, insanity tended to be absent among primitive societies. Edward Jarvis, on the other hand, believed that lower-class Irish immigrants were far more susceptible to this dreaded malady than native Americans—a view that was quite common among New Englanders at that time.[35] At the other end of the spectrum was the point of view that mental illness was a function of character defects and moral shortcomings and that, at times, such characteristics were transmitted to offspring in the form of an inherited disposition.

AR, I (1855), 12–13; Pennsylvania State Lunatic Hospital, AR, VIII (1858), 15–17, XXV (1875), 9–18; Butler Hospital for the Insane, AR, 1859, 24–27; Alabama Insane Hospital, AR, II (1862), 23–24; Northern Hospital for the Insane, Oshkosh, Wisconsin, AR, III (1875), 17.

34. Edward Jarvis, "Causes of Insanity," *Boston Medical and Surgical Journal*, XLV (November 12, 1851), 303–305.

35. Ohio Lunatic Asylum, AR, IV (1842), 18; *Report on Insanity and Idiocy in Massachusetts, by the Commission on Lunacy, Under Resolve of the Legislature of 1854*, Massachusetts *House Document No. 144* (1855), 61–62.

The character of mid-nineteenth-century psychiatric thought was not due to accident or chance; it arose rather out of a combination of circumstances. In the first place, superintendents were a homogeneous social group and tended to share common values. Part of this was a function of their background. Of eighty-one persons who served as superintendents of insane hospitals through 1875, no less than thirty-four (42 percent) were from New England, while an additional twenty-one (26 percent) were from Pennsylvania and New York. The overwhelming majority were Protestant, and most had been born and raised in small towns or rural areas; only five had come from a major urban center. Most superintendents, therefore, had grown up in small communities where they imbibed traditional Protestant values and an agrarian and antiurban outlook. It was natural for such men to view mental disease as the inevitable consequence of the violation of the immutable natural laws that governed humanity. Undoubtedly, they defined these laws in terms of the life-style of the group from which they came. "Be careful of your health," wrote Rufus Wyman, superintendent of McLean from 1818 to 1835, to his son who was studying medicine in Paris. "I need not caution you against the vices of a great city. Your own moral feeling will be your safe guide. I must entreat [you] not to make the Sabbath a day of mirth and frolic. Keep it after the New England fashion and you will find the gay city more like your native land for one day at least in each passing week."[36]

Nor did their experiences with the insane in any way contradict their own values and beliefs. Mentally ill persons, after all, *did* behave in odd and bizarre ways. Many had been ill for years and had spent extended periods of time in jails and almshouses before being transferred to public hospitals, and these experiences undoubtedly influenced their behavior. Some were filthy; some were violent; some showed no concern for either themselves or others; and most were poor or indigent. A significant proportion were from minority ethnic groups; in New England and elsewhere the Irish occupied a disproportionately high percentage of hospital spaces. To many superintendents it seemed as though these persons were paying the inevitable

36. Rufus Wyman to Jeffries Wyman, June 14, 1841, Jeffries Wyman Papers, CLMHMS.

price for their strange and aberrant ways and their apparent refusal to follow time-honored and traditional modes of behavior. Such attitudes, of course, were by no means unique to psychiatrists, but were rather characteristic of large numbers of their countrymen from similar backgrounds.

The breadth of the psychiatric critique of American society was also related to the young profession's confidence in its expertise and knowledge of human behavior. Having interpreted abnormal behavior as the inevitable consequence of improper institutions and immoral actions on the part of the individual (excluding those who had become insane through physical causes), it was natural for superintendents to assume a prophylactic and educational role in the hope that preventive means might prove to be the best way to cope with mental disease. Although he never occupied a hospital superintendency, the career of Dr. Edward Jarvis in this respect is revealing. An influential mid-nineteenth-century psychiatrist, he spent a good part of his life warning people that disease was the reward for sin and the violation of the natural laws which governed mankind. A New Englander by birth, Jarvis married many of his religious and moral beliefs about the proper conduct of life to the specialty of medicine. "God," he wrote in 1843, "has put our lives, partially at least, into our own hands. Whether we shall live to the fulness of our years, and give to each day its fulness of strength and pleasure, or whether we shall be miserable invalids, ever moving toward the grave and cut off in the morn, noon, or eve of life; these depend upon our obedience to those laws which God has stamped upon our frames."[37] The physical and moral order were simply parts of an organic whole, and it was impossible to separate health and morality because of the indissoluble bond between them.

Convinced that disease was the consequence of ignorance and sin, Jarvis devoted a considerable amount of his time to enlightening the public about proper modes of conduct. "There is a general ignorance of the laws of vitality," he informed the members of the Massachusetts Medical Society in 1849. "Men do not understand the connection between their conduct and vital force; and they feel but little responsibility for the mainte-

37. Jarvis, "Law of Physical Life," *Christian Examiner*, XXXV (September, 1843), 4.

nance of health. They lay their plans and carry on their operations, without much regard to the conditions of their existence. Life and its interests are not always paramount considerations; but they are made subordinate to matters of inferior importance."[38]

Physicians, Jarvis believed, had a special and grave responsibility for disseminating within all communities knowledge concerning the laws of health and illness. At the urging of Horace Mann, he published several books on physiology, the basic purpose of which was to provide the public with accurate information about proper behavior. Proper behavior meant much more than the mere observance of the laws of physiology; it included the entire behavioral pattern of the individual. Jarvis not only advocated a proper diet, fresh air, and other prerequisites of physical development but also condemned the use of tobacco and alcohol, the overuse of intellectual capacities, and the overzealous pursuit of material gain, among other things. His ideal, not surprisingly, corresponded to the ideal of the New England society into which he was born and lived.[39]

Jarvis's views were by no means atypical of the psychiatric profession. In their annual reports, in articles, speeches, and books, psychiatrists attempted to persuade their fellow countrymen to behave in accordance with certain norms. While the behaviorial norms of psychiatrists were no different from those of most native Protestant Americans, they were clothed with a scientific mantle—a fact made possible by the vagueness of contemporary etiological theory and the ardent desire to prevent disease and to promote health. Few aspects of American life were

38. Jarvis, "The Production of Vital Force," *Medical Communications of the Massachusetts Medical Society*, 2nd ser., IV (Boston, 1854), 23. Jarvis made much the same point in his review of the *Report of the Sanitary Commission of Massachusetts . . . 1850* [Shattuck Report], which appeared in the *American Journal of the Medical Sciences*, XXI (April, 1851), 391–409 (see especially 408–409).

39. Some of Jarvis's works written largely for the general public include *Lecture on the Necessity of the Study of Physiology, Delivered before the American Institute of Instruction, at Hartford, August 22, 1845* (Boston, 1845); *Practical Physiology: For the Use of Schools and Families* (Philadelphia, 1847); *Primary Physiology* (Philadelphia, 1848); *Practical Physiology. Or, Anatomy and Physiology Applied to Health*, rev. ed. (New York, 1852).

omitted from the searching critique of psychiatrists. Educators were told how to educate children; the ministry how to observe true religion; husbands and wives how to behave toward each other and how to raise children. Even the Civil War came under close scrutiny. To some Northern psychiatrists the nobility of the struggle diverted attention from the pursuit of material goals and strengthened the national character. "Before the rebellion," noted John S. Butler, "we were as a people sinking into a selfish materialism . . . [with] the consequent rapid increase of insanity. . . . Now in this new and higher life upon which we have entered, wealth seems as if deemed but the handmaid of a charity that never faileth. . . . A war, wisely conducted to a successful issue and in defense of the right, tends directly to the elevation and development of the nation conducting it."[40] Above all, psychiatrists were confident that their professional expertise gave them the inescapable duty to lay down the values that should govern the behavior of a society. Beneath their views of abnormal behavior and mental illness, therefore, lay a fairly clear conception of normative behavior.[41]

40. Connecticut Retreat for the Insane, *AR*, XLI (1865), 14–15. The psychiatric interpretation of the relationship between the Civil War and mental illness was largely a function of two variables; the sectional affiliation of the psychiatrist and victory/defeat. For a sampling of psychiatrists' comments about the Civil War see the following: McLean Asylum for the Insane, *AR*, XLIV (1861), in Massachusetts General Hospital, *AR*, 1861, 23–27; Iowa Hospital for the Insane, *BR*, II (1862/1863), 23–24; Utica State Lunatic Asylum, *AR*, XX (1862), 15–17; New York City Lunatic Asylum, Blackwell's Island, *AR*, 1862, 5–6; Illinois Hospital for the Insane, *BR*, VIII (1862), 26–28; Government Hospital for the Insane, *AR*, IX (1863/1864), 8–9; Kentucky Eastern Lunatic Asylum, *AR*, XL (1864), 13–14; Central Ohio Lunatic Asylum, *AR*, XXVI (1864), 18–20; Missouri State Lunatic Asylum, *BR*, VI (1864), 12–14; Michigan Asylum for the Insane, *BR*, 1861/1862, 24–27; Kentucky Western Lunatic Asylum, *AR*, 1865, 15–16; Virginia Eastern Lunatic Asylum, *AR*, 1866, 9; Texas State Lunatic Asylum, *AR*, 1866, 9. See also George M. Fredrickson, *The Inner Civil War: Northern Intellectuals and the Crisis of the Union* (New York, 1965).

41. Some selected examples of the prophylactic and didactic nature of mid-nineteenth-century psychiatric thought are: Amariah Brigham, *Remarks on the Influence of Mental Cultivation and Mental Excitement Upon Health*, 2nd ed. (Boston, 1833); Utica State Lunatic Asylum, *AR*, II (1845), 51–57; Maine Insane Hospital, *AR*, XXII (1862), 16–21; Butler Hospital for the Insane, *AR*, 1860, 20–25; Southern Ohio Lunatic Asylum, *AR*, XII

Psychiatrists were so confident of their expertise that they rarely considered the possibility of error. Indeed, they often pointed out that statistical data completely verified the validity of their analysis. Following the Jeffersonian and Enlightenment traditions, they believed that God had not been capricious or arbitrary in creating the universe; He had promulgated a series of laws whose operations were regular and predictable. Because they were regular and predictable, these laws lent themselves to scientific inquiry. Influenced by French medicine, they believed that the best way of deriving these laws was through a broad quantitative analysis of a large body of empirical data. As scientists, they had a special responsibility to aid in the collection of data that would serve as the springboard for further advances. Consequently, their annual reports were for the most part composed of statistical tables that included information on age, sex, ethnicity, occupation, finances, duration of illness, recovery rates, and length of institutionalization, to cite only a few. Jarvis was the most ardent advocate of this approach. He was the most active member of the American Statistical Association and was its president and driving force for more than three decades. Working for the federal government, he served as a consultant to the Census Bureau. He spent much of his time attempting to convert the members of the AMSAII to the cause of quantification in their research. Among his numerous publications, there were significant papers, books, and reports that utilized quantitative data. Jarvis, then, practiced what he preached.[42]

(1866), 10–13; George Cook, "Mental Hygiene," *AJI*, XV (January, April, 1859), 272–282, 353–365; Isaac Ray, *Mental Hygiene* (Boston, 1863); John P. Gray, "Mental Hygiene," *AJI*, XXXIV (January, 1878), 307–341. The Samuel B. Woodward Papers, AAS, are especially good on this subject.

42. For Jarvis's career see the critical introduction by Gerald N. Grob to *Insanity and Idiocy in Massachusetts: Report of the Commission on Lunacy, 1855 by Edward Jarvis* (Cambridge, 1971), especially 39–71. For evidence on the faith of early superintendents in statistics see Samuel B. Woodward to Pliny Earle, March 18, 1842, Earle Papers, AAS; William M. Awl to Woodward, April 18, 1842, Jarvis to Woodward, October 12, 1844, Woodward Papers, AAS; Woodward to George Chandler, May 14, 1843, Chandler Papers, AAS; Ohio Lunatic Asylum, *AR*, IV (1842), 37.

In their emphasis upon statistics, psychiatrists were following the lead of many contemporary scientists and political economists. The application

Although many psychiatrists continued to express their faith in quantitative data, some dissenting voices began to be heard. Isaac Ray, who possessed one of the keenest and most critical minds in the profession, expressed some doubts early in his career. In a long analysis of the statistical approach in 1849, he pointed out that many categories were too vaguely defined; the same category meant different things to different people, and too often inferences drawn from statistical data rested on dubious assumptions and illogical reasoning. Ray's criticisms were echoed by others, but before 1875 they had relatively little impact.[43] The resemblance between the statistical emphasis of European medicine and that of American medicine was a largely superficial one. American psychiatrists, unlike their European counterparts, collected data with the assumption that laws would become self-evident. Since American psychiatry was largely devoted to hospital management and administration, there was neither time nor incentive for superintendents to pursue research interests. Indeed, their administrative outlook in many ways militated

---

of a numerical method had been undertaken as early as the seventeenth century by mercantilists who hoped that the quantitative data of natural life would result in knowledge that would enhance the authority of the nation-state. By the eighteenth century the possibilities inherent in the statistical analysis of disease were being increasingly recognized by philosophers like Condorcet and physicians like Pinel. The philosophy of Ideology, with its empirical approach, markedly strengthened faith in analytical statistics. Industrial and technological changes, which gave rise to new social problems, also reinforced interest in the statistical analysis of the problems of health, and the numerical method of Pierre Louis and the Paris school of the early nineteenth century seemed to prove beyond a doubt the fruitfulness of a quantitative approach (even though the immediate result tended to be therapeutic nihilism). See George Rosen, "Problems in the Application of Statistical Analysis to Questions of Health: 1700–1880," *Bulletin of the History of Medicine*, XXIX (January–February, 1955), 27–45, and Richard H. Shryock, *The Development of Modern Medicine: An Interpretation of the Social and Scientific Factors Involved*, rev. ed. (New York, 1947), 157–169.

43. Isaac Ray, "The Statistics of Insane Hospitals," *AJI*, VI (July, 1849), 23–52, and his comments in the Maine Insane Hospital's *AR*, III (1842), 14ff.; Kirkbride to Pliny Earle, April 23, 1844, Kirkbride to Samuel Tuke, November 22, 1845, Kirkbride Papers, IPH; McLean Asylum for the Insane, *AR*, XXIII (1840), XXIV (1841), in Massachusetts General Hospital, *AR*, 1840, 13–14, 1841, 10ff.; Connecticut Retreat for the Insane, *AR*, XXII (1846), 34–36.

against an inquiring spirit, for experimentation and innovation were often the antithesis of internal order, efficiency, and rationality. The collection of statistical data characteristic of mid-nineteenth-century American psychiatry, therefore, became an end in itself and did not reflect an emphasis upon rigorous scientific inquiry.

IV

To define the nature and causes of mental illness was only a beginning, not an end. Psychiatrists then faced the question that had the greatest policy implication: what could be done to alleviate or cure mental disease? Despite their belief that mental illness was largely a function of individual and structural defects, they did not necessarily draw pessimistic conclusions; most superintendents were convinced that insanity could be cured. From their theoretical model they drew the conclusion that insanity was as curable as, if not more curable than, most somatic illnesses. If derangements of the brain and nervous system were the consequences of environmental pressures that led the individual to violate the natural laws governing human behavior (thus leading to lesions of the brain), it followed that a change in the environment could lead to a reversal of improper physical development. The prognosis for insanity was thus quite hopeful (provided that treatment was begun before the disease had entered the chronic stage). "Insanity," proclaimed Woodward, "of all diseases the most fearful, is found to be among the most curable." Indeed, it was common for superintendents to claim that as high as 90 percent or more of all recent cases (defined as being insane for one year or less) could be cured if treated promptly.[44]

44. Worcester State Lunatic Hospital, *AR*, VII (1839), 65. For similar statements see *ibid.*, III (1835), 35, VIII (1840), 68, XII (1844), 60; Vermont Asylum for the Insane, *AR*, II (1838), 12; Ohio Lunatic Asylum, *AR*, IV (1842), 57; Virginia Eastern Asylum, *AR*, 1843, 4–5; Friends' Asylum for the Insane, *AR*, XXXIV (1851), 14–15; McLean Asylum for the Insane, *AR*, XLII (1859), in Massachusetts General Hospital, *AR*, 1859, 31; Pliny Earle, *The Curability of Insanity: A Series of Studies* (Philadelphia, 1887), 18ff. The emphasis on curability was especially evident among those individuals and groups promoting the founding of hospitals. Obviously, superintendents were far less optimistic about the chances for recovery where insanity had followed organic changes not having environmental causes.

Along with an optimistic view about the prognosis of mental illness went a well-defined and carefully thought out rationale for care and treatment that closely reflected the profession's views on the nature and etiology of mental disease. Since insanity was in large part a product of behavior produced by an improper environment, naturally treatment had to begin with the creation of a new and proper environment. A patient could not be treated at home, simply because there was no way of checking those undesirable influences that had been responsible for the advent of disease. Consequently, virtually all superintendents—whatever their outlook on other matters—agreed that confinement in an institution was an absolute necessity for all insane persons. Institutionalization not only forced the patient to break with the obviously improper environment in which he lived but also provided the physician with the opportunity to establish and to manipulate the environment and therefore to change behavior. In effect, superintendents drew a sharp line between the community and the hospital; only the hospital could recreate an atmosphere free from the evils and temptations characteristic of society. Indeed, the AMSAII in 1851 recommended that no hospital be located less than 2 miles outside of a large town; otherwise the hospital could not evade the invidious influence of the community.[45]

Institutionalization, of course, represented only the first step in promoting recovery. Next came the arduous task of treating the afflicted individual. In general, superintendents divided therapy into two broad categories: medical and moral. Subscribing to the ancient axiom of a sound mind in a sound body, alienists believed that it was important to strengthen the patient's bodily condition in order to improve his mental state. Tonics and laxatives, therefore, were used with a high degree of frequency. Most psychiatrists, in addition, were strong advocates of the use of drugs as adjuncts to moral treatment. Where behavior was particularly active and violent, narcotics like opium and morphine were administered for many reasons: to quiet patients and to make them receptive to moral management; to avoid fatal exhaustion;

45. See, for example, Vermont Asylum for the Insane, AR, II (1838), 7; Utica State Lunatic Asylum, AR, VI (1848), 55–56; McLean Asylum for the Insane, AR, XXIV (1841), in Massachusetts General Hospital, AR, 1841, 22–23; AJI, IV (July, 1847), 1, VIII (July, 1851), 79–80.

15. Pliny Earle (1809–1892). Although launching his career during the optimistic decades of the 1830's and 1840's, he ended up on a pessimistic note. His book, The Curability of Insanity *(1887), which was begun while he was superintendent of the Northampton State Lunatic Hospital in Massachusetts, rejected the earlier belief in the curability of mental illness. Source: John Curwen,* The Original Thirteen Members of the Association of Medical Superintendents of American Institutions for the Insane *(Warren, Pa., 1885).*

to minimize the use of mechanical restraint; and to prevent harm from befalling the individual, other patients, or the staff. Psychiatrists, like most general medical practitioners, also used Dover's powder, digitalis, hyoscyamus, calomel, antimony, ipecac, and acta racemosa. Warm and cold baths, cold head compresses, and special diets likewise were often part of the medical regimen, though none were especially unique to the practice of psychiatry.[46]

Medical treatment of mental illness, however, was but an aid and adjunct to what was known in the nineteenth century as moral treatment. While susceptible to many interpretations, moral treatment meant kind, individualized care in a small hospital; resort to occupational therapy, religious exercises, amusements and games; repudiation in large measure of all threats of physical violence; and only infrequent application of mechanical restraints. Moral treatment, in effect, involved the reeducation of the patient within a proper moral atmosphere. Since disease was often a function of immoral or improper behavior, what was required was a change of atmosphere in order to help the individual change himself. The role of the superintendent was not fundamentally different from the role of the stern, authoritarian, yet loving and concerned father. A good father did not indiscriminately punish an erring child, but rather reasoned with the child in order to induce a moral reformation. Punishment, while necessary on occasion, was never arbitrary, capricious, cruel, or unjust. The superintendent was always supposed to appeal to

46. Worcester State Lunatic Hospital, *AR*, IV (1836), 50, VIII (1840), 81–82, IX (1841), 78–81, XII (1844), 70–82; Connecticut Retreat for the Insane, *AR*, XVIII (1842), 32–33; Northampton State Lunatic Hospital, *AR*, XIV (1869), 15–16; McLean Asylum for the Insane, *AR*, XLI (1858), in Massachusetts General Hospital, *AR*, 1858, 28; Friends' Asylum for the Insane, *AR*, LVI (1873), 21–22; *American Journal of the Medical Sciences*, n.s. XIII (January, 1847), 112–116; *AJI*, III (April, 1847), 353–358; Woodward, "Observations on the Medical Treatment of Insanity," *AJI*, VII (July, 1850), 1–34.

Many superintendents, nevertheless, were doubtful about the efficacy of medical treatment of mental illness. See Luther V. Bell to Dix, February 14, 1843, Dix Papers, HLHU; Rufus Wyman, "A Discourse on Mental Philosophy as Connected with Mental Disease, Delivered before the Massachusetts Medical Society, in June, 1830," in *Medical Communications of the Massachusetts Medical Society*, V, part I (Boston, 1830), 24; Maine Insane Hospital, *AR*, V (1844), 7–15; Iowa Hospital for the Insane at Mt. Pleasant, *BR*, I (1860/1861), 29–30.

the rational side of an insane person, and to treat the patient with consideration and respect in the hope of eliciting a response in kind. Nevertheless, if misbehavior persisted, the psychiatrist did not for a moment hesitate to invoke punishment of one variety or another. Basically, the goal was the inculcation, through habit and understanding, of desirable moral traits and values. The ideal hospital, in other words, was modeled along the lines of a closely knit and cohesive family. After more than a decade of service at the Worcester hospital, Woodward remarked that the 1,800 patients who had been and were under his care seemed *"like children and kindred."*[47] "By our whole moral treatment, as well as by our religious services," he noted in 1841 in words similar to those of most other superintendents,

> we inculcate all the habits and obligations of rational society. We think the insane should never be deceived; all their delusions and false impressions of character should be discouraged by removing, in the kindest manner, every badge of honor and distinction which they are disposed to assume, and by directing their attention to other subjects of interest. They may be held responsible for their conduct so far as they are capable of regulating it. By encouraging self-control and respect for themselves and others, we make them better men, more orderly and reasonable, before any impression is made upon their delusions.[48]

47. Woodward to Charles Sedgwick, January 16, 1844, in Woodward, "Collected Writings," vol. I, Library of Worcester State Hospital, Worcester, Mass.

48. Worcester State Lunatic Hospital, *AR*, IX (1841), 88. The nineteenth-century psychiatric literature describing moral treatment was very extensive. Selected examples include Virginia Western Lunatic Asylum, *AR*, X (1837), 29–32; Vermont Asylum for the Insane, *AR*, II (1838), 14–15, III (1839), 14–16; Maine Insane Hospital, *AR*, I (1840), 24–25, II (1841), 33; Worcester State Lunatic Hospital, *AR*, IX (1841), 81ff.; McLean Asylum for the Insane, *AR*, XXIV (1841), in Massachusetts General Hospital, *AR*, 1841, 22–32; Ohio Lunatic Asylum, *AR*, IV (1842), 67; Pennsylvania Hospital for the Insane, *AR*, II (1842), 22–45, VIII (1848), 26–29; Bloomingdale Asylum for the Insane, *AR*, XXVII (1847), Appendix, 4–5; New Jersey State Lunatic Asylum, *AR*, II (1848), 26–30; "The Moral Treatment of Insanity," *AJI*, IV (July, 1847), 1–15; "Report on Insanity," in American Medical Association, *Transactions*, XVIII (1867), 412.

Fuller discussions of moral treatment can be found in Dain, *Concepts of Insanity in the United States, passim,* and Gerald N. Grob, *The State and the Mentally Ill: A History of Worcester State Hospital in Massachusetts, 1830–1920* (Chapel Hill, 1966), 43–79.

Along with a rationale for care and treatment went a fairly elaborate vision of the structure of the ideal mental hospital.[49] There was general agreement that hospitals should remain small (250 or less); that superintendents should have complete control of the medical, moral, and dietetic treatment; and that all staff, professional and supporting, should remain under the unfettered control of the superintendent. Although each hospital obviously had to have a governing board having legal status, its role was to be limited to selecting the superintendent and to overseeing the finances and operations in order to give "to the community a proper degree of confidence in the correctness of its management."[50] In the ideal hospital the superintendent was clearly the dominant figure; his authority grew out of his expertise in and knowledge about mental disease.

The dominant position of the superintendent was reflected in the prevailing architecture of mid-nineteenth-century hospitals. Form, insisted the AMSAII in its famous propositions in 1851 and 1853 dealing with the construction and organization of hospitals, was to follow function; a building should not be constructed in a haphazard manner, but should rather reflect its essential functions. The ideal mental hospital, therefore, usually had a center building that housed the superintendent, his family, and the administrative offices and quarters. Extending laterally on both sides were the patient wings, which could be further divided into wards to house the different categories of patients. If additional accommodations were required, a similar structure could be repeated, either joining existing wings at right angles or else lapping on at the end and extending in a parallel line. Such a structure was based on the assumption that all patients were to be directly under the care of the chief medical officer; the floor plan was intended to provide him with easy access to all patients and thereby to maximize observation and control. This plan, noted Kirkbride in his classic work on hospital architecture in 1854, would provide

49. Cf. Pliny Earle, "The Psychopathic Hospital of the Future," *AJI*, XXIV (October, 1867), 117–130.

50. The AMSAII spelled out these details in 1853 in a series of propositions relative to the organization of mental hospitals. For the propositions see *AJI*, X (July, 1853), 67–69; for a discussion of them see Kirkbride, *On the Construction, Organization, and General Arrangements of Hospitals for the Insane* (Philadelphia, 1854), *passim*.

ample accommodations for the staff, "every thing requisite for the custody, comfort and enlightened treatment of the patients, and arrangements throughout that will allow the supervision to be thorough and effective, and the management liberal and at the same time strictly economical."[51] Mid-nineteenth-century American hospital architecture, then, reflected the prevailing psychiatric ideology in the following ways: separation of the patients from the community (a fact represented symbolically by the wall that often surrounded the hospital); emphasis upon a physical structure that would facilitate the creation of a new environment; and a floor plan which reflected the idea that the superintendent-psychiatrist was the dominant person in the institution.

Aside from spelling out the ideal form of hospital architecture, superintendents spent an extraordinary amount of time in providing the most minute details of construction. In their annual reports, in private correspondence, in articles and books, and in their discussions at the AMSAII, they analyzed sites, water supplies, sewerage, drainage, size of buildings, materials, heating and ventilating systems, lighting, support facilities—to mention but a few of the details. Their involvement in such minutiae reflected their view of the hospital as an institution that cured mentally ill people by providing them with a proper and moral environment. "The location of a hospital for the insane," wrote Kirkbride, "its general arrangements and official organization, must ever exert so important an influence on the comfort and happiness of all its patients, on the prospects for a recovery in those that are curable, and of the mental and physical well-being of those that are incurable, that no apology is required for any one, who having some practical knowledge of the subject, desires a general dissemination of the views and conclusions which have resulted from actual experience among those for whom these institutions are specially intended."[52] Since each new hospital was built only after committee visits to existing institutions and consultations among the same small group of superintendents, it was understandable that mid-nineteenth-century hospital architecture was uniform and homogeneous and reflected to an astonishing degree the role assigned to it by society and by the young profession.

51. Kirkbride, *On the Construction . . . of Hospitals for the Insane*, 37.
52. *Ibid.*, 2.

V

During the 1840's the individuals who were in charge of mental hospitals had begun to band together and to recognize their common concerns and interests. In so doing they laid the foundations for a professional self-identity and self-awareness. By most of the usual criteria, psychiatry—in the form of hospital management and administration—had begun the process of professionalization well before the Civil War. Its members had formulated a comprehensive body of theory about mental illness and mental hospitals; they claimed authority over all issues relating to this dreaded malady; they provided government and the public with information and policy recommendations; they had spelled out a code of ethics to govern their own behavior and even delineated the ideal personal qualities of practitioners; and they had organized themselves in order to enhance their authority in society. The problems they faced—both personal and public—only served to intensify their dedication to the cause of the mentally ill. Given a free hand and sufficient resources, they intimated over and over again, it was not impossible to conceive of a society where mental illness would be sharply reduced, if not eliminated entirely. Recognizing that their voices were just barely heard, the members of the young profession nevertheless looked forward to a brighter future when humanity would heed their admonitions, avoid dissipation and immorality, and live their lives in the manner stipulated by divine authority.

The legacy of the professionalization of psychiatry, nevertheless, was far more ambiguous and complex than its members realized. To most superintendents it was inconceivable that professionalization could have other than beneficial results. Since the ethics and goals of the profession appeared virtually indistinguishable from those of the community, they saw little need to go beyond the parameters of their immediate circumstances or to engage in a critical examination of their own beliefs and practices. Consequently, they were not always aware of the fact that their newly emerging specialty might ultimately be used by the community in ways that they themselves would not approve, or that their analysis of mental illness might reinforce policies toward dependent groups with which they had little sympathy. Nor did they recognize that if their goal of containing or eliminating mental disease remained largely unfulfilled, the quality of public institutional care might be further undermined by the ensuing reaction. Indeed, the limiting aspects of professionalization were to have significant unforeseen results during and after the 1850's when superintendents were forced to cope with problems for which their training and experience had not prepared them.

Chapter V

The Mental Hospital, 1830-1875: Dilemmas of Growth

I

IN FORGING THEIR PROFESSION, hospital superintendents spelled out in considerable detail an ideal model of a mental hospital. Although they differed often over minor details, they were in complete agreement regarding the main purpose of their institutions: to bring about, if possible, the total recovery of the patient. To be sure, they did not reject outright a custodial role, for this function on occasion was necessary in order to safeguard both the welfare of the community and the afflicted individual. Nevertheless, they viewed the mental hospital as a therapeutic institution with a constantly changing patient population as recovered persons were discharged and new ones admitted. In their eyes there were few differences between general and insane hospitals; both admitted patients for brief periods in order to provide appropriate treatment. Thus a mental hospital was simply a specialized institution caring for the mentally ill. Similarly, the function of the psychiatrist was precisely the same as that of the general physician or specialist—to diagnose the nature of the illness and to prescribe treatment.

No ideal model, of course, corresponds precisely with reality. In the case of the mental hospital, however, the gap between the ideal and social reality widened steadily in the decades that followed the establishment of a comprehensive system of public institutions. In place of moral treatment these hospitals increasingly provided custodial care for poor and indigent dependent persons, and their structure and functions resembled those of welfare institutions rather than general hospitals. Instead of reflecting the entire social structure, patient populations tended more and more to represent lower-class and minority ethnic groups. Intended to be relatively small, mental hospitals grew rapidly in size; by the twentieth century it was not uncommon for them to have 3,000 or more patients each. Ostensibly innovative and socially desirable institutions, mental hospitals by the 1860's and 1870's began to face a rising chorus of criticism that pointed to their supposedly dehumanizing character. In many respects, then, the mental hospital became the very antithesis of the ideals and hopes of its first founders and early leaders.

What accounted for this transformation of the mental hospital? Was it due to the character or ideology of the individuals who founded and then led such institutions? Did social activists assume that their task was finished once these institutions were established? Did superintendents as a professional group share the general hostility in America toward poor and minority groups—a hostility that contributed toward the reversal of the optimistic expectations regarding mental hospitals? Was the failure of mental hospitals part of a larger failure of institutions generally? Did not confinement—whether in a mental hospital, reform school, penitentiary, or almshouse—affect human qualities and diminish individual personality?[1] Or were the shortcomings of mental hospitals simply an accurate reflection of the shortcomings of a materialistic society that allocated too few resources and

1. The most brilliant sociological analysis along this line of thought is Erving Goffman's influential *Asylums: Essays on the Social Situation of Mental Patients and Other Inmates* (Garden City, New York, 1961). Recently David J. Rothman has presented a historical version of much the same theme. Americans in the early national period, he argues, turned to institutionalization as the general solution to the problems of crime, poverty, and deviancy in general. Thus the poor were sent to poor houses, criminals to prisons, mentally ill persons to hospitals, and orphans to orphan asylums. These institutions were especially liable to abuse because of their emphasis on authority, obedience, and regularity, which all too predictably turned into a mechanical application of discipline. David J. Rothman, *The Discovery of the Asylum: Social Order and Disorder in the New Republic* (Boston, 1971).

manifested little patience and sympathy to groups—including the mentally ill—that failed to make it on their own and were dependent upon others for their survival?

To some degree all of these explanations are true, but such a conclusion represents at best an oversimplification. To attribute bad results to evil people or to condemn an entire society may prove psychologically and intellectually satisfying, but both avoid the far more difficult task of analyzing the *process* by which the character of institutions is altered so that they eventually serve purposes antithetical to their original objectives. The history of the mental hospital provides an excellent case in point. In its early days it was conceived as, and in many respects was, a curative institution. But through a series of events, many of which were unanticipated and unpredictable, its later development was in a very different direction. To understand the process by which this occurred, an examination of the internal evolution of the mental hospital and the forces which brought it about is in order.

II

Prior to 1850 the gap between theory and practice of moral treatment was relatively narrow. Hospitals were organized in such a manner as to facilitate the creation of a therapeutic environment that would change the lives and behavior of patients. In many respects hospitals were self-contained and isolated communities, a fact that seemed to maximize opportunities to institute controls and minimize adverse external influences. However early mental hospitals may have been portrayed, it is clear that their internal structure and daily regimen were not haphazard, arbitrary, or capricious. On the contrary, they reflected to an astonishing degree the theoretical precepts of moral treatment.

The daily routine in early mental hospitals may be best characterized as orderly, predictable, and regular. Patients knew what was expected of them, and it was assumed that they would behave accordingly. Discipline for the most part was a function of self-control. Restraint, either through mechanical means or isolation, was imposed only as a last resort. The goal of most superintendents was not to force patients to behave, but rather to help them develop an internal sense of what was socially correct and proper. If behavior was controlled by an internal mechanism, as was believed, there was hope that the patient could be returned to society without a recurrence of the behavioral pattern that had led to commitment in the first place. Although most superintendents were defensive about any form of restraint, they felt it was impossible to run a mental hospital without resort to such measures. To avoid any abuses, however, they usually insisted that no patient be restrained without the explicit approval of a physician. "Restraint," noted Isaac Ray in typical words,

> is sometimes necessary. The patient must not be suffered to injure his person or his clothing, nor those of others; nor to mar, destroy, or molest. Our means of restraint, however, are so well contrived and adjusted, that they effectually accomplish our purpose without causing the slightest pain, and with the least possible degree of annoyance. No restraint can be applied, except by order of an officer; and whenever any is required, our standing rule is to apply no more and continue it no longer than is absolutely necessary. The patient is made to understand that it is not applied as a punishment—this has no place in our moral treatment—but is merely a necessary means to prevent him from committing injury. Every indulgence at our disposal likely to promote their comfort, is freely given, until forfeited by an abuse of our confidence; to be granted again when they have shown themselves worthy of another trial by a course of correct behavior. As soon as a patient becomes aware of this rule, he places a double guard upon his conduct, and is thus actuated by a powerful motive to self-control.[2]

2. Maine Insane Hospital, *AR*, II (1841), 48–49. For further evidence of Ray's views see *ibid.*, V (1844), 30–31; *AJI*, II (July, 1845), 49–54; Butler Hospital for the Insane, *AR*, XVI (1862), 14–25; Ray to Edward Jarvis, September 29, 1860, November 21, 1863, Jarvis Papers, CLMHMS.

The defensiveness of superintendents about restraint was evident at an early date. A resolution adopted at the first meeting of the AMSAII in 1844 arguing against the entire abandonment of the practice was later deleted from the published proceedings because it might be misunderstood (Kirkbride to Luther V. Bell, November 13, 1844, Kirkbride to Amariah Brigham, November 18, 23, 1844, Kirkbride Papers, IPH). Most superintendents were also critical of the so-called nonrestraint system in England (cf. John Conolly's *The Treatment of the Insane Without Mechanical Restraints* [London, 1856]). For some typical statements see Worcester State Lunatic Hospital, *AR*, VIII (1840), 79–81; McLean Asylum for the Insane, *AR*, XXV (1842), XXVII (1844), XXVIII (1845), in Massachusetts

The typical day at a mental hospital began in the early morning. Patients arose at six or earlier and attended to their personal needs. Following breakfast they were required to put their quarters in order. Cleanliness and neatness were regarded as necessary in an institution containing large numbers of people living in close proximity, if only to discourage epidemics. The superintendent and his assistant made rounds after the breakfast hour and spoke with the patients and attendants about matters regarding diet, employment, amusements, and medication. Throughout the day attendants usually remained with patients. After nine in the evening the quarters were locked and the supervisory staff relaxed its vigilance for the first time.[3]

Throughout the day there was a determined effort to provide as many patients as possible with some kind of useful occupation. Men were assigned to agricultural pursuits, carpentry, painting, and general maintenance work. Women performed many of the domestic chores. Virtually all superintendents agreed that productive labor was perhaps the most important element in moral management. Hospitals, wrote Ray with pride in 1844, were now "places of refuge for the unfortunate, where a spirit of industry is fostered, and a healthful mental activity maintained by various forms of useful employment," whereas in the past they had simply been "strong houses" for the safekeeping of those deemed dangerous to society.[4] If every employable insane person was provided

General Hospital, *AR*, 1842, 22–23, 1844, 14–15, 1845, 14–19; Ohio Lunatic Asylum, *AR*, IV (1842), 68; Utica State Lunatic Asylum, *AR*, I (1843), 51–52; Pennsylvania Hospital for the Insane, *AR*, II (1842), 38–42; Virginia Eastern Asylum, *AR*, 1845, 26–30; Pennsylvania State Lunatic Hospital, *AR*, II (1852), 17; Taunton State Lunatic Hospital, *AR*, I (1854), 40; *AJI*, XIII (January, 1857), 281–290; Kirkbride to Luther V. Bell, December 11, 1844, Kirkbride to Pliny Earle, July 8, 1845, Kirkbride Papers, IPH; Amariah Brigham to Earle, February 27, 1845, Earle Papers, AAS; D. D. Richardson to Edward Jarvis, April 22, 1858, Jarvis Papers, CLMHMS.

3. Cf. "Memorandum of the Superintendent," in *Report and Resolve Making Appropriations for the State Lunatic Hospital*, 18–22, in Massachusetts *Senate Document No. 62* (March, 1838); Worcester State Lunatic Hospital, *AR*, VII (1839), 86–91, VIII (1840), 77; New Jersey State Lunatic Asylum, *AR*, III (1849), 27–32.

4. Maine Insane Hospital, *AR*, V (1844), 25. For a similar comment by Luther V. Bell see his letter in Virginia Western Lunatic Hospital, *AR*, X (1837), 29–32.

with useful labor under intelligent and proper supervision, noted one superintendent, then the entire world would learn "that rational & useful work is a means of averting insanity; a means of keeping a sane mind sane; a means of lessening insanity of the mind & etc."[5]

A few hospitals permitted and even encouraged their patients to publish their own newspapers and journals. Beginning in 1837 the *Retreat Gazette* was published at the Hartford Retreat, though its life was a brief one. The Vermont Asylum for the Insane sponsored a similar venture in 1842; its *Asylum Journal* continued to appear for five years. Both the Utica Asylum and the Pennsylvania Hospital for the Insane had journals prepared by inmates during the 1850's. Written and edited by patients, such publications provided a means of occupation and served also to educate the outside community about mental illness. Indeed, the valedictory number of the *Opal*, published at the Utica institution, noted that the world was "wiser, if not better for our *Opal.*"

> It has cleared up so many doubts, dissipated so many errors and wrong opinions concerning monomania and insanity. It has taught outsiders how little difference in ideas there often is between those within and those without the walls. It has shown how very difficult it is to tell where melancholy ends and insanity begins; how narrow the boundary between eccentricity and lunacy, and it might tell how much better insane people behave under the asylum code of etiquette than the world's votaries often do.[6]

Most hospitals, in addition, built libraries for their patients. While superintendents were concerned with "excessive" use of one's intellectual faculties, they felt that "moderate" or "normal" use promoted sanity and sound mental health. A number of institutions provided lecture series for patients. The best program of long standing was instituted by Kirkbride at the Pennsylvania Hospital for the Insane. Begun in 1844, the series of two lectures

5. John Fonerden to Kirkbride, June 19, 1859, Kirkbride Papers, IPH.

6. Judson B. Andrews, "Asylum Periodicals," *AJI*, XXXIII (July, 1876), 42–49 (quote from 45); Vermont Asylum for the Insane, *AR*, IX (1845), 9–10; *Boston Medical and Surgical Journal*, XLV (August 27, 1851), 83; Earl D. Bond, *Dr. Kirkbride and His Mental Hospital* (Philadelphia, 1947), 69–77.

a week for the better part of the year was apparently an unqualified success, and a large room was converted into a permanent lecture hall. The topics were varied and included subects chosen from the sciences, medicine, literature, and history.[7]

Most hospitals resorted to regular religious observances as part of moral treatment. This was especially true during the 1830's and 1840's, for many of the early superintendents were themselves devout Christians. The inculcation of religious precepts, they believed, would exercise a powerful influence over a patient's mental state. Not only would religion affect the character and condition of the individual; it would also enable him to live a more normal life. Religion, therefore, was an important tool (in addition to its intrinsic worth) in helping the insane to learn and to recall the moral laws that governed humanity. "I wish them to attend religious worship," wrote Woodward, "to listen to instruction from the volume of truth, and receive encouragement to calm and quiet temper from its promises of reward to virtuous and upright conduct. Few individuals are so completely insane as to be beyond the reach of moral instruction, and perhaps may I add responsibility." Religious exercises, noted William H. Rockwell of the Vermont Asylum, served "to promote order," revive good habits and associations, and reinforce "that self-control which tends to their recovery." Devout Christians, moreover, tended to recover more quickly than nonbelievers. For these reasons many hospitals had chapels and services conducted by local clergymen.[8]

The goal of superintendents to a large extent was the promotion of close interpersonal relationships between staff and patients. "If there is any secret in the management of the insane," commented Woodward, "it is this: respect them and they will respect themselves, treat them as reasonable beings, and they will take

7. Edward A. Smith, *A Lecture Introductory to the Thirteenth Annual Course of Lectures and Evening Entertainment at the Pennsylvania Hospital for the Insane* (Philadelphia, 1857), *passim*.

8. Worcester State Lunatic Hospital, *AR*, IV (1836), 58; Vermont Asylum for the Insane, *AR*, III (1839), 15; Maine Insane Hospital, *AR*, I (1840), 24; Pennsylvania Hospital for the Insane, *AR*, II (1842), 36–37; Virginia Western Lunatic Asylum, *AR*, XV (1842), 34; South Carolina Lunatic Asylum, *AR*, 1842, 8–9.

every possible pains to show you that they are such; give them your confidence, and they will rightly appreciate it, and rarely abuse it."[9] To encourage close interpersonal relationships, superintendents tended to oppose large institutions, which, they believed, resulted in a decline in therapeutic successes. Luther V. Bell for one was quite emphatic in his belief that an institution having more than 200 patients was undesirable. "I believe," he wrote to Dix, "that if there is any circumstance which has elevated our American institutions to the present position of confidence before the community it is their moderate extent and having the head of the establishment domiciled with his family in the midst of his charge, where he can have a certain paternal relation to them, and can know their characters, feelings, connections and interests with a good degree of intimacy."[10]

As long as institutions remained relatively small, it was common for superintendents to follow the progress of each patient personally and to maintain contacts with the family. Kirkbride, to cite a typical example, requested a wife to visit her husband at the hospital and to make arrangements for his return home. "My own impression," he added, "is that if your husband lives at home—and not to go into much company and above all never to drink anything but water, that he would get along very well." In another case he suggested that a son not be removed prematurely. Then, three months after the young man had recovered, Kirkbride noted that only the young man's *"morbid feeling on the subject of his return home"* prevented his immediate release. The son, he wrote to the mother, should be persuaded to return home, where his interests "will be advanced by his return . . . & entrance into business."[11] Similarly, Woodward demonstrated patience and kindness in his relationships with inmates. He listened to their problems and noted carefully their symptoms and progress. At times he attempted to demonstrate the falsity of

9. Worcester State Lunatic Hospital, *AR*, VII (1839), 97.

10. Bell to Dix, February 14, 1843, Dix Papers, HLHU. See also William Wilson to Dix, February 11, 1843, Ray to Dix, February 20, 1843, *ibid.*

11. Kirkbride to Mrs. Philip Monis, October 9, 1842, Kirkbride to Richard Walker, December 15, 1842, Kirkbride to Mrs. Isabella Walker, March 31, 1843, Kirkbride Papers, IPH.

their delusions or hallucinations. Every patient was visited daily, and a regular and complete case history was kept in large bound volumes containing as many as 500 pages. It was also common for Woodward to receive correspondence from former patients with whom he had developed close ties.[12]

During the 1830's and 1840's superintendents claimed striking successes in curing mental illness, especially for individuals who had been ill for a year or less. William M. Awl and Woodward—the two most prominent men to promote the idea that mental illness, if treated in the early stages, was more curable than most diseases—claimed a recovery rate in recent cases of between 80 and 100 percent. In the first four years of operation, the Ohio Lunatic Asylum reported that it had received 171 individuals insane for one year or less; 69 between one and two years; 85 between two and five years; and 44 between five and ten years. The respective recovery rates within each group were 136 (80 percent), 24 (35 percent), 12 (14 percent), and 4 (9 percent). Between 1833 and 1846 2,583 cases were admitted to the Worcester hospital. During the same period 2,215 were discharged, of which 1,192 were listed as recovered. When one takes into consideration that those discharged as stationary represented old and chronic cases for the most part, the statistics regarding the chances of recovery of recent cases seemed imposing.[13]

How valid were these curability claims? Pliny Earle, an acquaintance of Woodward, subsequently maintained that the latter's statistics were void of meaning. In the first place, Earle argued, the proportion of cures represented the ratio of recoveries to cases discharged rather than to cases admitted. Secondly,

12. The various manuscript case histories in the case books kept by Woodward (Record Storage Section, Worcester State Hospital, Worcester, Mass.) offer convincing illustrations of these generalizations, as do the Woodward Papers, AAS. See also Gerald N. Grob, *The State and the Mentally Ill: A History of Worcester State Hospital in Massachusetts, 1830–1920* (Chapel Hill, 1966), Chap. II.

13. The statistics of the Worcester State Lunatic Hospital have been compiled from its annual reports between 1833 and 1846. Awl's figures can be found in Ohio Lunatic Asylum, *AR*, IV (1842), 57. For similar curability claims see Vermont Asylum for the Insane, *AR*, II (1838), 12–13; Virginia Eastern Asylum, *AR*, 1843, 4–5; Friends' Asylum for the Insane, *AR*, XXXIV (1851), 14–15.

Woodward's figures did not take into account readmissions; hence the total number of cases was considerably larger than the actual number of individuals. Finally, the fact that many individuals recovered more than once also threw Woodward's results into doubt.[14] Explaining such apparent distortions, Earle pointed out that at the time the Worcester hospital was opened, there were less than ten mental hospitals in the United States, and in many cases the chief medical officer was merely a visiting physician. Woodward, implied Earle, was concerned in part with building support for the founding of public hospitals, and a high curability rate would undoubtedly aid the cause.[15]

There is little doubt that Earle's strictures were justified—at least in part. Woodward and others *were* interested in building up public support for an expansion of the institutional system for the care and treatment of the insane. Thus they argued that it was more economical to cure mentally ill persons than it was to keep them in custodial and welfare institutions for long periods of time. "I think the statistics of insanity have done great good," wrote Woodward to Earle in 1842, "and the extensive and en-

14. Pliny Earle, *The Curability of Insanity: A Series of Studies* (Philadelphia, 1887), 9–22. This book was an outgrowth of studies undertaken while Earle was superintendent of the Northampton (Massachusetts) State Lunatic Hospital and published in the annual reports of that institution during the 1870's. In an article on curability in 1843, however, Earle did not manifest the disillusionment that marked his work in the 1870's. In his earlier work he admitted that definitions of recovery varied, and that physicians were not always in agreement about individual patients. A desire to remove patients sometimes led to a premature certification of restorative powers. Earle then noted that recovery seemed to be related to the age and sex of the patient; cause, type, and duration of the illness; season; and plan of medication. He also disliked the distinction between "recent" and "chronic" categories, and felt that recurrences of mental illness were probably greater in this disease than most others. Nevertheless, he did not directly dispute the notion of curability. See Earle, "On the Curability of Insanity," *American Journal of the Medical Sciences*, n.s. V (April, 1843), 344–363. The difficulties of determining recovery were spelled out by Isaac Ray in "Doubtful Recoveries," *AJI*, XX (July, 1863), 26–44.

15. Earle, *Curability of Insanity*, 25–26, and "A Glance at Insanity, and the Management of the Insane in the American States," Conference of Charities, *Proceedings*, VI (1879), 43–44.

thusiastic movements in favor of the insane in the United States has been produced by comparing the results of institutions and looking to the success of the best as given in the published statistics."[16] Woodward's definition of recovery, moreover, clearly influenced his already favorable statistics. He denied that a recurrence of insanity was necessarily a relapse; he argued instead that if a patient who had been discharged was free from the disease for one year or more, any recurrence should be attributed to a new cause, having occurred independently of the previous attack. Thus it was perfectly acceptable to have the same person recovering on a number of different occasions. "The institutions for the insane," he argued in 1842, "are blameless for the numerous recommittals, while those who have recovered from insanity will throw themselves into these channels of excitement, and seek rather than avoid these known causes of disease. This should not be so. If those who are predisposed to insanity would avoid these and many other known causes, they might safely pass on, and, in most cases, continue well."[17]

On the other hand, there exists some evidence to show that the record for treating the insane during the second third of the nineteenth century was marked by a considerable degree of success. In the 1880's Dr. John G. Park, then superintendent of the Worcester institution, undertook a follow-up study of persons discharged from the hospital as "recovered" on their only admission or last admission. Influenced by the pessimistic studies of Earle and the prevailing idea that insanity was largely incurable, Park argued that "there can be no doubt that the public have been hitherto widely misled as to the meaning of the word 'recovery,' as used in the hospital reports, and as to the permanency of cures from insanity."[18] Park, therefore, was predisposed against accepting Woodward's claims about the curability of insanity. Yet Park's study did not by any means dispute earlier claims concerning the curability of insanity. For example, in 1881 he reported

16. Woodward to Earle, March 18, 1842, Earle Papers, AAS. See also Worcester State Lunatic Hospital, *AR*, XII (1844), 60, and William M. Awl to Woodward, April 18, 1842, Woodward Papers, AAS.

17. Worcester State Lunatic Hospital, *AR*, VIII (1840), 47, IX (1841), 68, X (1842), 62.

18. *Ibid.*, XLIX (1881), 12–13.

that inquiries had been made regarding 211 patients discharged as cured prior to 1840. The 94 replies received indicated that 8 individuals were living and well, 40 had remained well as long as they had lived, and an additional 45 had become mentally ill again (7 of the 45 had committed suicide and 10 had been admitted to other hospitals).[19] In other words, slightly more than 51 percent of those discharged as recovered prior to 1840 had never again become insane—a record that compares quite favorably with mid-twentieth-century discharge rates from mental hospitals.[20] It is therefore possible to infer that the character and internal environment of many early mental hospitals together with the charismatic personalities of many superintendents had a beneficial impact upon their inmates.[21]

19. *Ibid.*, 13–14. Park did not indicate the status of 1 of the patients included in the total of 94 replies.

20. Park's study, which was not completed until 1893, eventually included follow-up results for 1,157 persons. Complete information was received in the cases of 984, of whom 317 were alive and well at the time of their reply, while an additional 251 had remained well until their death. Thus nearly 58 percent of those discharged as recovered had not had a relapse. See *ibid.*, LXI (1893), 70.

Much the same state of affairs seems to have been true for the Williamsburg hospital. Norman Dain has observed that perhaps one-third of all patients ordinarily admitted each year into a hospital would recover so long as certain minimum conditions prevailed; that insanity was regarded as curable; that patients were treated with some consideration; that the hospital was neither greatly understaffed or grossly overcrowded; and that not too many patients were chronic. The contribution of moral treatment, he observes, "may have been to help restore a significant proportion of a second third of the patients." Dain, *Disordered Minds: The First Century of the Eastern State Hospital in Williamsburg, Virginia 1776–1866* (Williamsburg, 1971), 45–46.

21. Recent studies have emphasized the importance of the attitude of both the therapist and the environment of the patient in successful treatment of mental illness. See the following: Milton Greenblatt et al., *From Custodial to Therapeutic Patient Care in Mental Hospitals* (New York, 1955); J. Sanbourne Bockoven, "Moral Treatment in American Psychiatry," *Journal of Nervous and Mental Disease*, CXXIV (August–September, 1956), 167–194, 292–321; *Action for Mental Health: Final Report of the Joint Commission on Mental Illness and Health 1961* (New York, 1961), 36–37; Jerome D. Frank, *Persuasion and Healing* (Baltimore, 1961); Karl Mennniger et al., *The Vital Balance: The Life Process in Mental Health and Illness* (New York, 1963).

III

The apparent success of early mental hospitals rested upon a series of circumstances: the small number and homogeneous nature of patients; the internal therapeutic atmosphere that arose from the enthusiasm and sometimes charismatic personality of superintendents; and close interpersonal relationships, to cite only some of the factors. Some of these circumstances, it should be noted, were difficult to replicate. A charismatic personality, for example, was in most respects incompatible with the process of institutionalization. Consequently, the problem of retaining the character of these early mental hospitals remained unresolved. In addition, changing circumstances began to contribute toward a transformation of the structure and functions of hospitals in a direction that had been neither anticipated nor desired.

During the early phases of the movement to establish facilities for the insane it was assumed that a therapeutic hospital had a transient population. Patients who recovered were immediately sent back to the community. An institution with the capacity to care for 200 patients at any one time, therefore, could accept two or three times that number annually, for those individuals who recovered generally did so in six months or less after being admitted (especially if the disease was of recent origin).[22] In practice, however, this assumption did not hold true. Superintendents for the most part found themselves unable to control the destinies

22. In his significant report on insanity in Massachusetts Edward Jarvis collected complete data pertaining to recovery for the Worcester and Virginia Western hospitals, and partial data for the New Hampshire, Kentucky, and Ohio institutions. In recent cases the average time in the hospital required for recovery in 2,775 cases was five months and nineteen days; at McLean the average figure after 1840 for 1,075 recent and old cases was five months and two days. *Report on Insanity and Idiocy in Massachusetts by the Commission on Lunacy, Under Resolve of the Legislature of 1854*, Massachusetts *House Document No. 144* (1855), 105, 191. See also Jarvis, *Insanity and Insane Asylums* (Louisville, 1841), 38-39; Pliny Earle, "On the Curability of Insanity," *loc. cit.*, 354-355; Friends' Asylum for the Insane, *AR*, XXXIV (1851), 12-13; Pliny Earle, *History, Description and Statistics of the Bloomingdale Asylum for the Insane* (New York, 1848), 112-113.

of their institutions in a manner prescribed by theory. Over the years an imperfect model gave rise to consequences that created a very different type of institution.

Consider first the type of patient sent to newly opened public hospitals (and many private ones as well). Prior to the establishment of such hospitals many mentally ill persons were confined in welfare and penal institutions, often for extended periods of time. They were placed there for a number of reasons: some were regarded as threats to the community; some were unable to support themselves and had no friends or family able to assume the burden; and some were institutionalized because their presence at home seemed to disrupt family relationships. Welfare and penal institutions, however, found it difficult to provide care for such cases. Their physical plant did not permit classification, and their personnel were not equipped to care for mentally ill persons. Officials in welfare and penal institutions were anxious to have such inmates cared for elsewhere not because they were unsympathetic, but because they simply lacked adequate facilities. Five months before the opening of the Worcester hospital, for example, the superintendent of the Boston House of Industry wrote to Horace Mann to inquire when the new facility would be ready to receive patients. Ten percent of the inmates at the House of Industry, he noted, were insane, and half of them required "constant confinement in close dormitories." More than half of the total number of persons admitted during the first year of operations at the Worcester hospital were individuals who had long histories of mental illness and who had been confined in welfare and penal institutions for extended periods of time. There was relatively little hope for these individuals (at least statistically); for them the hospital served a custodial role. Much the same was true at other hospitals.[23]

From the very beginning, therefore, hospitals found that a significant part of their capacity was being devoted to providing custodial care for chronic patients whose chances for recovery seemed at best remote. The normal accumulation of patients who

23. Artemas Simonds to Horace Mann, August 17, 1832, Mann Papers, MHS; Worcester State Lunatic Hospital, *AR*, I (1833), 5, 25; Maine Insane Hospital, *AR*, II (1841), 7, 10–11, 16; Utica State Lunatic Asylum, *AR*, I (1843), 6, II (1844), 6; New Jersey State Lunatic Asylum, *AR*, II (1848), 24; Indiana Hospital for the Insane, *AR*, I (1849), 13.

for one reason or another failed to recover further augmented the total number of chronic cases. The result was an inability on the part of many superintendents to devote themselves to therapeutic care; they invariably spent a great deal of time caring for large numbers of patients for whom there was little hope of improvement. Over the years the accumulation of chronic cases tended to mandate involuntary increases in the sizes of institutions. Such growth was haphazard and often occurred without either the consent of the institution or a commensurate expansion of staff and plant.

The chronic category included a broad spectrum of persons. In some cases the hospital found itself providing care for older persons afflicted with "senile dementia" whose families either did not or could not care for them at home. While this group accounted for less than 10 percent of the total number of admissions from 1830 to 1875, their presence invariably complicated the hospital's management. Superintendents argued without much success that such persons did not belong in a mental hospital. "The new and strange surroundings, the absence of familiar faces, the loss of comforts, the well-known easy chair, the old cozy room and bed, the accustomed food, and above all the kind offices of the faithful family physician," noted one superintendent, "give such a shock to their sensibilities as to render them objects of the utmost pity. There is great impropriety in committing this class to our care. They cannot recover under any circumstances, and but seldom improve. Kindness, sympathy, humanity, dictate that their waning existence should be made cheerful and attractive by all the delicate attentions of home, family and friends."[24] In a relatively young society where geographic mobility was high and institutions were fluid, however, comprehensive facilities for the care of old age groups were simply lacking. Under these circumstances the mental hospital assumed an unwilling role as an old age home for perhaps between 5 and 10 percent of the inmates.

24. Worcester State Lunatic Hospital, *AR*, XXV (1857), 55–56, XXXIV (1866), 67 (quote), XXXV (1867), 34; Insane Asylum of Louisiana, *AR*, 1858, 13; New York City Lunatic Asylum, Blackwell's Island, *AR*, 1861, 17; New Hampshire Asylum for the Insane, *AR*, XXIII (1864), 16; Utica State Lunatic Asylum, *AR*, XXXVIII (1870), 18–19; Western Pennsylvania Hospital, *AR*, 1871, 18–19.

Other classes of patients also contributed to the ranks of the chronic. Some individuals were sent to hospitals because of behavioral problems deemed dangerous to the security either of the family or of society. "A majority of the insane," reported the superintendent of the New York City Lunatic Asylum, "are necessarily retained in hospitals, for the protection of the public."[25] Others were sent to institutions because of alcoholism. Still others were committed because their aberrant behavior and poverty forced the community to accept responsibility for their welfare. In many of these cases the almshouse was deemed inappropriate. Within certain areas welfare institutions were lacking because of low population density and the mental hospital seemed to be the proper institution to care for such persons. Three years after Massachusetts opened its first institution a judge of the Boston Municipal Court asked to be relieved of certain duties relative to commitment. "It has subjected me," he wrote to the Speaker of the House, "to very frequent applications from many persons, who, regarding the Hospital as a great State Charity, and intended for all classes of the Insane, were desirous to relieve themselves from the burden of Lunatics under their care, and to throw it upon the Commonwealth."[26] In most states, especially after 1840, a high proportion of chronic patients were impoverished immigrants completely dependent upon public support. The commitment of insane criminals to hospitals also proved especially troubling to superintendents. Not only did this group contribute to the ranks of the chronic; it also required hospitals (prior to the establishment of separate institutions for insane criminals) to provide separate maximum security quarters. There was little doubt that general paresis (the advanced stages of cases of previous syphilitic infection of the brain) and other organic diseases accounted for part of the number of chronic patients. At the Utica institution, for example, 2.7 percent of the total number of persons admitted between 1850 and 1868 were afflicted with general paresis (and probably more, given the rudimentary nature of

25. New York City Lunatic Asylum, Blackwell's Island, *AR*, 1852, in New York City Governors of the Almshouse, *AR*, IV (1852), 79.

26. Peter O. Thacher to William B. Calhoun, February 6, 1834, Original Papers of Act of 1834, Chap. 150, Massachusetts Archives, State House, Boston, Mass.

contemporary diagnostic procedures). For these patients in particular as well as those suffering from other organic diseases, the hospital was a purely custodial institution.[27]

The increase in seemingly incurable patients was but one indication of the gap between the ideal mental hospital and the realities of the situation. Another was the rapid growth in the size of hospitals and a consequent diminution in therapeutic practices. Indeed, the recommendation of the AMSAII in 1851 was that no institution should have more than 250 (and preferably 200) patients, or else therapeutic care became virtually meaningless. Yet by 1870 public hospitals in Massachusetts had an average patient population of nearly 400; the Utica Asylum in New York had 629; the New Jersey Asylum 648; the New York City Lunatic Asylum on Blackwell's Island 1,252; the Iowa Hospital at Mt. Pleasant 441; the Indiana hospital 479; the California Asylum 1,047; the Southern Ohio Lunatic Asylum 481; and the Longview institution 544. Only in the South did institutions tend to be smaller (Louisiana had 163 patients, Texas 83, and Mississippi 160). But even in that section the two Kentucky asylums averaged over 400, the Virginia Western Asylum 335, and the Tennessee institution 352 (1871). The somewhat smaller size of Southern institutions, however, did not imply that they provided superior care or emphasized moral treatment, for such was not the case.[28]

27. For some selected examples of the broad range of chronic patients at American mental hospitals see the following: Boston Lunatic Hospital, *AR*, III (1842), 18ff., XI (1850), 14–16; New York City Lunatic Asylum, Blackwell's Island, *AR*, 1853, 6, 1858, 12; South Carolina Lunatic Asylum, *AR*, 1850, 6–7; New York Asylum for Insane Convicts, *AR*, I (1860), in Inspectors of State Prisons of the State of New York, *AR*, XIII (1860), 265ff.; Northampton State Lunatic Hospital, *AR*, VI (1861), 21–25; Illinois State Hospital for the Insane, *BR*, VIII (1862), 18–19; Insane Asylum of the State of California, *AR*, X (1862), 32–36; Kentucky Western Lunatic Asylum, *AR*, 1864, 11; Maine Insane Hospital, *AR*, XXIV (1864), 13–14, XXXIV (1874), 18–19; Utica State Lunatic Asylum, *AR*, XXVI (1868), 36; Kansas Asylum for the Insane, *AR*, VII (1871), 5; Western Pennsylvania Hospital, *AR*, 1871, 19; Taunton State Lunatic Hospital, *AR*, XVIII (1871), 27–29; Longview Asylum, *AR*, XVI (1875), 6; Committee of the Medical Society of the State of Pennsylvania, *Memorial* ("To the State Legislature in Reference to the Proper Care and Treatment of Insane Criminals") (n.p., n.d. [c. early 1870's]).

28. Figures compiled from the annual reports of these mental hospitals. In most cases the figures represent the total remaining in the institu-

The expansion of hospitals tended to accelerate the thrust toward greater reliance on institutional care of the mentally ill, which in turn increased the demand for more facilities. The result was a constant cycle of growth that resulted in larger and larger institutions, since the increase in the number of institutions did not keep pace with the number of commitments. It is important to note that the pressure for increasing institutional facilities came not only from reformers, social activists, and political leaders, but from the very groups that most used these facilities. Such pressure was exerted indirectly by the commitment process, which was usually inaugurated by a family unable either to cope with the disruptive behavior of one of its members or to support such a person.

The simultaneous leap in the number of chronic patients and the size of hospitals—which had marked effects upon care and treatment—was in part a function of the legal, financial, and administrative framework that governed the operations of mental hospitals. Before the establishment of a comprehensive system of public institutions in the early nineteenth century, little attention was paid to the precise structure of such a framework if only because the responsibility for the mentally ill lay with the family or local community. The rise of public institutions, however, forced legislatures to develop a system that would allocate funds for operating and capital expenditures and provide for the admission, retention, and discharge of patients. Having little experience to draw upon, most states adopted systems that appeared rational and reasonable and were intended to protect the community against dangerous mentally ill persons and to provide therapeutic care for the curable and custodial care for the chronic. That these systems were to have very different consequences from their goals simply was not foreseen at the time they were adopted.

Although the financial and legal structures governing hospitals varied slightly by state and region, most were quite similar in terms of their goals and operations. The experiences of Massachusetts were typical in many ways of what occurred in other states. When the Worcester hospital opened in 1833, it had facilities for 120 patients. The assumption at that time of the legislation gov-

---

tion at the time of the report; in a few cases the figure is the average number of patients resident during the year. Both figures are for all intents and purposes identical.

erning its operation was that annual turnover would range between two and three times total capacity, since the discharge of
recovered cases would make room for new admissions. Little leeway was allowed in the event that projected estimates of the number of insane persons proved too low; no provision was made for
the increase in mental illness relating to population growth; nor
was consideration given to the problem of patients who for one
reason or another failed to respond to therapy.

Almost from the first day that patients were admitted, the hospital proved incapable of meeting the demands placed upon its
facilities. The reasons for this situation were not difficult to understand. The existence of an alternative to family care or confinement in an almshouse or jail, a growing social acceptance of institutionalization, the increase in population, and the migration to
the United States of impoverished groups who used hospitals with
a far greater frequency than native groups all combined to increase sharply the pressure on the hospital to accept more patients.
As a result of enlargements of its physical plant in 1836 and 1844,
the average number of patients rose from 107 in 1833 to 359 in
1846.[29]

Not only had Bay State authorities grossly underestimated the
potential use of hospital facilities, but they had also failed to fore-
see the odd manner that the legal structure under which the institution functioned would markedly influence future developments.
In 1832 the legislature adopted a far-reaching law to govern the
operations of the hospital. Under its provisions all insane persons
deemed dangerous to the security of the community were required to be sent to Worcester and their cost paid for by the
respective towns or counties in which they resided. This stipulation was a logical extension of a system that mandated local responsibility for dependent groups generally. All other mentally ill
persons, including poor and indigent persons as well as those coming from more affluent families, could be sent to the hospital if
room were available. The localities assumed financial responsibility for all pauper insane having a legal settlement within their
boundaries, although the hospital could not charge more than the
actual cost of support. Similarly, those families sending private

29. Much of this section is based upon Grob, *The State and the
Mentally Ill*, Chap. III.

patients to the hospital were held financially liable, and in such cases no limit was set in regard to charges. Under this system the hospital was expected to receive sufficient revenue to meet the costs of its operations; legislative appropriations would be necessary only for capital expenditures.[30]

Although the hospital was supposed to care only for 120 patients, this ideal was made impossible by the law of 1832. Hospital authorities, for example, had no effective control over admission policies, since they were given no discretion about accepting or rejecting persons committed by the courts. In effect, this meant that the hospital was operating under a system that had a built-in escalation clause insofar as the number and type of patients were concerned. The law did not take into account any possible impact upon the internal operations of the institution. As population increased, so too did the number of mentally ill persons sent by the courts. Unless the superintendent and trustees refused to accept other patients or discharge some prematurely (policies that they vehemently opposed), they would be faced with a slow but steady rise in the average number of residents.

Besides forcing the hospital's officials to accept all cases referred by the judiciary, the law (which stipulated that all dangerous lunatics already confined in jails and houses of correction by court order be transferred to Worcester) had the inadvertent effect of placing obstacles in the path of the institution's therapeutic objectives. Many persons who had been incarcerated throughout the state in welfare and penal institutions constituted the oldest and most advanced cases of mental illness and had the least chance for recovery. Such patients, although unresponsive to therapy, were not eligible for discharge into the community because the law provided for their release only when the original cause of commitment ceased to exist. Given the accumulation of such cases over time and a finite physical plant, the hospital re-

30. This law was first suggested by the commissioners overseeing the construction of the hospital, and was probably the work of Horace Mann. See the *Report of Commissioners Appointed Under a Resolve of the Legislature of Massachusetts, to Superintend the Erection of a Lunatic Hospital at Worcester . . . 1832*, Massachusetts *Senate Document No. 2* (January 4, 1832), and Chap. CLXIII, Act of March 24, 1832, in *Laws of the Commonwealth of Massachusetts . . . Beginning May, 1831, and Ending March, 1833* (Boston, 1833), 466–470.

sorted to the dual expedient of refusing admission to some and discharging others prematurely or returning them to jail if they fell into the category of dangerous persons.[31]

Finally, the system which governed the hospital's finances also had an impact upon its operations. Under the law the charges for pauper patients were at a fixed rate. Until 1844 the charges could not exceed costs; after that date the legislature simply set a specific figure. When costs exceeded income (as frequently happened), the hospital had no recourse but to raise charges to private patients, given the legal requirement that it be a self-supporting institution. This feature had a dual impact: it served to exclude some persons because the cost of institutionalization were too high; and it tended to reinforce the influence of class, since private patients were given more comfortable quarters and living conditions on the grounds that they paid higher charges.[32]

Clearly, the administrative, legal, and financial structure established by Massachusetts had an extraordinary impact on the internal development of the Worcester institution. The number and type of patients, the time spent in the hospital, and the quality of care were all dependent to a significant degree upon the framework established by law. This framework, at least at the time of its creation in 1832, seemed reasonable and proper, given the goals of the new facility. Yet its actual operations gave rise to consequences that were not originally anticipated. When this occurred the legislature passed remedial laws, but often with little awareness of their long-range implications.

Nor was the situation appreciably different elsewhere in the country. Most legislatures provided the capital funds necessary for acquiring a site and constructing a physical plant, and also appropriated funds for renovations and expansion. But since welfare was still conceived of as a local responsibility, towns and cities were expected to pay to the hospital the actual costs of caring for dependent patients. The idea of a single appropriation by the state (based on the size of the hospital) was alien to mid-nineteenth-century legislators. In large part they were building on a system whose roots dated back to fifteenth- and sixteenth-

31. Worcester State Lunatic Hospital, *AR*, II (1834), 23, X (1842), 33–34; Trustees' meeting of February 22, 1842, in "Trustees Records, 1832 to 1849," Worcester State Hospital, Worcester, Mass.

32. Grob, *The State and the Mentally Ill*, 91–95, 205–208.

century English precedents and colonial experiences.

To be sure, practices varied somewhat from state to state. Some paid the salaries of hospital officers directly out of the state treasury; others provided subsidies so that localities would pay a sum below actual costs; some required local officials to pay for the costs of independent families which nevertheless could not afford the costs of protracted care; and some, as a result of experience, moved to assume the costs of supporting either poor and indigent patients or even all patients irrespective of their pecuniary status. In Vermont and New Hampshire the state helped to defray some of the costs of indigent patients, although localities were still liable for their share. After passing a law in 1857 which stipulated that poor insane persons were to be sent to the hospital but offered no funds for their support, New Hampshire provided a subsidy. In New York, New Jersey, and Pennsylvania the state paid the salaries of the officers; localities or families paid the rest. The Empire State mandated a system that made admission a function of county population, while Pennsylvania eventually provided some subsidies to lower the cost to localities. The situation in the South and West was equally mixed. Maryland made its counties responsible for the support of pauper patients, but because the amount the counties paid was insufficient to cover costs, the Maryland hospital set a limit on the maximum number of such patients. South Carolina followed basically the system adopted in Massachusetts; the hospital made up its deficit by charging private patients more than actual costs. North Carolina paid the hospital directly for the care of patients, and then charged 80 per cent of the total to the counties. In Illinois all patients were charged actual costs and the counties were held liable for those persons who could not afford to pay. Much the same was true in Missouri and Michigan.[33]

33. For descriptions of the systems in individual states see the following sources: *The Vermont Asylum for the Insane: Its Annals for Fifty Years* (Brattleboro, 1887), 28, 69–70; New Hampshire Asylum for the Insane, *AR*, XVI (1857), 8–9, 15–16; David M. Schneider, *The History of Public Welfare in New York State 1609–1866* (Chicago, 1938), 354–355; New Jersey State Lunatic Asylum, *AR*, III (1849), 10–11, V (1851), 33–34; *By-Laws Adopted by the Managers of the New Jersey State Lunatic Asylum* (Trenton, 1848), 34–35; Pennsylvania State Lunatic Hospital, *AR*, VI (1856), 2–3; Maryland Hospital, *AR*, 1853, 9–10, 1858 and 1859, 17–20 (1859); New York *Senate Document No. 20* (January 12, 1842), 148; Ohio

In less than a decade after the opening of most public institutions the defects inherent in the governing framework had become obvious. Hospitals found their facilities overtaxed by both the pressures to admit new patients and the simultaneous demand that chronic and dangerous individuals be retained. Few institutions, if any, had complete control over their admissions and discharge policies, and this situation made their destiny dependent upon external authorities or impersonal forces and events. While many legislatures ultimately provided expanded facilities, the lead time required for passage of an appropriation, planning, and construction was considerable. On many occasions the new quarters were inadequate to meet the demand by the time they were ready for the reception of additional patients.[34]

The nature of the legal, administrative, and financial framework established by states also created numerous financial problems that had severe repercussions upon individual hospitals. The sum paid for pauper patients was often insufficient or marginal; slow and delinquent payments by local authorities caused severe cash-flow problems; and inadequate or tardy state appropriations compounded existing difficulties. It was by no means unusual for

Lunatic Asylum, *AR*, IV (1842), 12–13, XVII (1855), 14, 16; *Reports of the Illinois State Hospital for the Insane 1847–1862* (Chicago, 1863), 38–39; Michigan Asylum for the Insane, *BR*, 1861/1862, 11; Missouri State Lunatic Asylum, *BR*, III (1856/1857), 39–40; Worcester State Lunatic Hospital, *AR*, XXX (1862), 18–22; Tennessee Hospital for the Insane, *BR*, I (1852/1853), 18–20.

34. For conditions at fairly typical institutions see Virginia Western Lunatic Asylum, *AR*, XV (1842), 21–22, XIX (1846), 34–36, *BR*, 1859/ 1860–1860/1861, 55–56; Virginia Eastern Asylum, *AR*, 1847, 8–10, 16–21; New Hampshire Asylum for the Insane, *AR*, VII (1848), 8–9, VIII (1849), 40; Indiana Hospital for the Insane, *AR*, VI (1854), 14–20, IX (1857), 5–11; South Carolina Lunatic Asylum, *AR*, 1850, 6–7, 1852, 6ff.; New Jersey State Lunatic Asylum, *AR*, VI (1852), 20–21; Maryland Hospital, *AR*, 1857, 5ff.; Tennessee Hospital for the Insane, *BR*, III (1855/ 1857), 46–47; *Reports of the Trustees and Building Commissioners of the Wisconsin State Hospital for the Insane. December, 1859* (Madison, 1859), 12–14; Mississippi State Lunatic Asylum, *AR*, 1859, 23–25; Insane Asylum of California, *AR*, IX (1861), 20–25; Pennsylvania State Lunatic Hospital, *AR*, IV (1854), 7–8, V (1855), 7–8, VIII (1858), 7–8; Missouri State Lunatic Asylum, *BR*, II (1853/1854), 32–37, IV (1857/1858), 18–19; Michigan Asylum for the Insane, *BR*, 1865/1866, 5ff.

hospital officials to borrow money or to issue scrip in order to keep their institution open. The superintendent of the Maryland hospital complained in bitter terms about this problem in 1858, and in 1867 the trustees of the Kansas State Insane Asylum, faced with pressing indebtedness, authorized its treasurer to sell scrip to county treasurers for as little as 92 cents on the dollar.[35] In Massachusetts and South Carolina private patients were charged above-average sums in order to compensate for the below-average payments for paupers. Jarvis, who had pointed this out clearly in his report on insanity in 1855, attempted to get the Massachusetts legislature to enact a law directing the Commonwealth to pay the full costs for state paupers in public hospitals. "It is a little remarkable," he wrote to Earle, "that our State, instead of finding means to lighten the burden on the families of the poor or in straitened circumstances should lay a heavy tax on them, when in the hospitals, by making them pay more than the actual cost, in order, that the Commonwealth may pay less for its patients, the Irish pauper!"[36]

The existing structure, moreover, also created a situation that led to continuous friction between hospital authorities and town and municipal officials. In many states the stipulation that localities were financially liable for their pauper insane made selectmen and overseers of the poor attempt to provide for such individuals in almshouses, where the cost was far less than in hospitals.[37] If, on the other hand, the state assumed complete financial responsibility for the care of paupers at its hospitals, localities were apt to reduce welfare costs by shifting the burden to the state and flooding hospitals with chronic cases.

Superintendents were by no means unaware of the residual

35. Maryland Hospital, *AR*, 1858 and 1859, 11–12; Trustees' meeting of June 14, 1867, "Record Book of the Trustees, 1865–1868," Library of Osawatomie State Hospital, Osawatomie, Kansas.

36. *Report on Insanity and Idiocy in Massachusetts*, 65–68; Jarvis to Pliny Earle, December 26, 1864, Earle Papers, AAS. See also Jarvis to Earle, February 10, 1865, Earle Papers, AAS.

37. Cf. Maine Insane Hospital, *AR*, II (1841), 27, IV (1843), 8–10, XIII (1853), 10–11, XIV (1854), 8–10; New Hampshire Asylum for the Insane, *AR*, VI (1847), 8–10, XIX (1860), 20–21; Pennsylvania State Lunatic Hospital, *AR*, I (1851), 4, VII (1857), 17–19; Grob, *The State and the Mentally Ill*, 87–91.

difficulties that accrued to their institutions under this system. Only a few years after assuming the superintendency of the Maine hospital (which was then only four years old), Isaac Ray addressed himself to the problem in a clear and incisive manner. Hospitals, he noted, were costlier than poor houses since their goals and objectives were different and required greater expenditures to implement. Expenses could be cut "by herding their inmates together in large numbers, and furnishing a scanty attendance." Or paupers could be provided with cheaper care and private patients with more expensive care. To both of these options Ray was opposed. He admitted that the burden on towns, especially small ones, was extremely heavy. If all expenses were assumed by the state, on the other hand, the tendency would be to send all mentally ill persons to hospitals, including those who were comfortable at home, forcing the hospital to accept some and reject others—a policy that would create "dissatisfaction and distrust." Ray's solution was to have the hospital charge a rate equal to the cost of home care, and then to have the state make up the deficiency. Although other problems would arise under this system, no patient would be "debarred from receiving the benefits of the institution by considerations of economy, while there will be no inducement to place in it those who are comfortable enough at home."[38] Ray's dissatisfaction was shared by other superintendents, for their experiences with local communities and dual financial responsibility did not differ in any fundamental way.[39]

Slowly but inexorably the ambiguities growing out of the administrative, financial, and legal framework were resolved by the centralization of responsibility for the mentally ill in the hands of the state. This did not mean, at least initially, that all mentally ill persons were placed under state jurisdiction. For a good part of the nineteenth century, as a matter of fact, the majority of such persons were still kept in local welfare institutions financed and

38. Maine Insane Hospital, AR, IV (1843), 22–25. See also ibid., II (1841), 27, XIII (1853), 10–11, XIV (1854), 9–10.

39. Cf. South Carolina Lunatic Asylum, AR, 1842, 23; Ohio Lunatic Asylum, AR, VII (1846), 43–44; New Hampshire Asylum for the Insane, AR, VI (1847), 8–9, XIX (1860), 20–21; Pennsylvania State Lunatic Hospital, AR, VII (1857), 17–19; Maryland Hospital, AR, 1857, 15; Missouri State Lunatic Asylum, BR, III (1856/1857), 39–40.

administered by local communities.⁴⁰ The results of a system whereby state institutions were partly dependent on revenue from private individuals and local governments proved so unsatisfactory, however, that ultimately many states moved to assume complete responsibility for all insane persons in public hospitals. This tendency was more evident in the West than in the East. By the time of the Civil War, for example, Ohio, Indiana, Illinois, Wisconsin, and California paid for the total costs of institutionalization irrespective of an individual's pecuniary status. Kentucky, Missouri, Louisiana, Tennessee, Mississippi, and Georgia accepted responsibility for all pauper insane persons (although Missouri charged its counties for the cost of clothing). While not all states moved as rapidly in this direction, a number began to modify their practices. Some agreed to pay part of the costs of upkeep, thereby relieving individuals and communities of the entire burden; some provided lump sum appropriations; and many paid for the salaries of the officers, which were usually not chargeable to communities or individuals.⁴¹ Nevertheless, progress was by no means automatic and backsliding was sometimes evident. Wisconsin in 1871 reverted to the older system when it made counties partly responsible for the support of its poor and indigent insane citizens in public hospitals and families partly responsible for the support of relatives. Not until 1904 did Massachusetts, which by all criteria was the most influential state in setting precedents for the care and treatment of the mentally ill in the nineteenth century, assume financial responsibility for its public institutions and relieve local communities of the burden.⁴²

The assumption by states of the responsibility of financing

40. In the northern Ohio hospital district in 1869, 302 insane persons were in local institutions, while the average population of the state hospital was 294. Northern Ohio Lunatic Asylum, *AR*, XV (1869), 4–5. In Michigan in 1873 far more were in local welfare institutions than in the state hospital. The Michigan County Superintendents of the Poor heard a report at their convention that was highly critical of the system, and urged a state takeover. Michigan Board of State Commissioners for the General Supervision of Charitable, Penal, Pauper, and Reformatory Institutions, *BR*, II (1873/1874), 70–71.

41. For a description of the practices of many states in the early 1860's see Worcester State Lunatic Hospital, *AR*, XXX (1862), 18ff.

42. Wisconsin State Hospital for the Insane, *AR*, XII (1871), 6–7; Grob, *The State and the Mentally Ill*, 330–332.

institutional care, however, did not appreciably alleviate the problems of mental hospitals. For by the time the takeover occurred, the structure and functions of most public hospitals had become fixed. Although the pressure of the initial governing framework was somewhat lessened by centralization, its residual impact remained evident for decades to come. Future generations, therefore, were always faced with the results of an imperfect system. Consequently, both psychiatrists and policy officials had to begin with an ongoing system that was extraordinarily resistant to change, a fact that had significant implications for the mentally ill during the latter half of the nineteenth century and well into the twentieth.

The most significant attempt to alter the manner in which states financed mental hospitals was undertaken by Dorothea L. Dix, who had a clear grasp of the issues involved. In 1848 she presented a lengthy memorial to Congress requesting legislation that would provide for the distribution of 5,000,000 acres of federal land to the states, the proceeds of which would be used for the support of the indigent insane. Precedents for such a subsidy already existed, since education and railroads had already benefited from federal land grants. Although some misunderstanding of her plan was evident, she quickly received support from the AMSAII and prominent reformers such as Horace Mann and others.[43]

For the next six years Dix labored strenuously to convince the members of Congress that the project was desirable and important. Initially legislators evinced little interest in the bill; the sectional conflict that had intensified after the close of the Mexican War absorbed most of their energies and time. Through her persistent lobbying, however, support for the bill began to mount. Nevertheless, the thirtieth Congress permitted the bill to lapse. At the next Congress Dix returned with a bill asking for more than 12,000,000 acres, and later requested an appropriation for an

---

43. *Memorial of D. L. Dix, Praying a Grant of Land for the Relief and Support of the Indigent, Curable and Incurable Insane in the United States. June 27, 1848*, 30th Cong., 1st Sess., *Senate Miscellaneous Document No. 150; Boston Medical and Surgical Journal*, XXXIX (August 2, 1848), 25–26; *AJI*, V (January, 1849), 286–287, VII (July, 1850), 86, VIII (July, 1851), 90; Horace Mann to Dix, December 15, 1849, Dix Papers, HLHU.

insane hospital for the armed forces to be situated in the District of Columbia. Much of the debate in Congress revolved around the constitutional question of whether or not the federal government had the legal authority to use the public domain for such projects. Finally, both houses in early 1854 passed a bill setting aside 10,000,000 acres to be used by the states for the indigent insane. Dix's ecstasy over her success proved of short duration, for the act met with a presidential veto. "I cannot but repeat what I have before expressed," wrote Franklin Pierce in his message to Congress, "that if the several States, many of which have already laid the foundation of munificent establishments of local beneficence, and nearly all of which are proceeding to establish them, shall be led to suppose, as they will be, should this bill become a law, that Congress is to make provision for such objects, the fountains of charity will be dried up at home, and the several States, instead of bestowing their own means on the social wants of their own people, may themselves, through the strong temptation, which appeals to States as to individuals, become humble suppliants for the bounty of the Federal Government, reversing their true relation to this Union." When the presidential veto was upheld by a wide margin, the issue of federal support disappeared as a viable alternative for decades to come, although the following year Congress enacted legislation that established the Government Hospital for the Insane in Washington.[44] For the remainder of the nineteenth and the early part of the twentieth century responsibility for the mentally ill would continue to be borne by the state and local communities.

44. The controversy can be followed in the *Congressional Globe*, 30th–33d Cong.; 31st Cong., 1st Sess., *House Report No. 487* (August 8, 1850); 33d Cong., 1st Sess., *Senate Report No. 57* (January 23, 1854); 33d Cong., 1st Sess., *House Report No. 125* (March 29, 1854); Francis T. Stribling to Kirkbride, September 23, 1850, August 21, 1852, Kirkbride Papers, IPH; Millard Fillmore to Dix, September 27, October 7, 1850, Ray to Dix, September 15, 1851, G. S. Hillard to Dix, May 6, 1854, Ellen D. Walker to Dix, May 10, 1854, M. T. Torrey to Dix, May 12, 1854, Anne E. Heath to Dix, May 22, 1854, Fillmore to Dix, May 26, 1854, Dix Papers, HLHU. For some reactions to the veto see the newspaper clippings in the Dix Papers, HLHU. There are also accounts in Francis Tiffany, *Life of Dorothea Lynde Dix* (Boston, 1890), 167–200, and Helen E. Marshall, *Dorothea Dix: Forgotten Samaritan* (Chapel Hill, 1937), 129–154.

IV

The increase in the size of mental hospitals and the accumulation of large numbers of chronic patients—both of which in part grew out of the general legal and administrative framework established by most states—in turn had a pronounced impact upon the internal structure and functions of most institutions. Both of these developments directly contradicted many of the cherished theoretical precepts of moral therapy, which assumed that hospitals—like families—would remain small, and that superintendents—like firm but loving fathers—would have the ability and flexibility to manipulate the environment in order to promote the mental health of their patients (i.e., their children). In the minds of most psychiatrists the objectives of moral treatment required close and intimate interpersonal relationships without many mediating influences between physician and patient.

As long as hospitals remained small, superintendents were able to supervise personally the care of their patients and conduct routine administrative duties as well. There was, after all, no inherent conflict between these two tasks. But as institutions grew in size and the nature of the patient body changed, superintendents found it increasingly difficult to meet both these responsibilities. No longer were they able to run their institutions in a loose and informal manner. With three, four, and five hundred patients the problems of social organization and adjustment were far more complex. The heterogeneous nature of the patient population merely compounded the problems arising out of growth, for each category of inmates seemed to require a different type of care and treatment. The needs of older patients, of chronic patients, of patients suffering from a somatic form of mental disease (e.g., general paresis), of insane criminals, of alcoholics, and of patients amenable to therapy all differed sharply in many respects and oftentimes proved antagonistic or irreconcilable with each other. The theory of moral treatment frequently did not offer answers or guidelines to cope with such problems, for it rested on largely individualistic premises. Since the theoretical framework of most mid-nineteenth-century psychiatrists did not provide for the coordination or rationalization of an individualistic-ally oriented therapy with the demands of a complex system with quite different and even opposing objectives, the tendency was for the demands of the social system to outweigh the requirements of moral treatment. Thus superintendents were faced with a cruel dilemma; their concern for the welfare of their patients increasingly came into conflict with the larger goal of maintaining order and administrative rationality in a complex social institution.

Many superintendents, though recognizing the ways in which their institutions deviated from their ideal, were unable to adjust their theoretical outlook in the light of changing circumstances. Instead they continued to reaffirm their faith in small therapeutic institutions modeled along familial lines. When queried by a legislative committee about the proper size of an institution, one superintendent provided a revealing answer that offered an analysis of his problems as well as an indication of his bewilderment. At the time his institution had an average daily census of over 400. "I confess my inability," he noted,

> to do justice to my feeling in its management. I cannot sufficiently keep myself acquainted with the various departments to act understandingly. I cannot know the daily changes in the symptoms of 450 patients—the operations on the farms and in the workshops —the domestic operations—direct the moral treatment—conduct the correspondence with friends—wait upon such visitors as demand my personal attention and various other things which are daily pressing upon the attention of this Superintendent. Many of these matters in large Hospitals must be attended to, if attended to at all, by those who do not and cannot act so faithfully and understandingly as the Superintendent could and would.

One man, he continued, was incapable of supervising a hospital that had more than 100 patients. While a large hospital had certain inherent advantages—better classification facilities, a large staff—its disadvantages far outweighed any possible benefits. "As mechanical business thrives best under the immediate eye of the master workman," he observed, "so it is with the management of the insane. The patients expect and desire frequent intercourse with the Superintendent for it is in his care they are placed. He, if any one, has their confidence and he can usually control them better than any one else. If he has under his charge more than one hundred he finds it difficult to know their personal history and the daily changes of their condition." Condemning any intermediaries between the superintendent and the patient, he recommended the establishment of small or moderately sized hospitals contiguous to the community they served.[45]

Outside pressure further compounded the difficulties faced by institutional psychiatrists. Hospitals, for example, played dual roles; they performed therapeutic and custodial functions. As long as they remained small, it was relatively easy for psychiatrists to combine both roles.[46] The gradual growth in the size of hospitals, however, made this more difficult. Superintendents, faced with an administrative structure that limited their authority over admissions and discharge policies and maximum institutional size, were increasingly confronted with the necessity of having to sacrifice one of their roles in order to perform the other. Given a choice, there is little doubt that therapeutic considerations would have been dominant. But superintendents could not be concerned only with the welfare of the patient; they had to take into account the demands of society for protection against those who ostensibly menaced the security of the community. "Hospitals," noted one superintendent, "are yet far too much regarded as mere places of confinement and their inmates as prisoners, and are supposed to be kept up more for the safety of the community and the convenience of friends who wish to be relieved of the trouble of taking care of them at home than for the welfare and benefit of the patients themselves."[47]

The growing internal complexity of the goals, structure, and functions of mental hospitals also hastened the transformation of psychiatry into a basically administrative and managerial occupation. An intricate social institution like a mental hospital required formal mechanisms to ensure order and efficiency; formal mechanisms, in turn, often defeated the aim of moral treatment, which

45. George Chandler, "On the proper number of patients for an institution . . ." (undated, c. 1848), Chandler Papers, AAS. See also Worcester State Lunatic Hospital, *AR*, XVI (1848), 39–40, XIX (1851), 13–14.

46. Cf. Ray's comment in Maine Insane Hospital, *AR*, II (1841), 36.

47. J. H. Worthington to Pliny Earle, January 16, 1872, Earle Papers, AAS. See also N. D. Benedict to Dix, May 16, 185?, Dix Papers, HLHU.

was based on the ability of the physician to manipulate the environment of the individual and group as the need arose. Custodial considerations merely reinforced administrative concerns, for custody required a tight and efficiently run institution governed by rational and clearly defined procedures. In effect, the rise of what might be conveniently designated as administrative psychiatry reflected the dominance of an institution in which therapeutic concerns were slowly being pushed into the background.[48]

Over a period of time psychiatry began to lose the charismatic aura of its early years and became endowed with some of the qualities often associated with managerial occupations—order, regularity, efficiency, rationality. "There is no institution," announced the superintendent of the St. Louis County Insane Asylum in 1870, "in which men and women are to be sequestered from the community where, so much as in an Insane Asylum, *perfect system* is required. 'Order is Heaven's first law,' and is the basis of all good results in the management of our institutions for the care or custody of the unfortunate. It has been our aim to impress all in their respective departments with the importance of this principle, as well as a strict compliance with the established rules."[49] Most individuals who served as superintendents, of course, were hardly aware of the transformation of their profession, largely because it occurred so slowly. For most of them it seemed easier to debate problems of administration, organization, architectural standards, occupational therapy, and efficient heating and ventilating systems, and to issue blanket condemnations of overcrowded conditions, than to experiment or to innovate within their institutions where they still retained a measure of autonomy.[50] One superintendent even came to the conclusion

48. I do not mean to imply that administrative psychiatry and therapeutic concerns are *necessarily* incompatible, but rather that the dominance of the former at a particular juncture in time and within a specific context set it in opposition to the latter. Ideally an administrative specialty must be viewed in terms of a means–end relationship; the basic problem is whether the specialty serves predetermined goals or becomes an end in itself.

49. St. Louis County Insane Asylum, *AR*, I (1869/1870), 4.

50. An examination of the *American Journal of Insanity*, the most authoritative journal of its kind in the United States, and the history of the AMSAII offers evidence of the managerial and administrative nature

that a steward was "of much more importance to me and the Hospital than a young physician."[51] Disclaimers to the contrary, administrative psychiatrists tacitly accepted the role defined for them by society; they became the agents charged with the responsibility of implementing the by now vague and multiple goals of mental hospitals.

Nowhere were the pressures on superintendents better revealed than in the heated nineteenth-century debate over the use of restraints. For if large institutions with heterogeneous patient populations were to be conducted in an orderly and rational manner, what should be done with those inmates whose behavior was disruptive and threatened either their own safety or that of others and resulted in property damage? Could mental hospitals be run so loosely and informally that no impediments would be placed in the way of those who attempted to flee their confines? What would be the response of the community, which after all had sanctioned and supported the institution, if seemingly dangerous persons could disrupt the routine or even escape?

In theory, of course, most superintendents agreed that internal self-control was the ideal check on behavior, and that rational persuasion was clearly preferable to the use of force. Nevertheless, there were circumstances when the use of restraints was indispensable. Restraint was justified if employed for "the positive benefit or safety of the patient" and never to facilitate the task of those staff members and attendants to whose care the patient

---

of nineteenth-century psychiatry. The pages of the journal were notable for the absence of articles embodying the results of original research. While French, German, and to a lesser extent British physicians were performing autopsies, correlating symptoms with pathological anatomy, studying the nervous system, and trying to observe the course and development of identifiable disease entities, their brethren across the Atlantic tended to be somewhat aloof from such concerns. Similarly, the annual conventions of the AMSAII were devoted to managerial and administrative issues. As late as 1872 Kirkbride introduced a long motion relative to overcrowding, which promptly stimulated a long discussion at the end of which time the resolution passed unanimously. The resolution in effect urged governing boards not to accept more patients than the hospital could effectively accommodate. Yet there was virtually no inclination to discuss possible structural alternatives in the care and treatment of the mentally ill. See *AJI*, XXIX (October, 1872), 179–201, 242–243.

51. J. A. Reed to Dix, January 17, 1860, Dix Papers, HLHU.

was entrusted.[52] In this respect American superintendents were extraordinarily hostile toward John Conolly and his so-called nonrestraint system that became popular in England in the 1840's and afterwards. Nonrestraint, they felt, was impossible to implement either in theory or in practice. Often what went under the name of nonrestraint was actually restraint. Indeed, they charged the British with a form of self-deception. Seclusion and isolation of patients in padded cells, which were among the techniques employed by British alienists, in many instances had a more adverse effect upon patients than restraints, American superintendents argued, since such practices removed them from virtually all human contacts. Or else, according to Ray, the English system was nothing more than bringing together "a mass of patients of every description, under no restraint, and *taking their chance for the result.*" Ray, on the other hand, preferred "the merit of anticipating an evil and providing for it." John Bull, he concluded, "like many other beasts is easily deceived by a little false show, especially when his self-complacency is gratified at the same time."[53]

Nevertheless, the growth in the size and heterogeneity of institutions and the problems of recruiting an effective and disciplined corps of attendants tended to increase reliance on the actual or potential use of restraint as a means of institutional control. This development was recognized by the trustees of the Worcester hospital, who regretted that circumstances did not permit adoption of the British system.

> But there was always a crowd of patients within the Hospital, and more pressing for admisssion. Those in charge deemed it necessary to use these [strong] rooms. Still, therefore, men and women were thrust into them, and made more furious by the

52. Pennsylvania Hospital for the Insane, *AR*, II (1842), 41. For similar comments see Worcester State Lunatic Hospital, *AR*, VIII (1840), 79–80; Maine Insane Hospital, *AR*, II (1841), 48–49, V (1844), 30–31; Ohio Lunatic Asylum, *AR*, IV (1842), 68; Utica State Lunatic Asylum, *AR*, I (1843), 51–52; Virginia Eastern Asylum, *AR*, 1845, 26–30; Pennsylvania State Lunatic Hospital, *AR*, II (1852), 17; Taunton State Lunatic Hospital, *AR*, I (1854), 40.

53. Ray to Jarvis, November 21, 1863, Jarvis Papers, CLMHMS. See also Ray's comments in Butler Hospital for the Insane, *AR*, XVI (1862), 14–25.

confinement; and still many others were restrained by straps and various mechanical contrivances, who might have had freedom of motion, and the use of their limbs, if sufficient space and sufficient means of medical and moral treatment had been at command, and if there had been fuller faith in the efficacy of milder measures. The principal evil, and that which seemed to justify the use of so much seclusion and restraint, was the crowd of patients.[54]

Many superintendents clearly preferred restraint to the alternative of relying on attendants to enforce a minimum of order, if only because the caliber of the nonprofessional personnel left much to be desired. Restraint was never arbitrary; its use was strictly limited and carefully regulated. More often than not the welfare of the patient was better served by its judicious use. While some superintendents attempted to reduce its frequency (especially if their institutions were new and small), they were unwilling to abandon it altogether. Luther V. Bell, for example, was able to experiment along this line in the 1840's precisely because of McLean's small size and select patient body,[55] and for a brief time Amariah Brigham attempted to emulate Conolly at Utica. "I have determined," he wrote to Earle, "to try the disuse of mechanical Restraint à la Conolly—and have hired additional help and got all hands ready to cooperate and will earnestly and fairly try it. I am inclined to think that although such restraints do good in some cases—(just as a few strokes of the whip would in some instances) yet the bad moral effect might counterbalance all good—so I will try."[56] But in most institutions, especially the larger ones, restraint remained an important means of ensuring order and efficiency. Indeed, some superintendents argued that institutionalization in any case was a form of restraint; the real debate, therefore, was over means, not ends.[57]

If anything, the use of restraint probably increased in the

54. Worcester State Lunatic Hospital, *AR*, XXII (1854), 30–31.

55. McLean Asylum for the Insane, *AR*, XXV (1842), XXVII (1844), XXVIII (1845), in Massachusetts General Hospital, *AR*, 1842, 22, 1844, 14–15, 1845, 14–19; Kirkbride to Bell, December 11, 1844, Kirkbride Papers, IPH.

56. Brigham to Pliny Earle, February 27, 1845, Earle Papers, AAS.

57. Cf. Tennessee Hospital for the Insane, *AR*, 1866, 8–9, and Ray to Jarvis, September 29, 1860, Jarvis Papers, CLMHMS.

years following 1850. While superintendents—for obvious reasons —were reluctant to make public statements, they found themselves impelled to rely on it as patient populations increased and the caliber of attendants remained poor or mediocre. "We are obliged to restrain many of our patients," noted the superintendent of the insane department of the Philadelphia Almshouse. "I think it a far more human plan than allowing them [to be] knocked down by assistants—which is the case in many Institutions where it is pretended that no restraint is used."[58] At the North Carolina hospital the superintendent reported that with the limited assistance furnished by the existing corps of attendants it was impossible to dispense with restraints.[59] Dr. Charles A. Lee, a critic of the use of restraints and an advocate of separate institutions for curable and chronic patients, felt that restraints were the rule rather than the exception. "I find in nearly all our asylums they are in pretty general use, and I could name some asylums in your State," he wrote to Jarvis, "where I have seen patients confined with iron chains nearly as large as *ox-chains,* and that within the last six months."[60] And Dr. John C. Bucknill, the distinguished British alienist who made an extensive tour of American mental hospitals in the mid-1870's, was especially critical of the reliance on restraint.[61]

While they staunchly advocated the necessity of restraint, most superintendents were usually defensive or apologetic in their tone. The first meeting of the AMSAII in 1844, for example, adopted a resolution stipulating that the best interests of the insane were not served by the abandonment of restraint. Brigham, Bell, and Kirkbride had second thoughts on including it in the published proceedings because they felt that it might be misunderstood and used by their critics. Lacking the power to re-

58. D. D. Richardson to Jarvis, April 22, 1858, Jarvis Papers, CLMHMS.

59. Edward C. Fisher to Jarvis, May 13, 1868, *ibid.*

60. Charles A. Lee to Jarvis, January 2, 1871, *ibid.* Cf. Joseph L. Bodine, "The Management of the Insane Without Mechanical Restraint," Conference of Charities, *Proceedings,* III (1876), 104–106.

61. John C. Bucknill, *Notes on Asylums for the Insane in America* (London, 1876), 65ff. Bucknill wrote the book as a response to the even harsher criticisms of American practices by *The Lancet.* See Bucknill to Henry I. Bowditch, January 23, 1877, CLMHMS.

word it, they deleted the resolution from the printed record of the proceedings.[62]

For the next three decades much the same tone was evident. Most institutional psychiatrists felt that the use of restraint was legitimate if it was intended for the benefit of the patient, but admitted that internal problems of management facilitated the frequency with which it was employed. There was unanimous hostility toward Bucknill at the convention of the AMSAII in 1877, even though his book (and a number of earlier statements as well) had defended American hospitals against the far more critical charges of *The Lancet*, a British medical periodical. In one of its editorials *The Lancet* indicted American psychiatrists for the way in which they conducted their hospitals. "It is surprising, but unhappily it is notorious," stated the journal, "that in the United States the treatment of lunatics can hardly be said to have made much progress even in the stage of development which we have reluctantly described as the 'humane.' The sort of humanity which sways too many governors of asylums in the United States might indeed be inspired by a rule similar to that said to have been made for the officers of Bethlehem Hospital after the removal to Moorfields in 1675:—'No keeper or servant shall beat or ill-treat a lunatic without he considers it absolutely necessary for the better governing of the lunatic.'" Bucknill, on the other hand, had discussed American practices in a less emotional tone and had argued that public distrust of asylums grew out of their modus operandi. After apologizing to his American brethren for criticizing them, he looked forward to the time when American institutions would also attempt to implement the principles of nonrestraint, which had gained widespread popularity in England and on the continent without harmful results to either patients or society. The superintendents who took part in the debate at the meeting, nevertheless, were unanimous in their conviction that Bucknill was in error, and they refused to concede that nonrestraint was a real possibility.[63]

62. Kirkbride to Luther V. Bell, November 13, 1844, Kirkbride to Amariah Brigham, November 18, 23, 1844, Kirkbride Papers, IPH.

63. The controversy can be followed in the following sources: Bucknill, "American Lunatic Asylums," *AJI*, XXXII (April, 1876), 582–585; *idem*, "Speech . . . 1876," *ibid.*, XXXIII (October, 1876), 324–329; *idem*, "Notes on Asylums for the Insane in America," *ibid.*, XXXIII (July, 1876),

The use of restraint as a means of institutional control represented in many ways a partial compromise of the tenets of moral treatment, for it reflected the growing administrative ethos of hospital superintendents, whose concern for internal order and rationality seemed to outweigh the individual and sometimes unique needs of patients. But the increase in size and heterogeneity of the patient population that had helped to foster this ethos was by no means the only development that had hindered the full application of the tenets of moral treatment. Another barrier to the implementation of these theoretical precepts lay in the character of the corps of attendants and nurses. In theory the ideal attendant and nurse (both of whom played vital roles in the therapeutic regimen) were remarkable individuals. They were kind, patient, and considerate; they were able to gain the confidence of patients; they could take even the most vile abuses without responding in kind; they were firm yet honest and open in their dealings with inmates; they were intelligent and informed; and they were completely obedient to the instructions of the superintendent. For as moral treatment succeeded brute force in the management of the insane, so were the positions of nurse and attendant correspondingly magnified in importance. "None should be employed for the delicate and difficult task," the regents of the South Carolina Asylum noted with approval in quoting their counterparts in New York State, "but well educated persons, of moral worth, actuated by a high sense of duty, and possessing sound discriminating judgment, firmness, sweetness of temper, conciliatory manners, unwearied patience, and inexhaustible kindness."[64] Since the implementation of the principles of moral management could not be left to the superintendent and his one or two medical assistants, it was clear that the major share of the responsibility would fall upon the shoulders of nurses and attendants.

21–41 (October, 1876), 137–160; *idem., Notes on Asylums for the Insane in America,* 65–88; *The Lancet,* November 13, 1875, 705–707, February 12, 1876, 254–255, 263–264; *Boston Medical and Surgical Journal,* XCIII (December 9, 1875), 681–686, XCV (August 31, 1876), 268–269; *AJI,* XXXIV (July, 1877), 27–58 (October, 1877), 217–243.

64. South Carolina Lunatic Asylum, *AR,* 1842, 7. See also Pennsylvania Hospital for the Insane, *AR,* II (1842), 42–43, XXIX (1869), 25–29; New York State Commissioner in Lunacy, *AR,* I (1873), 25.

In practice, of course, few attendants and nurses possessed all or most of the ideal qualities so eagerly sought. "They are in fact," noted Ray, "plain every-day men and women, with the common infirmities of the race, losing their temper under extraordinary irritations, and sometimes guilty of downright abuse of their trust. This is the truth, and there would be as little wisdom in denying it, as in expecting that persons on becoming attendants upon the insane, are transformed by some mysterious process, from ordinary men and women into angels."[65] A few institutions experienced only minor problems, but most found the difficulty so severe as to be a source of considerable concern. Nor were superintendents certain that it was possible to eliminate all abuse of patients by attendants; they simply hoped that constant vigilance on their part would minimize the possibility of such abuses.[66]

The problems posed by unqualified and generally inferior nurses and attendants were undoubtedly most acute at urban municipal institutions such as existed in New York, Brooklyn, Philadelphia, Cincinnati, and Boston. At the New York City Lunatic Asylum attendants were drawn from among the inmates of the penitentiary. These keepers and attendants, complained the physician in 1843, were

> criminals and vagrants, who have neither character nor discretion to take care of themselves. The bad effects of this system in the introduction of vulgarity and profanity into our halls, is painfully evident. Many of the patients are well aware of their character. Instead of respecting and loving their attendants, they become embittered against them, and consequently irritable and fretful— of course, much to their prejudice. . . .
>
> The impropriety of this arrangement, as well as its sad effect upon these wretched beings, must be apparent to every one. Man, in his best mental and moral condition, is ever apt to imitate and acquire bad habits; peculiarly is this the case in man who has lost the chart of reason. . . . [Without attendants] no occupation, work, or amusement can be entered upon. Had we every facility

65. Isaac Ray, "The Popular Feeling Towards Hospitals for the Insane," *AJI*, IX (July, 1852), 53.

66. Cf. Pliny Earle, "Answers to Interrogatories propounded by E. G. Miner, President of the Board of Trustees of the Illinois State Hospital for the Insane," c. September 9, 1867, copy in the Earle Papers, AAS.

for these, the patients could not be trusted to improve them, but must, as at present, be confined to their narrow halls, or, when the weather permits, be turned into their fenced enclosures, to bask in the sun, or saunter about in listless ennui.

Although the superintendents of the institution were adamant in their condemnation of the use of such persons as attendants, the practice persisted for decades in one form or another.[67] As late as 1875 the superintendent of the New York City Asylum for the Insane, Ward's Island (which had been founded a few years earlier to care for the city's male insane, while the Blackwell's Island institution cared for females), condemned the use of convicts whose presence had "a constantly and powerfully depreciating effect upon its tone and discipline." Moreover, the fact that political considerations played a role in the selection of the regular attendants aggravated the situation, while low wages and long hours hampered recruitment. Matters were further complicated by a chronic shortage of attendants; in the larger wards a single attendant had to take care of as many as sixty-five patients. The result was a turnover rate of astonishing proportions. In 1875, for example, the Ward's Island institution had only two attendants who had been serving in that capacity for more than one year. During the same year there were sixty changes; twenty-two resigned and thirty-eight were dismissed (sixteen for drinking, five for striking patients, and the remainder for various other infringements of the rules).[68] While the New York City institutions were clearly among the worst in the country, other municipal hospitals had similar problems. The size of these asylums and

67. *Report of the Resident Physician of the Alms-House Establishment*, New York City Board of Aldermen *Document No. 119* (May 8, 1843), 1405–1406; New York City Lunatic Asylum, Blackwell's Island, *AR*, 1848, 27–28, 1849, 23–24, 1850 (in New York City Governors of the Almshouse, *AR*, II [1850], 97–100), 1855, 6–7, 1875, 22, 29–30; "Account of a Visit to 9 institutions in 1845 by Dr. Thomas S. Kirkbride and Mr. Jacob Morris," ms. in the Kirkbride Papers, IPH.

68. New York City Asylum for the Insane, Ward's Island, *AR*, III (1874), 18–20, IV (1875), 21–25. For a description of the penal and eleemosynary institutions of New York, Boston, Baltimore, and Philadelphia see the "Report of Committee on Penal and Reformatory Institutions," in *Annual Report of the Public Institutions of St. Louis County, for the Fiscal Year Ending August 31, 1875* (St. Louis, 1875), 5–19.

small supervisory staffs tended to maximize opportunities for abuse. Bucknill was particularly hostile toward Northern municipal asylums; he was convinced that they were among the worst in the country.[69]

At many Southern hospitals, on the other hand, a different problem existed. The low sums appropriated by legislatures in some cases simply prevented hospital authorities from hiring staff. Such was the case in South Carolina, and in Tennessee the superintendent reported in 1847 that he had a total of one female and two male attendants. Virginia solved its problems by utilizing the services of black slaves. At the Williamsburg hospital hired slaves did all of the menial work and occasionally acted as attendants. Its superintendent believed that this practice made it easier to hire a "better class" of white personnel, since their status within the institution was higher than that of their Northern counterparts. Francis T. Stribling of the Western Lunatic Asylum attempted to convince his directors to allow the purchase of slaves; in this way he would be able to get blacks with the "proper requisites." How well this system worked at the Virginia institutions is unknown, although Woodward noted during his Southern tour that Stribling had "some serious obstacles to great success especially the employments of slave labor." And Stribling himself complained in 1844 that the rapid turnover among hired black slaves was working to the detriment of the hospital.[70] The superintendent of the Georgia institution, whose attendants consisted solely of hired black slaves, had equally strong reservations about this state of affairs. Where "every *word, look,* and *action,* may exercise an important influence upon the disordered, peculiarly

69. New York State Commissioner in Lunacy, *AR*, III (1875), 45–46; S. W. Butler to Kirkbride, June 25, 1860, Kirkbride Papers, IPH; William L. Peck to Dix, March 18, 1872, Dix Papers, HLHU; *Testimony Given before the Committee of the City Government, in the Case of Charles Frost; Together with the Argument of C. M. Ellis, Esq., Touching the Management of the Lunatic Hospital; November 10, 1865* (Boston, 1866), *passim;* Bucknill, *Notes on Asylums for the Insane in America,* 40–53.

70. South Carolina Lunatic Asylum, *AR*, 1849, 9; Lunatic Asylum of Tennessee, *BR*, 1846/1847, 4; Virginia Western Lunatic Asylum, *AR*, XVII (1844), 25–26, *BR*, 1855/1856–1856/1857, 53; Francis T. Stribling to Jonathan Bramson, July 20, 1858, Dix Papers, HLHU; Woodward to George Chandler, July 28, 1844, Chandler Papers, AAS; Dain, *Disordered Minds,* 43, 82–84, 157–158.

sensitive and impressionable mind, it will surely require no argument to show, that it cannot be otherwise than mischievous, to allow that negroes should be their frequent, indeed, at sometimes, almost constant associates, and often in circumstances requiring that they should (for the moment at least) exercise authority and assume control over them." He urged that the hospital be permitted to hire suitable white attendants, and also be permitted to purchase its own slaves for certain tasks (a policy that would presumably prove less costly to the state).[71]

While municipal and Southern institutions had specific problems that did not for the most part exist elsewhere, virtually every hospital in the country faced the general difficulty of recruiting and retaining qualified persons. As institutions increased in size the problem was exacerbated by the fact that more and more responsibilities fell on the shoulders of attendants, since the number of physicians in most institutions did not increase as rapidly as the number of patients. The growth of the responsibilities of attendants and nurses was not accompanied by efforts to upgrade the caliber of those hired and to provide some type of training. Although many institutions had a few faithful and competent persons, the norm was an extraordinarily high turnover rate that often ran between one-third and one-half of the staff annually. The positions of attendants and nurses were demanding ones; individuals who occupied them had to work long hours and were required to live on the hospital grounds. Salaries, even by contemporary standards, were low. In 1844 Kirkbride paid his male attendants $10 per month and females $8—sums that he felt were far too small to attract the type of persons he required. (New York City shoemakers, by way of comparison, received at this time between $4 and $6 per week and woodworkers between $5 and $8, and neither of these occupations was among the highest paid.) And Kirkbride's institution, being private, possessed somewhat more flexibility than its public counterparts. Indeed, even private institutions—which catered to a far more select clientele—had much the same problem as public institutions. "By and by in the good time certainly coming," wrote the superintendent of the Hartford Retreat in turning down a request to supply another institution with one of his attendants, "when *Brains* shall be more

71. Georgia State Lunatic Asylum, *AR*, 1846/1847, 11–12.

esteem'd than *Dollars*, the public will demand that we employ a higher grade of service and intelligent charity will supply the material."[72]

The inexperience and high turnover rate among nurses and attendants severely hampered attempts by superintendents to implement the principles of moral treatment. The growth of institutions was usually accompanied by the transfer of many of the superintendent's functions to the nonprofessional staff.[73] The result was an ironic situation, for the increasingly important role of the nonprofessional staff—which gradually assumed a mediating position between the patients and the superintendent (whose concerns were now largely administrative and managerial) and provided the latter with information vital to the effectiveness of the hospital—was not matched by a commensurate increase in its quality. The relative shortage of nurses and attendants at many hospitals further compounded existing problems.[74] "In general,"

72. Kirkbride to Luther V. Bell, September 14, 1844, Kirkbride to the Board of Managers of the Pennsylvania Hospital, September 26, 1844, Kirkbride Papers, IPH; John S. Butler to Edward Jarvis, July 4, 1859, Jarvis Papers, CLMHMS.

73. One superintendent who favored greater liberty for patients remarked that he had doubled the number of attendants and was contemplating further additions "because I find every additional attendant enables me to add to the privileges of the patient." W. S. Chipley to Dix, August 4, 1858, Dix Papers, HLHU.

74. For typical statements see the following: New Hampshire Asylum for the Insane, *AR*, VII (1848), 24–25; Kentucky Western Lunatic Asylum, *AR*, 1864, 11–12; Worcester State Lunatic Hospital, *AR*, III (1835), 29–30, XXII (1854), 85, XXXIII (1865), 55–58, XXXIV (1866), 77–78, XXXV (1867), 74; Tennessee Hospital for the Insane, *BR*, 1868/1869, 27; *Report of the Investigating Committee on the Hospital for the Insane, Made to the Governor of Illinois, December 1, 1867*, in *Reports Made to the General Assembly of Illinois at its Twenty-Sixth Session, Convened January 4, 1869*, III, 65–68; Brigham Hall, *AR*, 1872, 8–9; Pennsylvania State Lunatic Hospital, *AR*, XXII (1872), 10–11; Wisconsin State Board of Charities and Reform, *AR*, II (1872), 183–185; Wisconsin State Hospital for the Insane, *AR*, XIV (1873), 18–19; Missouri State Lunatic Asylum No. 2, *BR*, I (1875/1876), 34–36.

Existing evidence indicates that the quality of attendants declined between 1830 and 1875. The absolute and relative increase in the number of complaints during these decades is striking. See also Ray's discussion of this point at the meeting of the AMSAII in 1871, in *AJI*, XXVIII (October, 1871), 322–323.

according to the New York State Commissioner in Lunacy, "attendants come from that class of society which furnishes us our house-servants; and yet no house-servant would endure, in a private family, the onerous duties that devolve upon similar persons in an asylum. In an ordinary household, if one servant were assigned the care of a demented member it would be considered a sufficient task; whereas, in too many of our public asylums one attendant has to take charge of from eight to fifteen patients." He recommended that a system of promotions and rewards be instituted in order to attract and to retain desirable personnel.[75]

Aside from low pay, long hours, and low status, the role of attendants in mental hospitals was scarcely a challenging one. Although superintendents prior to 1875 were aware of the problem, few ever considered the possibility of offering training to nurses and attendants and giving them greater responsibilities within the institution. Treatment was the sole prerogative of the physician; at best lay personnel were useful auxiliaries. Since mental illness, like smallpox and other organic diseases, was a pathological condition of a patient, responsibility for his care and treatment had to remain within the hands of the psychiatrist. The doctor-patient relationship was an inviolate one that precluded, at least in theory, the intrusion of any third party. While psychological factors entered into etiology and therapy, the patient was still viewed as a passive agent who was active only in the sense that he followed or complied with the directions of the physician. Given such a medical model, it was easy to understand the fact that relatively few attendants were employed in a deliberately meaningful manner. An extreme (but by no means atypical) view was expressed by Andrew McFarland in a paper at the meetings of the AMSAII in 1860. McFarland, superintendent of the Illinois State Hospital for the Insane and president of the association, remarked that there was only one quality that disqualified an individual from assuming the duties of an attendant, namely, disobedience. "No individual," he maintained,

> should ever be trusted in this capacity, who cannot implicitly and promptly comply with the wishes of the head of the institution in which he is engaged. What might be a servility in other departments of hired service, is only a just and proper require-

75. New York State Commissioner in Lunacy, *AR*, I (1873), 26.

ment, in an employment so responsible as this. No superintendent of a hospital for the insane should omit, in his regular injunction of rules, to place the reasons for the most strict compliance with his wishes, in strong light upon those who are to execute them. If this should become more a usage in all our institutions, it would gradually bring up the tone of strict and healthful discipline, throughout our whole specialty. Certainly, the stern necessities of military service do not require any more prompt compliances than our own.[76]

The continued use of restraint, staff problems, and the transformation of psychiatry into a largely administrative specialty were not the only indications of the gap between the ideal hospital and reality. In other ways as well, the rapid increase in patient populations plus the lag in constructing commensurate facilities operated in ways antithetical to the expressed goals of mental hospitals. Occupational therapy was a case in point. Most superintendents made occupational therapy one of the foundation stones of moral treatment. But as institutional facilities were overtaxed, fewer and fewer patients were provided with meaningful work. Such a situation complicated behavioral problems. "In passing through the different wards of the asylum," observed some Michigan officials, "it seemed to the Board that the great lack of the institution was a want of the means to interest and occupy the attention of the inmates. Many of them were apparently without anything to divert the mind, or draw it away from the consideration of the malady that besets them. There seemed to be a dearth of occupation and amusement."[77] These comments were fairly typical, for superintendents themselves freely admitted that they were unable to provide employment for many of their patients. During a European tour in 1860 Edward Jarvis noted that Americans had much to learn from the Old World. European asylums, he reported, had occupational facilities of all sorts. Also, their institutions "dispensed with all means of restraint, more than we have. They have no strong

76. *AJI*, XVII (July, 1860), 55.

77. Michigan Board of State Commissioners for the General Supervision of Charitable, Penal, Pauper, and Reformatory Institutions, *BR*, II (1873/1874), 35.

rooms [and] no means of confining hand. . . . Some of the asylums have no grates or iron-protected windows."[78] In effect, the conditions under which growth occurred in the mid-nineteenth century together with its consequences intensified the process of institutionalization at mental hospitals.

V

By the 1860's the cumulative impact of rapid growth and the influence of the existing legal and administrative framework had combined to undermine many of the therapeutic goals of mental hospitals, a fact that was partially reflected in the decline in official curability rates. Faced with a structure that permitted them relatively little flexibility insofar as the number and type of patients was concerned, superintendents found the gap between theory and practice increasing rather than decreasing. As their hospitals took on more and more of a custodial character, they unwittingly transformed their own occupation into an administrative and managerial specialty, with a consequent loss of the élan and charisma that had marked the first generation of superintendents in the early part of the nineteenth century. Moreover, their unquestioned authority within hospitals and relative professional isolation served to reinforce their administrative and managerial outlook, making them unreceptive and often intolerant toward those with differing views. Institutional psychiatry, therefore, became a bulwark rather than a foe of the existing system, for it was difficult for its members to behave in ways contrary to the dominant standards of their own profession. Like countless generations of human beings, they saw impersonal forces beyond their control (and sometimes their comprehen-

78. Jarvis to Kirkbride, September 20, 1860, Kirkbride Papers, IPH. For another unfavorable comparison of American with British hospitals see H. B. Wilber, "Management of the Insane in Great Britain," New York State Board of Charities, *AR*, IX (1875), 175–220. Upon becoming superintendent of the Taunton hospital in Massachusetts, W. W. Godding wrote to Dix that "the great indoor amusement that never wears out or grows old here is lying on lounges and in bed. This seems to be thoroughly ingrained into their lives." Godding to Dix, September 13, 1870, Dix Papers, HLHU.

sion) overwhelming them and giving rise to developments they neither sought nor desired. And as mental hospitals deviated more and more from their early goals, American society would face grave and puzzling problems relating to the manner in which it provided for its mentally ill citizens.

Chapter VI

Class, Ethnicity, and Race
in Mental Hospitals

I

THE GROWING OBSTACLES that hampered the therapeutic activities of most public mental hospitals were undoubtedly related to the limitations placed upon the authority of the superintendent by the legal, administrative, and financial framework established by most states. Nevertheless, the character of these hospitals was by no means a function of external influences alone. On the contrary, internal practices and prevailing staff attitudes, both of which were related to the class, ethnic, and racial composition of the patient population, contributed also to the transformation of mid-nineteenth-century institutions in subtle ways.

The theoretical framework that governed the psychiatric profession and the formulation of public policy, of course, assumed the equality of all persons and their inalienable right of access to care and treatment on a nondiscriminatory basis. That private hospitals existed alongside public institutions made no difference; there were virtually no individuals advocating that the state discriminate or differentiate on the basis of class, ethnicity, race, religion, or in any other manner. Indeed, the means adopted by most states to support mental hospitals assumed equal access to public facilities; the costs were to be borne either by the local community or the family, depending on the individual's pecuniary situation.

A theoretical framework, of course, rarely corresponds precisely with reality; few persons behave in ways that are completely consistent with their ideals. In many instances the situational choices put individuals in morally ambiguous positions; in others behavior reflects affective factors that are often at variance with supposedly rational principles. Whatever the case, most human institutions generally fall far short of ideal types precisely because individuals and groups—often without a clear recognition of the sources of their conduct—behave in ways that appear inconsistent or in direct conflict with the principles that stipulate the manner in which they *ought* to behave. As institutions evolve, modifications are introduced that often compound rather than alleviate the difficulty. Furthermore, many ameliorative efforts are undertaken without either an adequate knowledge of the magnitude and complexity of the problem or an awareness that partial modifications within a total system influence and change the system itself in a frequently unpredictable manner.

The evolution of the mental hospital offers a good illustration of how a social institution established with the best and most honorable of intentions may be inadvertently transformed by the behavior of individuals and groups. In theory hospital officials never discriminated against patients on any basis whatsoever; all persons received identical care and treatment. Hospital practices, however, deviated from theory. Some superintendents manifested unconscious hostility toward patients coming from backgrounds different from their own; some structured the hospital in ways that inadvertently promoted discriminatory practices; and some shared many of the racial, ethnic, and class attitudes and prejudices of the larger society. Much the same was true of state legislators and public officials. It was also not at all uncommon for patients to behave in ways that ultimately defeated attempts to ensure that equal care and treatment would be made available for all Americans.

The pattern of differential care that ultimately prevailed at mental hospitals was not a simple phenomenon, for the influences of class, ethnic, and racial factors were not equal, nor did they operate independently of each other. It is possible, however, to spell out with some degree of precision the relationships between class, ethnicity, and race on the one hand and the quality of care and treatment on the other hand. In general, the best care was given native-born paying patients. On a descending scale, they were followed by native-born poor and indigent patients, and below them were poor and indigent immigrants. At the bottom were blacks, who received the lowest quality of care.

The persistence of practices that resulted in less than equal treatment for some groups was to have profound implications for the institutional care of the insane in the United States. For ultimately the mental hospital—precisely because it reflected many of the same class, ethnic, and racial antagonisms of the larger society—found itself incapable of providing the therapeutic care for which it was first established. As it lost its therapeutic character, the mental hospital was converted into a welfare receptacle that provided inexpensive custodial care for a variety of groups, including those deemed dangerous to the security of the community, the aged, the poor, and those individuals seemingly incapable of surviving unless within a highly structured environment. Moreover, the custodial character of most public hospitals contributed to the managerial nature of the psychiatric profession, since the overwhelming bulk of practitioners prior to 1880 were basically administrators whose outlook and values were molded by their institutional environment. Indeed, by 1875 critics could condemn the mental hospital on the grounds that it subverted rather than fostered humane values.[1]

II

In most public mental hospitals native-born poor and indigent patients did not receive the same care as patients who paid for

1. E. C. Seguin, "The Right of the Insane to Liberty," in Conference of Charities and Correction, *Proceedings*, VII (1880), 143ff.; Seguin, "Lunacy Reform—Historical Considerations," *Archives of Medicine*, II (October, 1879), 184–198, and "Lunacy Reform. II. Insufficiency of the Medical Staff of Asylums," *ibid.*, II (December, 1879), 310–318; William A. Hammond, "The Treatment of the Insane," *International Review*, VIII (March, 1880), 225–241; *National Association for the Protection of the Insane and the Prevention of Insanity* (Boston, 1880); Dorman B. Eaton, "Despotism in Lunatic Asylums," *North American Review*, CXXXII (March, 1881), 263–275. None of these writers cited were disinterested critics, for they were pushing their own alternatives (which will be discussed in Chapter VIII).

the costs of institutionalization. Yet the differences were contained within relatively narrow limits. In part this situation reflected the fact that superintendents and patients for the most part shared a common cultural and religious heritage. It should also be kept in mind that not all or even most of the mentally ill persons supported at public expense in hospitals were paupers; in many cases the family income level simply did not allow for an illness that required protracted institutionalization (particularly if the hospitalized individual was the principal wage earner). The values of superintendents, moreover, did not place a premium on wealth; most regarded excessive materialism (but not labor) as a prime cause of disease. Consequently, there was no conscious disposition to punish poor and indigent patients. The differential care that did exist arose largely out of two factors: a desire to maintain a heterogeneous patient body, which in turn helped to assure the broad community support such institutions required; and—a more subtly operating factor—a homogeneous ward structure.

While overt discrimination between patients coming from different class backgrounds was not immediately visible, a careful analysis of the manner in which hospitals functioned reveals its presence in many subtle ways. Inadvertent discrimination, for example, grew out of the manner in which hospitals were structured and administered. As hospital managers, superintendents had to organize their hospitals. Being physicians, they naturally thought in terms of the traditional divisions of general hospitals with their fairly elaborate system of wards to care for different types of cases (e.g., surgery, infectious diseases, pregnancy). So too mental hospitals were divided into wards. But upon what basis should wards be organized? One possibility was a series of wards corresponding to the diagnostic categories then in use. Most superintendents, however, were not especially impressed with the traditional division of insanity into mania, melancholia, and dementia, if only because the relationship of these categories to therapy was not at all clear. Another possibility was to assign patients to wards on the basis of their date of admission or even on a purely random basis. Neither of these alternatives was seriously considered because from a therapeutic viewpoint they did not appear to be based on a rational analysis.

Fortunately the principles of moral treatment offered to most superintendents a sure guide. If the creation of a new environment played a crucial role in the treatment of mental disease, then it followed logically that assignment of patients to wards was of vital importance because the internal environment was in part a product of the interaction of patients with each other. A rational system of classification thus became one of the cardinal tenets of moral management. Luther V. Bell in 1841 made classification one of his four indispensable principles of moral treatment (the other three being separation from the patient's previous environment, direction within the hospital, and occupational therapy), and Kirkbride in his classic work on hospital architecture also insisted on its importance.[2] Though minor disagreements on specifics existed, no superintendent was disposed to question the vital importance of proper classification.

If proper classification was an indispensable part of moral treatment, how could its effect be maximized? Obviously wards had to separate the sexes, given the fundamental physical differences between men and women and the need for discouraging illicit sexual relationships. Kirkbride, as a matter of fact, felt that in areas so populous as to require two hospitals, it was desirable to have separate institutions for each of the sexes (a plan actually implemented at the New York City municipal asylums in the early 1870's).[3] Beyond the separation of the sexes, there was general agreement that earlier practices both in the United States and abroad of placing patients in different wards on the basis of status or the amount paid for board was improper, for it brought together "the violent maniac, the drivelling idiot, and the tranquil monamaniac, the outrageous, profane, and noisy, the convalescent, the timid, and the sensitive."[4] The assignment of similar cases (e.g., violent with violent) to the same ward, while a better

2. McLean Asylum for the Insane, *AR*, XXIV (1841), in Massachusetts General Hospital, *AR*, 1841, 22–23, 30–31; Thomas S. Kirkbride, *On the Construction, Organization, and General Arrangements of Hospitals for the Insane* (Philadelphia, 1854), 58. For examples of similar statements see Virginia Western Lunatic Asylum, *AR*, XV (1842), 34–35; New Jersey State Lunatic Asylum, *AR*, VII (1853), 14–15; Friends' Asylum for the Insane, *AR*, XXXIX (1856), 15; Vermont Asylum for the Insane, *AR*, XXIV (1860), 12.

3. Kirkbride, *On the Construction . . . of Hospitals for the Insane*, 59–60.

4. Worcester State Lunatic Hospital, *AR*, XII (1844), 89.

method, still presented problems. The best and most rational system, in the words of Kirkbride, was "to associate in the same ward those who are least likely to injure and most likely to benefit each other, no matter what may be the character or form of their disease, or whether supposed to be curable or incurable."[5]

Such a system of classification appeared to provide all patients with an environment that promoted therapy and avoided any type of differential care. In practice, however, this system did not work out in line with the theory. In deciding to bring together patients who could benefit each other, superintendents were in effect adopting a system partly based on socioeconomic characteristics, for they often employed social, educational, cultural, and religious criteria for classifying patients. They were especially concerned—to quote Woodward—"that no one shall associate with those particularly obnoxious to him."[6] Another superintendent, although denying that he drew "unnecessary distinctions" among his patients, nevertheless argued that a patient's previous environment had to be taken into account if therapeutic aims were not to be subordinated to other goals. "It is certainly exceedingly unpleasant," he noted,

> to be almost compelled to associate with those whose education, conduct and moral habits, are unlike and repugnant to us. Because persons are insane, we must not conclude that they always lose the power of appreciating suitable associates, or are insensible to the influence of improper communications. This is by no means true. It is among our greatest perplexities here, to know how to quiet the complaints of those whose delicacy is shocked, whose tempers are perturbed, and whose quietude is annoyed by improper and unwelcome associates.[7]

The assignment of similar-type patients to particular wards was an understandable practice, for most individuals tended to move in homogeneous circles. This procedure, however, set the stage for other inherently unequal practices. Most psychiatrists felt that the hospital environment should replicate as closely as possible those features of the patient's home environment that had not played a part in bringing on mental disease. Consequently,

5. Kirkbride, *On the Construction . . . of Hospitals for the Insane*, 58.
6. Worcester State Lunatic Hospital, *AR*, XII (1844), 89.
7. Kentucky (Eastern) Lunatic Asylum, *AR*, 1845, 24.

patients from middle-class backgrounds as well as private patients tended to be assigned to more luxurious accommodations and receive greater privileges. At the Worcester hospital such patients were permitted to keep their trunks in their own rooms and take charge of their own clothing, books, and work.[8] Similar procedures were followed at other hospitals.

The fact that hospitals provided (within certain well-defined limits) differential care did not go unnoticed by the psychiatric profession. While recommending that more affluent patients be provided with certain luxuries if they so desired, one superintendent warned against the practice of drawing distinctions openly since it would destroy "the contentment of the many . . . for the indulgence of the few." He recommended that complete separation between paying and nonpaying patients was the only means of alleviating the problem and preventing it from hampering the therapeutic process.[9] Another superintendent insisted that invidious distinctions could only be abolished if all patients—irrespective of their financial condition—were admitted on a nonpaying basis.[10] Nevertheless, to the majority of superintendents there seemed clear and compelling reasons for differential care. Isaac Ray for one felt that patients from the "poor and laboring" class required less attention than those from "educated and affluent" backgrounds. The former were used to working and were content with simple pleasures such as a walk in the country or performing small tasks. The latter, on the other hand, could only "be satisfied by long and repeated interviews with the superintendent." Each class, therefore, required different forms of therapy.[11] With some isolated exceptions, most psychiatrists saw no reason why hospitals should not provide certain amenities to patients able and willing to pay for them.[12]

8. Worcester State Lunatic Hospital, *AR*, VII (1839), 89.

9. Kentucky (Eastern) Lunatic Asylum, *AR*, XXIII (1845), 24–25, XXIV (1846), 20.

10. Ohio Lunatic Asylum, *AR*, XIII (1851), 20–23.

11. Ray, "Observations on the Principal Hospitals for the Insane in Great Britain, France and Germany," *AJI*, II (April, 1846), 387–388.

12. Cf. Kirkbride, "Remarks on Cottages for Certain Classes of Patients, in Connection with Hospitals for the Insane," *AJI*, VII (April, 1851), 376; New Jersey State Lunatic Asylum, *AR*, IV (1850), 28; Maine Insane Hospital, *AR*, XII (1852), 34; Worcester State Lunatic Hospital,

The argument most frequently employed by superintendents in defending—even urging—the admission of private patients was that their presence was essential if hospitals were to retain broad community support and avoid any process of social deterioration. They were especially fearful of seeing their institutions converted into glorified poor houses. Aside from detracting from their own professional status, such a process was clearly not in the best interests of their patients. The best means of preventing mental hospitals from becoming pauper establishments was to attract a sufficiently large number of more affluent patients, who would then make the institution more acceptable and provide a strong base of support among articulate and influential groups. Although they recognized that a dual system of private and public hospitals was already in existence, they nevertheless felt that any further extension of the system would be detrimental to the interests of the mentally ill. Moreover, the group that would be hardest hit by the conversion of the hospital into a pauper institution would be those independent families who were neither rich nor poor; they could not afford the costs of private hospitals nor would they be willing to commit relatives to public welfare institutions. Justice and wisdom therefore required a proper mix in the patient population of all public hospitals. The directors of the Ohio Lunatic Asylum recognized some of the dangers of a dual system when they took the somewhat novel step, in 1851, of abolishing all charges for private patients. In defending this action, the superintendent recalled the results of the policy of requiring patients to pay the costs of institutionalization if they could so afford.

AR, XXV (1857), 57; Kentucky Western Lunatic Asylum, *AR*, 1864, 14; Insane Asylum of Louisiana, *AR*, 1866, 6.

The available evidence offers fairly conclusive proof that differential patterns of *care* (better physical quarters, privileges, etc.) existed at most hospitals. Evidence about differential *treatment* is far more difficult to come by, if only because there are virtually no descriptions of treatment in terms of what psychiatrists actually did with patients. Aside from drugs and other medication (which were probably administered on a nondiscriminatory basis), I have assumed that differential care inevitably involved differential treatment. If the success of moral treatment rested on the creation of a certain type of internal therapeutic environment, it is difficult to see how patients would not react adversely to clear patterns of differential care and how this reaction would not impair the effectiveness of moral management.

The distinction was invidious; its bad consequences were manifold, and far outweighed all pecuniary advantages. Often did our halls resound with the exclamation, "*You* are only a pauper, *I* pay for my board.". . . But if she [Ohio] does not pursue the course she has commenced—if she does not speedily make ample and free provision for *all* those of her insane requiring constant care —private establishments, where the luxury indulged in by the patients is graduated by the scale of weekly payments, will spring into being, and the distinction, so invidious and pernicious among individuals in the same hospital, will exist equally invidiously and perniciously between public and private institutions. These latter will most certainly attract nearly all whose relatives are able to pay the sum demanded for their maintenance in them; and *State institutions will sink to the level of pauper establishments.*[13]

A heterogeneous patient population, argued many superintendents, had other beneficial therapeutic effects. Although classification usually resulted in homogeneous patient wards, it was virtually impossible to maintain a rigorous and unyielding system of internal segregation on the basis of class. Consequently, there was considerable interaction among patients, often with positive results for all concerned. The superintendent of the New Jersey Asylum noted that many desirable behavioral traits could be secured "by a proper association of different individuals." Francis T. Stribling at the Virginia Western Lunatic Asylum employed classification as an incentive for good behavior. Paying patients who misbehaved were removed "to a circle better adapted" to their dispositions and habits. Such a system, he argued, induced patients "to efforts of self-control and self-respect, for the purposes of retaining their place or ascending still higher in the scale of distinction."[14]

Interestingly enough, superintendents in general evinced little overt hostility toward the native poor and indigent insane. While their theoretical discussions seemed to imply that mental disease

13. Ohio Lunatic Asylum, *AR*, XIII (1851), 22–23. For similar comments see Worcester State Lunatic Hospital, *AR*, XIII (1845), 45, XXVI (1858), 10; New Jersey State Lunatic Asylum, *AR*, IV (1850), 28; Kentucky (Eastern) Lunatic Asylum, *AR*, 1845, 27.

14. Virginia Western Lunatic Asylum, *AR*, XIV (1841), 56; New Jersey State Lunatic Asylum, *AR*, VII (1853), 15. See also Worcester State Lunatic Hospital, *AR*, XXVI (1858), 56–57.

was often self-inflicted by those who disobeyed the natural laws that governed their behavior and whose character was morally deficient, they did not necessarily draw the conclusion that poor and indigent persons who had become insane were therefore less deserving. As a matter of fact, they insisted that the state had a moral obligation to help such unfortunate persons in order that they might recover and become self-supporting. From a therapeutic point of view virtually no psychiatrist favored a policy that was basically penal in nature. Indeed, Ray maintained that the United States lacked a permanent pauper class such as existed in England. The British pauper, he wrote, "is a being sui generis. . . . He is born of paupers, lives a pauper, dies a pauper, and leaves behind him a train of pauper successors." The future for such persons promised no chance of improvement and hope was entirely absent; confinement in a mental hospital was a welcome relief from the vicissitudes of life. In America, on the other hand, poverty was "a casual condition, a temporary misfortune, the result of accident, disease, or mischance, and dies out with its unfortunate subject." Such differences made Americans far less deferential and far more independent; they simply would not observe the "distinctions of rank" characteristic of English society.[15] If this were true, then it would be difficult, if not impossible, to provide blatantly discriminatory care within hospitals.

III

Although native-born and indigent patients at mental hospitals did not receive the same precise care as private patients, their lot tended to be better than that of foreign-born inmates (especially those coming from Ireland). To put it another way, ethnicity—particularly of the non-Protestant variety—when combined with a lower-class background, increased the differential in care at many institutions. This was not true, of course, of private hospitals which did not receive poor patients from minority ethnic groups for the most part. The differential was greatest in New

15. Ray, "Observations on the Principal Hospitals for the Insane in Great Britain, France and Germany," *loc. cit.*, 344–347. For a similar analysis by Woodward see Worcester State Lunatic Hospital, *AR*, XIII (1845), 22.

England hospitals and least in institutions located in areas with small immigrant populations.

At precisely the same time that most states were establishing mental hospitals, the pace of immigration to the United States began to accelerate. The individuals who flocked to American shores between 1840 and 1860 were far less likely to be of Protestant descent than seventeenth- and eighteenth-century immigrants. About two-fifths of the nearly 2¾ million immigrants who entered the United States between 1847 and 1854 were Irish Catholics who had fled their native land following the devastating famines of that period. Another third were from Germany, and the remainder were from all other countries combined.

As a result of population growth from immigration and births, the number of institutionalized patients began to increase (a fact that also reflected the establishment of new hospitals and expansion of older ones). The rise in patient populations at public hospitals was often accompanied by a disproportionately high number of lower-class patients from minority ethnic groups. At the New York City Lunatic Asylum on Blackwell's Island—to cite the most extreme illustration—8,620 out of the 11,141 persons admitted between 1847 and 1870 were immigrants; of this number 5,219 were from Ireland and 2,056 from Germany. In the single year of 1850, 534 patients were foreign-born and only 121 were native Americans—this despite the fact that the foreign-born constituted slightly less than half of the city's population. Similarly, at the Longview Asylum, which served Cincinnati, 68 percent of the resident patients in 1875 were foreign-born, although this group constituted only 32 percent of the population. Urban institutions in particular, including those in New York, Boston, Philadelphia, Cincinnati, and St. Louis, had high percentages of foreign-born inmates, as did state institutions in Massachusetts. It is interesting to note that in states like New York, Ohio, Pennsylvania, and Missouri—all of which had urban-supported institutions—the percentage of foreign-born inmates at state institutions remained lower. This reflected both the pattern of locating state institutions centrally and the tendency to permit large urban areas to solve their problems on their own. Thus 77 percent of the patient population at the New York City Lunatic Asylum between 1847 and 1870 was foreign-born, while at the Utica hospital the comparable figure rarely exceeded one-third.

In Massachusetts, the differential between state institutions and the Boston Lunatic Hospital was narrower, but the latter still had a larger concentration of immigrants. The overall proportion of institutionalized immigrants in America was higher than their representation in the general population.[16]

The large number of Irish-born persons in public mental hospitals was by no means unique to these institutions. For example, at the New York City House of Refuge, an institution that cared for delinquent and neglected children, a disproportionate number of inmates were Irish. Not only did the Irish provide a far higher percentage of admissions to welfare institutions, but their death rate during cholera epidemics as well as during normal periods was significantly higher than that of native groups. The reasons are not difficult to understand. Many Irish arrived in the United States in a state of almost total destitution, which contributed to the partial disruption of the family unit. Fathers were often compelled to accept jobs as unskilled laborers away from their families on such projects as canal building, where the mortality rate from what officials called "canal fever" was abnormally high. The submarginal economic situation of most Irish families encouraged mothers and children to seek employment in

16. These figures and generalizations are based on an analysis of admissions and nativity statistics to 1875 (when available). They have been compiled from the annual reports of mental hospitals, many of which included on a regular or irregular basis detailed breakdowns of the origins of patients.

At present it is difficult to state precisely the relationship between the incidence of mental disease and class. There is little doubt that poor persons had a shorter life expectancy and suffered from various diseases associated with an impoverished environment. It does not necessarily follow, however, that the culture shock associated with immigration and the ensuing struggle for survival among lower-class and minority immigrant groups resulted in a higher incidence of mental disease. Statistically there are far more variables than class or ethnicity, including such factors as population, the level of employment in the economy, nutrition, and changing definitions of mental disease. Moreover, we know little about those individuals who migrated to the United States, as compared with those who remained behind. Definitive knowledge about the epidemiology of mental illness, as Hollingshead and Redlich have observed, is lacking at present, making it difficult to draw conclusions about the relationship between mental disease and socioeconomic factors. See August B. Hollingshead and Frederick C. Redlich, *Social Class and Mental Illness: A Community Study* (New York, 1958), 370–371.

order to survive. The result was a vicious cycle of poverty, disease, and delinquency among Irish immigrants, who then entered welfare and penal institutions at a significantly higher rate than their proportion in the general population.[17]

The growing number of foreign-born inmates at mental hospitals and welfare institutions was to have profound effects on the care of dependent groups generally. Although this was a nation of immigrants, many Americans by the early nineteenth century had begun to distinguish between desirable and undesirable types of immigration. The latter category included persons who for one reason or another were unable to assimilate and become sturdy, independent, and productive citizens. Such a distinction led toward an ambivalent value structure, which was soon reflected in the dilemma of welfare policy generally. Those who saw America as a land of equal opportunity and a haven for oppressed peoples sympathized with the newcomers and looked forward to the day when immigrants would be assimilated and share in the benefits of American society. Dependency was thus a momentary and transitory phase requiring a combination of public and private aid to help unfortunate persons overcome their problems. Others, however, were far less sanguine and feared the threat posed to American institutions by non-Protestant groups. Dependency, they argued, reflected innate character deficiencies, which public welfare simply perpetuated. Between 1830 and 1860 the older tradition of anti-Catholicism merged with the general hostility toward destitute immigrant groups, thereby contributing to the strong nativist movement of the antebellum decades.[18]

Hostility toward destitute immigrants (of which the Irish were the single largest group) was especially pronounced in the Northeast, particularly in areas where such groups constituted

17. Robert S. Pickett, *House of Refuge: Origins of Juvenile Reform in New York State, 1815–1857* (Syracuse, 1969), 1–20.

18. See Ray A. Billington, *The Protestant Crusade 1800–1860: A Study of the Origins of American Nativism* (New York, 1938); John Higham, "Another Look at Nativism," *Catholic Historical Review,* XLIV (July, 1958), 147–158; David Brion Davis, "Some Themes of Counter-Subversion: An Analysis of Anti-Masonic, Anti-Catholic, and Anti-Mormon Literature," *Mississippi Valley Historical Review,* XLVII (September, 1960), 205–224.

more than 10 percent of the population. As early as 1827 public officials had become concerned with the problem of destitute immigrants. "One of the greatest burthens that falls upon this corporation," remarked the members of a Philadelphia committee studying welfare policies in other urban areas,

> is the maintenance of the host of worthless foreigners, disgorged upon our shores. The proportion is so large, and so continually increasing, that we are imperatively called upon to take some steps to arrest its progress. It is neither reasonable nor just, nor politic, that we should incur so heavy an expense in the support of people, who never have, *nor never will* contribute one cent to the benefit of this community, and who have in many instances been public paupers in their own country. If ever the trite adage, "that charity begins at home," be adopted, as a rule of conduct, either by individuals or communities, it is especially under circumstances like the present, that it should be admitted in its fullest extent; and that the people of this district, should unresistingly suffer it to become the reservoir into which Europe may pour her surplus of worthlessness, improvidence and crime, exhibits a degree of forbearance and recklessness altogether inexcusable.[19]

The growing heterogeneity of patients in public mental hospitals that began to become evident by the 1840's was a factor of major importance; it contributed to the decline of the therapeutic institution, which assumed a harmonious and trusting relationship between doctor and patient, and helped to hasten its transformation into a custodial institution. So long as psychiatrists treated patients who came from a background similar to their own and who shared a common religion, values, and culture, no conflict ensued. But when these psychiatrists began to deal with patients—especially impoverished immigrants—whose customs, language, culture, traditions, and values seemed to diverge sharply from their own, they found themselves unable to communicate in the familiar manner to which they had grown ac-

19. *Report of the Committee Appointed by the Board of Guardians of the Poor of the City and Districts of Philadelphia, to Visit the Cities of Baltimore, New-York, Providence, Boston, and Salem* (Philadelphia, 1827), 28. See also Raymond A. Mohl, *Poverty in New York 1783–1825* (New York, 1971), *passim*.

customed. Even those psychiatrists who genuinely sympathized with the plight of less fortunate individuals found themselves in a difficult situation, for they recognized their inability to create the type of therapeutic relationship that was essential to success. "Our want of success in the treatment of their mental diseases," observed Ray with both chagrin and sympathy, "is in some degree to be attributed, I imagine, to our inability to approach them in a proper way. . . . Modes of address like those used in our intercourse with our own people, generally fall upon their ears like an unknown tongue, or are comprehended just enough to render the whole misunderstood, and thereby excite feelings very different from such as were intended."[20] "We are not so successful in our treatment of them [the Irish] as with the native population of New England," observed another superintendent. "It is difficult to obtain their confidence, for they seem to be jealous of our motives; and the embarrassment they are under, from not clearly comprehending our language, is another obstacle in the way of their recovery."[21]

The growing number of foreign-born patients in public institutions, which undoubtedly exacerbated internal problems of classification and management and rendered therapeutic relationships more difficult, led superintendents to question carefully whether or not immigrants who became insane could be cured as easily as native Americans. Was it possible that innate differences between the two groups were responsible for differential recovery rates? Had a state of chronic poverty and deprivation so impaired the mental faculties of foreigners that chances for recovery were at best remote? Or was the problem simply one of developing appropriate approaches to immigrant patients, who would then respond in the same manner as natives? These were but some of the issues that faced superintendents who had to confront immigrants not on an abstract level (as did many public officials), but rather on an everyday basis.

In general, there was no unanimity among superintendents whose heterogeneous patient populations made it difficult for them to evade some of the problems involved. Those who had small numbers of foreign-born patients had little or nothing to

20. Butler Hospital for the Insane, *AR*, 1849, 32.
21. Worcester State Lunatic Hospital, *AR*, XV (1847), 33.

say, if only because the questions seemed academic. Others saw mental illness among immigrants as an outgrowth of the process whereby individuals uprooted themselves from a familiar environment and migrated to a new and strange country some 3,000 or more miles away where they faced a multitude of problems and where their expectations far surpassed their actual achievements. Noting that over 70 percent of his patients were foreigners, one superintendent nevertheless explained this fact in terms of circumstances rather than as a consequence of natural disposition toward mental disease. "Regrets after parents, the absence of the cheering voice of friends, the cold indifference of strangers, difficulties, hardships, privations, and disappointments no doubt predispose many an immigrant to mental aberration, who, in the midst of relatives would never become the subject of insanity."[22] This point of view was held in one form or another by a number of superintendents, who found no innate, differences between foreign-born (including Irish) patients and native Americans.[23] Indeed, a few even felt that immigrants were far more susceptible to moral treatment than natives. One superintendent found German patients to be among the best; they possessed "a healthy and elastic mental constitution" and were "docile and affectionate under treatment, and grateful when they recover." The head of the New York City Lunatic Asylum was favorably disposed toward Irish inmates. Prior to their admission, he pointed out, they felt abandoned and friendless. But with sincere efforts by concerned physicians, "their complete confidence will be gained, and the great change from a hopeless and forlorn condition, gives an influence of the strongest character."[24]

Other superintendents, however, were less certain that lower-class immigrants became insane simply because of the trials and tribulations involved in the shock of moving to a strange and different land. Their contacts with such individuals had convinced them that more was involved, particularly in the case of the Irish,

22. Hamilton County Lunatic Asylum, *AR*, II (1855), 10.

23. Cf. Utica State Lunatic Asylum, *AR*, XII (1854), 25; Longview Asylum, *AR*, II (1861), 13, XVI (1875), 6; Kansas Asylum for the Insane, *AR*, VII (1871), 5.

24. Illinois State Hospital for the Insane, *BR*, *IV* (1853/1854), in *Reports of the Illinois State Hospital for the Insane 1847–1862* (Chicago, 1863), 159; M. H. Ranney, "On Insane Foreigners," *AJI*, VII (July, 1850), 56–57.

a group that provided a disproportionate number of admissions to mental hospitals and a seemingly lower recovery rate. Moreover, Irish patients presented more problems in hospitals and were less intelligent, independent, refined, and self-reliant than natives. These superintendents believed that a combination of ethnic characteristics and environmental influences was responsible for an apparently high rate of therapeutic failures and the ensuing accumulation of incurable cases. Such explanations, of course, had significant implications for the manner in which such patients were cared for within institutions as well as for the broad framework of public policy.

Few superintendents ever adopted a purely genetic explanation of the seemingly high incidence of mental illness among the Irish. Nevertheless, they found far greater problems with the Irish than with native patients. At a discussion on the subject at the AMSAII in 1857 one superintendent found foreigners to be "more noisy, destructive, and troublesome," while another commented on the low curability rate of the Irish, which he attributed to their nativity.[25] "It is the experience of all, I believe," wrote the superintendent of the Maine Insane Hospital, "who have had the care of insane Irish in this country, that they, from some cause or another, seldom recover." Isaac Ray noted that "very ignorant, uncultivated people" often failed to have any insight into their delusions and could not distinguish the subjective from the objective in their mental experience. This trait was especially common "among the lower class of the Irish."[26] The ambivalence that was inherent in such views was well expressed by Ralph L. Parsons, superintendent of the New York City Lunatic Asylum on Blackwell's Island. In discussing the differentials in curability rates between Irish and native patients, he refused to draw any hard and fast conclusions because of the complex issues involved. Many of the Irish in mental hospitals were "persons of exceptionably bad habits." In a new and strange country they experienced "many disappointments and hardships," especially at a time when they were separated from their families and friends. Their physical condition, in addition, had been severely impaired

25. *AJI*, XIV (July, 1857), 79, 103.

26. Maine Insane Hospital, *AR*, XII (1852), 19; Ray, "Doubtful Recoveries," *AJI*, XX (July, 1863), 33.

by their indigent straits, poor diet, substandard living conditions, and intemperance. "The majority of such patients," continued Parsons, "are of a low order of intelligence, and very many of them have imperfectly developed brains. When such persons become insane, I am inclined to think that the prognosis is peculiarly unfavorable."[27]

Nowhere did the combined influence of class and ethnicity have as great an impact upon care and treatment as in Massachusetts. The citizens and public officials of this state, where anti-Catholicism had a long tradition, were beginning to find by the late 1840's and 1850's that the number of destitute Irish at public institutions was increasing rapidly. At the Boston Lunatic Hospital the foreign-born inmates constituted by far the largest group. By 1846 no less than 90 of the 169 patients were immigrants; of this number 70 were from Ireland. Unhappy at this state of affairs, the board of visitors urged the state to relieve the city of responsibility of caring for immigrant paupers.[28] Much the same was true at state institutions. In 1846 only 12 Irish patients were admitted to the Worcester hospital; by 1854 this figure had risen to 96. Although the superintendent of the hospital initially attempted to avoid differential care, the pressures on him began to mount, particularly since the increase in immigrant inmates (many of whom were chronic cases) meant that fewer spaces were available for native patients. The hospital's trustees were particularly distressed that foreign patients were so numerous. The Worcester institution, they reported in 1854, "is fast becoming a Hospital for foreigners." As a result, fewer places were available for "the intelligent yeomanry" of the state—a development that they sharply condemned (although they reiterated their conviction that the state had a responsibility toward "all who congregate upon her shores"). "It is important and pertinent to the present subject," they continued,

> to bear in mind, that insanity does not change the nature of men and women; that it does not always blunt their sensibilities, or lessen their prejudices, but that, on the contrary, it often intensifies them. Among the insane of this State are wives and

27. *AJI*, XXVII (October, 1870), 158–159.
28. Boston Lunatic Hospital, *AR*, VII (1846), 2–5, 10–13. See also *ibid.*, IV (1843), 15–16, X (1849), 10–11, XI (1850), 14–16.

daughters, widows and orphans, of farmers, mechanics, ministers, schoolmasters, and the like. These women were taught in our public schools, trained up in our proverbially neat and orderly households, and accustomed to cultivated society; and, however ready and willing they might have been, when sane, to help the poor, and elevate the humble, of whatever race or color, they would have shrunk most sensitively from living next door even to a wretched hovel, and from intimate association with those who are accustomed to, and satisfied with filthy habitations and filthier habits. Now, they do not lose their sensibilities by becoming insane, and they ought not to have them wounded by being herded together in the same apartment with persons whose language, whose habits, and whose manners, offend and shock them. Besides, such associations do not promote the good of any patient, but may retard, and perhaps prevent, the cure of some.[29]

Similarly, in his famous study of insanity for the Massachusetts legislature in 1854, Edward Jarvis—noting that foreigners were enjoying the benefits of public hospitals to a far greater degree than natives—drew an unfavorable portrait of the Irish and recommended that they be sent to separate institutions. Coming from a different environment and holding dissimilar customs, attitudes, and religious beliefs, these aliens resembled the English poor rather than the native poor. The interests of all would best be served by keeping native and state paupers (Irish) apart. "Keeping in view that the style of life in the hospital should not differ so far from that to which the patients have been accustomed to at home as to offend their tastes and disappoint them," wrote Jarvis in justification of his recommendation, "and regarding the difference of domestic condition in the measure of comfort and convenience which they adopt when they have the means and the power to select for themselves, it is obvious that there may be, with equal advantage for the restoration of the curable, and the protection and comfort of the incurable, plainer and cheaper accommodations, and a smaller expenditure for the daily maintenance and management of the State paupers, than would be proper for the average of the other patients—the members of

29. Worcester State Lunatic Hospital, *AR*, XXII (1854), 10–11. See also *ibid.*, XIV (1846), 42, XV (1847), 3–4, XVI (1848), 33, XVIII (1850), 3, XIX (1851), 8–9, XX (1852), 6–7, 39–40, XXI (1853), 6–8, 52–54, XXII (1854), 73, XXIII (1855), 36.

the families of the farmers and mechanics in Massachusetts."[30] The most vehement denunciations of the situation at the Worcester hospital appeared in the pages of the influential *Boston Medical and Surgical Journal*. "Never was a sovereign State so grievously burdened," it remarked on one occasion. "The people bear the growing evil without a murmur, and it is therefore taken for granted that taxation for the support of the cast-off humanity of Europe is an agreeable exercise of their charity."[31]

Although specific descriptions of care and treatment within mental hospitals are almost nonexistent for this period, there is some circumstantial evidence that the relationships between physicians and especially Irish patients were hardly cordial, a fact that probably played a role in the effectiveness of therapy. The case histories at the Worcester hospital, for example, often in-

30. *Report on Insanity and Idiocy in Massachusetts, by the Commission on Lunacy, Under Resolve of the Legislature of 1854*, Massachusetts *House Document No. 144* (1855), 145–150. It should be noted that few of the hundreds of questionnaires received by Jarvis in taking the survey of mental illness expressed anti-Catholic or anti-immigrant sentiments (all of the correspondents were given an opportunity to give their own opinions). One of the few exceptions came from a Boston physician. "Very many of the foreign Irish population," he wrote, "say one in ten, imported into this city for the last six years, are idiots, or at least no better. Three fourths of the remaining Irish importations, are *monomaniacs*, being the *dupes* of *Catholic Priests*. One half of the whole receive aid from charitable institutions, the City or State." E. B. Moore to Jarvis, August 21, 1854, in "Report of the Physicians of Massachusetts. Superintendents of Hospitals . . . and Others Describing the Insane and Idiotic Persons in the State of Massachusetts in 1855. Made to the Commissioners on Lunacy," ms. in CLMHMS. In other words, Jarvis's hostility toward the Irish was not a product of the pressure of public opinion in any form (at least as regards the survey). See also Jarvis to Governor John A. Andrew, February 11, 1861, John A. Andrew Papers, MHS.

31. *Boston Medical and Surgical Journal*, XLV (January 28, 1852), 537. See also *ibid.*, XLII (March 20, 1850), 146, XLIV (July 9, 1851), 467, XLVI (February 25, 1852), 85. Luther V. Bell, superintendent of McLean, favored the establishment of a separate institution for Irish patients administered by an Irish superintendent and officers subject to a board of trustees. See the *Report of the Committee on Public Charitable Institutions*, Massachusetts *House Document No. 139* (April 5, 1848), 3, and Bell's article "Considerations on a New State Lunatic Hospital," *Boston Medical and Surgical Journal*, XLI (December 5, 1849), 349–355.

cluded descriptions of patient behavior that demonstrated some revulsion on the part of the physician. One Irish female, to take one example out of many, was described in 1854 in the following terms: "This girl is much of the time noisy and troublesome. Has nymphomania and exposes her person. . . . Is vulgar and obscene. . . . Is noisy destructive violent and vulgar."[32] By 1858 the superintendent had even reorganized the wards in order to maintain "a complete separation" of foreign and native inmates. Such a policy, he maintained, was not in any way motivated by considerations of economy or a desire to discriminate; treatment, though separate, was in all respects equal. In their daily life immigrants and natives lived apart and had few feelings in common. "Opposite in religion and all the notions of social life, it would not be well to class the two races in the same wards, where each must bear from the other what was considered troublesome and offensive while in health."[33] The superintendent of the Taunton hospital was of the same mind. Although his building did not permit separation on the basis of ethnicity, he kept urging that new facilities be constructed so as to permit him to segregate patients. In a like vein the head of the Northampton institution urged the state to consider some alternative policy so that hospitals would not become asylums for incurable foreign paupers.[34]

Although less pronounced and more subtle, the influence of ethnicity was especially evident in one form or another in most areas with large immigrant populations. The institutions in New York City, Philadelphia, Cincinnati, and St. Louis, all of which

32. Case No. 4710, Case Book No. 28, p. 240, Record Storage Section, Worcester State Hospital, Worcester, Mass.

33. Worcester State Lunatic Hospital, *AR*, XXVI (1858), 56–57. The *American Journal of Insanity* was especially critical of this innovation. "The complete separation in an asylum of patients of one nativity from those of another," it remarked, "is a measure for which our own experience does not suggest a sufficient motive, and which, if really necessary, indicates a state of things much to be lamented." *AJI*, XVI (July, 1859), 106–107.

34. Taunton State Lunatic Hospital, *AR*, I (1854), 8, 32–33, II (1855), 26, III (1856), 17–18, 25–26, IV (1857), 4–5, 14–15, 29, V (1858), 27–28, VI (1859), 3–4, VIII (1861), 12–13, XI (1864), 13–16, XV (1868), 14–15; Northampton State Lunatic Hospital, *AR*, VII (1862), 23–25, VIII (1863), 9–11.

had a proportion of foreign-born inmates as high as or higher than hospitals in Massachusetts, are a case in point. Like the Boston Lunatic Hospital, they were founded by their municipal governments because state-supported institutions simply did not serve the needs of these populous areas. Yet they were, as contemporary observers were quick to recognize, among the worst in the nation. They tended to be significantly underfinanced and understaffed and, as the superintendent of the New York City Lunatic Asylum noted, to be used by native and middle-class groups only infrequently precisely because of their character. Indeed, on a number of occasions this same individual complained bitterly about the fact that the Commissioners of Emigration (a state body) accepted fiscal responsibility for immigrants for only five years after their arrival; thereafter such persons were thrust upon the city for support. "There is no good reason," he remarked in 1856, "why the city of New York should be especially compelled to maintain them. The same condition of things occurring in any other country would make it clamorous for redress, by assistance from the state." Moreover, the city was in effect supporting the Utica State Lunatic Asylum through the taxes its citizens paid while deriving little or no benefit from this institution. Although he opposed differential care and insisted that all insane persons should have equal access to treatment, he noted that the crowded state of the New York City institution "destroys all efforts at classification, bringing in close proximity the violent, the filthy, the stupid, the sensitive, each mutually irritating the other."[35]

The situation in New York City as well as in other urban areas rapidly gave rise to a widespread belief that municipal hospitals served as receptacles for large numbers of undesirable elements. On occasion psychiatrists contributed unwittingly to this belief by reporting that a substantial number of inmates had previously been confined in foreign asylums. "No doubt some of these persons," noted one superintendent, "in undertaking, under the circumstances, so hazardous an experiment, were guided by advice dictated by sincere convictions as to its probable utility,

35. New York City Lunatic Asylum, Blackwell's Island, *AR*, 1853, 6, 1855, 12–15, 1856, 5–6, 11–12, 1858, 11–17.

and which indeed has often proved salutary; but with regard to the beneficiaries, there is reason to suspect that their guardians were actuated rather by a desire to be rid of costly and troublesome burdens."[36] Given the hostilities between native Americans and immigrants, it was not at all surprising that urban mental hospitals provided the lowest quality of care for patient populations composed largely of impoverished immigrants.

IV

The most significant differentials in care and treatment during the nineteenth century were clearly related to race. Blacks who became mentally ill were either denied admission to mental hospitals or else were segregated within existing institutions (where the quality of care provided them was inferior to that accorded lower-class immigrants). Yet the clear differentials that existed were—with a few exceptions—not the product of a systematic body of theory that related race and mental illness. While the scientific community in the mid-nineteenth century was engaged in an extended debate over the relative mental capabilities and the unity or separate origins of the different races,[37] superintendents rarely discussed the issue in theoretical terms.[38] As administrators, they were involved in managerial issues and spent little

36. Kings County Lunatic Asylum, *AR*, 1866, 13.

37. For discussions of racial theories see William Stanton, *The Leopard's Spots: Scientific Attitudes toward Race in America 1815–59* (Chicago, 1960), and John S. Haller, Jr., *Outcasts from Evolution: Scientific Attitudes of Racial Inferiority, 1859–1900* (Urbana, 1971).

38. Even the census of 1840, which aroused a heated controversy among some Northerners and Southerners because it purportedly showed (largely by employing data of dubious accuracy) extraordinarily high rates of insanity among free blacks, was not a subject of interest to most Northern hospital superintendents. For this controversy see the following: Albert Deutsch, "The First U.S. Census of the Insane (1840) and its Use as Pro-Slavery Propaganda," *Bulletin of the History of Medicine*, XV (May, 1944), 469–482; Stanton, *The Leopard's Spots*, 58–66; Leon Litwack, *North of Slavery: The Negro in the Free States, 1790–1860* (Chicago, 1961), 40–46; Gerald N. Grob, *Insanity and Idiocy in Massachusetts: Report of the Commission on Lunacy, 1855 by Edward Jarvis* (Cambridge, 1971), 44–48.

time in speculating about such abstract problems. Consequently, the treatment of black mentally ill persons was inevitably a function of prevailing community attitudes and practices rather than a product of the application of a body of ostensibly scientific and objective knowledge.

Outside of the South the issue of mental illness among blacks did not arouse any sense of urgency among hospital or welfare officials, if only because the proportion of blacks in the general population was low.[39] The general practice in most areas was either to exclude blacks or else to provide them with separate facilities. In this respect the policies of public mental hospitals were not fundamentally different from those of other welfare and medical institutions. At the Massachusetts General Hospital, for example, the trustees were confronted with the "painful necessity" of rejecting black applicants because of the "unwillingness of the ward patients to admit among them individuals of that description."[40] At the New York City Almshouse, on the other hand, a separate and clearly unequal building was set aside for black inmates. Such was its character that almshouse officials described it in the following terms:

> In the Building assigned to colored subjects, was an exhibition of squalid misery and its concomitants, never witnessed by your Commissioners in any public receptacle, for even the most abandoned dregs of human society. Here, where the healing art had objects for its highest commisseration, was a scene of neglect, and filth, and putrefaction, and vermin. Of system or subordination, there was none. The same apparel and the same bedding, had been alternately used by the sick, the dying, the convalescent, and those in health, for a long period, as we were informed by inmates. The situation of one room was such, that it would have created contagion as the warm season came on; the air seeming to carry poison with every breath. It was a scene, the recollections of which are too sickening to describe.[41]

39. In 1860 there were 4,097,111 blacks and 7,033,973 whites in the South; the comparable figures for the rest of the nation were 344,719 and 19,888,-564. See U.S. Bureau of the Census, *Negro Population, 1790–1915* (Washington, D.C., 1918), 44–57.

40. Massachusetts General Hospital, *AR*, 1836, 4.

41. *Report of the Commissioners of the Alms House, Bridewell and Penitentiary*, New York City Board of Aldermen *Document No. 32* (1837), 204. See also Boston Prison Discipline Society, *AR*, IX (1834), 87–88;

The availability of facilities for blacks tended to vary from state to state and institution to institution. In Massachusetts the new Worcester hospital received several black patients shortly after it opened in 1833. The trustees, including Horace Mann, were in agreement that "Africans . . . ought not to mingle with the other female patients," and resolved the issue by constructing separate lodgings for the former in the brick shop.[42] Others followed the practice of providing separate quarters. Such was the case at the Government Hospital for the Insane in Washington, D.C. In California the state asylum set aside a ward for black and Chinese patients. In Indiana, on the other hand, the state hospital rejected black applicants on the grounds of chronicity and the fact that they were not considered to be citizens. This policy came under sharp attack by the superintendent. Recognizing the existence of deeply ingrained prejudices among whites, he nevertheless insisted that the state construct separate quarters for black patients. Similarly, blacks were refused admission at Ohio state hospitals, while in Cincinnati the county jail served as the place of confinement.[43]

Prior to 1875 the number of blacks in hospitals outside the South was never large. A survey undertaken in 1863 by the American Freedmen's Inquiry Commission provided some specific data. In Maine, Michigan, Illinois, Iowa, New Hampshire, Pennsylvania, and Vermont the number admitted from the time that their respective institutions had opened to 1863 was less than 10 per hospital. At the time of the survey 3 out of 531 residents

Pennsylvania Board of Commissioners of Public Charities, *AR*, III (1872), xxxiv; Philadelphia Alms House (Hospital), *Annual Reports of the Insane and Hospital Departments*, Report of the Secretary of the Medical Board, 1870, 1–2.

42. Bezaleel Taft, Jr., to Horace Mann, April 14, 1833, William B. Calhoun to Mann, June 28, 1833, Mann Papers, MHS; Worcester State Lunatic Hospital, *AR*, XXXVII (1869), 70.

43. *Report of the Superintendent of the Government Hospital for the Insane* (Washington, D.C., 1855), 3, 5; *Majority Report of Assembly Committee on State Hospitals in Relation to Assembly Bill No. 226* [California] (n.p., n.d. [c. 1863]), 4; Indiana Hospital for the Insane, *AR*, 1854, 36–37; Richard Gundry to George T. Chapman, September 10, 1863, R. Hills to Chapman, September 21, 1863, American Freedmen's Inquiry Commission Mss., HLHU; Longview Asylum, *AR*, I (1860), 16; Central Ohio Lunatic Asylum, *AR*, XXIX (1867), 7–8.

at the Utica hospital were black; the comparable figures at the New Jersey institution were 4 and 340. Of 8,411 admissions to the Northampton State Lunatic Hospital in Massachusetts 12 were black; the figures for the Boston Lunatic Hospital were 1,764 and 30, respectively. The largest number of blacks were admitted to the New York City Lunatic Asylum; between 1853 and 1862 the institution had 98 black patients as compared with 3,813 whites. The pattern at private hospitals did not differ in any significant respects. The Friends' Asylum, Pennsylvania Hospital for the Insane, Brigham Hall, and Mount Hope Institution never accepted any blacks; McLean admitted 2 and the Hartford Retreat 6 in about four decades; Bloomingdale had cared for 1 black patient between 1852 and 1863; and the number of blacks at Butler was too small to estimate.[44]

It is difficult, however, to draw precise conclusions from these statistics. The figures dealing with the incidence of mental illness among blacks prior to 1880 were notoriously inaccurate; statistically the sample is too small; and it is not known whether blacks were discouraged from applying for admission to mental hospitals. Nevertheless, the number of admissions of black insane persons was not fundamentally different from their proportion in the general population. In New York City blacks constituted slightly more than 1.6 percent of the population as compared with 2.5 percent of the total admissions at the municipal lunatic

44. W. S. Chipley to George T. Chapman, September 17, 1863, H. M. Harlow to Chapman, August, 1863, William H. Stokes to Chapman, August 24, 1863, John Fonerden to Chapman, August 26, 1863, C. Nolker (?) to Samuel Gridley Howe, April 22, 1864, William H. Prince to Chapman, August 26, 1863, John E. Tyler to Chapman, August 24, 1863, E. H. Van Deusen to Chapman, August 28, 1863, John S. Butler to Chapman, September 7, 1863, Andrew McFarland to Chapman, August 28, 1863, R. J. Patterson to Chapman, August 28, 1863, H. A. Buttolph to Chapman, August 24, 1863, J. P. Bancroft to Chapman, August 24, 1863, J. B. Chapin to Chapman, September 4, 1863, John P. Gray to Chapman, December 4, 1863, D. T. Brown to Chapman, August 24, 1863, Moses H. Ranney to Chapman, August 24, 1863, Richard Gundry to Chapman, September 10, 1863, R. Hills to Chapman, September 21, 1863, J. A. Reed to Chapman, August 27, 1863, Kirkbride to Chapman, August 23, 1863, J. H. Worthington to Chapman, August 24, 1863, John Curwen to Chapman, August 24, 1863, Ray to Chapman, August 24, 1863, W. H. Rockwell to Chapman, August 24, 1863, American Freedmen's Inquiry Commission Mss., HLHU.

hospital; comparable figures for Maine were 0.21 percent and 0.15 percent, for Boston 1.7 percent and 1.7 percent, for New Jersey 3.8 percent and 1.2 percent, and for Michigan 0.9 percent and 1 percent. The statistics in most other Northern states were similar. This is not in any way to imply that black patients, once admitted to hospitals, received the same care as whites; in most institutions—if they were not excluded—they were cared for in separate facilities, which usually constituted de facto evidence of differential care because of their inferior quality.

Curiously enough, Northern superintendents, although artic-ulate on many issues, tended almost completely to ignore ques-tions involving mental illness among blacks. Outside of an occasional reference to the subject, they did not argue that blacks were more or less prone to insanity than whites, nor did they attempt to defend the obvious differentials in care and treatment in racial terms. Like their fellow citizens, they accepted the pre-vailing belief that separate facilities were required for white and black, a view summed up by Charles H. Nichols, a superintendent who was to become president of the AMSAII. "I think yr views & mine," he wrote to Kirkbride in 1855,

> in regard to what is a suitable provision for col'd insane agree, & that our views are that it *is the duty* of all State, County, & City Hospitals for Insane, situated in communities composed in any considerable part of blacks, whether slave or free, to receive col'd patients; that they sh'd be accommodated in special cottages or lodges situated near the main ediface for whites, but so entirely distinct from it that all desirable separation of the races may be maintained; that such an arrangement may be carried into effect without prejudice to either party, & that entirely separate Hospi-tals for col'd insane is not practicable nor even desirable.[45]

Even when the American Freedmen's Inquiry Commission under-took its survey in 1863, only a few of the more than two dozen superintendents did more than provide data about black insane persons in their institutions. John S. Butler of the Hartford Re-treat, however, remarked that the "constitutional cheerfulness"

45. C. H. Nichols to Kirkbride, April 24, 1855, Kirkbride Papers, IPH. See also Nichols to Kirkbride, April 14, 1855, *ibid.*, and *AJI*, XII (July, 1855), 43.

of blacks made them less prone to mental illness, while the superintendent of the Friends' Asylum, drawing on the familiar view
that insanity was a consequence of advancing civilization, said
that they were less liable to become insane because they were
"less educated and it might be said less civilized." Isaac Ray, an
individual noted for his skepticism, wrote that his institution had
received too few black patients for him to draw any conclusions
pertaining to incidence.[46]

Unlike their Northern brethren, Southern superintendents
were never able to ignore the problems posed by mental illness
among both free and slave blacks. Although the incidence of insanity seemed far lower among Southern blacks than among
Southern whites before 1860,[47] most hospital officials in that
section still had to contend with substantial numbers of applications for admission from either slave owners or free black
families. Given the large black population, the fact that close
contacts between black and white were unavoidable, and the
belief that whites had an obligation toward blacks, it is understandable that there was more concern with the problem in the
South than in the North.

46. John S. Butler to George T. Chapman, September 7, 1863, J. H.
Worthington to Chapman, August 24, 1863, Ray to Chapman, August 24,
1863, American Freedmen's Inquiry Commission Mss., HLHU.

47. A number of explanations of the low rate of mental illness among
slaves may apply, assuming that the incidence (as opposed to hospitalization) *was indeed low.* First, Southerners believed that slaves were not
prone to mental disease since they were not subject to the pressures of an
advanced civilization; they also tended to see bondsmen as possessing a
childlike nature. Consequently, whites may have been less prone to see
aberrant black behavior in terms of mental disease, since their perceptual
framework told them that mental illness among blacks was rare. Moreover,
childlike behavior, which might have led to a diagnosis of insanity among
whites, may have been regarded by whites as closer to black normative
behavior. Secondly, an operative factor may have been the unwillingness
of whites to commit their slaves to a hospital; not only would the labor
of the slave be lost, but the owner would be financially liable for the costs
of institutionalization. Finally, it may be argued that slavery was such a
closed and authoritarian system that slaves who behaved in strange and
deviant ways were treated so harshly that they were forced to conform to
normative standards for their group. Evidence as to the validity of all of
these explanations, however, is presently lacking.

The pattern of institutional care for blacks in the South varied from state to state. The Maryland hospital did not segregate patients, for the superintendent saw no reason for such a policy. Charles H. Nichols, however, regarded this practice as "a sort of corollary of a low view of management generally." The Kentucky Western Lunatic Asylum admitted limited numbers of slaves when the costs were borne by their owners and "when there was accommodation for them such as would prevent indiscriminate mingling of white and black." The Kentucky Eastern Lunatic Asylum, on the other hand, refused to accept slaves because the institution had no separate accommodations and, as the superintendent remarked, "it would be manifestly improper to mingle these persons with our own race." He nevertheless urged the legislature to make some provision for such individuals. The costs of maintenance, he pointed out, were nonexistent, since slave owners would have to pay the full costs of institutionalization.[48]

Without doubt the most curious situation existed in Virginia. When the Williamsburg institution opened in the late eighteenth century, the law stipulated that it would receive all "persons," but it made no mention of slaves. During its early decades the institution accepted free blacks. It is not known whether slaves were admitted then; if so, the institution was an oddity and an exception. Under John M. Galt, who became superintendent in 1841, the hospital did accept insane slaves as patients. Galt was firm in his belief that separate institutions for black and white were unfeasible and uneconomical; he was convinced that blacks could be cured either in a separate or in a completely integrated building. At his hospital black females were housed in a separate structure, while black males were kept in integrated wards with whites. Since all of the hospital's servants were black slaves, noted Galt, white patients regarded black patients "pretty much in the same light as they do the servants." By 1856, however, the hospital no longer accepted slaves, and the following year Galt, probaably under public pressure, retreated from the flexibility that he

48. Maryland Hospital for the Insane, *AR*, 1851, 7–8; Charles H. Nichols to Kirkbride, April 14, 1855, Kirkbride Papers, IPH; Kentucky Western Lunatic Asylum, *AR*, 1865, 14; Kentucky Eastern Lunatic Asylum, *BR*, XXXIII/XXXIV (1856/1857), 24.

had demonstrated in regard to the mixing of black and white.[49]

A quite different policy prevailed at the Virginia Western Lunatic Asylum. When that institution first opened in 1828, a free black was denied admission on the grounds that he was a harmless idiot; the directors argued that they accepted only dangerous persons and those amenable to therapy. Nevertheless, the institution did not accept free blacks or slaves falling into the admissible category.[50] Francis T. Stribling, the superintendent for many years, took the position that black and white should be cared for in separate and distinct institutions, although for economic reasons both could be under the authority of the same officers. "It would be mutually prejudicial to both whites and blacks," he remarked, "but especially to the former, were the two classes blended in one Asylum, or within the same enclosure. The principal reasons for this opinion are based upon a knowledge of the relation which most of the patients in our State institutions sustained to colored persons previous to their mental affliction, connected with the consideration that the prejudices existing when in health, have been aggravated, in all probability, by the morbid state of feeling which insanity mostly engenders." Stribling's policy and recommendations probably represented the feelings of citizens residing in the western part of the state, most of whom opposed public expenditures for slaves (90 percent of whom were located east of the Blue Ridge).[51]

Elsewhere in the South the pattern was equally mixed. Georgia made no provision for black insane persons, although its governor and those connected with the state asylum favored entirely

49. Virginia Eastern Asylum, *AR*, 1846, 4, 1848, 23–29, 1849, 5–6, 17; Norman Dain, *Disordered Minds: The First Century of Eastern State Hospital in Williamsburg, Virginia 1766–1866* (Williamsburg, 1971), 19, 105, 109–113.

50. *Report of the Court of Directors of the Western Lunatic Hospital, December, 1828*, document appended to the *Journal of the House of Delegates of the Commonwealth of Virginia, Begun . . . the First Day of December, One Thousand Eight Hundred and Twenty-Eight* (Richmond, 1828), 5; Virginia Western Lunatic Asylum, *AR*, XVII (1844), 26, *BR*, 1867/1868–1868/1869, 6–7; C. H. Nichols to Kirkbride, April 14, 1855, Kirkbride Papers, IPH.

51. Virginia Western Lunatic Asylum, *AR*, XVIII (1845), 7–8, 29–31, XXI (1848), 4–5, 32–34, *BR*, 1867/1868–1868/1869, 6–7.

separate buildings to care for the small number of such cases. The same held true for Tennessee and Mississippi. Louisiana, on the other hand, accepted free blacks and some slaves as patients. Similarly, the South Carolina legislature in 1848 authorized its hospital to accept black patients, and soon afterwards separate facilities (inferior to those provided white inmates) were constructed. Nevertheless, by 1860 the hospital was accepting only black females.[52]

After 1865 the South was confronted with far more serious problems regarding the care and treatment of black insane persons. The end of slavery had given blacks—at least in theory if not in practice—the same rights and privileges enjoyed by all citizens. Yet virtually every Southern state faced conflicting internal pressures. Most blacks and some whites were demanding a nondiscriminatory policy. While most whites were unwilling to accede to such demands, their paternalistic attitude toward their former bondsmen made them receptive to the idea that some provision had to be made for insane blacks. Finally, there was an element of fear among some public officials that the incidence of mental disease among blacks would rise sharply and surpass that of whites.[53] "Unrestrained freedom," noted a Maryland official

52. Georgia State Lunatic Asylum, *AR*, 1858/1859, 15; Tennessee Hospital for the Insane, *BR*, I (1852/1853), 21; Mississippi State Lunatic Asylum, *AR*, IV (1858), 11–12, V (1859), 24; Stanford Chaillé, *A Memoir of the Insane Asylum of the State of Louisiana, at Jackson* (New Orleans, 1858), 8–9; Insane Asylum of Louisiana, *AR*, 1866, 6; South Carolina Lunatic Asylum, *AR*, 1844, 5, 1850, 12, 1851, 8–9, 1858, 12–13, 1860, 13.

53. Antebellum Southerners were receptive to the belief that slavery made blacks relatively immune to insanity. "From many of the causes affecting the other classes of our inhabitants," noted Galt in 1848, "they [slaves] are somewhat exempt; for example, they are removed from much of the mental excitement to which the free population of the Union is necessarily exposed in the daily routine of life; not to mention the liability of the latter to the influence of the agitating novelties in religion, the intensity of political discussion, and other elements of the excessive mental action which is the result of our republican form of government. Again, they have not the anxious cares and anxieties relative to property, which tend to depress some of our free citizens. The future, which to some of our white population may seem dark and gloomy, to them presents no cloud on its horizon. Moreover, not only are they less exposed to causative influences of a moral character, but the mode of life which they lead

in 1877, "has had the effect of multiplying their [blacks'] desires and wants, but together with them it has also multiplied greatly their disappointments, and in very many instances the price of liberty to them has been the prison, the almshouse and the insane asylum."[54]

In general, a consensus among Southern superintendents emerged relatively early on the question of facilities for black insane persons. They insisted that the state had a legal and moral obligation to provide care and treatment for blacks. On this point there was little evidence of disagreement; most superintendents were opposed to efforts that might be made to evade this obligation. A few emphasized the potential threat to the community posed by the increase in the number of black insane persons; but most used the same arguments that had been traditionally employed in justifying the need for new and expanded facilities for all mentally ill persons.

These superintendents, on the other hand, were convinced that it was impossible to provide care and treatment in integrated wards. In this respect Southern superintendents shared the views of most Americans, Northerners and Southerners alike. While there were some subtle differences, there was absolutely no disposition to question the basic assumption itself. "I must confess," wrote the superintendent of the Kentucky Western Lunatic Asylum in words similar to those used by most of his colleagues, "that I have an insurmountable prejudice against any such show of equality of races, and fancy there are few or none, sane or insane, in this State, but indulge in the same feeling." Neverthe-

tends to strengthen the constitution, and enable it to resist physical agents, calculated to induce insanity." Virginia Eastern Asylum, *AR*, 1848, 25. For examples of similar statements see Virginia Western Lunatic Asylum, *AR*, XIV (1841), 38–43; "Reflections on the Census of 1840," *Southern Literary Messenger*, IX (June, 1843), 340–352; C. B. Hayden, "On the Distribution of Insanity in the U. States," *Southern Literary Messenger*, X (March, 1844), 179–181; *The Works of John C. Calhoun*, ed. by Richard K. Crallé, 6 vols. (New York, 1870–1876), V, 333–339.

54. *Report on the Public Charities, Reformatories, Prisons and Almshouses, of the State of Maryland, by C. W. Chancellor, M.D., Secretary of the State Board of Health, Made to His Excellency, John Lee Carroll, Governor. July, 1877* (Frederick, 1877), 14–15.

55. Kentucky Western Lunatic Asylum, *AR*, 1865, 14.

less, he insisted that equal but separate treatment facilities be provided for blacks.[55] "We have two classes—white and colored," noted the superintendent of the Mississippi hospital.

> In some States, as in Mississippi, the colored have a majority of the population. Now the claims of both press alike upon us. We must provide with equal care for both. Can we treat both classes with the best chances for success in the same institution? We know too well that a feeling of caste exists between the two races, and that all those feelings and inborn ideas are intensified in the insane mind. Whether right or wrong, it is no less a fact; and as men of science and alienists, we cannot and must not ignore it in our calculations for the proper care and treatment of the insane. . . . Each race will be better off in every respect if treated and managed separately.[56]

The broad consensus among superintendents reflected to a considerable degree developments in most Southern states after 1865. The majority of states set aside separate quarters for blacks either in the same building used by whites or in a separate one, although usually of inferior quality. Some states—including North Carolina, Mississippi, and West Virginia—were slower than others in authorizing the establishment of segregated facilities. Others, like Kentucky, provided accommodations that were limited in scope. The general policy, however, was clearly to move in the direction of segregated care. A few states carried this policy to its logical conclusion by founding entirely separate and distinct institutions for blacks. Tennessee opened a Hospital for the Colored Insane shortly after the end of the war. This facility

56. Mississippi State Lunatic Asylum, *AR*, 1872, 21. For the consensus among Southern superintendents, see the following: *ibid.*, 1871, 20–21; Alabama Insane Hospital, *AR*, XV (1875), 18; Kentucky Eastern Lunatic Asylum, *AR*, XLII (1866), 17; Kentucky Western Lunatic Asylum, *AR*, 1866, 12–13; Lunatic Asylum of the State of Georgia, *AR*, 1865, 7, 1867/ 1868, 10–11; Missouri State Lunatic Asylum, *BR*, VIII (1867/1868), 15–16; St. Louis County Insane Asylum, *AR*, I (1869/1870), 18; Insane Asylum of North Carolina, *AR*, X (1865), 2–3; Tennessee Hospital for the Insane, *BR*, 1868/1869, 24; Texas State Lunatic Asylum, *AR*, 1866, 10; Virginia Western Lunatic Asylum, *AR*, 1866, 11, *BR*, 1867/1868–1868/1869, 37–45; South Carolina Lunatic Asylum, *AR*, 1869, 6, 1872, 24–26; West Virginia Hospital for the Insane, *AR*, IV (1867), 24–25, IX (1872), 16.

was located adjacent to the Tennessee Hospital for the Insane and remained under a common administration. Virginia, on the other hand, eventually converted a black general hospital founded by the Freedmen's Bureau into the first truly separate hospital for black insane persons. Whatever the individual policy, the facilities provided blacks rarely equaled those for whites. Indeed, the superintendent of the South Carolina Lunatic Asylum thought it necessary to apologize in 1871 for the facilities for black patients. Nevertheless, there was a gradual improvement during the 1870's in the accommodations for black persons in most Southern states.[57]

Interestingly enough, those Northern areas with relatively large concentrations of blacks pursued policies not fundamentally different from those in the South. Cincinnati, for example, initially refused admission to black applicants at its municipal hospital, which opened in 1860. In 1866, however, the Longview Asylum was authorized to admit black patients. Because of strong prejudices, its authorities purchased a separate building for blacks. Since state institutions excluded all blacks, an arrangement was worked out with municipal officials in Cincinnati whereby the "colored department" at Longview served the entire black com-

57. Alabama Insane Hospital, *AR*, VII (1867), 8–9, IX (1869), 8, X (1870), 11, XII (1872), 25–26, XV (1875), 18; Lunatic Asylum of the State of Georgia, *Report*, 1865/1866, 7, 1866/1867, 7–8, 1867/1868, 10–11; Kentucky Eastern Lunatic Asylum, *AR*, XLII (1866), 17, XLIV (1868), 7–8, XLIX (1873), 14; Kentucky Western Lunatic Asylum, *AR*, 1865, 14–15, 1866, 12–13; Central Kentucky Lunatic Asylum, *AR*, II (1874), 19, III (1875), 9–11, 18; Mississippi State Lunatic Asylum, *AR*, 1871, 20–21, 1872, 15–23; Missouri State Lunatic Asylum, *BR*, VII (1865/1866) (in *Missouri Senate Journal*, 24th General Assembly, 1867, Appendix), 443–444, VIII (1867/1868), 15–16; Insane Asylum of North Carolina, *AR*, X (1865), 2–3, XI (1866), 10, XX (1875), 3–18; South Carolina Lunatic Asylum, *AR*, 1868, 5–6, 1869, 6, 1871, 27, 1872, 24–25, 1873, 10, 1875, 13; Tennessee Hospital for the Insane, *Report*, 1865/1867, 15–17, *AR*, 1866, 6, *BR*, 1868/1869, 24, VIII (1869/1871), 17; Texas State Lunatic Asylum, *AR*, 1866, 10–11, *Semi-Annual Report*, I (August, 1866–March, 1867), 8–9; Virginia Western Lunatic Asylum, *AR*, 1866, 11, *BR*, 1867/1868–1868/1869, 6–7, 37–45; Virginia Eastern Lunatic Asylum, *AR*, 1868, 4–6, 1870, 28, 1873, 18; Virginia Central Lunatic Asylum, *AR*, I (1870), 4–10, II (1871/1872), 6–13, III (1872/1873), 13–26; West Virginia Hospital for the Insane, *AR*, IV (1867), 24–25, IX (1872), 16, 21, *BR*, XII (1875/1876), 5, 34–35; *AJI*, XXXI (October, 1874), 155–157, XXXV (July, 1878), 125–127, 129–130.

munity in Ohio. Not until the early 1870's did the state open its facilities to blacks. This arrangement was sharply criticized by one state superintendent. "In my judgment," he wrote, "anxious as I am for the best interests of all concerned, this unnatural admixture in the hospitals is of very doubtful propriety."[58]

By the late nineteenth century, therefore, more hospital facilities were beginning to be made available to blacks, although in most areas these facilities were segregated and often below the quality of those that served poor and indigent whites as well as other ethnic minorities. Like the overwhelming majority of most white Americans, virtually no member of the psychiatric profession was willing to challenge the dominant separate but equal doctrine that was the basis of public policy. Most psychiatrists not only accepted the assumptions underlying this policy but proved to be among its staunchest supporters. A few who might have been opposed took the position that their function was to provide care and treatment and not to educate the public on racial issues (although they never refrained from offering their opinions on other topics). Concerned also that integrated hospitals and wards might undermine public and legislative support for their institutions and their profession, they followed what appeared to be a reasonable and logical policy.

V

In theory public mental hospitals were beneficent medical institutions serving all groups. In practice, however, the quality of care was partially dependent upon class, ethnicity, and race, with the last of these playing a more significant role (at least quantitatively) than the other two. Ultimately all three, operating simultaneously and reinforcing each other, would have a significant influence over the entire system of public mental hospitals (as well as over the broad range of health-care facilities), for the degree to which institutions catered to predominantly

58. Longview Asylum, *AR*, I (1860), 16, III (1862), 16–17, IV (1863), 4, VII (1866), 3–4, 9–11, VIII (1867), 8, IX (1868), 10, X (1869), 10–11, XI (1870), 8–9, XII (1871), 7, XIII (1872), 7; Central Ohio Lunatic Asylum, *AR*, XXIX (1867), 7–8; Northern Ohio Lunatic Asylum, *AR*, XIV (1868), 7 14; Western Ohio Hospital for the Insane, *AR*, XX (1874), 23.

lower-class, ethnic minority, and nonwhite groups was inversely related to their reputation, level of funding, and quality of care and treatment. It must also be emphasized that while class, ethnicity, and race played important roles in shaping the configuration of hospitals, few psychiatrists (or policy officials for that matter) were completely cognizant of this fact. Most were unable to see the ways in which their personal social attitudes influenced the manner in which they structured their institutions. They were convinced that if their intentions were honorable, the results of their policies could not help but be good and beneficial to all concerned.

Chapter VII

Centralization and Rationalization: The Evolution of Public Policy, 1850-1875

I

By THE 1850's there was a growing awareness that the mere founding of hospitals had not solved the difficult problems posed by mental illness. The gap between the therapeutic goals and the internal practices of hospitals had widened rather than narrowed; the increase in the number of mentally ill persons had not been arrested; the number of insane persons in almshouses and other welfare institutions still exceeded by far the number in hospitals; and the costs of care and treatment, rather than stabilizing or diminishing, continued to rise. All of these facts made it painfully clear that the potential benefits of institutionalization to both the individual and the community had not been realized.

The growing public concern with the inability of hospitals to live up to their therapeutic goals was by no means an isolated or unique phenomenon. By the 1850's, as a matter of fact, many of the institutional structures that had been created during the second quarter of the nineteenth century had also become objects of public scrutiny. Despite the proliferation of almshouses, penitentiaries, hospitals, schools, and houses of correction, neither illness, dependency, nor crime seemed to be on the wane; if anything all were on the rise. The massive increases in the activities and expenditures of state governments, many charged, had not produced commensurate benefits. Why was this the case? More important, how could this dismal state of affairs be reversed? Above all, upon what basis could a sound and economical public policy rest?

The disillusionment of several decades of social innovation gradually led to a searching examination of the foundations of public policy. Responding to the broad current of dissatisfaction with existing structures, a number of legislatures authorized detailed studies that would provide them with the data and recommendations that would serve as the basis for a more enlightened and effective social policy. Out of these studies came the establishment of new state agencies possessing broad investigatory and regulatory authority. These agencies were given mandates to systematize and to rationalize the existing chaotic and often self-defeating policies toward dependent groups in order to make certain that the large investments in hospitals, for example, were not wasted. In their early years their members were responsible for the collection and analysis of data and the development of comprehensive policy recommendations for the legislative and executive branches of government. In time, however, the authority of these agencies was sharply broadened, and slowly but surely they became the vehicle by which states imposed a rationalized, centralized, and bureaucratic framework upon its welfare institutions.

The movement to centralize and to rationalize public welfare had a profound impact upon mental hospitals, most of which were under the jurisdiction of these new state agencies. This development tended to place these hospitals on the same precise footing as strictly welfare institutions as far as their funding and reputation were concerned. With their character and status thus defined, they were to suffer serious disabilities that hampered the fulfillment of their therapeutic mission. The bureaucratic structure imposed upon hospitals, in other words, solidified their custodial character and made it increasingly difficult to differentiate their functions from those of other welfare institutions dealing with a broad range of distressed and dependent groups.

II

The inclusion of the mental hospital as an integral part of a centralized and bureaucratic apparatus financed and controlled by the state took place in several distinct stages and without any particular awareness of the eventual outcome. The initial stage was marked by an emphasis on the amassing of information and the publicizing of the alleged shortcomings and problems of mental hospitals. Investigations by existing or special legislative committees became more common, and exposés by former patients or other individuals who for one reason or another were dissatisfied with the performance of mental institutions began to receive more and more attention.

The most famous legislative study of mental illness was the one undertaken by Edward Jarvis in 1854 at the behest of the Massachusetts legislature, which was becoming more and more concerned with the problem. Six years earlier a special legislative committee had studied the deteriorating conditions at the Worcester hospital. After rejecting proposals that the state establish separate institutions for Irish and native patients as well as for curable and incurable persons, it recommended the creation of a second hospital. Following affirmative action by the legislature, the new hospital (located in Taunton) opened in 1854. By that time, however, conditions at Worcester were so bad that the trustees suggested that the existing plant be demolished and an entirely new facility be constructed. In addition, the number of mentally ill persons still exceeded by a wide margin available institutional space. Dismayed by its inability to develop effective policies to deal with the insane, the legislature decided to appoint an impartial commission to study the problem and to recommend the adoption of a "general and uniform system."[1]

1. *Report of the Joint Committee of the Legislature of Massachusetts, Appointed April 20, 1848, on the Subject of Insanity in the State, and Directed to Sit During the Recess of the Legislature, and to Report at the Early Part of the Session of 1849,* Massachusetts *Senate Document No. 9* (January 15, 1849), 3–27, Massachusetts *Senate Document No. 60* (March 9, 1854), 1–8; Worcester State Lunatic Hospital, *AR*, XXII (1854), 8–36; *Re-*

Aside from conducting what was easily the most authoritative statistical survey of mental disease up to that time, Jarvis provided an analytical framework that related mental disease to class and ethnicity and recommended that the state establish separate institutions for native and foreign-born patients. In the short run the result of his report was simply the establishment of a third public hospital in the Bay State. In the long run, however, his report contributed to a growing tendency to identify mental hospitals in terms of welfare-related problems. His study, for example, had shown a higher incidence of insanity, idiocy, and crime among poor and pauper groups than among independent groups. Nor was the association between poverty and insanity a statistical accident. On the contrary, both were traceable to the same source, namely, an "imperfectly organized brain and feeble mental constitution" which carried with it "inherent elements of poverty and insanity." Moreover, his statistical data had seemed to indicate that most insane persons could not be cured. The result of his study, therefore, was to blur somewhat the potential differences between hospitals and strictly welfare institutions.[2]

While its magnitude and relative sophistication gave the *Report on Insanity and Idiocy in Massachusetts* a unique charac-

_____

port of the Committee on Public Charitable Institutions, Massachusetts Senate Document No. 83 (March, 1854), 1–8; Acts and Resolves Passed by the General Court of Massachusetts, in the Year 1854 (Boston, 1854), 438. For a detailed analysis see Gerald N. Grob, The State and the Mentally Ill: A History of Worcester State Hospital in Massachusetts, 1830–1920 (Chapel Hill, 1966), 145ff.

2. Report on Insanity and Idiocy in Massachusetts, by the Commission on Lunacy, Under Resolve of the Legislature of 1854, Massachusetts House Document No. 144 (1855), 45, 52–56. All of the manuscript returns, some of which contain comments as well, can be found in the "Report of the Physicians of Massachusetts, Superintendents of Hospitals . . . and Others Describing the Insane and Idiotic Persons in the State of Massachusetts in 1855. Made to the Commissioners on Lunacy," ms. in the CLMHMS. For a lengthy discussion of Jarvis's career and an extended analysis of his report see the critical introduction by Gerald N. Grob in Insanity and Idiocy in Massachusetts: Report of the Commission on Lunacy, 1855 by Edward Jarvis (Cambridge, 1971), 1–72. This volume also reprints the entire text of the report itself.

ter, it was by no means the only legislative inquiry on the subject. Four years earlier Thomas R. Hazard had presented his report on the poor and insane to the Rhode Island legislature, which had authorized the study at its previous session. Hazard, who retired from business at the age of forty-three after a successful career in textile manufacturing, spent the remainder of his life pursuing educational reform, abolition, and women's suffrage. His report recommended that the state adopt a mixed form of poor relief whereby impoverished persons lacking a home or family would be cared for in an institution, while all others would receive outdoor assistance. He also insisted on certain administrative and procedural safeguards for the poor. With respect to the insane, he saw no reason why chronic cases should not be kept in local welfare institutions, which, unlike mental hospitals, were under no significant pressure to restrict the personal liberties of their inmates. Recent cases, however, had to be treated in a hospital. As a result of his efforts, the General Assembly enacted legislation providing for partial subsidization of the pauper insane at the Butler Hospital. Unlike Jarvis, Hazard did not distinguish between natives and immigrants, nor did he view poverty in terms of character deficiency; his analysis was sympathetic in nature. Yet its influence remained minimal, perhaps because few persons were concerned with developments in Rhode Island.[3]

In New York State, on the other hand, the issue was thrust upon the legislature by local welfare officials. At a state convention in 1854, the county superintendents of the poor began to discuss inadequate public provision for the insane poor. The following year they urged the state to provide ample and suitable accommodations for such persons; in their view almshouses were inappropriate places of confinement. Their memorial to the legislature sharply opposed the practice of allowing a single circumstance—poverty—to govern the care of the insane in welfare institutions. The Utica hospital alone was clearly inadequate to the task at hand; for every space there were seven insane persons. Noting that poverty often followed insanity, they insisted

3. Thomas R. Hazard, *Report on the Poor and Insane in Rhode Island; Made to the General Assembly at its January Session, 1851* (Providence, 1851), 85–108.

that economic, scientific, and humanitarian considerations all dictated an expansion of state facilities for the mentally ill.[4]

The legislature immediately referred the superintendents' memorial to a select committee, which agreed that there were important distinctions between the poor and the insane poor. The former required food, clothing, and shelter "which physical inability disqualifies him from obtaining"; the latter, though possessing the physical ability, had "wants, arising from mental disease, which he is unable to supply." Strongly in favor of an expansion of institutional facilities, the committee recommended that a three-member board of commissioners be established to supervise the location and establishment of new public facilities, thereby avoiding the parochialism that had defeated earlier efforts to expand public hospitals.[5] A month before the select committee reported, three of its five members were authorized to visit all of the state's charitable institutions and all city and county welfare and penal institutions during the legislative recess. Their report generally supported the recommendations of the superintendents of the poor and employed most of the same arguments. But their report also went far beyond previous studies in one important respect—it urged the establishment of a state commission to supervise all public welfare institutions in order to prevent abuses and to oversee the efficient expenditure of public funds.[6] Although nothing specific resulted from this brief flurry of legislative concern, it was clear that pressures for change were beginning to mount.

While most states did not undertake comparable investigations, all faced a welfare system that appeared increasingly disorganized because of the seeming absence of a clearly defined rationale and structure. In the case of mental hospitals, capacity tended to lag far behind applications for admission. Confronted

4. *Report and Memorial of the County Superintendents of the Poor of this State on Lunacy and its Relation to Pauperism, and for Relief of Insane Poor*, New York *Senate Document No. 17* (January 23, 1856), 1–16.

5. *Report of the Select Committee on Report and Memorial of County Superintendents of the Poor, on Lunacy and Its Relation to Pauperism*, New York *Senate Document No. 71* (March 5, 1856), 1–21.

6. *Report of Select Committee Appointed to Visit Charitable Institutions Supported by the State, and all City and County Poor and Work Houses and Jails*, New York *Senate Document No. 8* (January 9, 1857), 22–23.

with continuous pressure to admit recent and curable cases and required to retain persons deemed dangerous to themselves or to the community, most hospital officials had only two options: they could either discharge chronic cases or halt all further admissions. Whatever course they followed, the result was the same —a further accumulation of mentally ill persons in welfare institutions such as almshouses, which in turn increased the protests of local welfare officers, who felt that they had neither the facilities, the training, nor the experience to care for such cases.[7]

The chaotic pattern of hospital and welfare administration that began to become evident during the 1850's and 1860's was also accompanied by a body of criticism of mental hospitals themselves. In part this criticism was a reaction to the extravagant promises held out by the early founders of hospitals and the claims of superintendents. Although insisting that mental illness was as curable as if not more curable than other diseases, they were unable to deliver on their promises. Indeed, by the 1850's a decline in official curability rates had begun to become evident. This fact left hospital officials particularly vulnerable to charges of mismanagement. In addition, the growing internal bureaucratization and regimentation that accompanied the increase in the size of hospitals contributed still more ammunition to those individuals and groups who were dissatisfied with the existing state of affairs.

Criticisms of mental hospitals took several different forms. One was the publication of exposés by former patients who claimed that they had been illegally incarcerated despite the fact that they were sane. The most spectacular revelations were those published by Mrs. E. P. W. Packard, who charged that she had been committed to the Illinois State Hospital for the Insane for three years by her husband. One result of this and other attacks on mental hospitals was a drive to secure passage of legislation that would more effecively guard the rights of patients and circumscribe the powers of hospital officials. Another result was an increase in the number of legislative investigations into the

7. The most detailed analysis of this problem was made by Sylvester D. Willard, in his *Report on the Condition of the Insane Poor in the County Poor Houses of New York*, New York *Assembly Document No. 19* (January 13, 1865). For a detailed discussion of this report and the consequences for mental hospitals see Chapter VIII.

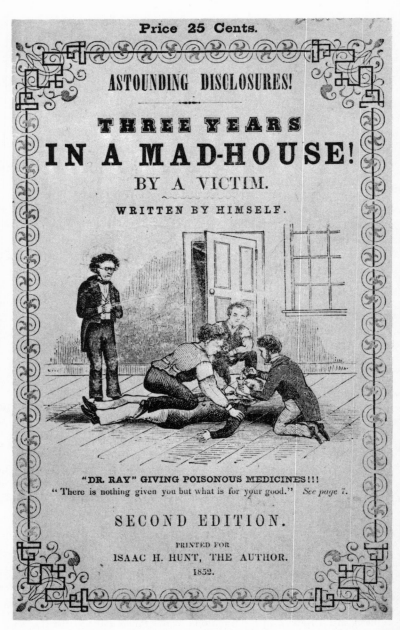

16. *Three Years in a Mad-house! Written by Isaac H. Hunt, this pamphlet was one of the first illustrated publications attacking mental hospitals in the early 1850's. Source: Isaac H. Hunt,* Three Years in a Mad-House! *(1852).*

internal activities of mental hospitals and alleged abuses of patients. Although neither patient exposés nor legislative investigations were unknown during the 1850's, the number and scope of both accelerated sharply during the 1860's.[8]

Unquestionably the most spectacular controversy occurred in Illinois. The state hospital there faced a host of problems that began almost from the very day that it received its first patients in 1851. Dissension among the trustees led to the dismissal of the superintendent, who had involved himself in the internecine struggle. In 1854 Andrew C. McFarland, then head of the New Hampshire Asylum for the Insane, was hired as superintendent. During his sixteen years in office, he and the hospital were continuously involved in public controversy, part of which was related to McFarland's domineering personality. After Packard's charges, the General Assembly enacted a personal liberty law in 1867 that provided for jury trials in sanity proceedings. The legislature also authorized an extensive investigation of the hospital; the result was a report highly critical of the superintendent. When the trustees supported McFarland, a bitter conflict followed that did not end until he resigned from office. The situation in Illinois received national publicity, in part because the issues of unfair and involuntary commitments, the abuse of patients, and the question of the rights of the insane were by this time of concern in other states as well.[9]

8. Two of the earliest exposés of mental hospitals—both of which were directed against McLean—were Robert Fuller, *An Account of the Imprisonments and Sufferings of Robert Fuller, of Cambridge* (Boston, 1833), and Elizabeth T. Stone, *A Sketch of the Life of Elizabeth T. Stone, and of Her Persecutions, With an Appendix of Her Treatment and Sufferings While in the Charlestown McLean Asylum, Where She was Confined Under the Pretence of Insanity* (n.p., 1842). For Mrs. E. P. W. Packard's charges see her books *Mrs. Packard's Reproof to Dr. McFarland, for His Abuse of His Patients . . . Nov. 12th, 1860* (Chicago, 1864), *Great Disclosures of Spiritual Wickedness!! In High Places. With an Appeal to the Government to Protect the Inalienable Rights of Married Women*, 4th ed. (Boston, 1865), and *Modern Persecution, or Insane Asylums Unveiled, as Demonstrated by the Report of the Investigating Committee of the Legislature of Illinois*, 2 vols. (Hartford, 1873).

9. Andrew McFarland to Kirkbride, March 24, 1855, Kirkbride Papers, IPH; C. H. Rammelkamp, ed., "The Memoirs of John Henry: A Pioneer of Morgan County," *Journal of the Illinois State Historical Society*, XVIII (April, 1925), 65–66; Illinois State Hospital for the Insane, *BR*, III (1851/

Kidnapping Mrs. Packard.

"Is there no man in this crowd to protect this woman!" See page 59.

No. 1.—"And this is the protection you promised my Mother! What is your gas worth to me!" See page 61.

No. 2.—"I will get my dear Mamma out of prison! My Mamma shan't be locked up in a prison!" See page 62.

17. *Mrs. E. P. W. Packard. Mrs. Packard launched one of the first personal freedom crusades for individuals committeed involuntarily to mental hospitals. Source: E. P. W. Packard,* Modern Persecution, or Insane Asylums Unveiled, as Demonstrated by the Report of the Investigating Committee of the Legislature of Illinois *(2 vols.: Hartford, 1873), vol. I.*

Although no hospital received as much publicity as the one in Illinois, indications of dissatisfaction were evident everywhere. In Massachusetts several petitions by Samuel Sewall and other prominent citizens led the legislature to authorize the appointment of a commission to examine the laws relating to mental disease and commitment proceedings. Five years later the House passed a bill establishing a commission on lunacy whose basic function was to protect the insane against abuses, but the bill died in the Senate.[10] Throughout the 1860's and 1870's the furor over the alleged abuses of the rights of the insane continued unabated. Indeed, Iowa passed a law in 1872 (in part the result of Packard's crusade) that gave patients complete freedom to write to whomever they desired and which forbade the superintendent or staff to open and to censor mail. This law merely added fuel to the fire.[11] When the Rhode Island legislature was

1852), IV (1853/1854), in *Reports of the Illinois State Hospital for the Insane 1847–1862* (Chicago, 1863), 101–109, 149–152, VIII (1861/1862), 22–24, XI (1867/1868), 8–11, 30–32; McFarland to Edward Jarvis, January 2, August 12, 1868, Jarvis Papers, CLMHMS; *Report of the Investigating Committee on the Hospital for the Insane, Made to the Governor of Illinois, December 1, 1867*, in *Reports Made to the General Assembly of Illinois at its Twenty-Sixth Session, Convened January 4, 1869*, vol. III (Springfield, 1869), *passim; Special Report of the Trustees of the Illinois State Hospital for the Insane, in Review of a Report of a Legislative Committee Appointed by the Twenty-Fifth General Assembly* (Springfield, 1868); *AJI*, XXVI (October, 1869), 204–229, XXVII (October, 1870), 260–262; William W. Burke, "The Supervision of the Care of the Mentally Diseased by the Illinois State Board of Charities (1869–1909)" (unpubl. Ph.D. dissertation, University of Chicago, 1934), Chap. VI.

10. Massachusetts *House Document No. 57* (February, 1862), 1–8; Massachusetts *Senate Document No. 10* (January, 1863); Massachusetts *Senate Document No. 72* (February 23, 1864), 1–20; Massachusetts *House Document No. 397* (May 13, 1869), 1–5; Massachusetts *House Document No. 496* (June, 1869), 1–4.

11. Iowa Hospital for the Insane at Mt. Pleasant, *BR*, VII (1872/1873), 27–31, 38–39, VIII (1874/1875), 24–25; *AJI*, XXIX (October, 1872), 249–258, XXX (April, 1874), 481–489; Massachusetts Board of State Charities, *AR*, XI (1874), 98–100; New Hampshire Asylum for the Insane, *AR*, XXXIV (1875), 31–32; Mark Ranney to Dix, February 1, 1873, Dix Papers, HLHU; Ellen Collins to Pliny Earle, August ?, 1877, Earle Papers, AAS. For examples of problems and investigations at other hospitals see the following: Vermont Asylum for the Insane, *AR*, XVI (1852), 10–11; Insane Asylum of California, *AR*, XIII (1865), 28–35; *Report of the Joint*

considering a similar proposal, Isaac Ray expressed his own anger, which probably reflected the views of the overwhelming majority of the psychiatric profession:

The legislation those people seek is anomalous & utterly indefensible. You may challenge them to show any malpractice or abuse that should furnish a ground for it, or any complaint or petition for it. It is not the custom to legislate in this high handed manner against evils not shown to exist. And let them look at the working of these arrangements. The boxes [for letters written by inmates], I suppose, are to be under the control of an outside & independent board. Are they to open the letters, & then send or withhold them, according to their discretion? If so, how can their judgment be better than that of the officers who have an intimate acquaintance with the writers and know all about their friends & connections. The only reply possible is, either that "we cant trust you to do the right thing," or that, "we know better how to manage these things than you with all your long experiences." The boxes themselves would be a standing proclamation

---

Committee of Senate and Assembly to Investigate the Affairs of the Insane Asylum at Stockton (n.p., n.d.), 4–35; Pennsylvania Hospital for the Insane, *AR*, XXVIII (1868), 38–50, XXIX (1869), 31–40; *Remarks of Hon. S. D. Hastings, Chairman of the Committee Appointed to Investigate the Affairs of the State Hospital for the Insane, Before the Board of Trustees at Madison, June 4th, 1868* (n.p., n.d.); Wisconsin State Hospital for the Insane, *AR*, IX (1868), Appendix, 3–393; *Report of the Commissioners of Investigation of the Insane Asylum, Made to the Governor and Council by Order of the Legislature. January, 1868* (Augusta, Maine, 1868); *AJI*, XXIX (April, 1873), 590–595; *Report and Correspondence Relating to the Release from the Government Hospital for the Insane of Certain Persons Admitted Thereto Upon the Order of the Authorities of the District of Columbia* (Washington, D.C., 1875); John W. Sawyer to Dix, March 20, 1875, J. P. Bancroft to Dix, March 20, 1875, Mrs. S. L. Nichols to Dix, April 8, 20, 26, 1876, C. H. Nichols to Dix, April 15, 1876, F. M. Gunnell to Dix, April 21, 1876, W. W. Godding to Dix, May 21, 1876, Dix Papers, HLHU; *Review of the Report of the Commissioners of the Insane, By the Officers of the Vermont Asylum for the Insane 1876* (Brattleboro, 1876); *Report on the Public Charities, Reformatories, Prisons and Almshouses, of the State of Maryland, by C. W. Chancellor, M.D., Secretary of the State Board of Health, Made to His Excellency, John Lee Carroll, Governor, July, 1877* (Frederick, 1877).

to the patients that the officers were unworthy of their confidence, and they must look to the outside Board for protection against the Superintendent, assistants, & Trustees who are combined for the purpose of depriving them of their liberty.[12]

Nor were the more exclusive private hospitals in any way exempted from the growing chorus of criticism. Kirkbride and the Pennsylvania Hospital for the Insane remained on the defensive for more than five years beginning in 1868 when on a number of occasions writs of habeus corpus freed several patients. These cases resulted in sharp newspaper attacks on the hospital and its officers. A similar situation occurred at the Bloomingdale Asylum at about the same time. The most serious affair took place in Baltimore when a jury indicted the chief medical officer (Dr. William H. Stokes) and the general manager (Sister Mary Blenkinsop) of the Mount Hope hospital on the charge of inducing people to commit individuals "by means of the false pretences, representations and allegations aforesaid, to the common injury of the liege inhabitants of this State, to the evil example of others, and against the peace, government and dignity of the State." Although the charges were dismissed by the court, the affair was symptomatic of the rising public suspicions of the conduct of mental hospitals.[13]

12. Ray to John W. Sawyer, February 21, 1875, ms. in the Butler Hospital Library, Providence, R.I. See also Ray's earlier report at the meetings of the AMSAII, "American Legislation on Insanity," *AJI*, XXI (July, 1864), 21–62, 131, 143–150, and the comments by John E. Tyler in McLean Asylum for the Insane, *AR*, XLVI (1863), in Massachusetts General Hospital, *AR*, 1863, 38–50.

13. Earl D. Bond, *Dr. Kirkbride and His Mental Hospital* (Philadelphia, 1947), 122–137; *Boston Medical and Surgical Journal*, LXXXI (October 14, 1869), 191–193, LXXXVII (September 5, 1872), 173; New York Hospital and Bloomingdale Asylum, *AR*, 1872, 11–12, 15–21; *AJI*, XXIX (April, 1873), 591–595, XXX (October, 1873), 241–244; *Report of the Trial of Dr. Wm. H. Stokes and Mary Blenkinsop, Physician and Sister Superior of Mount Hope Institution, Before the Circuit Court for Baltimore Co., Md. Held at Towsontown, Tuesday, February 6, 1866. By Eugene L. Didier, Stenographic Reporter* (Baltimore, 1866), 20 *et passim*; Mount Hope Institution, *AR*, XXIII (1865), 3–14, also reprinted in the *AJI*, XXIII (October, 1866), 311–329.

III

The second stage of the process that ultimately placed mental hospitals within a bureaucratic regulatory structure was characterized by a concerted effort by a number of states to rationalize what seemed to be their chaotic welfare systems. During this stage there was no direct effort to single out the mentally ill or differentiate the mental hospital in terms of its unique mission; the focus instead was on the development of a general policy that would simultaneously help to contain dependency, safeguard the recipients of welfare and medical services, and also ensure the most efficient use of public expenditures. With virtually no resources at hand but with a firm conviction that a better system was possible, small groups of government officials and concerned citizens began to seek alternatives to the seeming chaos and inefficiency that marked the care of dependent and distressed persons.

From the very beginning the movement to transform public welfare assumed an administrative mantle. Few of those directly involved were hostile to the system itself; they simply believed that it was possible to introduce greater accountability and efficiency by instituting tighter and more effective controls. The emphasis on administration and management was accompanied by the methodical collection of aggregate data, which would illuminate existing problems and facilitate the development of comprehensive policies. Although the collection of such data was by no means novel, there had been little previous effort to base policy decisions and the determination of priorities on such information, if only because the organizational components that would formulate and implement social policy did not exist. The reformers of the 1860's, on the other hand, were imbued with the desire to articulate comprehensive public policies, and they set out to create the organizational structures that would make this possible. The result of their efforts was the beginnings of an administrative and managerial transformation at the state level—especially in welfare-related and social policy matters—that eventually stimulated the growth of governmental bureaucracies. Although few of these activists were bureaucratically minded (or even aware of the concept), their ideals of order, rationality, and efficiency in the long run proved to be especially conducive to the bureaucratic phenomenon.[14]

Prior to 1860 some of the larger urban areas with a high proportion of immigrants and complex social problems began to experiment with administrative reorganizations in the hope of improving welfare services. In 1849 the New York legislature authorized the establishment in New York City of a municipal board of governors with authority over outdoor relief, the three city jails and penitentiary, the almshouse, lunatic asylum, nurseries, and the Bellevue Hospital. Eleven years later this body was replaced with another agency—the Department of Public Charities and Correction. Yet neither reorganization accomplished the desired goal of improving the pattern of public welfare. In many instances competing private agencies inhibited public welfare or aroused hostility among immigrants and other lower-class groups distrustful of the middle- and upper-class Protestants who dominated these organizations. The emergence of an urban political machine and the proverbial "Boss" in New York City during the mid-nineteenth century alleviated somewhat the plight of lower-class groups who became the recipients of numerous services. But this development occurred only at the expense of weakening efforts to reorganize public welfare. In a similar vein Boston attempted to bring its eleemosynary institutions under some sort of central control by establishing a municipal Board of Directors of Public Institutions in 1857. The results, however, were no different from those in New York.[15]

Although there was growing concern with the problem of welfare at the state level, the movement to rationalize and centralize the administration of public welfare did not emerge in a self-conscious and mature form before the Civil War. Prior

14. Cf. Franklin B. Sanborn, "The Work of Social Science in the United States," *Journal of Social Sciences*, VII (July, 1874), 36–45, and "The Work of Social Science, Past and Present," *ibid.*, VIII (May, 1876), 23–39.

15. New York City Governors of the Almshouse, *AR*, I (1849), 1–13; New York City Commissioners of Public Charities and Correction, *AR*, I (1860), vii–x; Boston Board of Directors of Public Institutions, *AR*, I (1857), *passim*. See also Seymour J. Mandelbaum, *Boss Tweed's New York* (New York, 1965), and Alexander B. Callow, Jr., *The Tweed Ring* (New York, 1965).

to that date certain states, however, had begun to experiment with regulatory mechanisms in response to the massive influx of immigrants during the 1840's and 1850's. The goal of such efforts was often to prevent the entry of individuals who for one reason or another were incapable of becoming self-supporting. Both New York and Massachusetts, which received large numbers of impoverished immigrants, led the way in attempting to contain the social and economic problems growing out of immigration. In 1847 New York passed legislation that included among its provisions the establishment of a Board of Commissioners of Emigration. The first permanent agency to be involved in poor relief, the new board was given responsibility for making certain that immigrants would not become a public charge within five years of their date of entry into the state. Similarly, Massachusetts in 1848 provided for the appointment of a superintendent of alien passengers in each town and city to perform the same function. Three years later the state created a Board of Alien Commissioners, which was given responsibility for enforcing laws dealing with aliens and the support of state paupers. In neither state, however, were these boards especially effective; friction with local authorities, inadequate powers, and administrative shortcomings sharply inhibited their development. Nevertheless, their very existence and involvement in welfare-related issues was a portent of things to come.[16]

The crucial step in the growing centralization of welfare was taken in 1863, when Massachusetts founded the first Board of State Charities in the nation, the predecessor of modern state departments of welfare. By the late 1850's the welfare activities of Massachusetts had become complicated and diverse. The Commonwealth had in operation three mental hospitals, a reform school for boys, an industrial school for girls, three almshouses, and a hospital for sick and disabled aliens. Four other eleemosynary institutions received public subsidies. In most instances these institutions had been in existence for less than a decade, and each functioned under a different administrative system;

16. David M. Schneider, *The History of Public Welfare in New York State 1609–1866* (Chicago, 1938), 295–316; Gerald N. Grob, *The State and the Mentally Ill: A History of Worcester State Hospital in Massachusetts, 1830–1920* (Chapel Hill, 1966), 175–179.

central direction was almost completely absent. Moreover, welfare expenditures had risen rapidly. In 1832 the state spent $60,000 for welfare-related purposes; by 1855 the figure had risen to over $300,000, and there was every indication that it would continue to increase.[17]

Concern over spiraling costs of welfare and anti-immigrant sentiment led the legislature in 1858 to authorize the appointment of a special joint committee "to investigate the whole system of the public charitable institutions of the Commonwealth, and to recommend such changes, and such additional provisions, as they may deem necessary for their economical and efficient administration." Within nine months the committee was ready with its report to the legislature. Pointing to the unsystematic and haphazard nature of state welfare, its members recommended that a permanent Board of State Charities be established and "intrusted with the duty of constantly supervising the whole system of public charities, in order to secure the greatest usefulness, without unnecessary expense." By mid-nineteenth-century standards this proposal was novel, for no other state had such an administrative agency. The committee maintained that the autonomy of individual institutions would not be undermined, for the authority of the new board would be limited to investigatory and fact-finding functions; its only substantive power would be its authority to transfer persons from one institution to another.[18]

Much of the report was devoted to a discussion of the general problem of pauperism in the state. Curiously enough, the committee took the position that the state should not maintain its welfare responsibilities on a permanent basis. But it held also that an immediate and abrupt return to local responsibility was equally unwise. The committee therefore favored a continuation of existing state welfare responsibility under the new board, "but always with a view to its abolition at the earliest day that may be consistent with the public welfare." The function of the pro-

17. *Report of the Special Joint Committee Appointed to Investigate the Whole System of the Public Charitable Institutions of the Commonwealth of Massachusetts, During the Recess of the Legislature in 1858,* Massachusetts *Senate Document No. 2* (January, 1859), table between 152 and 153.

18. *Ibid.,* 1–8.

posed agency, in other words, was to begin the long process of dismantling the state's welfare apparatus.[19]

Although the legislature did not act on the recommendations of its special joint committee, the pressures for retrenchment continued to mount. In 1861 the legislature's Committee on Public Charitable Institutions suggested that chronic insane paupers be kept at state almshouses, and that two of the three state hospitals accept only paupers, while the third confine its admission to private cases. The following year the committee reiterated its proposal. The cost to the state, argued its members, would be reduced, since paupers could be supported at a lower figure than paying patients without any real injury to them. "Comforts and luxuries are now provided for the paupers at the Insane Hospitals, which, in their best state, the foreign insane paupers have never known and cannot appreciate, and which are not called for in their medical treatment."[20] That same year another special committee was appointed to consider the abolition of state welfare. Although its recommendations were not acted upon prior to adjournment, its report was in much the same tradition as those of its predecessors. Condemning the Bay State's "hospital palaces" for the insane, its members asked in revealing words: "Whence comes the host of paupers and madmen? What are the causes which are making Massachusetts the great lazar-house of the whole world? for there is hardly a nook or corner of it not unrepresented in our 'ragged congress of nations.' "[21]

The constant discussions and investigations of pauperism and insanity were making a profound impression upon the legislature and public in a state where ethnic tensions were probably the strongest in the nation. Since 1848 there had been a steady succession of legislative studies. While few had resulted in the adoption of significant structural or policy changes, the issues had been kept alive because of a desire to economize and hostility toward dependent immigrants. It mattered little that many

19. *Ibid.*, 17–34.

20. *Report of the Committee on Public Charitable Institutions*, Massachusetts *Senate Document No. 167* (April 3, 1861), 2; *Report of the Committee on Public Charitable Institutions*, Massachusetts *House Document No. 269* (April 11, 1862), 2–6.

21. Quoted in Massachusetts *House Report No. 277* (April 20, 1863), 3–4.

of the collected data were capable of being interpreted in several different ways;[22] most legislators and several governors saw this evidence as confirmation of their own attitudes regarding Irish immigrants. But as the social problems of pauperism and mental illness mounted, it became more difficult to continue along old and familiar paths. At the end of March, 1863, therefore, the legislature created another special joint committee to investigate the possibility of reducing the expenses of the state's charitable institutions. Within one month the committee was ready with a report. Conceding that no new system of management had been considered, its members nevertheless insisted that existing institutions could be run more efficiently. In the past, the increase in indigency had been accompanied by increased expenditures. What could be done to alter this pattern? The first step involved a simplification in administration and the establishment of a central agency to coordinate the state's varied activities and thus hopefully reduce expenditures. "No one," the committee wrote, "desires of course to deal with any harshness towards the unfortunate poor of the Commonwealth; no one wishes or expects to be relieved from the burden of their support; but the errors, inconsistencies and unnecessary expenses of a *wrong system* should be pointed out and corrected."[23]

After consulting with the heads of most state institutions, the members of the committee introduced a bill to reorganize the

22. Jarvis's statistics on the high incidence of institutionalization among Irish insane immigrants, for example, could have been explained in terms of the stress and economic difficulties faced by an impoverished group that was attempting to be upward mobile. A forthcoming book by M. Harvey Brenner (to be published by Harvard University Press) establishes with considerable authoritativeness that changes in the economy are inversely related to the use of mental hospitals; the rate of hospitalization increased sharply during periods of unemployment and depression. For some of his preliminary findings see M. Harvey Brenner, "Economic Change and Mental Hospitalization: New York State, 1910–1960," *Social Psychiatry*, II (November, 1967), 180–188; M. Harvey Brenner, Wallace Mandell, Sheldon Blackman, and Richard M. Silberstein, "Economic Conditions and Mental Hospitalization for Functional Psychosis," *Journal of Nervous and Mental Disease*, CXLV (November, 1967), 371–384; and M. Harvey Brenner, "Patterns of Psychiatric Hospitalization among Different Socioeconomic Groups in Response to Economic Stress," *Journal of Nervous and Mental Disease*, CXLVIII (January, 1969), 31–38.

23. Massachusetts *House Report No. 277* (April 20, 1863), 4–11.

administration of public charities. Drawing upon the report of the special joint committee of 1858, they recommended the establishment of a State Board of Charities. The proposed board would have wide investigatory powers; it would report annually to the legislature on conditions at state institutions and would recommend appropriate policies. The board, however, would not supersede existing boards of inspectors or trustees. It would serve instead in a largely advisory capacity. Since it was not to be involved in the minutiae of daily routine and administration, it would possess a breadth of vision that individual trustee and administrative groups invariably lacked. The board would also have substantive authority over state paupers and could send or transfer them to the most appropriate institution. Its membership would be composed of five unsalaried individuals, a full-time general agent for outdoor work, and a secretary to keep records and make reports. Finally, the Board of Alien Commissioners would be abolished and its functions and powers transferred to the new body. Within two weeks the legislature passed a bill that included virtually every suggestion of the committee.[24]

Although it was not immediately apparent, the legislation establishing the first Board of State Charities was to prove a major landmark in the history of American welfare. It is true that several earlier regulatory organizations had been created in other states,[25] but none came close to the comprehensive nature of the new agency. While its authority was sharply circumscribed and limited and its staff minimal, the new board had the potential for rapid growth—a potential that was to be quickly realized by its first members and secretaries. By the very fact that its functions were largely in the policy-making rather than the administrative domain, it quickly overshadowed the individual welfare institutions, which over the years were slowly relegated to a subordinate

24. *Ibid.*, 12–14.

25. Massachusetts and New York, of course, had created the Board of Alien Commissioners and the Board of Commissioners of Emigration, respectively. Vermont, on the other hand, had authorized the appointment or election of a Commissioner of the Insane in 1845 to visit the Vermont Asylum for the Insane and report on its condition to the legislature (see Vermont Asylum for the Insane, *BR*, 1873/1874, 27–29). None of these bodies, however, had been given a comprehensive mandate, nor did they attract the type of organizationally minded individuals that boards of state charities did after their establishment.

position within a comprehensive system. That the board was intended to preside over the dismantling of the state's welfare apparatus proved of little consequence. Its early leaders were strong-willed and organizationally minded men who were determined to introduce an element of rationality into welfare. In so doing they inadvertently began to create a bureaucratic apparatus that steadily increased its role and authority despite the fact that this trend was in direct contradiction to the original intent of the legislation.

While Massachusetts was the first to move directly toward centralization and rationalization of its welfare system, other states were not far behind. In New York State a legislative committee had urged as early as 1857 the enactment of legislation providing for "a more efficient and constant supervision of all the charitable and reformatory institutions which participate in the public bounty, or are supported by taxation." A bill embodying this proposal failed to pass, and subsequent efforts to establish a state supervisory body also proved unsuccessful. In 1867, however, the governor in his annual message urged the legislature to establish a central supervisory agency. Shortly thereafter the legislature authorized the establishment of a Board of State Commissioners of Public Charities. By then the example of Massachusetts was well known, since the first members of its Board of State Charities—including Samuel Gridley Howe and Franklin B. Sanborn—proved extraordinarily energetic and effective in maximizing the relatively meager powers at their disposal. The New York board was modeled along the lines of its Massachusetts counterpart; it had general investigatory authority, and was required to determine whether or not public funds were judiciously and economically expended.[26] Similarly, the Ohio legislature, at precisely the same time as New York, created a Board of State Charities to investigate public charitable and correctional institutions and to recommend changes deemed necessary for an "economical

26. *Report of Select Committee Appointed to Visit Charitable Institutions Supported by the State, and All City and County Poor and Work Houses and Jails*, New York *Senate Document No. 8* (January 9, 1857), 22–23; New York Board of State Commissioners of Public Charities, *AR*, II (1868), ix–x; *AJI*, XXIV (October, 1867), 244–246; David M. Schneider and Albert Deutsch, *The History of Public Welfare in New York State 1867–1940* (Chicago, 1941), 14ff.

and efficient administration." Unlike Massachusetts and New York, however, the Ohio board was not provided with an appropriation for a paid secretary, sharply inhibiting its work (the members of the board were also not compensated for their services). By 1871 the board had gone out of existence; it was not reestablished on a firmer basis until 1876.[27]

During 1869 four more states—Pennsylvania, Illinois, Rhode Island, and North Carolina—established central boards. The pattern was again much the same as in Massachusetts and New York; the desire to impose order and efficiency upon public welfare was clearly the paramount element. Individual variations in different states, of course, existed. In Illinois, for example, the controversy over commitment procedures growing out of the charges made by Packard led to a legislative investigation in 1867. Although the governor seemed to favor the trustees and superintendent of the Illinois State Hospital for the Insane, both bore the brunt of the legislature's criticisms. Concern over alleged abuses, especially in the care and treatment of the mentally ill, undoubtedly played a role in the establishment of the Board of State Commissioners of Public Charities. The selection of Frederick H. Wines, destined to become a significant figure in late-nineteenth-century American welfare, ensured the success and growing importance of the new body. The North Carolina Board of Public Charities, established under circumstances similar to those in other states, remained in existence for only four years; the lack of any appropriation sharply circumscribed its work by forcing it to rely on the voluntary efforts of public-spirited citizens.[28]

Rhode Island, on the other hand, had from the outset one of the most powerful central boards in the nation. The reason for this, oddly enough, grew out of the fact that the state lacked any central facilities for the mentally ill and other dependent groups;

27. Ohio Board of State Charities, *AR*, II (1868), in Ohio Executive Documents, 1868, part II, *AR*, III (1869), *ibid.*, 1869, part II, *AR*, I (1876), *ibid.*, 1876, part I.

28. Pennsylvania Board of Commissioners of Public Charities, *AR*, I (1870), x–xii, II (1871), iii–vi, cxiff.; Illinois Board of State Commissioners of Public Charities, *BR*, I (1869/1870), xiii–xv, 1–9, II (1871/1872), 216–220; Burke, "The Supervision of the Care of the Mentally Diseased by the Illinois State Board of Charities (1869–1909)," Chap. I; North Carolina Board of Public Charities, *AR*, I (1869), 3–5, III (1871), 1–3.

responsibility had remained in the hands of local communities. The Butler Hospital accepted some patients on a contractual basis, but the overwhelming majority of the insane were kept in local almshouses and asylums. A state investigation of the latter two in 1865 was critical of certain aspects of their management, especially the lack of facilities to ensure proper classification of dependent groups and the absence of means for the systematic employment of inmates. Several years later the legislature began to discuss the possibility of establishing a state asylum for the insane. Out of the recommendations of a special joint committee came legislation establishing at one central location a state house of correction, workhouse, almshouse, and an asylum for the in-curable insane. The same legislation also authorized the creation of a Board of State Charities and Correction, which, in addition to general investigatory and advisory powers, was given direct control over the new state facilities.[29]

During the early 1870's a number of other states joined the ranks of those who had moved toward centralization. Michigan and Wisconsin both acted in 1871. Two years later Connecticut and Kansas adopted legislation creating state boards, but in Con-necticut the board was largely inoperative until a reorganization in 1881. After the surge in the early 1870's the movement perceptibly decreased, and not until the 1880's and 1890's (with the exception of Nebraska) did it resume again. The drive toward centralization and rationalization was strongest in the older and more populous regions of the Northeast and Midwest; it was weakest in the South.[30]

The legislation defining the responsibilities and powers of most of these early boards varied from state to state. Some states gave them authority to investigate penal and correctional as well

29. *Report of the Commissioner to Visit Almshouses and Asylums, for the Insane Poor, Indigent Persons, or Paupers,* Rhode Island *Public Docu-ment No. 20* (1865), Appendix, 3–10; Rhode Island Board of State Charities and Correction, *AR,* I (1869), 12–34, 43–47.

30. Michigan Board of State Commissioners for the General Supervision of Charitable, Penal, Pauper, and Reformatory Institutions, *BR,* I (1871/1872), 5–9, II (1873/1874), 5; Wisconsin State Board of Charities and Reform, *AR,* I (1871), 5–9, II (1872), 5–10, III (1873), 278–287, IV (1874), 9–10; Connecticut State Board of Charities, *AR,* I (1881), 5, III (1883), 3–4; A. M. Shew to Pliny Earle, April 28, 1881, Earle Papers, AAS.

as welfare institutions; some exempted private mental hospitals and other institutions from inspection; and none had precisely the same administrative structure. A few states developed their own unique variations. New York, for example, in 1873 gave the State Board of Charities licensing powers in regard to the care of the insane and provided for the appointment of a state commissioner in lunacy who was an ex-officio member of the board and reported directly to it. His function was to prevent abuses in commitment proceedings and care, and he was given broad investigatory powers.[31] There was also a general tendency for most state boards to press for greater authority, and in some states the individual welfare institutions and mental hospitals came directly under the administrative control of the board.[32]

The similarities between these central boards, however, completely overshadowed any differences. All of them represented the growing belief that welfare, if it was not to destroy the nation, had to be placed on a "scientific" basis. Scientific philanthropy, however, did not imply a new departure in the basic meaning of welfare. Indeed, as we shall see shortly, the approach of most boards was fundamentally no different from many antebellum voluntary and private benevolent organizations. By a scientific approach to welfare the reformers of the 1860's and 1870's generally meant a new managerial and administrative system that would impose far greater controls in the hope of first containing and then eliminating welfare. The Civil War, which had placed many welfare institutions in a precarious position and had also promoted an emphasis on administration, undoubtedly reinforced this trend. Once set in motion, the thrust toward greater state intervention by means of administrative agencies proved irresistible. Within six years after the founding

31. New York Board of State Commissioners of Public Charities, *AR*, VI (1872), 14; New York State Commissioner in Lunacy, *AR*, I (1873), 5–6; Schneider and Deutsch, *History of Public Welfare in New York*, 22–24.

32. See F. B. Sanborn, "Work Accomplished by the State Boards: Report of the Standing Committee on State Boards of Charities," in National Conference of Charities and Correction, *Proceedings*, XIV (1887), 75–105; Oscar Craig et al., "History of State Boards: Report of Committee," in *ibid.*, XX (1893), 33–51; Samuel E. Sparling, "State Boards of Control with Special Reference to the Experience of Wisconsin," in American Academy of Political and Social Science, *Annals*, XVII (January, 1901), 75–91.

of the first Board of State Charities, Massachusetts created a State Board of Health, a Railroad Commission, and a Bureau of Labor Statistics. All of these agencies were based in part upon the belief that right-minded, intelligent, and educated men, when placed in responsible managerial positions, would be able to deal effectively with social problems and thereby ensure the preservation of a fundamentally moral and healthy society.[33] Much the same thrust was evident in other states, which also began to create a series of regulatory agencies.

The managerial emphasis was clearly the dominant theme in the movement toward greater state control. After observing that it would be difficult to dismantle the system of public charity that had been so laboriously constructed over a long period of time, Franklin B. Sanborn, secretary of the Massachusetts board and a figure of national significance, argued that precisely because it could not be immediately abandoned it required "a careful, comprehensive, and wide supervision," but always with the view of its eventual abolition.[34] The president of the Wisconsin board noted that his agency had come into existence because of the impression that the annual reports of public institutions were unreliable and misleading. "We shall not strive to fall into this error," he wrote to Pliny Earle. "For the present our work is largely to bring order and system and economy out of chaos and its necessary concommitant, extravagance. We hope to accomplish this and then to be able to give not a little attention to the general methods of internal management."[35]

The common interests and common concerns of the early personnel of the new boards led inexorably toward the creation of a national forum to provide a vehicle for the dissemination of their views and an opportunity to meet at regular intervals and exchange ideas. In 1874 the members of the boards of New York, Massachusetts, Wisconsin, and Connecticut met jointly with the American Social Science Association (which was largely the creation of Franklin B. Sanborn and the Massachusetts Board

33. Cf. Barbara G. Rosenkrantz, *Public Health and the State: Changing Views in Massachusetts, 1842–1936* (Cambridge, 1972), Chap. II.

34. Franklin B. Sanborn, "The Supervision of Public Charities," *Journal of Social Science*, I (June, 1869), 72.

35. George W. Burchard to Pliny Earle, August 22, 1881, Earle Papers, AAS.

of State Charities) and founded the National Conference of Charities and Correction. This organization ultimately became the professional organization of social workers and played a major role in publicizing the doctrines of "scientific" philanthropy and professional social work. Dominated by representatives of public and private charitable agencies, the new organization—reflecting its constituency—emphasized administration and practice rather than scientific inquiry. By the 1870's, therefore, it was evident that the care of the mentally ill would be determined less by superintendents of individual institutions and more by centralized boards seeking to develop comprehensive and unified policies toward dependent groups of all kinds.

IV

While the substantive powers of most of the early state boards of charity were sharply limited, their strategic position within state governments (which grew out of the fact that they spoke not on behalf of a particular constituency such as the insane, the aged, or the poor, but on behalf of all dependent groups) as well as their ideological outlook ensured that they would be given an increasingly important role in the determination of welfare policies. Indeed, their growth potential was so promising that they often attracted extraordinarily able, articulate, and competent persons. Franklin B. Sanborn in Massachusetts, William P. Letchworth in New York, and Frederick H. Wines in Illinois were among the best known of the late-nineteenth-century figures in the history of public welfare; but their activities were matched by other less known but equally competent and able individuals.

If anything characterized the new boards in the 1860's and 1870's, it was their passion for order, efficiency, and rationality. The problem in their eyes was not that the American people had been lax in their responsibilities toward dependent persons, for such was not the case. Indeed, the proliferation of public and private philanthropy was clear evidence of the nation's generosity. The problem of welfare was rather an administrative one requiring first a hard analysis of the issues, which was to be followed by the development of appropriate and efficient policies. The role of state boards, therefore, was to define the basic issues—

especially the causes of dependency—and then to recommend a clear and incisive policy that would eliminate waste and inefficiency.

Since the powers of most boards in the 1860's and 1870's were limited, their members spent a considerable proportion of their time in compiling and analyzing the data pertaining to welfare and dependency. The power to investigate was clearly their most significant weapon, and they proceeded to make the most of it. When their investigatory work was combined with their organizational efforts at both the state and national level, the result was an irreversible trend toward centralization of authority. This was a trend that individual institutions were powerless to halt and one that also was furthered by the glaring deficiencies and problems inherent in most local programs. Out of these activities there slowly developed a rationale and an administrative apparatus whose growing influence reflected the increasing substantive powers of the boards themselves.

In the eyes of most boards, welfare had entered a critical phase. Poverty and pauperism led inexorably toward crime and degeneracy, and there was abundant evidence that these factors were increasing more rapidly than population. "The ratio of crime in this country has increased faster than the population," warned the Pennsylvania board in its second report. Nor was its perception of the threat of pauperism and crime idiosyncratic, for the Massachusetts and North Carolina boards took much the same position.[36] Indeed, Sanborn saw a veritable "epidemic of crime" that endangered the very foundations of the established order.[37] The moral was clear; unless corrective action was taken quickly and decisively, the American people were in danger of losing the unique character that had separated them from the older and more corrupt nations of the world.

Identifying the existence of a crisis, of course, was only a beginning, though it did have the added merit of magnifying the role that central boards might play. More important was the task of identifying the causes and magnitude of dependency.

36. Pennsylvania Board of Commissioners of Public Charities, *AR*, II (1871), lxxxiv–lxxxv; Massachusetts Board of State Charities, *AR*, II (1865), xxxivff.; North Carolina Board of Public Charities, *AR*, II (1870), 4ff.

37. Massachusetts Board of State Charities, *AR*, II (1865), 213ff.

The boards' annual reports, therefore, tended to be long documents replete with extensive collections of aggregate data and conclusions drawn from these data. While those associated with central boards prided themselves as having inaugurated a new era in which science replaced ignorance or sentimentality in public philanthropy, their analysis was neither new nor novel. As a matter of fact, their reports reflected the traditional ambiguity that was characteristic of Americans. Most of these documents combined sympathy, compassion, and understanding on the one hand with a fervent belief that poverty and pauperism were associated with character deficiencies and shortcomings on the other hand.

The second report of the Massachusetts Board of State Charities was in many ways typical. Written largely by the redoubtable Samuel Gridley Howe, it nevertheless had the full concurrence of Sanborn, who clearly represented the rising administrative-managerial viewpoint. Howe began by identifying two distinct categories of persons—dependents and destructives. The dependents were a heterogeneous group: included were those who could not support themselves because of infirmity, sickness, or feeblemindedness; those who would not support themselves, preferring instead a parasitic status; and those who remained idle because of bad training and evil habits. The destructives included "the hideous army of drunkards, with its foul purveyors," and "the destructives—the parasites of the body social,—some of whom wander up and down, pilfering and stealing; others sit and contrive ways and means of gambling, cheating, fraud and mischief of various kinds; while others distil and deal out poison to keep the whole crew excited and active." Both the dependent and destructive classes were the cumulative result of inherited organic imperfections, which in many cases had begun as functional disturbances. Imperfections, according to Howe, were of two different types: the first, which affected mainly the dependent class, was notable for the absence of vital force arising from improper nutrition, use of stimulants, or abuse of functions; the second included inherited tendencies to vice arising from "vicious habits of thought and action" and was characteristic of the destructive class, whose members had less of an "ability for self-guidance." The dependent class lacked bodily and mental vigor; the vicious and criminal class lacked the higher faculties, which controlled the lower ones. The former did not have the power to get along in life; the latter had the power but inevitably misused it.[38]

Yet Howe was not pessimistic about the future. Animals could be improved by proper breeding, and so could human beings. What was required was not merely a moral and religious reformation of the individual, but an environmental transformation that would inevitably alter behavior. Thus he urged "improvement of dwellings; encouragement to ownership of homesteads; increased facility for buying clothing and wholesome food; decreased facility for buying rum and unwholesome food; restriction of exhausting labor; [and] cleanliness in every street, lane and yard which the public arm can reach." In addition, the American people had to be better informed about the natural laws that governed behavior. Then they would understand that many individuals in the pauper and criminal classes "are no more responsible for being in those classes than lunatics are for being insane; that all of them are open to outward influences; and that the best and ablest men should be called to care for them, and to devise ways and means for cutting off the sources whence those classes draw their recruits." Howe believed that all institutions should be enlisted in the task of social regeneration, and that care and confinement in public welfare institutions was only a last resort.[39]

Howe's sentiments were by no means atypical of those expressed by other boards. This is not to imply that differences did not exist. In New York, for example, Charles S. Hoyt, secretary of the State Board of Charities, conducted a lengthy investigation of pauperism and came to the conclusion that the majority of paupers reached that condition "by idleness, improvidence, drunkenness, or some form of vicious indulgence." These vices in many cases were the result of inherited attributes. The number of persons in almshouses who had been reduced to poverty by forces beyond their control, he noted, was surprisingly small. "The whole policy of the State," Hoyt concluded, "should move in the direction of caring for the really unfortunate and worthy sick poor in hospitals, while a vigorous system of labor should be

38. *Ibid.*, xix–xxxvi.
39. *Ibid.*, xxxi–xxxix, xliv–xlv.

organized and administered for the vicious and unworthy."[40] Since not all states faced similar problems, each board had to take into account unique circumstances. The North Carolina board had to confront—as Massachusetts and other Northern states did not—the problems posed by thousands of freedmen who had previously been subject to the absolute authority of the slave owner rather than the law and who now came under the jurisdiction of the state in all welfare-related cases.[41] Despite their differences, most central boards tended to be deeply ambivalent on the subject of welfare. Their solutions, therefore, vacillated among assistance, education, and punishment. Many of their policy recommendations, it should be noted, were not directly related to the empirical data they had collected. Indeed, most of the statistics that appeared in their annual reports were collected in aggregate form; there was little effort to break down the various categories of dependents or to shed light on the specific roots and forms of dependency.[42]

The tendency to approach welfare and dependency in all-encompassing terms had significant implications for the mentally ill, since overall responsibility for this particular group tended to fall within the province of the new state boards of charity. That these boards from their very inception regarded the insane as falling within their jurisdiction was natural. Many of the issues related to mental illness, after all, were of public concern not only because of the presumed threat to society, but because they often involved protracted periods of institutionalization at a cost beyond the ability of individuals to pay—to say nothing about the economic impact of mental illness upon family structure. The fact that mental hospitals traditionally cared for large numbers of dependent persons thus facilitated their absorption into a general welfare structure. Nor did the ideological framework of most American psychiatrists inhibit such a development. On the con-

40. Charles S. Hoyt, "The Causes of Pauperism," in New York State Board of Charities, *AR*, X (1876), 287–288.

41. North Carolina Board of Public Charities, *AR*, II (1870), 6–8.

42. Cf. Illinois Board of State Commissioners of Public Charities, *BR*, I (1869/1870), 15–34, IV (1875/1876), 195–209; New York State Board of Charities, *AR*, VIII (1874), 131–159; Massachusetts Board of State Charities, *AR*, I (1864), 409–410, II (1865), 213–220, III (1866), 199–208, IV (1867), 129–144, V (1868), xix–xli, IX (1872), xvii–li, XI (1874), 107–112.

trary, the psychiatric belief that mental illness followed a violation of the natural laws governing behavior paralleled the belief
of many members of state boards that dependency was largely
self-inflicted. The prevailing concepts of insanity held by most
superintendents also tended to make them oblivious to the impact
of broad organizational and administrative changes on their institutions. Indeed, the establishment of boards of charities in most
states took place without arousing any feelings—either positive or
negative—among superintendents or the medical profession despite the fact that these new agencies were given mandates that
involved them in health-related problems.

Between 1863 and 1875 most state boards of charity emphasized the investigation of conditions at public institutions, the
collection of data, and the development of broad policy recommendations. While not ignoring the problems of individual mental
hospitals, their members and staff were for the most part more
concerned with the overall dimensions of social policy toward
mental illness. Consequently, their influence rapidly exceeded that
of the superintendents of individual institutions, whose problems
tended to be local and immediate in nature and whose activities
and interests were far removed from the policy-making activities
of state governments. The responsibility for the formulation of
policy toward the mentally ill, therefore, increasingly became a
function of central state agencies, a trend that increased in intensity during the twentieth century.

The basic thrust of boards of charity was clearly in the direction of the centralization of authority and the application of
rational guidelines in order to introduce greater effectiveness and
efficiency into the entire welfare system. Centralization, however,
was not merely a function of the drive of these boards to increase
their own authority, although this undoubtedly played a role.
Much more significant was the fact that the system of local responsibility for welfare-related problems had not lived up to
expectations. Indeed, contemporary observers were convinced
that in many respects it was a disaster. Since the possibility of ending welfare in the short run seemed to be virtually nonexistent,
the tendency was to move toward the imposition of greater state
regulation in the hope of ultimately eliminating the conditions
that made welfare a necessity.

Most state boards were adamant in their conviction that the

dual system of confining insane persons in local welfare institutions and state mental hospitals was a complete failure. A few were critical of both poor houses and hospitals—the former because of their inhumane environment and indiscriminate mixing of dependent persons, and the latter for their crowded conditions, lack of suitable employment for inmates, reliance upon restraint, and the tendency of superintendents to push for facilities that were unnecessarily costly. Most boards, however, were sympathetic toward mental hospitals and placed responsibility for their alleged shortcomings upon a system that mandated overcrowding and a patient population composed largely of chronic cases. They developed a number of policy proposals intended to improve conditions, including expansion of existing facilities and the construction of new hospitals, as well as a dual system that included therapeutic institutions for the curable and custodial institutions for the chronic. Several boards attempted to move in a different direction; they urged their states to establish decentralized or cottage institutions modeled loosely after the famous colony for the insane in Gheel, Belgium, in order to minimize the loss of freedom that inevitably accompanied institutionalization of any type. Some of these proposals, as we shall see later, aroused the hostility of the AMSAII and led to protracted conflict over the shape of public policy.[43]

The significance of central boards, however, was not only a function of their investigatory and policy-recommending authority. Indeed, many of their recommendations were similar if not

43. For the discussion by state boards of the problems relating to the care and treatment of the insane see the following: Massachusetts Board of State Charities, *AR*, I (1864), xiv–xv, xli–xliii, 363–366, II (1865), c–cxii, III (1866), 204–205, IV (1867), xxxvi–lx, 141–144, VI (1869), lxiv–ciii, VII (1870), xl–xlvii, IX (1872), xxx–xxxi, X (1873), 19, XII (1875), xi–xxxvii, 131–133; New York Board of State Commissioners of Public Charities, *AR*, IV (1870), 30–33, V (1871), 24–30; New York State Board of Charities, *AR*, VII (1873), 20–21, VIII (1874), 25–28; North Carolina Board of Charities, *AR*, I (1869), 22, 106–109, IV (1872), 11–12; Illinois Board of State Commissioners of Public Charities, *BR*, I (1869/1870)), 82–101, II (1871/1872), 119–121, IV (1875/1876), 73–78; Michigan Board of State Commissioners for the General Supervision of Charitable, Penal, Pauper, and Reformatory Institutions, *BR*, I (1871/1872), 58–65; Pennsylvania Board of Commissioners of Public Charities, *AR*, II (1871), 17–18, IV (1873), cxxxviii–ccx; Wisconsin State Board of Charities and Reform, *AR*, I (1871), 94–97, 310–314, V (1875), 102.

identical to those advanced on various occasions by superintendents of the AMSAII. Even when boards came into conflict with institutional psychiatrists, the lines of demarcation were never clearcut or distinct; on a number of occasions individual superintendents disassociated themselves from the majority of their professional brethren on key issues. In some states, moreover, board members enjoyed close and fruitful ties with superintendents and often relied upon them for information and advice. In Massachusetts, for example, Sanborn had a close relationship with Pliny Earle, who had assumed the superintendency of the Northampton State Lunatic Hospital in 1864 with the backing of the State Board of Charities, and after the latter's death wrote a biography dealing with his long career in psychiatry.[44] Nor did the members and staff of such boards hold views on the nature and etiology of insanity markedly different from those of the psychiatric profession. Although most state officials were skeptical of the curability of mental illness, they were simply reflecting the decline in the notion of curability within the ranks of psychiatrists themselves.[45]

The importance that central boards played in the evolution of public policy toward the mentally ill was rather a consequence of the organizational framework in which they were first conceived and within which they grew to maturity. The basic function of these boards—which was accurately expressed in the names given them—was to provide a comprehensive solution for the problems related to poverty and dependency. Their involvement in health-related issues was a consequence of their concern with the care of dependent groups generally. Thus their jurisdiction over the mentally ill did not arise out of medical considerations, but rather out of the fact that mental illness had the highest incidence among lower-class groups and ethnic minorities. Among these groups the family had no resources to pay for the costs of care and treatment. If the principal wage earner became insane, the family situation then became even more desperate. And if the person

44. Franklin B. Sanborn, *Memoirs of Pliny Earle, M.D.* (Boston, 1898), Chap. XII.

45. The classic attack on the idea of curability was the studies done by Earle at the Northampton hospital in the 1870's and 1880's and then issued in book form under the title *The Curability of Insanity: A Series of Studies* (Philadelphia, 1887).

afflicted was an elderly parent or relative, the fact that in many instances children and parents worked made it difficult to maintain the individual outside of an institution.

The inclusion of the mentally ill within the jurisdiction of state boards of charity, however, subjected this group to all of the strains and ambiguities that marked public welfare in the United States. The members of these boards rarely attempted to differentiate between the various categories of dependency and often lumped together a variety of different problems indiscriminately. Sanborn, in one of his annual reports to the legislature of Massachusetts, for example, organized one part under the heading "Pauperism, Crime, Disease and Insanity." In the section dealing with the latter two, he noted that all of the categories were "so closely connected as to make any exact separation of them difficult. Pauperism and Crime; Pauperism and Disease; Crime and Disease; Insanity and Crime; Insanity and Pauperism, —how frequent are the permutations and combinations of these evils! Like Sin and Death, in Milton's allegory,—what are they indeed but forms of sin and death?—they breed from each other a mixed and woeful progeny. Insanity, to be sure, is but a species of disease, but for convenience, it may be treated separately."[46]

Admittedly, sentiments such as those expressed by Sanborn and others were not necessarily typical. The Pennsylvania board, for example, noted that the majority of the insane owed "their poverty to insanity and not their insanity to their poverty."[47] Nevertheless, the bureaucratic changes in state governments that occurred during the latter part of the nineteenth century formalized the inclusion of the mentally ill within a welfare framework. This development was to have considerable influence even after separate state agencies for the mentally ill came into existence and the state assumed exclusive jurisdiction over care and treatment facilities. Basically, the fate of the mentally ill became inextricably involved with the fate of all dependent groups. And during the last three decades of the nineteenth century public welfare in America, despite all attempts at rationalization, remained as unsystematized as it had been earlier. During this same time the tendency of charity reformers was to oppose

46. Massachusetts Board of State Charities, *AR*, III (1866), 199, 204.

47. Pennsylvania Board of Commissioners of Public Charities, *AR*, IV (1873), cxlv.

relief and to treat poverty partly in pathological terms. The result, as Roy Lubove has noted, was a vast amount of rhetoric about the necessity for scientific investigation together with a series of moral judgments about the nature and character of many poor groups. While most charitable organizations found it impossible to dispense with relief in one form or another, existing welfare programs were further fragmented, especially as the newly emerging profession of social work moved away from outdoor relief.[48]

The thrust of public welfare in the late nineteenth century was not without an impact on mental hospitals, since these institutions were part of an administrative structure responsible for the care of dependent groups. In other words, structure tended to determine function rather than follow it. Given the low priorities accorded to welfare programs and the fact that hospital populations tended to be composed largely of lower-class groups and ethnic minorities, it was not at all surprising that mental hospitals would be treated much as were other welfare institutions. The resurgence of nativism in the late nineteenth century together with the prevailing belief in the existence of innate and distinct ethnic characteristics simply added to the problems of public hospitals, since there was a tendency of policy officials to see welfare and immigration as directly proportional to each other. The New York State Board of Charities on one occasion took under advisement proposals designed to limit immigration since, as John N. Pomeroy noted, large numbers of "convicts, habitual criminals, paupers, lunatics, persons of unsound mind, persons generally unable or unwilling to support themselves by means of bodily or mental infirmity" were dumped on American shores.[49]

Although there was no effort whatsoever to diminish the role of state governments in providing hospital facilities, a concerted movement was begun by many state boards during the 1870's to reduce expenditures, especially in the construction of expanded or new facilities. At the annual meetings of the Conference of Charities members of state boards often denounced mental hospitals for

48. See Roy Lubove, *The Professional Altruist: The Emergence of Social Work as a Career 1880–1930* (Cambridge, 1965), 7, and Blanche D. Coll, *Perspectives in Public Welfare: A History* (Washington, D.C., 1969), *passim.*

49. New York State Board of Charities, *AR*, VIII (1874), 141.

relying too heavily on mechanical and medical restraint and not providing meaningful occupational therapy, while at the same time they charged that these hospitals were unnecessarily extravagant insofar as their physical plants were concerned.[50] Hospital superintendents found themselves in an anomalous position, for they were charged with both incompetence and extravagance and simultaneously urged to improve institutional care and reduce the costs of hospitals to the public.

The fact-finding activities of state boards of charities also tended to confirm rather than to deny the identification of poverty, pauperism, and crime with mental and other diseases. Although the annual reports of most boards did not necessarily treat them as inseparable, the very fact that all were discussed within a single document was itself of no minor insignificance. Since most state legislatures did not as yet possess the supporting staff and elaborate committee structure that their twentieth-century successors did, they tended to rely to a considerable extent upon the state boards of charities for the data that would serve as the basis for legislation. This situation tended to hurt rather than to help mental hospitals, which saw their fate tied to a welfare system that aroused considerable public and legislative antipathy.

V

Prior to the establishment of central state agencies, state hospitals managed to retain a high degree of autonomy. Most were under the authority of an independent board of trustees appointed by the governor. Policy decisions were usually the result of internal agreements between the board and the superintendent. Relationships between the hospital on the one hand and the executive and the legislature on the other were direct; no agencies were interposed between them, for few states had begun the process of bureaucratization. It is true that the general legal, administrative, and financial environment had a significant impact upon the hospital, but in terms of internal policy and the use of

50. See Francis Wells, "Hospital Building," in Conference of Charities, *Proceedings*, III (1876), 114ff.; H. B. Wilbur, "Buildings for the Management and Treatment of the Insane," in *ibid.*, IV (1877), especially 146ff.; Conference of Charities and Correction, *Proceedings*, VII (1880), 120–121.

resources most institutions had considerable leeway to determine their own future.

Although a loose administrative system gave hospitals freedom and autonomy, within prescribed legal limits, and minimized conflict with other public agencies (if only because relatively few regulatory agencies existed at the state level), it also meant that a clearly defined public policy toward mental illness was absent. Policy was the aggregation of individual decisions and events; it did not follow from a conscious and rational consideration of alternative priorities. In this respect the lack of a policy framework toward mental illness reflected the localized nature of American society for much of the nineteenth century. Yet it was becoming increasingly evident that structural and technological changes were slowly but surely moving many states toward greater controls at both the policy-making and the administrative levels. Certainly the new state boards were one step in this direction. Even though it was clear that none of them (given their size, structure, and personnel) had attained maturity, all of them possessed the potential to evolve over a period of decades into highly organized and complex structures.

The process of centralization and rationalization was by no means devoid of friction and conflict. Individual hospitals had grown accustomed to considerable autonomy in managing their internal affairs. At the same time the AMSAII assumed the role of the preeminent authority on the subject of mental disease. Both individual hospitals and the AMSAII found it difficult to adjust to any diminution in their role; they resisted attempts to impose controls by external authorities. The result was several decades of bitter conflict.

Although the first state boards of charity had relatively few substantive powers, their thrust was clearly in the direction of centralization of authority. The formation of the Conference of Charities (now the National Conference on Social Welfare) was further evidence of this trend. Its annual conventions became a constant source of attacks on mental hospitals and demands for greater regulatory authority. The fact that the Conference and the AMSAII were two clearly distinct organizations with differing memberships and without any means of formal liaison contributed to the growing struggle for control. The former clearly had the advantage, for its members were able to attract support from various dissident individuals and groups, while the isolation of the latter placed it at a serious disadvantage.

The case for the imposition of greater governmental controls was spelled out on a number of occasions at Conference meetings. In 1876 Dr. Hervey B. Wilbur put the issue in a very succinct form. A pioneer in the care and education of the feebleminded, Wilbur was superintendent of the New York State Asylum for Idiots. He had been invited to talk at the AMSAII and had appeared, but since that organization included only superintendents (even assistant physicians were not members until the end of the nineteenth century), he was never admitted to membership. By the mid-1870's Wilbur had joined the ranks of the critics. This role was formalized by his election in 1880 to the presidency of the newly founded National Association for the Protection of the Insane and the Prevention of Insanity. Wilbur's talk at the Conference of Charities in 1876 was concerned with the need for governmental supervision of the insane. He vigorously condemned the "supreme control and somewhat arrogant guardianship" of superintendents. Such men, he noted, were chosen for political or social reasons; they frequently neglected their duties because of their services to courts as expert witnesses and their lucrative outside consulting practice. In many instances they lacked administrative ability and feared meaningful innovation. Pointing to the recent investigation of Dr. Charles H. Nichols at the Government Hospital for the Insane in Washington, D.C., Wilbur argued that proper and efficient government supervision would have prevented the abuses that existed at that institution. While not concerned with the specific form of such regulation, he advocated an expansion in the authority of state boards of charity, which seemed to be the logical supervisory agency.[51]

The movement toward central regulation quickly aroused the ire of the AMSAII. During the 1860's, when the controversy over commitment procedures first began in earnest, the association unanimously passed a resolution strongly opposing "Lunacy Commissions" or any other forms of government supervision as "not only wholly unnecessary, but injurious and subversive of

51. Hervey B. Wilbur, "Governmental Supervision of the Insane," Conference of Charities, *Proceedings*, III (1876), 82–90.

the present efficient system of control by Boards of Trustees or Managers appointed by the State Executives or the proper authorities of Corporate Institutions, and performing their prescribed duties without pay or emolument." During the discussion over the resolution there was virtually no support for any form of supervision or regulation. Even John P. Gray, who was often critical of his fellow superintendents, explained that he had favored the creation of a state commission on lunacy under the office of the secretary of state. The powers of such a commission, however, should be limited to the inspection and regulation of poor houses, almshouses, and jails containing insane persons. Like all members of the AMSAII, he was unalterably opposed to the establishment of any agency "having any oversight, charge or control of State or corporate institutions."[52]

Hidden from view was the broader philosophical problem posed by the claims of a profession for autonomy against the claims of the society that had established and supported mental hospitals. Who, for example, should determine the structure and functions of such institutions? Granted that society had the right to establish the level of funding and the priorities involved; but once it had made that decision was it to abrogate all other responsibilities to a professional group responsible only to its own members? On the other hand, was society competent to decide medical and technical issues, thereby assuming a function for which it had no training or experience? Such basic questions were rarely faced openly or directly. Instead the discussions tended to revolve around immediate considerations that arose at one time or another and seemed to require an urgent resolution, a development that often blurred or obfuscated basic policy issues.

In 1875, for example, Isaac Ray, who had never been favorably disposed toward external regulation, introduced a series of resolutions at the meetings of the AMSAII. While several were specifically concerned with those laws that limited the authority of the superintendent to censor patient mail, some were addressed to the broader subject of interference in the internal affairs of hospitals. Ray's resolutions were phrased largely in terms of the professional expertise of superintendents in the management and treatment of the mentally ill, and they rejected the notion that

52. *AJI*, XXI (July, 1864), 152–155 (October, 1864), 266–267.

supernumerary functionaries "with the privilege of scrutinizing the management of the hospital" or controlling it either by the direct exercise of power or indirectly by "stringent advice" could accomplish "an amount of good sufficient to compensate for the harm that is sure to follow." Ray's resolutions received the overwhelming support of the membership of the AMSAII; only two dissenting votes were cast against them.[53]

Throughout the 1870's and afterwards superintendents remained on the defensive against both their critics and those who would impose external controls upon their internal authority. "All our newspapers, the best as well as the worst," complained Ray, "take intense satisfaction in pitching into hospitals on every occasion, with an utter lack of intelligence, fairness, & honesty."[54] Ray's sentiments were echoed by other beleaguered colleagues. Kirkbride charged that the unjustified attacks upon the integrity of the profession came from "irresponsible sources, to be based on the most unsupported assertions, and to be written, as has been now and then honestly avowed, more from a belief that the public likes to hear stories of the kind, than from any desire to discover and correct abuses."[55] Most superintendents agreed with Ray and Kirkbride; they saw a combination that included a sensationalist press, an incipient but growing state bureaucracy, and well-intentioned but misinformed individuals leading the attack on their integrity.[56]

Despite opposition, the movement to impose more stringent controls over the autonomy of individual hospitals and superin-

53. *AJI*, XXXII (January, 1876), 345–355.

54. Isaac Ray to Judge Charles Doe, September 20, 1870, ms. in Butler Hospital Library, Providence. R.I.

55. Pennsylvania Hospital for the Insane, *AR*, XXXII (1872), 32–44.

56. Cf. Isaac Ray, "Confinement of the Insane," *American Law Review*, January, 1869, reprinted in Ray's *Contributions to Mental Pathology* (Boston, 1873), 168–202; Iowa Hospital for the Insane, *BR*, IV (1866/1867), 69–73, VIII (1874/1875), 17–22; Taunton State Lunatic Hospital, *AR*, XX (1873), 31–36; Mississippi State Lunatic Asylum, *AR*, 1873, 38–39; Asylum for the Insane of the State of Kansas, *AR*, IX (1873), 8–9, X (1874), 27–29; Worcester State Lunatic Hospital, *AR*, XLIII (1875), 25. See also the interesting exchange, "A Modern Lettre de Cachet," *Atlantic Monthly*, XXI (May, 1868), 588–602, and "'A Modern Lettre de Cachet' Reviewed," *ibid.*, XXII (August, 1868), 227–243.

tendents slowly but surely gained momentum. More and more hospital officials found that the determination of policy had passed into the hands of individuals who were immersed in welfare-related problems and whose outlook was dominated by concerns involving administrative rationality and efficiency. Since such individuals had a far broader constituency and were not involved in the minutiae of daily institutional life, they found it fairly easy to present a convincing case to justify an expansion of their powers. Their promises of lower expenditures also proved appealing. The authority of individual superintendents, on the other hand, slowly receded into the background, for they were unable to present their case without being involved in complex issues that often tried the patience of legislators and policymakers or to avoid the suspicion that their recommendations would inevitably mean larger appropriations for the care and treatment of the insane.

The thrust toward centralization was accompanied by considerable friction. From the very moment that the new state boards of charity were established, there was conflict between their members and hospital officials. The struggle involved a variety of issues that often differed from state to state. In some cases the boards charged hospital administrators with extravagance and financial mismanagement; in other cases there was a divergence of opinion as to the proper function of mental hospitals. Sooner or later, however, individual differences were reduced to a single issue: centralized versus decentralized control. Yet the problem of locating authority was never the subject of an open and direct debate; personal and professional antipathies completely overshadowed policy issues, which consequently were never presented in a clear or lucid manner.

Pennsylvania is a case in point. In that state an open struggle took place between the members of the central board and the individual public hospitals that seemed to involve personalities as much as issues. In their annual reports (parts of which were also circulated in pamphlet form), the Board of Commissioners of Public Charities had criticized the state's public institutions for accepting private patients and neglecting those persons unable to pay for the costs of hospitalization. The result was that many in the latter category were languishing in local poor houses and almshouses, which had neither the knowledge nor the facilities to provide adequate care. In pointing to this problem, the commissioners hinted that a desire for respectability on the part of the superintendents and officers was partly responsible, since these persons did not want to be associated with "an institution of mere paupers." They urged that state hospitals be required to give preference to insane poor persons as a matter of policy.[57]

The members of the board, moreover, were extremely incensed at the fact that mentally ill criminals as well as persons acquitted of crimes by reason of insanity were confined in prisons and jails; they strongly urged that a separate department connected with one of the state hospitals be established for such cases. They also sought the support of the AMSAII in 1873 for their proposal. For some unknown reason the letter of the president of the board to the association was suppressed at the association's convention, although the organization did pass a resolution condemning the incarceration of insane convicts in jails and mental hospitals and urging the establishment of separate facilities for such cases. Until this could be done, insane convicts could be cared for in a hospital connected with some prison, and not in the wards or a separate building of a mental hospital. The association made no attempt to take a general position in regard to the criminally insane. In presenting its case, the Pennsylvania board also attempted to define the limits of professional competency. "We . . . feel constrained to suggest," its members noted,

> —and we do it with much hesitation, and with sincere respect for all parties—that, in forming a judgment on this scheme, a preponderating weight ought not to be attached to the opinions of parties who may have any personal interest or convenience involved in the question, however respectable they may be, and even though they present themselves in the character of experts. THE AUTHORITY OF EXPERTS IS LIMITED to their particular professional sphere. Their proper office is to serve as

57. Pennsylvania Board of Commissioners of Public Charities, *AR*, IV (1837), cxxix–clv, 439–446, V (1874), 46–65, 297–304; Pennsylvania Board of Public Charities, *A Plea for the Insane in the Prisons and Poor-Houses of Pennsylvania* (Philadelphia, 1873), 6–27, and *Addenda to a Plea for the Insane in the Prisons and Poor-Houses of Pennsylvania* (Philadelphia, 1873), 3–16.

witnesses and not as *judges*; and any intelligent and disinterested layman, who by personal observation, and thorough study, has made himself acquainted with the condition of the insane in our penitentiaries, jails, poor houses and hospitals, is as well (perhaps better) qualified to judge, as they are, of the broad features of any plan proposed for ameliorating their condition—to judge what is consistent with or demanded by the dictates of justice, humanity and the public good.[58]

The board's allegations aroused the anger of some superintendents as well as the trustees of the Pennsylvania State Lunatic Hospital. The trustees published a specific rejoinder categorically denying that paying patients were given preference over poor patients; they also went on record in support of the position of the AMSAII on the issue of facilities for insane convicts. The basic problem, concluded the trustees, was that the people of Pennsylvania "have not been roused to a proper understanding of their full duty to the insane until within a recent period, and since they have been aroused, they find the work so large that their finances will not allow them to push forward the work of providing the remedy as rapidly as the necessity of the case seems to demand." The superintendents of Pennsylvania's mental hospitals supported the trustees against the board. In reviewing the entire controversy, the *American Journal of Insanity* noted that there did not seem any irreconcilable differences between the parties on the issues involved. The journal urged the board to expend its energies in promoting changes rather than becoming involved in personalities.[59]

Aside from the open and heated controversy over policy questions, a more serious struggle occurred behind the scenes in 1876 between the board and Dr. John Curwen, longtime superintendent of the Pennsylvania State Lunatic Hospital and a lead-

58. Pennsylvania Board of Commissioners of Public Charities, *AR*, IV (1873), cliv–ccvi; Pennsylvania Board of Public Charities, *A Plea for the Insane*, 27 ff.

59. *Statement of the Trustees of the Penn'a State Lunatic Hospital, in Regard to Certain Charges of the Board of Public Charities of the State of Pennsylvania with an Appendix* (Harrisburg, 1874), 3–15; *AJI*, XXX (April, 1874), 499–502.

ing member of AMSAII. Curwen felt that the board was seeking to curtail his power because it opposed his efforts to secure additional accommodations for the insane. His relations with the board continued to worsen; five months later he charged that the board was seeking his ouster. Curwen accused the commissioners of seeking to economize at the expense of patients, and he was sharply critical of their activities.[60]

Similar friction arose in Massachusetts, which—because of Sanborn's presence—had perhaps the most prestigious and influential charity board in the nation. By the early 1870's the board was pushing vigorously for an expansion of its authority. The legislature, it argued, was incapable of regulating and coordinating the activities of individual institutions. Only a central board clothed with the requisite powers could perform this function. "The vast sums expended by the State for charitable and correctional purposes," it remarked in words calculated to appeal to the legislature, "never can be properly economized; the great machinery for keeping her army of dependents can never work well to a common end; the immense moral power put forth through the various boards of trustees, inspectors, superintendents and officers, can never accomplish what it might do, until some central board shall be clothed with power to co-ordinate the existing forces, and make them work harmoniously to a common end."[61] In seeking to expand its role, the board quickly encountered opposition from individual superintendents. When it criticized the seemingly high death rate at the Worcester hospital, it aroused an angry but private response from Dr. Barnard D. Eastman. On another occasion Dr. J. P. Brown, superintendent of the Taunton hospital, attacked Sanborn for emphasizing economy at the expense of therapy. "Mr. S.," he wrote to Dix, "seems ambitious to gain favor with politicians by cheapening everything and would reduce the expenses of our Hospitals to Poor House Rates. It is like a wet blanket to all our institutions. I have not known him to commend a single thing that has been done here to increase the comforts and make

60. John Curwen to Dix, February 14, July 19, 1876, Dix Papers, HLHU.

61. Massachusetts Board of State Charities, *AR*, X (1873), xxxiii–xxxv.

more cheerful the daily lives of our patients. The burden of his inquiry is, 'how much is it costing you this quarter'?"[62]

VI

Although superintendents continued to fight against the growing authority of central boards, their struggle was essentially a rear-guard action. At no point did they take the initiative to limit the power of these agencies, nor did they offer any alternative organizational plans that would enable their institutions to function in a more autonomous manner. Perhaps their years of service as administrators had eroded their will to resist. Perhaps the similarity of their ideological framework to that of state welfare officials inhibited their power to protest. Whatever the reasons, it was clear that the role of hospital superintendents in the determination of public policy toward the mentally ill would continue to diminish.

The decline in the status and power of hospital superintendents was accompanied by a corresponding increase in the authority of central boards. This is not in any way to imply that central boards attempted to dictate standards of care and treatment involving professional judgments, for such was not the case. The thrust of state regulation was toward greater cohesiveness and economy in public policy, not toward a definition or resolution of professional issues. Nor was the diminution of local autonomy necessarily an evil or retrogressive development; in many instances central boards were responsible for change and innovation. Yet the most significant result of the drive toward centralization and rationalization was the formal inclusion of the mental hospital within a welfare structure, imparting to the former the intrinsic character of the latter. On the one hand, the mental hospital was ostensibly a medical institution providing care and treatment for all groups irrespective of their ability to pay for extended insti-

62. *Ibid.*, XI (1874), xlix–li; Worcester State Lunatic Hospital, *AR*, XLII (1874), 22–23, XLIII (1875), 7; Barnard D. Eastman to Pliny Earle, January 31, 1876, Earle to Eastman, February 29, 1876, Earle Papers, AAS; *AJI*, XXXV (July, 1878), 109; J. P. Brown to Dix, February 17, 1880, Dix Papers, HLHU.

tutionalization. On the other hand, it was an institution that cared for a patient population composed predominantly of lower-class groups and ethnic minorities, giving it an appearance similar to other welfare but nonhealth-related institutions. Its ambivalent character reflected to an astonishing extent the entire framework of public policy toward welfare and dependency with all of that policy's inconsistencies, tensions, and conflicts. For better or worse, the fate of the nation's mentally ill population would continue to depend largely on external circumstances beyond the control of those physicians and administrators specializing in the care and treatment of the insane.

Chapter VIII

The Search for Alternatives

I

By 1860 THERE WAS VIRTUALLY no disagreement with the principle that society had a moral obligation toward the mentally ill. While the Civil War seriously impaired the ability of some hospitals to carry out their mission and inhibited the founding of new ones, the interruption proved to be temporary. Between 1870 and 1880 nearly thirty new institutions were opened, including fifteen in the Midwest, ten in the Northeast, and two each in the South and Far West. For the remainder of the nineteenth century the movement to expand public facilities continued unabated; not until the twentieth century was there a clear diminution in the opening of new hospitals.

The existence of a general consensus, however, did not at all imply that disagreements and conflicts were absent. On the contrary, there were sharp divergencies of opinion over the means by which a general principle was to be translated into actual policies. These differences became even more clearly defined as disillusionment with existing hospitals mounted in intensity. The result was the beginning of an often bitter and acrimonious debate that had as its goal the formulation of more effective policies toward the mentally ill.

To a large extent the impetus for change came from outside the ranks of institutional psychiatrists. In some cases the search for alternatives was initiated by individuals associated with the state boards of charity; in others the issue was raised by individuals having only a tenuous connection with existing institutions. Whatever the case, it was clear that hospital superintendents (and their professional association) no longer occupied the position they had held for several decades as the preeminent authority on the subject of mental disease.

The challenge that dissident individuals and groups presented to hospital superintendents was heightened in importance because of the changing social context. Before 1860 policy was little more than the sum total of individual decisions, partly because the structure of state legislatures was not conducive to a consideration of long-range solutions and partly because of the absence of permanent state agencies concerned with broad social planning and engineering. The founding of state boards of charity, however, sharply altered the picture. Unlike hospital superintendents, the members of these boards were primarily interested in the problems arising out of distress and dependency. Consequently, their approach toward the mentally ill reflected their own goal of providing care for dependent groups in the most efficient and economical manner possible. Together with some younger psychiatrists, they sought to develop new organizational models for hospitals in order to fulfil their mandate to control the rising costs of dependency and yet provide humane care for groups requiring public assistance.

In the two decades following 1860 psychiatrists, charity reformers, and public officials engaged in a long debate over the proper structure, functions, and goals of mental hospitals and the way in which society should fulfil its responsibilities toward the insane. Yet the debate, which was bitter and acrimonious, produced more heat than light, more rhetoric than substantive changes. As late as 1880—nearly two decades after many states had begun to rationalize and centralize the structure of public welfare—a coherent and effective policy to deal with mental illness was only a hope and not an established fact.

II

In the three decades after 1830 superintendents had occasionally discussed among themselves alternative models of mental hospitals that might alleviate the problems of overcrowding and the continued accumulation of chronic patients that threatened the therapeutic character of their institutions. The one idea that aroused some interest involved the establishment of separate hospitals for the incurably insane. Such institutions would accept persons who did not respond to therapeutic care, but who required continued institutionalization. Hospitals for incurables would not only relieve the pressure on therapeutic institutions, but they would end once and for all the practice of confining insane persons in welfare and penal institutions and also ensure the most efficient use of public funds.

Generally speaking, the majority of superintendents were not favorably disposed toward a policy that differentiated between curable and incurable cases. To most superintendents the defects of institutions for incurables far outweighed any potential virtues. They were not at all convinced that it was possible to determine with any degree of precision when a person was curable or incurable. Nor would it be easy to prevent abuses in custodial hospitals. The only advantage was the relative inexpensiveness of such institutions, and this claim had validity only if humanitarian obligations were completely ignored.[1] In his classic and influential work on hospital architecture in 1854, Kirkbride summed up the case against separate facilities for incurable cases:

> The first grand objection to such a separation is, that no one can say with entire certainty who is incurable; and to condemn any one to an institution for this particular class is like dooming him to utter hopelessness. . . . When patients cannot be cured, they should still be considered under treatment, as long as life lasts; if not with the hope of restoring them to health, to do what is next in importance, to promote their comfort and happiness, and to keep them from sinking still lower in the scale of humanity. Fortunately, almost precisely the same class of means are generally required for the best management and treatment of the curable and incurable, and almost as much skill may be shown in caring judiciously for the latter as for the former. When the incurable are in the same institution as the curable, there is little danger of their being neglected; but when once consigned to receptacles specially provided for them, all experience leads us to

1. Cf. Amariah Brigham to Dix, January 14, 1844, Dix Papers, HLHU.

believe that but little time will elapse before they will be found gradually sinking, mentally and physically, their care entrusted to persons actuated only by selfish motives—the grand object being to ascertain at how little cost per week soul and body can be kept together—and, sooner or later, cruelty, neglect and suffering are pretty sure to be the results of every such experiment.[2]

Before 1860 the issue of separate institutions for incurable patients aroused relatively little controversy. In the early days of hospitals the accumulation of such cases was not as significant as it later would become; superintendents were probably adverse to the subect because any discussion might contradict their optimistic curability claims. Isaac Ray—one of the few who favored such differentiated institutions—felt that the size of a hospital was of far greater significance. And William M. Awl, while concerned about the potential impact that a gradual accumulation of incurable patients might have on his hospital, simply suggested that county almshouses be encouraged to care for them and that officials be given greater discretionary authority in deciding which patients would be accepted and which would be rejected.[3] Immersed in the internal problems of hospital management and the creation of a profession, few superintendents gave serious consideration to the implications that the establishment of institutions for incurables might have for public policy. The lack of external pressure further diminished the possibility of establishing custodial hospitals. While proposals for such hospitals were advanced from time to time, they were not a major source of discord.

After 1860, on the other hand, the continuous rise in the number of resident chronic patients had all but obliterated the therapeutic goals of many hospitals. Of 158 residents at the Western Pennsylvania Hospital for the Insane in early 1865, to

2. Thomas S. Kirkbride, *On the Construction, Organization, and General Arrangements of Hospitals for the Insane* (Philadelphia, 1854), 59.

3. Ray to Dix, February 20, 1843, Dix Papers, HLHU; Ohio Lunatic Asylum, *AR*, VI (1844), 30, VII (1845), 38–39. By the 1850's Ray had modified his position in regard to separate institutions for incurable persons, and by the 1860's he had reversed his earlier stand as a result of his experiences as a superintendent.

cite a fairly typical illustration, 10 had been insane for less than six months, 12 less than one year, 62 from one to five years, and 74 for periods ranging between five and thirty years. Nor was the situation different elsewhere; virtually every hospital in the nation was confronted with a problem whose magnitude was clearly increasing rather than diminishing.[4] One superintendent noted with a touch of sarcasm that the problem in his state was that "we are all born philanthropists each one with a scheme of his own for the amelioration of the race, including the insane. When we get all these schemes in operation Massachusetts will be a pleasant place to live in. . . . We are also to have a Commission. Mass. is wholly given over to Commissions—sit through the summer and, in addition to drawing their salary, try to find out what revision is necessary in our charities and their administration. Meanwhile the insane are a positive fact with us."[5]

Compounding the situation was the serious overcrowding at most hospitals. While many states continued to expand the number of public institutions, the demand always exceeds the supply at any given time. The financial and administrative environment in which hospitals functioned, as we have already seen, gave their officers little leeway to deal with the problems arising out of overcrowding and the accumulation of incurable patients.[6] Given the decline in curability rates that was clearly evident by the

4. Western Pennsylvania Hospital for the Insane, *AR*, VIII (1864), 16–19. See also Michigan Asylum for the Insane, *BR*, 1861/1862, 22–23, 28ff., 1863/1864, 18–20; New Jersey State Lunatic Asylum, *AR*, XVIII (1864), 13, XXVII (1873), 13–14; Utica State Lunatic Asylum, *AR*, XXIV (1866), 14–15; Indiana Hospital for the Insane, *AR*, XVII (1865), 5–6, XVIII (1866), 6–8, 13–14; Wisconsin State Hospital for the Insane, *AR*, VI (1865), 5–6; New Hampshire Asylum for the Insane, *AR*, XXVII (1868), 17; Southern Ohio Lunatic Asylum, *AR*, XV (1869), 10–11; Connecticut General Hospital for the Insane, *AR*, III (1869), 12–13; Asylum for the Insane of the State of Kansas, *AR*, VI (1870), 5–6, VIII (1872), 8; Insane Asylum of Louisiana, *AR*, 1870, 5; Mississippi State Lunatic Asylum, *AR*, 1871, 11; Virginia Western Lunatic Asylum, *AR*, 1871/1872, 9–10; Alabama Insane Hospital, *AR*, XII (1872), 35–36; West Virginia Hospital for the Insane, *AR*, IX (1872), 17–18.

5. W. W. Godding to Dix, May 7, 1877, Dix Papers, HLHU.

6. The annual reports of most mental hospitals during the 1870's offer ample evidence on this point.

1860's and 1870's as well as the growing distrust of mental hospitals, it was understandable that pressure for change would mount in intensity. Superintendents now found themselves in the uneasy position of having to answer for their inability to live up to their earlier claims about the curability of insanity. Although they could—with considerable justification—point to factors beyond their control that contributed to the therapeutic ineffectiveness of their hospitals, they usually were at a disadvantage during public and legislative policy discussions precisely because of the subtlety and complexity of their case.

The problems arising out of overcrowded conditions and the accumulation of chronic patients appeared earliest in those states with the oldest public institutions. Yet even in these states there were few conscious efforts prior to 1860 to adjust policy to the realities of the situation. Where changes were introduced, they tended to be piecemeal in nature. Massachusetts, for example, began to innovate not because of its concern for the mentally ill, but because of its fear of alien paupers. In 1854 the Bay State opened several state almshouses for foreign-born paupers. Shortly thereafter one of the almshouses (located at Tewksbury) established a separate department for incurably insane immigrant paupers. The inspectors of the almshouse approved of this development on the grounds that it benefited other public hospitals in the state and also offered inexpensive care for the alien insane. Conditions at the Tewksbury almshouse, however, deteriorated rapidly; its only redeeming virtue was that its cost per patient per year by 1861 was $52, as compared with $130 at the three state hospitals. By 1866 separate accommodations for the insane had been constructed and the asylum for chronic cases given semiautonomy within the administrative structure of the almshouse. Although the new facility received the support of the American Medical Association in 1867 as well as that of the superintendents of the state's public mental hospitals, conditions there remained below minimum standards for at least a decade. Even after startling revelations about Tewksbury had been made public in the mid-1870's, the practice of separating the alien pauper incurably insane was not abandoned. The state simply renamed the institution as the Tewksbury Asylum for the Chronic Insane, although it still remained a part of the Tewksbury almshouse. The new institution, however, continued to receive incurable aliens exclusively.[7]

Unlike Massachusetts, New York attempted to cope with the problems of the insane in a direct and open manner. As early as 1854 the county superintendents of the poor had criticized the state for allowing the pecuniary status of an individual to determine the quality of care and treatment. Although several legislative committees agreed with these local officials about the impropriety of dealing with the mentally ill within the framework of state welfare, no concrete changes followed.[8] In 1864, however, the New York legislature authorized Sylvester D. Willard, secretary of the Medical Society of the State of New York, to investigate conditions among the insane poor throughout the state. After several months of intensive study, Willard completed his report. He pointed to the obvious defects in the existing system, and was especially critical of the "gross want of provision for the common necessities of physical health and comfort, in a large majority of the poor houses where pauper lunatics were kept." Attendants in many cases were drawn from among the inmates of such institutions. "Paupers," noted Willard, "who in many instances are depraved by vice, cold, sordid, selfish from

7. Massachusetts State Almshouse at Tewksbury, *AR*, III (1856), 5–6, V (1858), 4–5, VIII (1861), 14, XI (1864), 5, 13, XII (1865), 7, 12, XIII (1866), 6–7, XIV (1867), 12–13, 28–33, XV (1868), 5–6, 29–31, XVI (1869), 3, XVIII (1871), 10–11, XXI (1874), 9–13, 33–34; Taunton State Lunatic Hospital, *AR*, XII (1865), 11–12, XIII (1866), 10–12; Massachusetts Board of State Charities, *AR*, I (1864), 265–266, II (1865), 149–150, III (1866), 150–151, X (1873), liv, XII (1875), lviii–lxi, XIII (1876), ix–xvi; Franklin B. Sanborn, *The Public Charities of Massachusetts during the Century Ending Jan. 1, 1876*, in Massachusetts Board of State Charities, Supplement to the *AR*, XII (1875), clii–clv; Pliny Earle to W. H. Lathrop, March 16, 1876 (copy), Earle Papers, AAS.

8. *Report and Memorial of the County Superintendents of the Poor of this State on Lunacy and its Relation to Pauperism, and for Relief of Insane Poor*, New York Senate Document No. 17 (January 23, 1856); *Report of the Select Committee on Report and Memorial of County Superintendents of the Poor, on Lunacy and its Relation to Pauperism*, New York Senate Document No. 71 (March 5, 1856); *Report of Select Committee Appointed to Visit Charitable Institutions Supported by the State, and all City and County Poor and Work Houses and Jails*, New York Senate Document No. 8 (January 9, 1857).

poverty, utterly incapable of taking care of themselves; these are employed to oversee and apply moral and physical means of restraint for the insane!" The report concluded by recommending the establishment of an institution for incurable persons in order to relieve local welfare institutions of responsibilities which they were ill equipped to meet. The legislature concurred with this proposal in 1865, and four years later the Willard Asylum for the Insane was opened for the reception of chronic cases.[9]

The action by the New York legislature in approving an institution for the incurably insane immediately precipitated a debate both within and without the psychiatric profession that lasted for over a decade. This debate covered far-ranging and fundamental issues and aroused sharp antagonisms between individuals and groups. To many hospital superintendents the new institution threatened their integrity, for the legislation had seemed to act contrary to their professional judgments. Critics of hospital officials, on the other hand, tended to support the new institution, and they were joined by those whose first concern was with welfare. The debate in general brought to a head a number of long-simmering issues. While generating heat as well as light, the controversy soon involved the contours of public policy, for the founding of the Willard institution was to have serious implications for the future.

The opening round of the debate was begun with the publication of an unsigned article in the *American Journal of Insanity* in October, 1865. Representing the views of John P. Gray, editor of the journal and superintendent of the Utica hospital, the article was critical of the legislature's action on a number of counts. First, the law made the Utica hospital responsible for all cases of insanity of less than one year's duration. Since a hospital tended to serve the adjacent community to a disproportionate extent, it was clear that Utica simply could not meet the needs of the state. Secondly, the Utica institution already contained 600 patients. Recognizing that moral treatment was extraordinarily arduous and time-consuming, the article emphasized that the conversion of Utica into a totally therapeutic institution would make unreasonable demands upon the staff. Thirdly, cus-

9. Sylvester D. Willard, *Report on the Condition of the Insane Poor in the County Poor Houses of New York,* New York *Assembly Document No. 19* (January 13, 1865), *passim.*

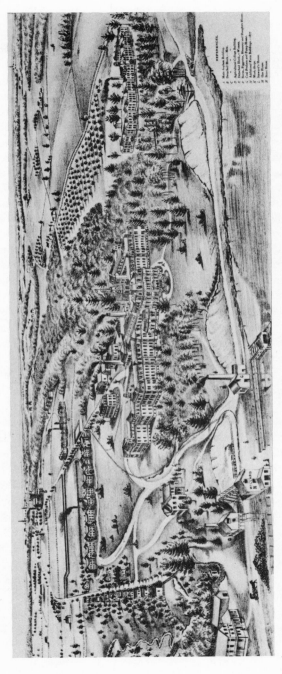

18. *The Willard Asylum. Opened in 1869 for chronic mentally ill persons, the Willard asylum became one of the largest hospitals in the nation and aroused the opposition of many prominent superintendents of mental institutions. Source: Willard Asylum for the Insane, Annual Report, IX (1877).*

todial care did not involve the abolition of treatment. On the contrary, medical and dietetic treatment remained as important as ever. Fourth, institutions for incurable patients tended to become unwieldy; treatment often vanished; recent cases were submerged in an undifferentiated mass; an unhealthful atmosphere was created because of the absence of hope; and above all, incurables tended to be affixed with the stigma of pauperism, even though pauperism was the result rather than the cause of insanity. Finally, many families would refuse to incarcerate relatives in such institutions. What was needed, the article concluded, was not an institution for incurables, but additional hospital facilities judiciously distributed so as to serve all geographic areas in the state.[10]

Meanwhile, a behind-the-scenes attempt was mounted to induce the legislature to reverse the principle of separate care for the chronic insane. The movement for repeal was spearheaded by Gray, who served briefly on the committee to locate the hospital but resigned when it became apparent that the legislature would not change its mind. Opposition to the new facility was also expressed by Dix, who threw her prestige into the fray. The controversy on occasion became so heated that a number of personal relationships were sorely strained. John B. Chapin, one of the strongest supporters of Willard (and later its first superintendent), felt that he was being unjustly malinged by Gray, while George Cook, an ally of Chapin, vigorously defended the new institution and expressed disappointment at the position taken by Dix.[11] "Those of us," Chapin wrote, "who have ventured to urge something better than poor houses for them [the chronic insane] will probably not abandon their position and are sure to have the public with them if they but persevere. It is idle to suppose all will ever be placed in *hospitals* though the Journal of Insanity proposes to *cure* all. Something must be conceded in style and expense of buildings and accommodations to the economic views

10. "The Willard Asylum, and Provision for the Insane," *AJI*, XXII (October, 1865), 192–212.

11. George Cook to Dix, March 15, 1866, D. T. Brown to Dix, March 31, April 7 (two letters), 1866, John B. Chapin to Dix, February 11, 20, 1867, John P. Gray to Dix, January 10, 1869, Dix Papers, HLHU; John P. Gray to Kirkbride, August 29, 1866(?), Kirkbride Papers, IPH.

of our people. In the essentials of care we ask that the standard may be elevated."[12]

The new departure in policy attracted the attention of the AMSAII. Most of those present at the convention of the association in 1865 clearly disapproved of separate institutions, but rather than act immediately they voted to refer the subject to a committee with instructions to report back the following year.[13] In 1866 a heated debate took place. The case for separate institutions was presented by George Cook of Brigham Hall, a small private hospital in New York State. Cook maintained that the new departure was intended to rectify the failures of localities to meet their responsibilities toward the insane. The shortsightedness of most communities had already created a dual system in fact, while all efforts to convince the legislature to found additional facilities had failed. The establishment of the the Willard hospital, therefore, would upgrade care and move in the direction of unitary state responsibility for the insane. Nor would chronic cases be neglected, for the new facility would provide occupational therapy. The result would be better care at a lower cost. "It is not well to sneer at political economy in its relations to the insane poor," he informed the association, "whether we think it right or not, the question of cost has determined, and will continue to determine their fate or weal or woe."[14]

After Cook had presented his paper, the committee appointed at the previous convention introduced a series of resolutions. The resolutions stipulated that the state should make adequate provision for all its insane; that hospitals be centrally located and geographically distributed; that it was wrong to attempt to make the labor of the insane remunerative rather than therapeutic; and that all insane persons (with the exception of cases of chronic and advanced dementia) should be cared for in hospitals. Separate facilities could be provided for demented persons, but always under close supervision to prevent abuses.[15]

12. John B. Chapin to Edward Jarvis, April 24, 1868, Jarvis Papers, CLMHMS.

13. *AJI*, XXII (July, 1865), 69–74.

14. George Cook, "Provision for the Insane Poor in the State of New York," *ibid.*, XXIII (July, 1866), 45–75.

15. *Ibid.*, 147–149.

The debate over Cook's paper and the resolution proved vigorous and lengthy. What emerged was a division not so much on the abstract issue (for even the proponents of Willard were unwilling to base their case on the absolute necessity of that type of institution), but rather on the more pragmatic consideration as to how far principle could be bent without being broken. The dilemma was especially evident in the anguished comments of Dr. Clement A. Walker, superintendent of the Boston Lunatic Hospital. To go before legislatures and ask for expensive accommodations for all insane persons, he declared, was hopeless. Yet the profession could not abandon its responsibilities and permit communities—which admittedly were "weighed down and overburdened with expenses"—to deal with the problem on their own. The profession, Walker concluded, had to lead the way in developing policies that took into consideration both the needs of the individual and the resources of the community.[16]

The convention in the end adopted five resolutions. The first four, which passed unanimously, supported a plan to divide states into geographic districts, each to be served by one comprehensive mental hospital having facilities for proper classification, and reaffirmed the propositions governing the construction, organization, and management adopted at the conventions of 1851 and 1853. The fifth resolution, which passed by a narrow margin, modified the association's position on the size of the ideal mental hospital by increasing the number of patients from 250 to 600.[17]

The controversy over separate institutions for the curable and incurable continued to rage over the next decade. The AMSAII remained unalterably opposed to institutions for incurable persons; it defended its position by reaffirming its members' vision of the ideal therapeutic hospital and refusing in any way to compromise their principles. Men like Kirkbride, Ray, and others had never surrendered their faith in the efficacy of moral management, and they tended to see insanity as a curable disease. The basic issue in their eyes was the size of institutions and the availability of sufficient resources for the fulfillment of a therapeutic mission. Critics of the AMSAII, on the other hand, tended to be much

16. *Ibid.*, 220–221. The entire debate is produced on 147–250.
17. *Ibid.*, 248–250.

younger and for the most part were not affiliated with mental hospitals. Their concern was more with those mentally ill persons in welfare institutions; they felt strongly that allegiance to principle would prove a disaster. "So much has been said by the members of the profession against our proceedings here," wrote Chapin, that "I have felt little interest in saying much of our plans. This asylum [Willard] has proved an entering wedge to break up forever I hope, at a distant day, the County house system of care of the insane poor in this state. If this result is accomplished I shall be content by whatever name called—it is of small consequence."[18] Men like Chapin, moreover, represented the somatic viewpoint that was rapidly becoming dominant in both medicine and psychiatry during the second half of the nineteenth century. As Chapin himself remarked in 1877: "The majority of the insane are not likely to, and, as a matter of fact, do not recover. . . . In the judgment of the medical profession, further advance in our knowledge of the pathology of structural changes is best assured in the revelations which the microscope will furnish."[19] While a somatic interpretation of disease promised much in the future, the immediate result was therapeutic nihilism; until it was possible to correlate lesions with abnormal behavior, no therapy—physical or psychological—was possible. Most physicians, interestingly enough, viewed therapeutic nihilism in optimistic terms; it was the prelude to the momentary discovery of remedies for a somatic illness. Government officials and the general public, on the other hand, saw it as confirmation of their distrust of mental hospitals.

Opponents of the AMSAII also argued that hospitals could be constructed more economically and that legislatures would be generous if their members could be convinced that public funds were not being wasted. Recognizing that the odds of changing the AMSAII were not especially good, they attempted instead to gain the support of organizations like the American Medical Association and the Conference of Charities. There was, however, no clearcut division between the AMSAII and other groups on this issue. The New York State Board of Charities, for example,

18. Chapin to Jarvis, February 6, 1872, Jarvis Papers, CLMHMS.
19. Conference of Charities, *Proceedings*, IV (1877), 7, 9.

sided with the AMSAII in opposing the Willard concept, while its Wisconsin counterpart favored such institutions.[20] And even within the AMSAII unanimity did not exist, for some superintendents favored differentiated institutions. Indeed, as early as 1863 one Ohio superintendent was jubilant over his success in getting support for the establishment of receptacles for chronic cases. "I have taken a step in my report," he wrote, "that I anticipate some condemnation of from my brethren of other Hospitals but I am *entrenched* behind impenetrable walls of common sense and logic—*as I think*—I have broken ground for the establishment of *large*—yes *large*—receptacles,—yes *receptacles*—for the incurable—yes, *large, receptacles for the incurable insane*—If my visions in this direction are ever realized Ohio will feel proud of her stride in the progress of humanitarian work and other states will bless her for giving the example to them."[21]

Yet to interpret this controversy in terms of reformers and conservatives, as many have done, is both misleading and inaccurate, for both sides had different concerns. Superintendents, immersed in the day-to-day details of administration and management, defined their policies within the context of their institutional problems. Aware of the unsatisfactory results of the separation of curable and incurable cases in England and on the continent, they felt that hospitals for chronic persons would always deteriorate, and they were unwilling to compromise the principles of care and treatment that had been so laboriously constructed over several decades.

Their critics, on the other hand, were less concerned with mental hospitals than with the fact that so many mentally ill persons were confined amidst the unsanitary and cruel surroundings of local receptacles. They did not believe that it was feasible to provide facilities for all insane persons, since neither legislatures nor policy officials were about to give a high priority to the care and treatment of the mentally ill. Most were primarily interested in welfare and dependency rather than in mental illness per se; they believed that it was possible to provide humane care at a

20. New York Board of State Commissioners of Public Charities, *AR*, V (1871), 24–30; New York State Board of Charities, *AR*, VII (1873), 20–21, VIII (1874), 25–28; Wisconsin State Board of Charities and Reform, *AR*, V (1875), 102.

21. R. Hills to Jarvis, November 7, 1863, Jarvis Papers, CLMHMS.

lower cost through efficient administrative and managerial techniques. "It appears to me," noted Frederick H. Wines, the very
influential secretary of the Illinois Board of State Commissioners
of Public Charities, "that the pressing problem with regard to
the future of the insane in this country is: how can the chronic
insane pauper be most cheaply cared for, consistently with a
proper regard to humanity? and must this work be done by the
state or by the several counties?"[22] Institutions for incurables
seemed to him and other critics of the AMSAII a better solution
than mere continuance of the unsatisfactory status quo.[23]

22. Frederick H. Wines to Pliny Earle, April 26, 1879, Earle Papers,
AAS.

23. For a sampling of the literature of the controversy see the following: Charles A. Lee to Jarvis, March 12, 1867, Jarvis Papers, CLMHMS;
John Curwen to Dix, February 7, 1867, Ray to Dix, December 29, 1869,
H. A. Buttolph to Dix, January 5, 1870, Kirkbride to Dix, January 7,
1870, Dix Papers, HLHU; Charles A. Lee to Earle, January 28, 1872, Earle
Papers, AAS; *AJI*, XXIII (July, 1866), 252–260, XXIV (July, 1867), 29–42,
91–95, 113–114, XXVII (October, 1870), 224, 254–258, XXVIII (October,
1871), 320–340; John B. Chapin, "Report on Provision for the Chronic
Insane," in American Medical Association, *Transactions*, XIX (1868), 191–
201; Charles A. Lee, "Report on Insanity," *ibid.*, 161–188; John Curwen,
"Report on the Proper Treatment of the Insane," *ibid.*, XXI (1870), 127–
143; Conference of Charities, *Proceedings*, III (1876), 17–20, 62–65, VII
(1880), lxxiv–lxxvi; Michigan Board of State Commissioners for the General Supervision of Charitable, Penal, Pauper, and Reformatory Institutions,
BR, III (1875/1876), 81–93; [California] *Majority Report of the Assembly
Committee on State Hospitals in Relation to Assembly Bill No. 226* (n.p.,
n.d. [1863?]), 1–4; John S. Van Voorhis, *Management of the Insane: A
Paper Read before the Fayette County Medical Society, on the 4th Day of
October, 1870* (Pittsburgh, 1870); Central Ohio Lunatic Asylum, *AR*, XXV
(1863), 18–23; Southern Ohio Lunatic Asylum, *AR*, XI (1865), 20–23;
Pennsylvania State Lunatic Hospital, *AR*, XV (1865), 17–20; Pennsylvania
Hospital for the Insane, *AR*, XXV (1865), 25–32; Illinois State Hospital
for the Insane, *BR*, X (1865/1866), 26–33; Utica State Lunatic Asylum,
AR, XXIV (1866), 17–20, XXV (1867), 16–19, XXIX (1871), 72–79; Butler
Hospital for the Insane, *AR*, XIX (1865), 13–27; Connecticut Retreat for
the Insane, *AR*, XLI (1865), 16–23; McLean Asylum for the Insane, *AR*,
L (1867), in Massachusetts General Hospital, *AR*, 1867, 56–60; Maine Insane
Hospital, *AR*, XXVIII (1868), 8–15; Michigan Asylum for the Insane, *BR*,
1869/1870, 20–28; Willard Asylum for the Insane, *AR*, II (1870), 7–10, III
(1871), 9–19, 38–39, IV (1872), 14–16, V (1873), 25, VI (1874), 11–15, VII
(1875), 33–35; Hudson River State Hospital for the Insane, *AR*, VI (1872),
25–31; West Virginia Hospital for the Insane, *AR*, X (1873), 7–9; Insane

The fact that the theoretical model of mental illness of both groups bore little or no relationship to the structure and functions of mental hospitals reinforced the preoccupation of the debate with administrative and organizational concerns. Theoretical vagueness also made it possible for individuals to adopt positions for which there was little or no compelling evidence and then to legitimate their claims on "scientific" grounds. Existing differences of opinion, in other words, reflected differences in occupational affiliation and ideology rather than competing scientific claims.

What is also noteworthy about the controversy is the fact that the debate on occasion was carried on in a bitter and acrimonious manner. Frequently there was an unwillingness to concede that the opposition might have valid points. Both sides defined the issues in terms of unyielding moral principles. The result was a polemical struggle in which the objective often appeared to be the portrayal of the absolutely evil nature of the opposition rather than the modification of public policy. Given the emotional tone of the debate, it was perhaps not surprising that the actual impact on public policy was minimal. Most states did not follow the example of the Willard institution, nor did they provide sufficient hospital facilities to take care of all of their mentally ill citizens.

This controversy also demonstrated the gap that existed between the recommendations of a profession dealing with one particular issue and public policy as exemplified in legislation. It was easy enough for a profession to lay down principles and standards and to define the ideal policy. Dealing with one type of issue—no matter how complex—presented relatively few obstacles even though sharp disagreements might exist within the profession. Legislators, on the other hand, were in a quite different situation, for they were confronted with seemingly endless pressures from a bewildering multiplicity of groups, many of which could make a perfectly good case for their demands. On what

---

Asylum of North Carolina, *AR*, XIX (1874), 10–44; Northern Hospital for the Insane, Oshkosh, Wisconsin, *AR*, II (1874), 15–22; Northampton State Lunatic Hospital, *AR*, XIX (1874), 42–51; Minnesota Hospital for the Insane, *AR*, IX (1875), 24–25; Central Kentucky Lunatic Asylum, *AR*, 1875, 16–17.

basis were these legislators to determine public priorities? And if priorities could indeed be determined, what assurance was there that one solution to a given problem might not have adverse effects elsewhere? The very concepts of public priorities and broad social planning, it should be noted, were entirely absent for most of the nineteenth century. Such concepts presupposed a paramount position for government, for no other institution could have served as the vehicle for the determination of social priorities and the formulation of budgets that would reflect these priorities. Given the absence of any significant support for such a governmental model, it was understandable that there was no mechanism with the authority to develop consistent and cohesive policies and then implement them in a systematic manner.

The one specific result of the controversy over institutions for incurable cases was to accelerate the end of local responsibility for the mentally ill. Both sides had demonstrated beyond a reasonable doubt that bad as state hospitals may have been, local institutions were invariably far worse. Pressures for economy and retrenchment were always most intense at the local level, for citizens could see for themselves the relatively clear and direct relationship between spending and taxation. When given an option, they usually chose to maintain or to lower existing taxation levels rather than to provide services to deal with dependent groups such as the mentally ill. The shortcomings of community control of welfare, then, led inevitably to the assumption by the state of responsibility for dependent groups, including the care and treatment of the mentally ill. At the state level the relationship between expenditures and taxation was not as direct as at the local level (it was also far more complicated). Following 1870, therefore, responsibility for all insane persons was increasingly concentrated in the hands of state agencies.[24]

III

At the very same time that the controversy over institutions for incurable persons was raging, another debate was taking place

24. See Albert Deutsch, *The Mentally Ill in America: A History of Their Care and Treatment from Colonial Times* (Garden City, New York, 1937), Chaps. XII–XIII.

over the internal structure and organization of mental hospitals. Since the 1840's relatively few changes had occurred within mental hospitals, although as they grew in size the role of the trustees tended to diminish in importance. The AMSAII, which had codified existing practices in its famous propositions in 1851 and 1853, had if anything become even more devoted to them. The only significant modification occurred in 1866, when the acceptable maximum size was reluctantly increased to 600. The fact that the AMSAII was a relatively small organization whose outstanding members (including Ray, Kirkbride, and Earle, to mention only a few) had been active since its founding in 1844 and were largely responsible for the formulation of professional standards contributed undoubtedly to its steadfast adherence to principle. Whatever the reasons, the association continued to insist that small hospitals (geographically distributed) were better than larger and more centralized ones, and that the authority of superintendents should not in any way be weakened.

What seemed reasonable and proper in the early years of the movement to found hospitals had by the 1860's become an apparent anachronism. The growth in the size of patient populations, the constantly increasing number of incurable cases, the attacks on mental hospitals, and the thrust toward greater economy, efficiency, and centralization had made the propositions of 1851 and 1853 appear obsolete and irrelevant. Slowly but surely, therefore, a movement began to get under way to develop alternative means of structuring and organizing mental hospitals so that they would be better prepared to meet the problems and challenges facing them.

Between 1840 and 1860 a few superintendents had on occasion suggested that alternative models of mental hospitals be considered alongside existing centralized institutions. William M. Awl, head of the Ohio Lunatic Asylum, thought that detached cottages would be highly appropriate for private institutions like the Pennsylvania Hospital for the Insane and the McLean Asylum. He was doubtful, however, about their suitability for public institutions, which lacked access to the type of resources enjoyed by their private counterparts.[25] More far-reaching proposals were

25. William M. Awl to Kirkbride, August 30, 1847, Kirkbride Papers, IPH.

offered by John M. Galt of the Virginia Eastern Asylum during the mid-1850's. Aware of developments abroad, he became interested in the farm of St. Anne, an experiment conducted at Bicêtre, the famous French hospital, and the system caring for the insane at Gheel in Belgium. Concerned with providing an orderly transition for patients who would eventually return to their homes as well as with the care of chronic cases, Galt offered a series of suggestions that would have sharply modified existing hospitals. Chronic cases could be placed as boarders in families living in communities adjacent to the hospital, while some patients could be paroled to live and work in the nearby community. Every institution, he argued, should also have an attached farm with cottages to serve both convalescent and chronic persons. Such innovations would reduce construction and maintenance costs and permit funds to be used to hire sorely needed staff. Galt insisted on maintaining the absolute authority of the superintendent because "the greater the degree of liberty allowed, the more is required in so entire and unbroken a system as can only result from a single controlling power, which shall make all things tend in one and the same direction." At the same time he insisted that "the insane, generally, are susceptible of a much more extended liberty than they are now allowed," and that his proposals would increase rather than decrease the freedom of patients. In contrast to European institutions, he noted, New England hospitals "appear mere prison-houses, notwithstanding their many internal attributes of comfort and elegance, and a general management and systematic action in which they are superior to the asylum referred to, and, in fact, have few equals anywhere."[26]

Such proposals, however, were ignored or else met with considerable opposition. Galt, who did not attend the convention of the AMSAII in 1855, came under sharp attack by his colleagues for his comments in the *American Journal of Insanity*. D. Tilden Brown, for example, regretted that Galt had not been restrained either by *"esprit du corps* or by literary comity" from

26. John M. Galt, "The Farm of St. Anne," *AJI*, XI (April, 1855), 352–357; Virginia Eastern Asylum, *Report*, 1853/1854 and 1854/1855, 24, 1855/1856 and 1856/1857, 20–30. See also Norman Dain, *Disordered Minds: The First Century of Eastern State Hospital in Williamsburg, Virginia 1766–1866* (Williamsburg, 1971), 128ff.

libeling New England hospitals, while Kirkbride, whose recently published book on hospitals had taken an entirely different tack on organizational issues, was especially annoyed. "I deny," he categorically stated,

> that the institutions of New England have the appearance that they are represented to have. Nor can I believe that there is not about as much liberty generally allowed as is safe and proper. The idea of mixing up all colors and all classes, as is seen in one or two institutions of the United States, is not what is wanted in our hospitals for the insane, although it may be regarded by that writer as a desirable kind of liberty. . . . Gentlemen who have the care of few but chronic demented cases have little idea of the restraint really necessary for recent cases, or of the restrictions which it is proper to place on their movements and actions.[27]

Privately, Galt came under even sharper criticism.[28] Having labored long and hard to establish professional standards, most superintendents rejected proposals which seemed to reflect adversely on their own judgment and integrity.

Such debates, however, were not characteristic of the decades before 1860. Psychiatrists were most concerned with expanding the existing system, placing their own institutions on a firm and stable foundation, and creating a professional self-identity; they were not especially interested in innovating or experimenting with their relatively young hospitals. The loose system suggested by Galt seemed to resemble the pattern of neglect characteristic of the prehospital era, and it clearly minimized the role of the physician. Consequently, a loose and decentralized hospital structure was viewed as a step backward, and there were few willing to move in a direction that appeared manifestly retrograde rather than progressive.

The growing criticisms of hospitals after 1860, combined with the thrust toward centralization and rationalization, however, markedly altered the environment in which such institutions

27. The debate appears in *AJI*, XII (July, 1855), 42ff. (quotation from pp. 43–44).

28. Cf. D. Tilden Brown to Kirkbride, May 3, 11, 1855, Charles H. Nichols to Kirkbride, April 14, 24, July 3, October 10, 1855, Kirkbride Papers, IPH.

functioned. The goal of a broad-based system of relatively small and geographically distributed therapeutic hospitals receded further and further into the background as the new state boards of charity relentlessly defined the objectives of public policy in terms of efficiency and economy. Superintendents, moreover, were increasingly on the defensive against critics who placed responsibility for the failure of the mental hospital to live up to its promise squarely on their shoulders. Having based much of their case upon the belief that insanity was curable, superintendents found that their inability to deliver on their promises, for whatever reasons, had seriously impaired their prestige and authority as preeminent spokesmen on this subject. The relative decline in their influence, together with the fact that institutional care and treatment had never had an especially high priority, left mental hospitals in a somewhat vulnerable position.

To criticize the existing structure of mental hospitals was only a beginning, not an end. Those individuals and groups dissatisfied with the performance of mental hospitals also faced the task of offering alternative proposals. One possibility involved the total abolition of institutional care; such a policy was never seriously considered since it ran counter to developments throughout the western world. Nor did anyone seriously entertain the possibility of terminating public responsibility for the mentally ill; that principle had become too firmly established. Given the permanence of state institutions, reformers adopted as their basic goal a fundamental internal restructuring of mental hospitals that would presumably result in better care, distinguish more clearly between chronic and curable cases, and use public resources more efficiently and economically. Although critics of institutional psychiatry were not always in accord on specifics, they agreed essentially that the existing system was extravagant and uneconomical, and that change would have to be imposed by outside authorities.

The debate over the proper structure of mental hospitals proved just as bitter and acrimonious as the one over separate institutions for curable and incurable persons. Indeed, in most respects it was a continuation of that controversy and involved much the same personnel; but the focus had shifted away from the establishment of institutions for incurables toward a consideration of the proper internal structure and organization of hospitals. Outwardly it seemed to pit a reactionary AMSAII against the forces of reform (including many of the state boards of charity and the Conference of Charities). Wines of Illinois—to cite the individual most committed to a decentralized cottage-type hospital—put the issue very simply in a paper at the Conference of Charities in 1878. The AMSAII, he charged. was "a close[d] corporation" committed to an inflexible type of institution characterized by "uniformity, verging on monotony, and the ease with which each individual patient may be subjected to any degree of restraint approved by the judgment of the medical officer in charge." Its members insisted that they were the only group competent to advise state authorities and that any deviation from their recommendations would obviously have adverse results. Wines noted that disagreement existed within the association, for some of its older members dissented from recent declarations, while younger members did not assent to all of the older declarations. Nevertheless, the voices of the latter tended to be muted, while assistant physicians, many of whom were less conservative than their superiors, were excluded from membership. The shape of public policy, insisted Wines, involved nonmedical issues and therefore could not be left in the hands of superintendents. Given the reluctance of legislatures and tax-payers to spend money lavishly for the maintenance of chronic paupers in extraordinarily expensive hospital facilities, he concluded, the policy and principles advocated by the AMSAII were "driving the chronic insane back into county jails and poorhouses, simply because they persist in their adherence to 'propositions,' framed to meet an entirely different condition of public sentiment of affairs."[29]

A closer examination of the issues, however, reveals that the categories of reactionaries and reformers are incapable of being applied to the two sides. As in the debate over institutions for incurables, each was responding to a different set of pressures. Men like Wines and others were concerned with welfare generally; they echoed their constituency when they insisted that the care of dependent groups could be done more efficiently and at a lower cost. Hospital superintendents, on the other hand,

29. Frederick H. Wines, "Hospital Building for the Insane," Conference of Charities, *Proceedings*, V (1878), 143–150.

were responding to the internal exigencies of their institutions, and they were unwilling to concede that the charge of extravagance was in any way justified. If anything, Americans had never allocated even minimal resources to deal with the problems arising out of mental illness. The result was again a somewhat confusing debate precisely because of the multiplicity of voices. Complicating the situation still further was the fact that neither the membership of the AMSAII nor the ranks of its critics were united; internecine warfare within both was common.

Interestingly enough, the earliest proposals for changing the internal structures of mental hospitals came from within the psychiatric profession. Most superintendents were aware of the heterogeneous nature of asylums in England and on the continent either from personal observation or from a careful reading of the foreign literature. By the latter part of the nineteenth century psychiatry was in most respects a profession that transcended national boundaries; there were vigorous exchanges of ideas, practices, and beliefs on an international basis. Consequently, some superintendents became interested in the applicability of European practices to American conditions. Without doubt, the mode of care that most attracted them was the colony system of Gheel in Belgium. More than a thousand years old, the town had become famous as a religious shrine where insane persons were sent in the hope that divine intercession would restore their reason. The inhabitants of the town soon became accustomed to the presence of lunatics among them and accepted responsibility for their welfare on a community basis. The community's religious commitment was passed down from generation to generation, and made the locale peculiarly adaptable to the cottage system of treatment. By the mid-nineteenth century Gheel had acquired a formal administrative system. A medical superintendent was given overall responsibility for the mentally ill in the town. Each lunatic was placed under the charge of a cottager with whom he boarded and strict safeguards were designed for the prevention of abuses. The diet was simple but ample, and there was more than enough work for all. Whenever possible, patients were granted freedom of action and movement.

Before 1850 Gheel was relatively unknown among American

hospital superintendents, although Esquirol had visited it in 1821 and published an account the following year. Probably the first American alienist to visit Gheel was Pliny Earle, who spent some time there in the summer of 1849. Two years later Earle's account appeared in the *American Journal of Insanity*. Though kindly disposed toward this unique community, Earle did not believe that it could be replicated in the United States. "I believe," he remarked, "the *system* is liable to greater abuses than can possibly occur in well ordered institutions, and that the interests of the patients now at Gheel would be advanced if they could be placed in public Asylums."[30] From time to time there were sporadic discussions of the Gheel example, but the "cottage system" did not become a focal point of debate among superintendents or others before the Civil War.

During the 1860's interest in the possible applicability of certain aspects of the Gheel model began to mount. Superintendents were concerned with the growing number of incurable patients and growing criticism of their institutions for supposedly depriving patients of personal liberties and relying exclusively on restraint. A decentralized mental hospital with detached cottages seemed to offer at least a partial solution to their problems. Moreover, Gheel was already the subject of a wide-ranging debate in England and Europe, where mental hospitals and asylums faced problems comparable to those of their American counterparts; most superintendents in the United States were reasonably well informed about this controversy.[31] The financial difficulties faced by many states as a result of the Civil War made it abundantly clear that the chances of drastically expanding institutional facilities for the mentally ill were nonexistent. This situation served to strengthen the search for an alternative policy that would not involve higher costs but would ensure a more comprehensive and effective system.[32]

30. Pliny Earle, "Gheel," *AJI*, VIII (July, 1851), 67–78.

31. See the discussion by Dr. J. Parigot, "The Gheel Question: From an American Point of View," *AJI*, XIX (January, 1863), 332–354. Parigot, a native of Belgium, had migrated to the United States after extensive involvement with European hospitals. The article reported on the differences of opinion among European and British psychiatrists.

32. For some early discussions see Central Ohio Lunatic Asylum, *AR*, XXIV (1862), 24, XXV (1863), 18–23, XXVI (1864), 20–23; Maine Insane

The establishment of a number of state boards in the years following 1863 gave added urgency to the issue. Their members were attracted by the Gheel model; its emulation could conceivably help to end once and for all local and county care of the insane, provide custodial care for the incurable and thereby alleviate one of the most serious problems facing American hospitals, and also reduce the high costs of therapeutic institutions with large numbers of chronic patients. Slowly but surely the leading figures on several of the more influential boards began to throw their prestige and authority into the struggle in order to modify the structure of any new facilities that might be constructed in their states.

The Illinois and Massachusetts boards played the most significant part in the controversy over the internal structure and organization of mental hospitals. Both states faced the impending prospect of adding new facilities, and disillusionment with existing institutions gave impetus to the efforts of those who preferred to innovate in hospital design. Wines in Illinois threw his prestige into the struggle, while in Massachusetts Samuel Gridley Howe played a leading role. Each of these states had at least one experienced superintendent who for one reason or another leaned toward a Gheel-type experiment.

In Illinois the founding of the central board took place at approximately the same time that the legislature authorized the establishment of two new state hospitals. The young and energetic Wines, secretary of the board, had managed to convene a conference dealing with insanity in November, 1869. Attended by hospital officials and trustees from within and without the state as well as the members of the Illinois Board of State Commissioners of Public Charities, the meeting was confined largely to a discussion of the relative merits of the congregate and segregate (or family) system in order to help to determine the future shape of the new institutions. Prior to the actual meeting Wines had written to all the superintendents in the nation soliciting their opinions on the different systems of hospital organization. The responses tended to vary in nature. Strong opposition to segregate hospitals was expressed by the majority of correspondents, including D. Tilden Brown, Edward R. Chapin, John P. Gray, William H. Rockwell, and William L. Peck. A few either favored segregate hospitals or else thought, as Pliny Earle put it, that alternative models might provide interesting comparative yardsticks to measure the achievements of traditional hospitals.[33]

The conference itself opened with an address by Andrew McFarland, superintendent of the oldest public hospital in Illinois. McFarland was particularly critical of existing congregate hospitals, which were constructed to restrain a relatively small number of persons and which ignored the majority of patients who did not require close supervision. Their lack of occupational facilities and the variety of stimuli required by all human beings was further evidence of their sterility. These disadvantages could be overcome by structural modifications. Hospitals should have both a large central facility and a group of two-story houses each capable of accommodating forty inmates. Each of the latter would be under the management of a married couple and several attendants. A firm believer in the principle that all asylums should be organized on an "industrial basis," McFarland urged that the domestic labor be performed by female patients and mechanical and agricultural work by males. Such a system, he noted, could be adequately supervised and would offer a far better alternative to existing congregate hospitals.[34]

McFarland was followed by Wines, who described in approving tones the colony of Fitz James, a private institution for the insane at Clarmont, France, some 50 miles north of Paris. At Fitz James an agricultural colony had been established about three-quarters of a mile from the parent asylum. All patients were provided with sufficient work; no coercion was practiced; and all intractable inmates were returned to the central facility. After lengthy discussion, the conference went on record supporting the idea of adding cottages to existing congregate institutions on the grounds that "it would increase both the economy and efficiency of asylums for the insane."[35] Although the work of

33. Illinois Board of State Commissioners of Public Charities, *BR*, I (1869/1870), 82–85.

34. *Ibid.*, 84–91.

35. *Ibid.*, 91–101.

the conference had no immediate effect, its deliberations later contributed to the establishment in 1877 of a new hospital at Kankakee, Illinois, where small buildings accommodating a hundred patients were grouped around a large building.[36]

In Massachusetts the initial suggestion for a modification of the large congregate system came from the superintendent of the Worcester hospital. Although the leading public institution in the nation following its opening in 1833, the hospital had begun to decline in the late 1840's and 1850's as a result of overcrowding, the accumulation of chronic patients, and the problems arising out of its heterogeneous patient population. In 1865, therefore, Dr. Merrick Bemis, superintendent for nearly a decade, began to propose major structural changes. His proposals were given added urgency by the fact that it had become increasingly evident that the hospital would shortly require an entirely new physical plant.[37] Bemis received strong and influential support from Howe, who traveled in Europe during 1867 and was favorably impressed by the colony at Gheel. To Howe Gheel had three major advantages. In the first place, it furnished employment for all patients in the company of sane persons. Secondly, the insane were provided with those "social and family relationship[s] with sane persons" that nourished "unperverted sentiments and affections," and thus helped to restore the "mental and moral balance." Finally, its managers gave the insane the greatest degree of personal freedom, which promoted mental health by emphasizing self-respect. As chairman of the Board of State Charities, Howe was in a position to make his views felt. In its annual report for 1867 the board began to move in a new

36. Henry M. Hurd, ed., *The Institutional Care of the Insane in the United States and Canada*, 4 vols. (Baltimore, 1916–1917), II, 222–233. See also *Recollections of Richard Dewey: Pioneer in American Psychiatry*, ed. by Ethel L. Dewey (Chicago, 1936), 130–140. Yet by the 1890's conditions at Kankakee were no better than those at large congregate hospitals. For a revealing description of Kankakee see Adolf Meyer (then a member of the staff) to G. Stanley Hall, December 7, 1895, Clark University Library, Worcester, Mass. This letter is reprinted in Gerald N. Grob, "Adolf Meyer on American Psychiatry in 1895," *American Journal of Psychiatry*, CXIX (June, 1963), 1135–1142.

37. Worcester State Lunatic Hospital, *AR*, XXXIII (1865), 4, 58–63, XXXIV (1866), 78–80, XXXV (1867), 5–6, 76–78.

direction when it supported a proposal to board out patients then confined in state institutions (although the hope of economy was a prime consideration in this suggestion).[38]

During a trip abroad in 1868, Bemis visited a number of mental hospitals in France, Switzerland, Germany, England, Scotland, Ireland, and Belgium. He was especially impressed by Gheel, where patients, although not in their own homes, nevertheless "have a home, live in a family and are members of a society, useless it may be, but still they are identified as part of a community." By 1869 Bemis had convinced the trustees to support his plan for a new hospital, and also received the endorsement of the Board of State Charities, the governor, and the Executive Council. Specifically, Bemis's plans involved the creation of a decentralized hospital. The main building would have space for no more than one-third of the patients; the remainder would be kept in small houses accommodating twelve to fifteen persons. As patients improved, they would be moved to houses further and further away from the main building, thus facilitating their adjustment to society. Under Bemis's system no patient would ever be confined in a lunatic hospital if proper control and care could be assured without institutionalization. Indeed, the majority of patients would remain outside the hospital proper, although all would live close enough to enable qualified physicians to care for them. To prevent abuses and neglect, the state could also assume responsibility for all mentally ill persons, whether institutionalized or not. An important byproduct of the new system, Bemis emphasized, was the fact that the hospital would be able to recruit a more competent staff by providing better working conditions and greater responsibilities for them.[39]

By 1870 the legislature had approved of the proposal for the new hospital and the trustees had purchased nearly 300 acres of land in an outlying section of Worcester. Yet the project was not without its opponents. As it became clearer that the new facility would involve greater rather than smaller costs than a comparable

38. *Ibid.*, XXXVI (1868), 69–70; Harold Schwartz, *Samuel Gridley Howe: Social Reformer 1801–1876* (Cambridge, 1956), 286–287; Massachusetts Board of State Charities, *AR*, IV (1867), xli–xlii.

39. Worcester State Lunatic Hospital, *AR*, XXXVI (1868), 54–83.

congregate hospital, the Board of State Charities began to retreat from its initial enthusiasm. At the end of 1870 its members specifically rejected the claim that they had ever advocated the introduction of the Gheel system into Massachusetts. Instead they recommended that the Commonwealth should maintain the existing closed asylum system and gradually board out harmless chronic patients.[40] Despite their disclaimers to the contrary, it was evident that they had moved away from their previous stand.

The greatest opposition to Bemis, however, came from within the psychiatric profession itself. The individual who took the lead was Pliny Earle, and his position was supported by Ray and Kirkbride. The project thus faced the united opposition of the three most distinguished superintendents in the nation. In 1871 Earle used his annual report as superintendent of the Northampton hospital as the means of making known his views. During the year he had spent several months abroad, and had visited no less than forty-six institutions in nearly a dozen European states. Two institutions—the new Whittingham Asylum in England and the colony at Gheel in Belguim—resembled most closely the plans for the new Worcester hospital. Both were based upon an expansion of the limits of a hospital for a given number of patients. The Whittingham Asylum had no less than sixteen separate buildings connected with each other by covered corridors, while Gheel was spread out not only in the village but among the peasantry throughout the commune. Admitting that the mental hospital had by no stretch of the imagination reached a final state of perfection, Earle argued that all types had to be judged by the results of their "practical application and operation." As far as he was concerned, a decentralized hospital had objections as well as advantages. The principal objections were higher construction and maintenance costs. More employees were needed because of the greater distances involved, and heating costs—a consideration of particular interest in cold areas—were very high. On the other hand, smaller edifices were more easily ventilated; they also permitted a wider separation of the different classes of patients. Toward the end of his discussion Earle made quite clear his own feelings. Favoring hospitals of 250 patients each located

40. Massachusetts Board of State Charities, *AR*, VII (1870), xli–xlii.

geographically throughout the state, he condemned all plans modeled after the Gheel example.[41]

Earle's remarks probably made a considerable impression upon individuals in policy-making positions. Certainly Ray was pleased with Earle's comments. "I read your report," wrote Ray,

> with an unusual degree of interest, especially your observations respecting the family and cottage methods of caring for the insane. These projects I regard as the offspring of that class of men (to be found in every community) whose only chance of achieving notoriety is to find fault with everybody else and who suppose they magnify themselves by depreciating others. It is a curious illustration of the prevalent spirit of altruism that while one community, frightened at the cost of furnishing hospital accommodation for all its insane, is disposed to acquiesce willingly in those primitive institutions, the poor house and county jail, another is advocating architectural arrangements far more costly than the old hospital.[42]

Earle made his hostility to the Gheel model even clearer in 1872. Repeating his previous criticisms, he emphasized that a cottage hospital would complicate immensely the surveillance of patients by hospital officials. Ideally, a superintendent observed closely every division, and a decentralized system would simply impose barriers. As the superintendent's duties were restricted, "his office would soon degenerate . . . to that of 'keeper.'" Earle questioned Bemis's claim that there would be much less restraint in the cottages. Pointing out that the plans called for a high wall surrounding the farm, he argued that such a wall constituted a perpetual restraint to all patients. But even if the wall were eliminated it would make little difference; an inmate who had his freedom in a cottage could also have it in a large building. Nevertheless, Earle was not convinced that liberty was necessarily good for an insane person, for discipline was often a significant ele-

41. Northampton State Lunatic Hospital, *AR*, XVI (1871), 28–39. Earle expressed much the same views in an address before the Massachusetts Medical Society in 1868 entitled "Prospective Provision for the Insane." It was published in the *AJI*, XXV (July, 1868), 51–65, and also circulated under the same title in pamphlet form (Utica, 1868).

42. Ray to Earle, February 18, 1872, Earle Papers, AAS.

ment in therapy. Finally, Earle took exception to the claim that a cottage system recreated a familial environment conducive to therapy. If this were true, such an atmosphere could easily be created in a hospital ward. But was a homelike atmosphere really desirable? If so, why did not insane persons recover at home? Earle's hostility toward a decentralized hospital was evident throughout his report.[43]

By itself the controversy over the proposed hospital was not particularly important. What made it so was the fact that a precedent might be set that would in all probability influence the future direction of public policy in the Bay State. Any significant policy shift was bound to have influence elsewhere, since Massachusetts still retained a preeminent position as a leader in social innovation. If the new hospital at Worcester were built along decentralized lines, there was every likelihood that it might become a model for other institutions. The controversy, in other words, involved opposing viewpoints that embodied quite different philosophies. Not only was the psychiatric profession vitally concerned over the outcome of the dispute, but the public and its representatives were also implicated because broad social and financial considerations were involved.

The importance of the debate over the Worcester hospital was further magnified in importance by the fact that a comparable discussion was taking place in Boston as well. Since the 1850's the inadequacy of the Boston Lunatic Hospital had been clear. Any major renovations in its physical plant were virtually impossible because land for expansion or new construction was unavailable. The Board of Directors of Public Institutions, therefore, moved to secure authorization for a completely new hospital on a new site that would meet the needs of a growing urban population. A heated debate developed after a new location was chosen. Although the project met with a veto in 1869, the controversy did not subside. The strongest opposition to a new hospital came from Howe, who believed the congregate system to be "radically wrong in some of its features." Howe suggested that most of the problems could be solved by committing all new applicants to state institutions, removing all private

43. Northampton State Lunatic Hospital, *AR*, XVII (1872), 36–42.

patients not citizens of Massachusetts, constructing small houses adjacent to state hospitals for quiet harmless patients, and completing the asylum for incurables at Tewksbury as rapidly as possible. In this way the Boston Lunatic Hospital could eventually be closed down and the care of the mentally ill relegated to the state, where it belonged in the first place.[44]

The discussions over the Worcester and Boston examples could have been the occasion for a full and open debate that might have clarified the issues arising out of mental illness and their implications for the formulation and implementation of public policy. Such was not the case, for the issues were never put in a coherent manner and peripheral concerns and internal conflicts further obfuscated the situation. At the Worcester hospital, for example, a conflict between Bemis and the trustees resulted in the trustees' resignation (probably involuntarily) and a decision to reverse the earlier approval of a decentralized hospital and construct instead a large congregate institution.[45] The responses to this turn of events were varied. Ray and Kirkbride breathed a sigh of relief. "I am glad," wrote Ray, "the coup de grace has been delivered at his preposterous cottage scheme, for I feared.

44. For the controversy over the Boston Lunatic Hospital see the following: *Report of a Committee of the Board of Directors for Public Institutions in Relation to the Condition of the Lunatic Hospital, Made May 23, 1862* (Boston, 1862); Board of Directors for Public Institutions of the City of Boston, *AR*, VIII (1864), 84–104; *Report of the Committee on Institutions, on a Site for a New Lunatic Hospital. 1865*, Boston *City Document No. 97* (November 13, 1865); Boston *City Document No. 105* (1867); Boston Lunatic Hospital, *AR*, 1868, in Boston Board of Directors for Public Institutions, *AR*, XII (1868), 28–29, 56–57; *Modified Plans and Estimates of the Boston Hospital for the Insane, at Winthrop. 1868*, Boston *City Document No. 75* (1868); *Dissenting Opinion of Mr. Cobb, A Member of Board of Directors, for Public Institutions, Relative to a Site for a New Lunatic Hospital*, in Boston *City Document No. 107* (1869); *Boston Medical and Surgical Journal*, n.s. IV (December 30, 1869), 398–399, n.s. VIII (October 19, 1871), 257–259; Samuel G. Howe, *Objections to the Proposed Plan for a City Hospital for Lunatics at Winthrop; With Answers to the Article by J. Putnam Bradlee, in the "Daily Advertiser," November 6* (Boston, 1871).

45. For a detailed analysis of the conflict over the Worcester hospital see Gerald N. Grob, *The State and the Mentally Ill: A History of Worcester State Hospital in Massachusetts, 1830–1920* (Chapel Hill, 1966), 208–228.

at one time, it would be adopted."[46] "The fact that Worcester has given up the scheme," wrote Kirkbride, "is an indication that Brother Bemis is no longer there, and also, of returning reason among these good people."[47] The Board of State Charities, on the other hand, was critical of a divided system of authority in the state's public institutions and emphasized "the lack of any prevailing and persistent principle even in the same establishment."[48]

Yet few issues had been clarified during the controversy. Earle had argued that a decentralized hospital was theoretically undesirable and too expensive, while Howe had taken the opposite position. Given the divisions among psychiatrists and public officials, it was not surprising that policy remained vague and often included contradictory features. The multiplicity of voices undoubtedly left legislators equally confused when it came to establish meaningful and comprehensive policies. Had presumed "experts" been in agreement, the problems posed by mental disease might have been easier to confront; that they were not merely compounded existing difficulties. Even on the issue of the relative costs of congregate and segregate institutions there was little hard information; statements presented as facts were often opinions. Nor did a consensus emerge on a pluralistic policy that would have permitted both types of institutions to exist alongside each other, thereby providing an opportunity to evaluate the merits and costs of each. Indeed, the very concept of systematic evaluation was entirely absent; both sides assumed the validity of their ideas and the invalidity of those of their opponents. And while Gheel became the symbol of the disagreements, few of the proposals to establish segregate hospitals resembled the Belgium system even remotely.[49] Most superintendents and public officials had a completely distorted and inaccurate picture of Gheel, which itself had a very stormy history for much of the nineteenth century. Nor was it made clear during

46. Ray to John Sawyer, February 15, 1873, ms. in Butler Hospital Library, Providence, R.I.

47. Kirkbride to Earle, March 3, 1873, Earle Papers, AAS.

48. Massachusetts Board of State Charities, *AR*, X (1873), xxxiv.

49. After the failure of Bemis's plans, the Worcester hospital was rebuilt on an entirely new site along traditional congregate lines. The old plant was then converted into an institution for the chronic insane. See Grob, *The State and the Mentally Ill*, Chap. VII.

the debate that most insane persons requiring institutionalization in Belgium were sent to traditional mental hospitals.

The debates in Illinois and Massachusetts over the proper shape of mental hospitals and public policy were by no means atypical, for comparable discussions occured in most other states as well as in various professional organizations. Proposals involving the establishment of cottage hospitals or of boarding out chronic patients were the subjects of vigorous debates among superintendents during the 1860's and 1870's. The majority were clearly opposed to such experiments on the grounds that neither the interests of the insane nor those of society were served. Unwilling to stamp large numbers of mentally ill persons with the stigma of incurability, they rejected as well the allegation that therapeutic care was necessarily more costly than custodial care. Nor would they accept the argument that the insane would receive greater freedom in decentralized institutions or among private families, or even that such freedom was necessarily beneficial; the major result would simply be a pattern of malevolent neglect. The basic problem in their eyes was the refusal by the public and their representatives to allocate sufficient funds to provide facilities for all mentally ill persons, curable and incurable. "I am not sure," Ray once remarked,

> that it would be so far beyond their means as to be utterly impracticable. It is with communities as it is with individuals,—what they ardently desire, and feel the need of by practical experience of its want, that they generally contrive to have. . . . Until therefore, it appears that the maintenance of all the incurably insane in regular hospitals is clearly beyond the means of our people— to be achieved, in short, at the expense of some great interest —we have no right to feel that the line of our duty to these unfortunates lies only in providing for them by some inexpensive method, when it shall be discovered.[50]

There is little doubt that the older members of the AMSAII played an important role in forging a strong and articulate opposition to proposals that undermined the structure and functions of their institutions. Men like Ray, Kirkbride, Earle, and

50. Butler Hospital for the Insane, *AR*, XIX (1865), 26–27.

others were fearful that desires to economize rather than strictly professional considerations were behind the thrust for change. Having entered institutional psychiatry when the overwhelming majority of the mentally ill were confined in jails and almshouses, they had spent most of their lives fighting for the expansion of hospital facilities for all insane persons requiring institutionalization. Segregate institutions and boarding-out plans also threatened their professional authority and integrity, for both impaired or negated the central role of the psychiatrist as stipulated by the basic precepts of moral treatment. Consequently, most superintendents bitterly resisted what they regarded as illegitimate attacks or encroachments on themselves and their institutions.[51]

Their opponents, on the other hand, were a more heterogeneous group, and included some younger psychiatrists, a few hospital trustees, and many welfare officials. These groups defended proposals intended to modify the structure of mental hospitals as necessary compromises with reality, although they believed too that real benefits would follow the implementation of their proposals. For example, Winthrop B. Hallock, a young assistant physician at the Connecticut General Hospital for the Insane (an institution that had begun in the early 1870's to experiment with cottages for a limited number of its patients), defended a decentralized hospital on the grounds that states would never authorize sufficient accommodations in congregate hospitals because of the enormous costs involved. Many insane persons, including chronics and convalescents, however, did not require close surveillance

51. For defenses of the congregate hospital see the following: Butler Hospital for the Insane, *AR*, XIX (1865), 13–27; McLean Asylum for the Insane, *AR*, L (1867), in Massachusetts General Hospital, *AR*, 1867, 40–44; Taunton State Lunatic Hospital, *AR*, XIV (1867), 10–12; "Hospital and Cottage Systems for the Care of the Insane," *AJI*, XXVII (July, 1870), 80–103; Pennsylvania State Hospital for the Insane, *AR*, XXXI (1871), 40–43; Wisconsin State Hospital for the Insane, *AR*, XII (1871), 23–42; New York City Asylum for the Insane, Ward's Island, *AR*, II (1873), 8–11; Insane Asylum of North Carolina, *AR*, XIX (1874), 19–44; Northern Illinois Hospital and Asylum for the Insane, *BR*, III (1873/1874), 5–7; John Curwen, *Report on the Proper Treatment of the Insane* (Philadelphia, 1870); and the debate at the convention of the AMSAII in 1879 in *AJI*, XXXVI (1879), 160ff.

in large institutions; they could be cared for in small detached wooden structures that could be constructed at fairly low costs. In such facilities patients would have greater freedom and would in all probability be willing to engage in productive labor, thereby reducing costs still further. Hallock was especially critical of the AMSAII for its reluctance to give up the "traditional idea of prison-like walls indiscriminately surrounding the insane" and the fact that it had convinced public authorities of the necessity of providing "for their pauper class the same grand and luxurious establishments as the rich are supposed to need." "What the latter prefer and need in the way of a building does not concern us here, and it is immaterial, since they can pay for what they have," he concluded. "But what the poor need and prefer is, not the stately hospital, but rather the real home-comforts of life."[52]

Such arguments were especially appealing to state boards of charity, since they promised both less expensive and more beneficial care. The Massachusetts board—clearly one of the two or three most influential ones in the nation—was critical of the legislature for not heeding its protests "against the waste of the people's money in costly and needless structures for the criminals and paupers of Massachusetts." The board specifically pointed to the new hospitals at Worcester and Danvers, which provided the pauper insane with quarters and care "more luxuriously than the average tax-payer, who supports himself and them by his labor." Such sentiments were frequently echoed by the members of other state boards at the annual meetings of the Conference of Charities.[53]

52. Winthrop B. Hallock, "Accommodation for the Insane on the Cottage Plan," *New York Medical Journal*, XVIII (December, 1873), 582–595, XIX (January, 1874), 1–9. See also Connecticut General Hospital for the Insane, *AR*, VI (1872), 11–12, VII (1873), 11–12.

53. Massachusetts Board of State Charities, *AR*, XII (1875), xi–xvii. For earlier discussions of Gheel see *ibid.*, IV (1867), xxxvi–lx, VI (1869), lxiv–ciii, VII (1870), xl–xlvii. For examples of the type of paper given at the Conference of Charities see Diller Luther, "The Extent to Which the State Should Assume the Care of the Indigent Insane" and F. H. Wines, "Hospital Building for the Insane," both in the Conference of Charities, *Proceedings*, V (1878), 90–101, 143–150.

Yet the heated debate over the merits of competing types of hospitals produced few substantive changes in the existing system. One of the reasons for the futility of the debate was the absence of any organizational component capable of translating recommendations into actual policy and practice. The boards of charity might have been the logical vehicle, but their members were often in conflict with hospital officials and immersed in the problems of welfare generally. Because of their remoteness from the everyday life of mental hospitals, they were not especially sympathetic toward the daily problems faced by superintendents. These boards, moreover, were not concerned with social planning or social innovation; their thrust was in the direction of economy and efficiency, and they manifested a distinct tendency to judge results in terms of dollars and cents. The structural weaknesses (or voids) within state governments, therefore, reinforced the inchoate and inconsistent nature of policy and practice.

The lack of an organizational component to both determine and implement policy, of course, was by no means the only or even the most significant reason for the absence of change during a decade of conflict and ferment. There were other operative factors that played a significant role as well. The decentralized nature of American society, for example, made social planning difficult, since the decision-making process was neither clear nor comprehensive in scope. Most state and local governments invariably dealt with issues individually and not as part of an interrelated and complex system. Even where specific problems were placed within a general context (e.g., mental illness within the framework of welfare and dependency), the tendency was to avoid making fine distinctions. Thus the care and treatment of the mentally ill became inextricably entangled in the controversy over welfare and dependency. Although mental illness and dependency were obviously related, they were not identical; yet policy often represented a peculiar amalgam of both. The controversy over alternative institutional forms was also marked by a curious alliance between those who wanted to economize and those who wanted to innovate, even though their rationales differed in most respects. Two decades of ferment and controversy, then, did not result in significant changes.

IV

By 1875 it had become apparent that the hopes and aspirations of those who had led and taken part in the struggle to improve the lot of the mentally ill had fallen far short of the mark. The early reformers had envisioned an essentially therapeutic institution caring for all mentally ill persons irrespective of class, ethnicity, or color. They had pressed vigorously for a rapid expansion of public facilities so that all who required institutionalization would be accommodated. Above all, they had insisted that a generous public policy would result in a sharp diminution of the incidence of this dreaded malady, provided that proper treatment was begun before the acute state of the disease had passed. Within a relatively brief period their work had resulted in the establishment in most states of public mental hospitals. The opening of such institutions also set the stage for the emergence of psychiatry as a profession—and by 1844 its members had achieved sufficient cohesiveness and self-awareness to enable them to found a national organization to represent their interests and outlook.

Yet the institutional system that came into being during the first half of the nineteenth century did not approximate the one envisioned by reformers, psychiatrists, or public officials. A variety of circumstances by the 1850's had converged to give rise to an institution that deviated sharply from the ideal type. Superintendents had conceived of their institutions in therapeutic terms; from the very beginning they were forced to accept large numbers of chronic insane persons, who eventually came to constitute a significant proportion of the institution's total population. Hospitals were intended to remain small in order to promote the types of relationships deemed conducive to recovery; instead they grew in size, thereby hastening the transition from a charismatic-type hospital to one dominated by administrative concerns. In theory all patients received the same quality of care; in practice class, ethnicity, and race played a significant role in the evolution of differential care and treatment. Conceiving of their own role in medical terms, superintendents were rapidly transformed into administrators who were concerned with largely managerial problems; considerations of order and efficiency often overshadowed their therapeutic concerns.

Regarded as a self-contained medical institution, the mental hospital was unable to retain any significant degree of isolation from the larger society in which it existed. Public policy remained a legislative responsibility, and hospital officials found that their autonomy was limited in significant ways by the general legal, administrative, and financial environment. The decentralized and prebureaucratic nature of mid-nineteenth-century American society inhibited the formulation of consistent policies; hospitals were often caught up in the vortex of change and confusion and saw their therapeutic goals subverted by circumstances beyond the control of their officials. Nor did local governments bring any measure of stability or continuity to policy issues; community control and participation—at least as far as the mentally ill were concerned—were inversely related to quality of care and degree of funding. The fact that the problems arising out of mental illness were not separated from the broader issues of dependency also had major implications for hospitals. While many states moved to centralize and rationalize their welfare systems in the last third of the nineteenth century, the net result was to further enmesh mental hospitals in an ambiguous system that alternated between compassion and hostility for dependent groups. Under these circumstances the functions of hospitals remained pluralistic rather than unitary; they continued to care for a heterogeneous patient population that included a significant proportion of poor and indigent persons, chronic cases, old age groups, and individuals who were deemed dangerous to society or who seemed to require a structured environment, in addition to providing care and treatment for acute cases for relatively short periods of time. By 1875, then, the structure and functions of mental hospitals and the general framework within which they functioned had been institutionalized; future generations, for better or worse, would have to deal with the mentally ill within the parameters that had been laid down by earlier generations.

The care of the mentally ill, then, tells us much about the operations of complex social processes generally in nineteenth-century America. It is easy, of course, to attribute the fact that the overwhelming majority of mental hospitals fell far short of their stated objectives to evil or shortsighted human beings or to a society lacking in sympathy and understanding for less fortunate groups. Yet a careful analysis does not substantiate such interpretations. Indeed, the most impressive fact is the relative absence of malevolence or for that matter consistency of behavior. What emerges more closely resembles a tragedy, in which most participants, to a greater or lesser degree, were well intentioned but their actual behavior gave rise to less than desirable results. For the history of the care and treatment of the mentally ill in American society is surely fraught with all of the elements of tragedy. Within such a perspective, any definitive judgment must contain some room for a measure of understanding and even compassion for all concerned—patients, psychiatrists, and the larger society. Perhaps the accomplishments of mental hospitals fell far short of their goals, but surely they had accomplished at least some things of value. In this respect mental hospitals were not fundamentally dissimilar from most human institutions, the achievements of which usually fall far short of the hopes and aspirations of the individuals who founded and led them.

Appendix I

The Founding of State Mental Hospitals to 1860

I

ALTHOUGH THE SURGE in the founding of state mental hospitals followed the action of Massachusetts in opening the Worcester hospital in 1833, several states had created such institutions earlier. Yet the public institutions in existence before 1830 had few of the characteristics deemed necessary and appropriate for the proper conduct of mental hospitals. In most cases their founders were uninformed of contemporary psychiatric theory and its emphasis upon the therapeutic role of the mental hospital. Consequently, they were little more than specialized almshouses and their influence on public policy was negligible.

The examples of Kentucky and South Carolina (which opened their public hospitals in 1824 and 1828, respectively) offer ample evidence for these generalizations. In neither state was any sustained thought given to the problem of classification of inmates or of structuring the hospital in such a way as to facilitate implementation of therapeutic goals. The objects of both hospitals were ill defined from the very beginning; internal authority was divided between a lay keeper and an attendant or resident physician; and the system for financing these hospitals bore little relationship to their mission. Both institutions, therefore, differed little from almshouses. The first medical superintendent of the Kentucky hospital (who was not appointed until 1844) found that only 18 of the 236 patients represented recent cases of mental illness; 182 had been insane for periods ranging from five to forty years. The patients, he noted,

> were generally from the lower classes of society—the poorer and least enlightened members of the community. Where sufficient reason remained to direct or sustain, in some degree, mental or moral effort, there appeared to be no desire for mental or moral enjoyment. Books had no charms for them. Music, games, dancing, and many other of the lighter and enlivening amusements, which those of a more elevated rank, or favorable circumstances usually mingle with the cares and drudgeries of life, exerted no power over their benumbed sensibilities. . . .
>
> Appalling indeed was the spectacle, to the rational mind, upon entering the halls of our Asylum, to behold the promiscuous and heterogeneous assembly of associates. . . . The same gallery resounded with the discordant sounds of maddened ravings, giddy laughs, senseless chatter, sepulchral moanings, earnest prayers, fiendish oaths and pious songs. . . .
>
> Then [sic], with cases generally of the most hopeless character, a house unadapted to classification, ignorance of the history of any case, and attendants unacquainted with the true mode of managing the insane, were a few, among the many serious obstacles, we had to encounter at the commencement of our duties.[1]

Similarly, the South Carolina hospital prior to 1836 performed the functions of a poor house, and even after that date continued to be plagued by serious internal problems that sharply curtailed the achievement of any therapeutic goals.[2]

1. Kentucky Eastern Lunatic Asylum, *AR*, 1844, 19–21.

2. My generalizations about the early history of the Kentucky hospital are based on the following sources: "Insanity in Kentucky," *Boston Medical and Surgical Journal*, XXIV (April 21, 1841), 166–168 (though unsigned, this article was probably written by Edward Jarvis); Samuel Theobold, "Some Account of the Lunatic Asylum of Kentucky, with Remarks, &c.," *Transylvania Journal of Medicine and the Associate Sciences*, II–III (November, 1829–February, 1830), 91, 509–511; Edward Jarvis, "Insanity and Asylums for the Insane," *Western Journal of Medicine and Surgery*, IV (December, 1841), 469–471; Kentucky Eastern Lunatic Asylum, *AR*, XLV (1869), 12–13; E. S. Abdy, *Journal of a Residence and Tour in the United States of North America, from April, 1833, to October, 1834*, 3 vols. (London, 1835), II, 346; *Boston Medical and Surgical Journal*, XXXI (December 11, 1844), 386. The comparable sources for South

Maryland and Virginia were the only other two states to have an institution that approximated a mental hospital before 1830. In the case of the former the hospital came into existence more by accident than by design. In 1797 a hospital for sick and insane persons was opened in Baltimore with the proceeds of contributions from both private and state sources. Although under the control of municipal authorities, the institution proved less than successful. Between 1808 and 1836, therefore, the Maryland hospital was leased to several private physicians. Three years after the state assumed control in 1836, the institution was converted into a hospital for the insane. Small in size (between 1835 and 1840 the hospital cared for fewer than four hundred cases) and beset by severe financial difficulties, the Maryland hospital prior to 1840 served largely as a custodial institution for poor and dependent insane persons.[3]

Carolina include Daniel H. Trezevant, *Letters to His Excellency Governor Manning on the Lunatic Asylum* (Columbia, 1854); Malvena G. S. King, "The South Carolina State Hospital and It's Treatment of Mental Disease" (unpubl. M.A. thesis, University of South Carolina, 1930), 2–4; *Acts Concerning the Lunatic Asylum of South Carolina; and By-Laws for its Government, Revised and Passed by the Board of Regents . . . 1850* (Columbia, 1851); South Carolina Lunatic Asylum, *AR*, 1842, 6–7, 18–19, 32–42, 1847, 8–9, 1848, 10–11, 1849, 9, 1850, 6, 1852, 6–8, 12, 1853, 9–15, 1855, 5–14.

3. This account of the Maryland hospital is based on the following sources: Maryland Hospital, *AR*, 1843, 5–7, 1852, 5–8, 1857, 5–8; William F. Steuart, "History of the Maryland Hospital," ms. in bound volume entitled *Report of the President and Board of Visitors of the Maryland Hospital*, National Library of Medicine, Bethesda, Md. (see also Steuart to J. S. Billings, January 31, 1871, in *ibid.*); "Historical Sketch of the First Hospital in Maryland for the Insane," Maryland Lunacy Commission, *AR*, XXIV (1909), 45–54; *Report on the Public Charities, Reformatories, Prisons and Almshouses, of the State of Maryland, by C. W. Chancellor, M.D., Secretary of the State Board of Health, Made to His Excellency, John Lee Carroll, Governor, July, 1877* (Frederick, 1877), 33ff.; *Report of the Trustees of the State Lunatic Asylum, with the Documents Accompanying the Same, Persuant to the Act of the Legislature Passed May 26, 1841,* New York *Senate Document No. 20* (January 12, 1842), 50. Between 1834 and 1839, when the hospital cared for patients with all diseases, the total number of patients admitted was over a thousand. Illinois Board of State Commissioners of Public Charities, *BR*, I (1869/1870), tables between 288 and 289.

In some ways Virginia could have led the way in providing public facilities for mentally ill persons. It had established the first public hospital before the American Revolution; it was also the initial state to have more than one public institution, since the Western Lunatic Asylum was founded in 1825 and opened in 1828. Yet Virginia's influence did not extend beyond its own borders. Its institutions remained very small; there was no evidence that they were conducted in accordance with the principles of moral treatment; and the Old Dominion made no effort to act as a catalyst by publicizing its activites. Consequently, Virginia's two hospitals remained parochial institutions; their influence was negligible during the 1830's when the hospital movement gained national momentum.

Prior to 1841 the Eastern Asylum, though never crowded, was isolated from the mainstream of contemporary psychiatric practice. Administration was haphazard; the keeper lacked authority, which remained in the hands of the directors. Not until 1822 was the institution required to report annually to the legislature, a fact that reinforced its parochial nature. Before 1826 the keeper kept virtually no patient records of any type. During the 1830's the recovery rate fell sharply and the number of chronic cases rose. Dr. John M. Galt, who began the process of transforming the institution upon his accession to the superintendency in 1841, reported the following year that 54 patients (out of a total of under 100) had been in the hospital for more than five years.[4] In the 1820's and 1830's, therefore, the Williamsburg hospital had little or no influence outside of the state.

Similarly, the Western Lunatic Asylum (which was founded in order to reduce the extraordinarily high costs of transporting patients from the western part of Virginia to Williamsburg) provided only custodial care for its first eight years of operations. Shortly after assuming control of the medical department, Dr. Francis T. Stribling (who later became superintendent and presided over the modernization of the hospital) condemned conditions at Staunton in harsh words. While the hospital was neat and clean, he noted, it compared unfavorably with other institutions

4. Virginia Eastern Asylum, *AR*, 1842, 4–5. This description of the Williamsburg hospital is based largely on Norman Dain's *Disordered Minds: The First Century of Eastern State Hospital in Williamsburg, Virginia 1766–1866* (Williamsburg, 1971), Chap. II.

because of the lack of facilities and resources to implement a systematic program of moral treatment. The hospital's managers demonstrated "a degree of *illiberality* utterly incompatible with, and destructive of, the very objects which they should desire to promote. . . . Every thing has been provided, which humanity could prompt, for the protection and support of the insane; but nothing has been done for the purpose of removing their affliction and enabling them to resume the care of themselves." Consequently, the number of cures was "trifling." "This institution," charged Stribling, "deserves no higher appellation, than *a well-kept prison*."[5]

II

The drive to found mental hospitals initially proved strongest in New England. By 1833 Massachusetts and Connecticut each had a distinguished private institution and Massachusetts a new public hospital; during the succeeding decade Vermont, Maine, and New Hampshire followed suit and opened their own hospitals. In all three states, however, the institutions that came into being were financed partially by private contributions, for public enthusiasm was not especially strong. In New Hampshire, for example, the legislature requested that all towns discuss and vote on the proposed hospital. The results proved astonishing; with the exception of the larger towns (which had greater numbers of insane persons), sentiment was decidedly negative. A majority of towns and a small majority of voters opposed a publicly supported hospital. Rural citizens saw no reason why they should have to pay for an institution that would not directly benefit them.[6] In most states, as a matter of fact, the movement to found

5. Virginia Western Lunatic Hospital, *AR*, IX (1836), 7, 9–10. For the founding of the institution see the *Report of the Court of Directors of the Western Lunatic Hospital* [December 13, 1826], document appended to the *Journal of the House of Delegates of the Commonwealth of Virginia*, 1826; *Report of the Court of Directors of the Western Lunatic Hospital, December, 1827*, document appended to *ibid.*, 1827; *Report of the Court of Directors of the Western Lunatic Hospital, December, 1828*, document appended to *ibid.*, 1828.

6. Boston Prison Discipline Society, *AR*, XII (1837), 7–8; *Extracts from Newspapers and Periodicals in Relation to the Condition of the*

mental hospitals was led by relatively small groups that included governors, physicians, and socially prominent persons who saw these institutions as expressions of noblesse oblige and the fulfillment of a religious and moral obligation by society toward distressed persons.

In Maine and New Hampshire concern over the plight of the mentally ill was first raised by the governor. In his annual message to the legislature in 1832, the chief executive of New Hampshire pointed out that while poor houses and jails provided security for the community, they were not adapted to humane care or therapy. "The public," he noted, "may, indeed, in this way, be secured from danger, but the protection is generally purchased by the sacrifice of the miserable victim."[7] In both states, nevertheless, it was nearly a decade before state hospitals were opened. Even when the legislatures gave their assent to the projects, their members insisted that a large proportion of the costs be borne by private contributors. Maine appropriated $20,000 contingent on an equal sum's being raised by donors within one year, while in New Hampshire the fact that control of the institution seemed to rest in the hands of private individuals caused a conflict that was not resolved until the state assumed control two years before the first patient was received. In neither state was there evidence that a public hospital had broad community support. Indeed, the greatest concern of local communities was the potential impact on their tax structure, for there was little enthusiasm at the prospect of spending larger sums to support the indigent insane at a hospital when such cases could be cared for in a cheaper manner at local welfare institutions. The arguments marshalled in favor of hospitals often reflected this fact. While the obligation of society toward the insane was always conceded, those who supported hospitals also insisted that the security of the community would be enhanced and that in the long run it would be cheaper to cure such persons than to confine them indefinitely.[8]

Insane in New Hampshire, Previous to the Erection of the N.H. Asylum for the Insane (Concord, 1890), 25–26.

7. Boston Prison Discipline Society, *AR*, VII (1832), 9.

8. For the founding of the New Hampshire Asylum for the Insane see *ibid.*, 8–10, XII (1837), 7–8; *Report of the Select Committee to the House of Representatives Upon the Subject of Building an Insane Hospital,*

In Vermont the movement to establish a hospital was initiated by a bequest of $10,000 by a wealthy widow who died in 1834. The legislature immediately accepted the money and established a hospital under the control of a self-perpetuating board of trustees, with the judges of the Court of Chancery serving as a board of visitors with the power to correct abuses. It also granted an appropriation of $2,000 per year for five years; eventually the state's contribution amounted to $23,000. The Vermont Asylum for the Insane, then, represented a compromise between a public and private hospital. At the outset patients paid $3 per week, and the trustees agreed to accept a stipulated percentage of indigent cases (defined as individuals having an estate valued at less than $100), whose confinement was not to exceed six months. For eight years following its opening in 1836 the relationship between the hospital and the state remained vague. During this period the hospital accepted poor and indigent persons, while the state provided funds to enlarge the physical plant. No provision, however, was made for the maintenance of such cases in the hospital. At the urging of the trustees, the legislature in 1844 finally passed "An Act for the Relief of the Insane Poor," which provided funds to pay for the confinement of the insane poor at the hospital. In effect, the relationship between the state and the hospital was a contractual one; the latter remained neither exclusively private nor public in character.[9]

In New Hampshire and Maine the care of the mentally ill did not have an especially high priority. A relatively low population density undoubtedly was an important factor, since the care of dependent persons remained the responsibility of the family and local community. A similar situation prevailed in both Connecti-

---

2nd ed. (Concord, 1832); *Report Made to the Legislature of New Hampshire on the Subject of the Insane. June Session, 1836* (Concord, 1836); *Extracts from Newspapers and Periodicals in Relation to the Condition of the Insane in New Hampshire;* New Hampshire Asylum for the Insane, *AR,* I (1840), 6, XXI (1862), 8–17. For the Maine institution see Henry M. Hurd, ed., *The Institutional Care of the Insane in the United States and Canada,* 4 vols. (Baltimore, 1916–1917), II, 484–485, and the Boston Prison Discipline Society, *AR,* X (1835), 6.

9. *The Vermont Asylum for the Insane. Its Annals for Fifty Years* (Brattleboro, 1887), 1–18, 70–71. For the superintendent's justification of mental hospitals see Vermont Asylum for the Insane, *AR,* III (1839), 14.

cut and Rhode Island. In the former the existence of the Hartford Retreat seemed to mitigate the urgency of the problem. Yet in 1837, upon receiving a memorial from the directors of the Retreat, the General Assembly appointed a committee to take a census of the insane. In the spring of the following year the committee reported its findings. Of 136 towns in the state, 118 had provided the required data. The findings revealed a minimum of 707 insane persons; of these, 321 were fully destitute and completely dependent upon public support, 145 were partly dependent, and 241 were supported through charitable giving; only 59 were actually confined (the remainder were cared for in various ways, including placing them with families who received a public subsidy). Moreover, there were at least 372 cases of intemperance; the fact that some of these were occasionally dangerous led the committee to recommend that provision be made for their care. Although the report strongly favored the establishment of a public hospital, the General Assembly took no further action. It preferred instead to inaugurate a system whereby the Hartford Retreat would accept some indigent patients in return for state aid. Connecticut being a state that had a relatively low rate of population growth and received only small numbers of immigrants, its leaders did not think it necessary to found a public hospital until after the Civil War.[10]

Also in Rhode Island, the smallest state in New England, the establishment of a mental hospital was the work of private philanthropy. In 1841 Nicholas Brown, a wealthy merchant, philanthropist, and benefactor of Brown University (which was renamed after him), left a bequest of $30,000 for a mental hospital. Since the sum was insufficient for the project, it became necessary to find other donors. Upon the urging of Dorothea L. Dix, Cyrus Butler, a wealthy friend of Brown, agreed to give an additional $40,000 if an equal sum could be raised from other sources. By the end of 1845 the money had been collected, and two years later the Butler Hospital for the Insane was opened in Providence.

10. *Report of the Committee on the Insane Poor in Connecticut, to the General Assembly, May Session, 1838* (New Haven, 1838), 3–17. This report was also reprinted by the Boston Prison Discipline Society in its *AR,* XIII (1838), 17–24. For criticism of Connecticut's backwardness in founding a state hospital see *ibid.,* XI (1836), 26–27, XV (1840), 21, and "Lunatic Asylums in the United States," *AJI,* II (October, 1845), 173.

Although its trustees set the price of board at the low figure of $2 per week in the hope of encouraging localities to use the facility, they found that they received only the most difficult cases. Many others remained in their communities because it was presumably cheaper to care for them locally than it was to send them to the hospital. For nearly two decades the Butler institution cared for poor and indigent cases, and beginning in 1850 the legislature began to provide subsidies for those persons unable to pay for their upkeep at the hospital. Not until after the Civil War did the state establish a public facility; prior to that time the Butler institution retained its mixed character and cared for indigent and private cases.[11]

III

The relatively slow growth of public hospitals that was characteristic of New England also prevailed in the populous states to the south of that region. New York and Pennsylvania, for example (which contained about 25 percent of the nation's population in 1830), were both beginning to encounter the problems of dependency that accompanied growth and urbanization. Neither the Bloomingdale Asylum in New York City nor the old Pennsylvania Hospital in Philadelphia was capable of caring for more than a fraction of the total number of mentally ill persons in its state, especially those from lower- and middle-income groups. In New York concern with mental illness was evident in both the

11. *Charter of the Butler Hospital for the Insane* (Providence, 1847), 3–5, 10–15; *Circular of the Trustees of the Butler Hospital for the Insane, in Providence, R.I.* (n.p., 1847); Butler Hospital for the Insane, *AR*, 1847, 4, 7, 1848, 8–10, 1851, 13–16, 27–36. Although Dix's biographers have generally given her the credit for inducing Butler to give money for the establishment of the hospital, there is some evidence that her efforts were not decisive. Isaac Ray in his contemporary account ("The Butler Hospital for the Insane," *AJI*, V [July, 1848], 1–20) did not mention Dix, nor does her name appear in the Butler Hospital Papers (John Carter Brown Library, Brown University, Providence, R.I.). Traditional accounts can be found in Francis Tiffany, *Life of Dorothea Lynde Dix* (Boston, 1890), 100–102, Helen E. Marshall, *Dorothea Dix: Forgotten Samaritan* (Chapel Hill, 1937), 100–104, and Franklin B. Sanborn, ed., *Memoirs of Pliny Earle, M.D.* (Boston, 1898), 307–308.

Yates report on the poor in 1824 and the passage of a law in 1827 that attempted to classify the mentally ill with dependent rather than criminal groups. Three years later the governor recommended to the legislature that the state establish a public institution to protect the community and to provide care for those unable to pay the high costs of protracted institutionalization. This recommendation quickly stimulated the legislature to appoint a committee to undertake a comprehensive study of both the Bloomingdale Asylum and the broad framework of public policy. In its report the committee concluded that public hospitals possessed inherent advantages over their private counterparts, especially on the issue of accountability for their actions. The state, insisted its members, had an obligation toward the indigent and poor insane. Yet New York had never adopted a comprehensive policy on the subject of mental illness, leaving local communities to deal with the problem as best they could. "Public establishments for the reception and cure of the insane poor," concluded the committee, "are both necessary and proper."[12]

In Pennsylvania the issue of a public hospital was not raised until 1838 when a group of prominent private citizens, including a number of physicians, published an appeal to the public and the legislature on behalf of the insane. The legislature responded immediately by appointing an investigating committee. In its report the committee indicated that the number of cases of mental illness, if anything, had been sharply underestimated. Those lunatics confined in existing welfare institutions were in many instances treated as well as could be expected, especially in larger ones able to provide special facilities. Nevertheless, hospitals were far better suited for the care of the insane than welfare institutions. The members of the committee, moreover, demonstrated a high degree of sensitivity toward the problems of the insane poor, refusing even to condemn those whose personal folly had led to the advent of the disease. "Poverty itself,—" they noted,

12. New York *Assembly Document No. 263* (March 10, 1831), 5–37; Utica State Lunatic Asylum, *AR*, IV (1846), 59–61; Stanley B. Klein, "A Study of Social Legislation Affecting Prisons and Institutions for the Mentally Ill in New York State 1822–1846" (unpubl. Ph.D. dissertation, New York University, 1956), 265ff.

when abject and hopeless enough to seek relief from public charity, is a bitter portion, at least to one whose pride and self respect have not been extinguished by vicious habits. To be miserably poor and at the same time to be shut out from every pleasant and cheerful prospect, and to be denied the alleviation of sympathy and hope, is an intense aggravation. But to have the mind diseased, distracted and tormented; and to endure, beyond all this neglect, abuse and cruelty, without the power of resistance, or the opportunity of complaint, presents a picture of human woe, which few can contemplate without a tear of pity.

Even if every case of suffering could be traced to the folly or sin of the victim, the appeal to our compassion would still be irresistible.

Without any hesitation or equivocation, the committee strongly urged that Pennsylvania establish a state lunatic asylum.[13]

Although sentiment in New York and Pennsylvania appeared favorable, the drive for public hospitals did not move rapidly. Despite the continued urgings of the governor and some of its own members, the New York legislature procrastinated, partly because of inertia and partly because of political rivalry and strife. In 1836 the State Medical Society threw its weight behind the project, and the legislature finally authorized the establishment of a hospital. By the time the Utica State Lunatic Asylum opened in early 1843, however, the number of insane persons had risen so sharply that the relative position of the state was not appreciably improved. Within a year Dorothea Dix had entered the state and undertaken a careful survey of conditions. Convinced that much remained to be done, she suggested that the state consider a variety of alternative policies, including the founding of four to six custodial asylums, which would permit Bloomingdale and Utica to function exclusively as curative institutions. Her proposals, however, were never seriously considered and her activities were not always viewed with favor, partly because of her strong and compelling personality. Public policy, therefore, remained lacking in definition; there was no effort to place the

13. *An Appeal to the People of Pennsylvania on the Subject of an Asylum for the Insane Poor of the Commonwealth* (Philadelphia, 1838); *Report in Relation to an Asylum for the Insane Poor* (Harrisburg, 1839), 3–24.

problem within a broad context or to develop comprehensive policies.[14]

Much the same situation existed in Pennsylvania. Although both houses of the legislature acted favorably on a proposal for a new hospital, the governor reluctantly vetoed the bill on the grounds that depressed economic conditions made retrenchment a necessity. The group of private citizens who had originally raised the idea of a public hospital continued to be active, but the project languished until 1844, when Dix arrived in Pennsylvania. After a careful survey of conditions, she presented one of her lengthy memorials to the legislature and began to lobby actively among key members of that body. In spite of the support she received from prison reformers and others, the struggle was not without internal friction. Kirkbride, for example, was accused of maneuvering to have the state hospital located on the grounds of the Pennsylvania Hospital for the Insane. He vehemently denied that he had ever entertained such a proposition and insisted that the state needed at least two institutions, one in Philadelphia and the other in the western part of Pennsylvania. "I should really be glad to know," he complained to Dix, "the name of the individual so exceedingly silly or so very malicious, as to make to you assertions as respects myself, [that] are utterly destitute of the shadow of a foundation." In 1845 the legislature finally acted. It was six years, however, before the Pennsylvania State Lunatic Hospital in Harrisburg was actually opened. Even after the decision to build a public hospital had been made, its supporters were fearful that the desire to spend as little as possible would be a paramount consideration in the construction of a physical plant.[15]

14. Utica State Lunatic Asylum, *AR*, IV (1846), 61–72, XXV (1867), 43–58; Dorothea L. Dix, *Memorial. To the Honorable the Legislature of the State of New York,* New York *Assembly Document No. 21* (1844), 56; Amariah Brigham to Kirkbride, March 3, 1845, Kirkbride Papers, IPH; Klein, "A Study of Social Legislation . . . in New York State," 286–351.

15. *A Second Appeal to the People of Pennsylvania on the Subject of an Asylum for the Insane Poor of the Commonwealth* (Philadelphia, 1840), 3ff.; Dix, *Memorial Soliciting a State Hospital for the Insane, Submitted to the Legislature of Pennsylvania, February 3, 1845* (Harrisburg, 1845); *Journal of Prison Discipline and Philanthropy,* I (January, 1845), 60–65 (July, 1845), 207–253; Kirkbride to Dix, July 27, 1845, Kirkbride to Samuel B. Woodward, July 17, 1845; Kirkbride to Rev. Louis Dwight, July 30, 1845, Kirkbride Papers, IPH.

In New Jersey the movement to provide a public facility for the mentally ill resembled somewhat its counterparts in both New York and Pennsylvania. Although New Jersey had made some provision for its blind and deaf, it had neither public nor private facilities for any mentally ill persons; responsibility for their well-being remained with the local community. The initiative for a hospital came first from the president of the Medical Society of New Jersey and its members in 1838. The following year the legislature authorized the establishment of a commission to study the problem. Four of the five commissioners were physicians, for in the early stages of the struggle the state's medical profession played a leading role. Their report in 1840 did not differ appreciably from comparable investigations elsewhere. It was prepared in a rapid and hasty manner, and included a rough statistical survey of the number of insane persons, a statement on conditions in local welfare institutions, and an analysis of activities in other states—particularly the example of the Worcester hospital in Massachusetts. The arguments marshalled by the commissioners likewise were familiar ones. A state hospital, which they strongly favored, "will be intended principally for that class of unfortunates, who for the want of such an establishment, are committed to jails, because the community is unsafe when they are at large." Moreover, only in such an institution could the insane receive proper care and treatment, thus maximizing the chances for recovery. Finally, the state had a moral and humanitarian obligation toward these unfortunates.[16]

The following year a legislative committee reported favorably on the proposed hospital; its members were convinced that in the long run confinement in a public institution would prove the most economical way of dealing with pauper lunatics. The legislature, however, took no action, partly because of reluctance to incur a state debt. In 1843 it passed an act requiring county officials to study conditions among their pauper insane and to send curable ones to hospitals in neighboring states. The lack of enforcement mechanisms plus the reluctance of other states to

16. *Report of the Commissioners Appointed by the Governor of New Jersey, to Ascertain the Number of Lunatics and Idiots in the State* (Newark, 1840), *passim;* H. A. Buttolph, "Historical and Descriptive Account of the New Jersey State Lunatic Asylum, at Trenton," *AJI*, VI (July, 1849), 1–2.

accept responsibility for noncitizens made the law little more than a verbal exercise. With the arrival of Dix in the state in 1844 the drive for a public hospital was revived. In 1845 she presented her case to the legislature and began to lobby intensively to win individual lawmakers to her side. "I am exhausted under this perpetual effort and exercise of fortitude," she wrote to one of her friends. "Some evenings I had at once twenty gentlemen for three hours' steady conversation." Those who opposed her efforts did not necessarily do so for selfish or partisan reasons. One legislator, for example, opposed a state debt and indicated his belief that the education of children had a higher priority. Nevertheless, the bill establishing a state lunatic asylum passed without difficulty. The struggle was not yet over, for supporters of the hospital then faced the danger of an insufficient appropriation as well as an effort to have the superintendent appointed directly by the legislature (thereby involving the hospital in political and partisan conflict). The latter proposal aroused the firm opposition of the young psychiatric profession, especially Kirkbride, who insisted that it would *"never do to have the Physician appointed by the Legislature."* The proposal was eventually defeated and the hospital opened in 1848.[17]

IV

Concern with the problems posed by mental disease was by no means confined to the more populous Northeast. On the contrary,

17. Dix, *Memorial Soliciting a State Hospital for the Insane, Submitted to the Legislature of New Jersey: January 23, 1845*, 2nd ed. (Trenton, 1845); Tiffany, *Life of Dorothea Lynde Dix*, 110–120; Marshall, *Dorothea Dix*, 104–108; Kirkbride to E. H. Cooley, January 31, 1846, Kirkbride to Rev. Louis Dwight, June 30, 1845, Kirkbride to Samuel B. Woodward, July 17, 1845, Kirkbride to Amariah Brigham, August 21, 1845, Kirkbride Papers, IPH; James Leiby, *Charity and Correction in New Jersey: A History of State Welfare Institutions* (New Brunswick, 1967), 49–51.

Curiously enough, the superintendent of the New Jersey hospital was unhappy with those critics who opposed charging $3 per week for pauper and indigent patients. "I have resolutely set my face against the custom of State institutions in cheapening the rate of charge down to *Poor-House* prices." H. A. Buttolph to Kirkbride, February 6, 1849, Kirkbride Papers, IPH.

the movement to provide institutional care was national rather than sectional in scope, for all states (particularly as population and the number of urban centers increased) were attempting to develop policies to deal with welfare and dependency. Indeed, what is remarkable about the drive to found hospitals was its national character and the relative ease with which its supporters, both lay and professional, could move about the country irrespective of the section from which they came or their personal outlook.

The pattern of hospital-founding in the newer states of the West, for example, was almost identical with that in the East. Ohio, which during the first half of the nineteenth century was the fastest growing of the east north central states, is a case in point. Between 1800 and 1830 its population grew from less than 50,000 to nearly 1 million. Even before Ohio became a state, the territorial government found it necessary to make provision for the guardians of insane persons. By 1815 the legislature had adopted a comprehensive statute that provided for the confinement of dangerous lunatics and affirmed the responsibility of the overseers of the poor for the pauper insane. During the 1830's, however, dissatisfaction with informal modes of care began to mount. The initial impetus for change came from the young medical profession in the state. At the first session of the state medical convention in 1835 a memorial was prepared and sent to the legislature urging that provision be made to establish a public lunatic asylum. In less than three months the necessary legislation had been passed. Modeled directly on the example of the Worcester institution, the Ohio Lunatic Asylum received its first patients toward the end of 1838.[18]

In neighboring states the course of events was similar. Early legislation touching upon the mentally ill was concerned with legal guardianship and pauperism. From time to time the question of proper provision for the insane arose, usually without any visible result. Indiana, for example, set aside land in its new capital of Indianapolis for a state lunatic hospital in the 1820's. Although this action was reaffirmed in 1831, the project languished. A

18. Boston Prison Discipline Society, *AR*, XI (1836), 76–78; *Report of the Directors to Whom was Committed the Charge of Erecting a Lunatic Asylum for the State of Ohio December 24, 1838* (n.p., n.d.), 5; Ohio Lunatic Asylum, *AR*, IV (1842), 9–11, XVII (1855), 9–10.

decade later interest in the project was reawakened, again with no visible results. The turning point came toward the end of 1843 when the senate rejected an unfavorable report by its Committee on Education relative to a public hospital. As pressure mounted from groups composed of physicians and private citizens, sentiment in the legislature for favorable action grew stronger. In early 1845, therefore, the required legislation passed both houses and received the governor's signature. In Illinois also the need for a mental hospital had been emphasized during the 1840's by physicians and others. By 1845 a coalition was actively seeking legislative support for the project. Its efforts were bolstered by the appearance of Dix the following year, and in 1847 the required legislation passed. That same year a state institution was founded in Missouri under similar circumstances.[19]

In time other Midwestern and Western states moved to open their own mental hospitals. Between 1851 and 1875 California, Michigan, Wisconsin, Iowa, Kansas, Minnesota, Nebraska, and Washington also established public facilities.[20] On occasion the pattern tended to deviate from the norm. Michigan and Iowa are cases in point. In Michigan pressure from private individuals and superintendents of the poor led to legislative approval of a bill founding a mental hospital in 1848. The subsequent history of the institution, however, proved somewhat unique. Under the provisions of the law a single board was given authority over the asylums for the insane and the deaf and dumb and blind. The board was empowered to select suitable sites and erect buildings. The legislature, however, appropriated no funds for the project; it granted instead eight sections of salt lands which were to be sold and the proceeds used for the asylums. This plan proved extraordinarily difficult to implement, and in the seven years

19. Indiana Hospital for the Insane, *AR*, IV (1852), 5–16, V (1853), 9–10; "Memorial of Miss Dix, January, 1847," in *Reports of the Illinois State Hospital for the Insane 1847–1862* (Chicago, 1863), especially 10ff.; William W. Burke, "The Supervision of the Care of the Mentally Diseased by the Illinois State Board of Charities (1869–1909)" (unpubl. Ph.D. dissertation, University of Chicago, 1934), 200–219; Hurd, *Institutional Care of the Insane*, II, 876.

20. The details of the founding of mental hospitals in most states can be followed in their annual reports. The bibliography at the end of this volume lists by state the reports that provide the basis for some of my generalizations.

following 1850 the hospital finally began to receive direct financial support by the state. The legislature also amended the original act and gave each institution its own governing board in 1857. Hopes of opening the hospital were momentarily dashed in 1859 when its center building was completely destroyed by fire. Using the remaining structures, the Michigan institution received a small group of female patients in 1859, and the following year began to accept some male patients. The opening of the hospital, nevertheless, ended few of its difficulties, and the coming of war in 1861 merely compounded its problems. Within a few years after its opening the institution had to exclude private patients and accept only indigent persons, causing a substantial decline in operating funds.[21]

Iowa, on the other hand, first attempted to rely on out-of-state facilities for its citizens. When it could no longer depend on hospitals elsewhere, the legislature moved to establish its own institution. Instead of providing a direct appropriation, however, it emulated Michigan's plan and authorized the use of all revenues derived from the sale of its salt lands (in the nineteenth century it was common to use the proceeds from the sale of the public domain for socially desirable projects). In this case the procedure proved inadequate. The portion of these revenues authorized by the legislature for construction was insufficient, and when the building commission decided on a more expensive plan the project became a source of political friction. The end result was a delay of six years before the hospital actually received patients.[22]

V

The thrust toward institutional care of the mentally ill in the decades following 1830 was also evident in most Southern states. Yet Southern hospitals as a group provided the lowest quality of care, received the lowest level of funding of any group of state hospitals, and were plagued by far more severe internal problems.

21. Michigan Asylum for the Insane, *BR*, 1857/1858, 6–19, 1865/1866 (*Building Commissioner's Report*), 5–47.

22. Iowa Hospital for the Insane, *BR*, I (1860/1861), 14; A. W. McClure, "The State Hospital at Mt. Pleasant," *Bulletin of Iowa Institutions*, III (1901), 305–309.

A number of factors contributed to this situation. The absence of clinical and training centers (which were common in the more urbanized Northeast) kept the South somewhat isolated from the mainstream of contemporary psychiatric theory and practice. The more rural nature of Southern society further inhibited the development of a cohesive profession. It is notable, for example, that the most influential figures in American psychiatry between 1830 and 1870 were from the Northeast; not a single Southerner served as president of the AMSAII between 1844 and 1870. Equally significant, the movement to establish and improve facilities in the South tended to be more derivative; none of the famous nineteenth-century psychiatric reformers were from that section. Above all, the tradition of public support for welfare, education, and other socially desirable projects was weakest in the South (although the proportionate differences between states narrow when per capita income and wealth are taken into account). Consequently, Southern hospitals as a group took on a somewhat different character as compared with those in other sections.

In the three decades prior to the Civil War most Southern states moved to found their own mental hospitals. Georgia, one of the first states to take such a step in the 1830's, had a long history with respect to the problem. Settled as the last of the thirteen original colonies, Georgia in the eighteenth century soon faced problems of poverty and disease. Given the fact that the founders of the colony were hoping to employ the settlement as a place where Englishmen imprisoned for crimes such as the nonpayment of debts might get a chance to start a new life, pauperism was an especially acute problem. Mental illness became a public issue when questions of property and guardianship arose, or when aberrant behavior seemed to threaten the safety of the community. Early legislation reflected these concerns; the care of the mentally ill was made a responsibility of the local community, the unit of government liable for the welfare of dependent groups.[23] Lacking specialized facilities, local officials often employed jails as undifferentiated welfare institutions.

23. For a description of welfare practices in the South see Elizabeth Wisner, *Social Welfare in the South: From Colonial Times to World War I* (Baton Rouge, 1970).

The initial request for a public hospital came in 1834 from Governor Wilson Lumpkin, who urged the legislature to pay serious attention "to idiots, lunatics, and insane," who "deserved to be among the first objectives of legislative care and attention." The result was a law establishing formal procedures to determine sanity and provide for legal guardianship. The issue was kept alive by several physicians in Milledgeville (then the seat of government and also the residence of an influential group of socially prominent and wealthy individuals). In 1836 the next governor reiterated the need for a public hospital. The following year the legislature acceded to his request and appropriated $20,000 for a new institution. After a site near Milledgeville had been selected, an architect (originally from Maine) was chosen. He promptly visited a number of Northern institutions and then prepared plans based on the design of the McLean and Worcester hospitals.[24]

Interestingly enough, the new facility was intended for the idiotic and epileptic in addition to the mentally ill. This feature gave it a unique character. Nevertheless, there is little evidence that the legislature or the promoters of the project were especially well informed about contemporary psychiatric theory and practice. The result was an institution plagued with more than the usual difficulties for the first three decades of its existence. Initially the legislature vested authority in a three-member board of trustees; it made no provision for a superintendent. Since all three trustees were physicians living in Milledgeville, they each took turns in visiting the hospital, thereby providing some medical care. In 1843 Dr. David Cooper was elected superintendent. Although apparently not lacking in ability, he proved highly eccentric. His first published report in 1845 was an astonishing document. In describing the finances of the institution, for example, he commented as follows:

> Also the facts we are in possession of in regard to the amounts the different counties from which pauper patients have been sent to the Asylum have heretofore paid out of the poor or charity

24. Lunatic, Idiot and Epileptic Asylum of the State of Georgia, *AR*, I (1842/1844), 25ff.; Hortense S. Cochrane, "Early Treatment of the Mentally Ill in Georgia," *Georgia Historical Quarterly*, XXXII (June, 1948), 105–118.

funds of the counties, sustain us in the assertion, that in a pecuniary and politico economical point of view, it will be to our
financial interests, the Archemedian lever to oscillate the incubus
beam of deranged, and depressed fiscal oppression which has shed
its blighting effects upon the monitary [sic] affairs, and financial
operations of the State Treasury for so many years, by lightening,
the onerous burthens of Taxation from the shoulders of the poor
and destitute, and afford bread to those who are ready to perish;
these are not anagogical suppositions and without veritous foundation, or demonstrable illustration, but susceptible of proof by the
introduction of a few prolegominous deductions, and the aid of
a few arithmetical prolepses.[25]

Cooper's words led the *American Journal of Insanity* to
comment that its initial impulse had been to question the genuine-
ness of the document. And Dr. D. Tilden Brown remarked that
Dix had written that she had been informed that Cooper "is really
insane, but being harmless, the Trustees consent to his remaining
in charge of the Institution."[26] Dr. Thomas T. Green succeeded
Cooper in 1847 as superintendent, a position he retained for over
thirty years. Despite his long tenure, the hospital continued to
have serious problems and remained considerably below the level
of other public institutions. As late as 1872 two physicians who
conducted a study for the legislature were moved to write that
"we have commended nothing, and for the very simple reason,
that we saw nothing to commend. . . . We can say nothing about
the Asylum but that in the past it has been a failure, and now
needs a thorough reorganization."[27]

The experiences of Georgia were by no means atypical. In
Tennessee a similar situation prevailed. By the 1820's a vigorous
penal reform movement had taken shape and had begun to stimu-

25. Lunatic, Idiot and Epileptic Asylum of the State of Georgia, *AR*,
I (1842/1844), 8-9.

26. *AJI*, II (October, 1845), 165-171; D. Tilden Brown to Pliny Earle,
January 22, 1846, Earle Papers, AAS.

27. *Reports of Jas. F. Bozeman, M.D., and Wm. Henry Cumming,
M.D., on the State Lunatic Asylum, Under Resolution of the General
Assembly, Passed January, 1872* (Atlanta, 1872), 29. See also Georgia State
Lunatic Asylum, *Report*, 1846/1847, 7-13; Thomas T. Green to Edward
Jarvis, December 26, 1855, Jarvis Papers, CLMHMS; Peter Bryce to Dix,
December 12, 1860, Dix Papers, HLHU.

late awareness of the fact that the line separating prisons and welfare institutions was almost nonexistent. In 1831, therefore, a group of private citizens petitioned the legislature to convert a wing of the newly erected penitentiary into a "sort of Hospital" for those lunatics in jails and poor houses. In response to rising pressure, the legislature in 1832 voted to establish a hospital for the insane, although it appropriated only $10,000 for the project. Hampered by inadequate funding, the new project proceeded at a snail's pace. In 1836 Dr. James Overton, who had visited a number of Northern institutions in his capacity as a special agent for the building commissioners, called attention to the possibility of curing the mentally ill rather than simply providing facilities for their confinement—a point that had not been previously emphasized. The following year the governor threw his support behind the project and with some additional funds the asylum opened in 1840.[28]

The Tennessee institution from its very inception proved almost as inadequate as its Georgia counterpart. The physical plant was completely unsuited for use as a hospital; its heating system was defective; it had no water supply; and its layout severely hampered a rational system of classification. "If it is intended merely to convert the house into a great State prison," observed an informed critic in 1841, "into which the unfortunate and unhappy lunatic is to be incarcerated for safe keeping, and simply administer to his animal wants and comfort and such accidental disease as may supervene, this plan may answer." As late as 1847 the institution employed one female and two male attendants, thus sharply restricting the number of patients it could admit.[29]

28. The movement to establish a mental hospital in Tennessee is dealt with in E. Bruce Thompson, "Reforms in the Care of the Insane in Tennessee, 1830–1850," *Tennessee Historical Quarterly*, III (December, 1944), 319–334.

29. *Remarks and Facts in Relation to Insanity and the Insane Asylum. Directed to the Members of the General Assembly of the State of Tennessee* (n.p., c. 1841), 5–9; Lunatic Asylum of Tennessee, *BR*, 1846/1847, 4. See also the adverse comments in the *Boston Medical and Surgical Journal*, XXXIII (December 24, 1845), 425, and XXXIII (January 7, 1846), 463–464.

By 1847 pressure to transform the asylum had mounted. At this juncture Dorothea Dix entered the state, and within a short period of time prepared a comprehensive memorial. In private she was even more damning than in public; the superintendent, she wrote Kirkbride, was an inebriate. "What a state," responded Kirkbride, "the insane must be in in the Nashville Institution when—they not only have not water to bathe or wash but not even to drink—this rather surpasses the dryest institution I have ever heard of. Maybe the want of water may account for a disposition you spoke of in your letter to indulge in something stronger than nature's beverage. I doubt that brandy can be substituted for water with safety by the Superintendent of a Hospital for the Insane."[30] Early in 1848 the legislature authorized the establishment of a new hospital for the insane and appropriated $40,000 for its construction. The new facility was completed four years later, whereupon all of the inmates at the old hospital were transferred to the new one.

In Louisiana the movement to found a public mental hospital had somewhat different origins. In the early eighteenth century a New Orleans resident had left a bequest to found a hospital in that city. After opening, Charity Hospital—as it was called later— served as both an almshouse and a refuge for the indigent sick. As New Orleans grew in size, the institution began to assume greater responsibilities for providing medical care. In 1816 the city council inquired into the possibility of having Charity Hospital accept insane patients, and by 1820 the state legislature had passed a law requiring the hospital's administrators to erect a separate building for the mentally ill. Two decades later the role of Charity Hospital was further expanded when the legislature appropriated $25,000 to erect a building for the insane provided that the hospital accept lunatics from anywhere in the state. Lack of adequate operating revenues and difficulties arising out of the confinement of insane persons within a general hospital led the board of administrators to petition the legislature to make separate provision for the insane. Although conditions at Charity were somewhat better than those at other Southern hospitals, the

30. Thomas Kirkbride to Dix, April 9, 1848, in Earl D. Bond, *Dr. Kirkbride and His Mental Hospital* (Philadelphia, 1947), 89–90.

legislature in 1847 acceded to the request and provided for the construction of a state facility in Jackson, some 30 miles from the state capital at Baton Rouge.[31] Within a year and a half after the legislature had acted, the new asylum began receiving patients. Although its board of administrators spoke in glowing terms about the new facility, Dix was incensed at what she saw. In an effort to save money a house carpenter who had never seen a hospital devised the plans for the building. No provisions were made for a water supply, bathing rooms, ventilation and warming, or quarters for physicians, officers, nurses, and servants. Only three years after the hospital had opened the administrators were requesting additional funds for expansion. The state, they noted, had given only $30,000 for construction—a sum far below the national average. Consequently, the institution could accommodate only eighty patients, or about 20 percent of the number requiring institutionalization in Louisiana.[32] As a result of insufficient facilities at Jackson, New Orleans was forced to maintain next to its jail a part of a building which it called the Temporary Asylum for the Indigent Insane. "Call it a lock-up, calaboose or man-kennel, if it so please you," remarked one observer, "for surely no benevolent lexicographer could so outrage humanity and the English language, as to justify our city fathers in terming this place an *Asylum*."[33] In addition to the defects in its physical plant, the Insane Asylum of Louisiana tended to receive predominantly chronic patients, leading its physician to remark in 1854 that from its inception the institution "has been more an alms house than an Insane Asylum." Plagued with a host of problems, the institution for the first twenty-five

31. *New Orleans Medical Journal*, I (May, 1844), 72–77 (July-September, 1844), 105–106; *AJI*, V (July, 1848), 73–74; Bond, *Dr. Kirkbride*, 100–101; Elizabeth Wisner, *Public Welfare Administration in Louisiana* (Chicago, 1930), 80–87; Francis R. Packard, *History of Medicine in the United States*, 2 vols. (New York, 1931), I, 261ff.

32. Dix to Kirkbride, March 6, 1848, in Bond, *Dr. Kirkbride*, 101; Insane Asylum of Louisiana, *BR*, II (1848/1849), 5–10, III (1850/1851), 8–12.

33. Stanford Chaillé, *A Memoir of the Insane Asylum of the State of Louisiana, at Jackson* (New Orleans, 1858), 11–12 (reprint of an article in the *New Orleans Medical and Surgical Journal*, XV [January, 1858], 103–124).

years of its existence remained a place of confinement distinctly below the caliber of public institutions in other parts of the country.[34] During the 1850's other Southern states, including Alabama, Mississippi, North Carolina, and Texas, also established mental hospitals. Within North Carolina the issue of psychiatric reform first arose in the 1820's as a byproduct of the agitation for a state penitentiary. Although successive governors supported the idea of a public hospital, the movement did not take cohesive form until the arrival of Dix in the state in 1848. In the legislative debate that preceded and followed her activities, the economy issue proved dominant. Many Democrats, believing in the theory of a negative state, balked at the prospect of an expenditure of $100,000 (at that time the annual revenue of the state—excluding the Literary Fund [which was intended for educational purposes] —was less than $200,000), while the Whigs were fearful that their political fortunes would be diminished if they pushed the bill through the legislature. In 1849 the law providing for the establishment of a mental hospital finally passed, though it was seven years before the institution was ready to receive patients. The delay in large measure was a result of the method adopted to finance the hospital; the legislature authorized a special land and poll tax, and the funds for the construction of the hospital could be spent only as the money was received.[35]

In Mississippi and Alabama the founding of public institutions was the result of the efforts of a coalition of physicians, a series

34. Insane Asylum of Louisiana, *AR*, 1854, 8, 1870, 4–6, 1875, 4–6; *Memorial of the Late Board of Administrators of the Insane Asylum at Jackson; Together with the Reply of the Present Board of Administrators, and the Report of the Special Committee to Whom was Referred the Memorial of the Late Administrators* (Baton Rouge, 1858); Wisner, *Public Welfare Administration in Louisiana*, 99–106.

35. Dix, *Memorial Soliciting a State Hospital for the Protection and Cure of the Insane, Submitted to the General Assembly of North Carolina. November, 1848* (Raleigh, 1848); Tiffany, *Life of Dorothea Lynde Dix*, 134–136; Margaret C. McCulloch, "Founding the North Carolina Asylum for the Insane," *North Carolina Historical Review*, XIII (July, 1936), 185–201; Clark R. Cahow, "The History of the North Carolina Mental Hospitals, 1848–1960" (unpubl. Ph.D. dissertation, Duke University, 1967), 23ff.

of governors, and the redoubtable Dix, who was able to lobby effectively among individuals possessing both influence and authority. In both states, however, the projects were sharply underfunded. The Mississippi legislature, for example, granted only $10,000 when it approved the establishment of a state mental hospital in 1848. The difficulties that followed were hardly unexpected, and succeeding legislatures had to increase sharply the original grant. Further complications arose when the state penitentiary failed to furnish the bricks required for construction. Not until 1855 was the hospital finally opened. A comparable situation developed in Alabama. There the groundwork had been laid first by Dix's visit. The cause was then taken up by the Medical Association of the State of Alabama, which undertook a census of the insane and then sent a detailed and impassioned memorial to the legislature in 1851. Citing the statistical results of its census as well as the words of virtually every prominent authority in mid-nineteenth-century psychiatry, the memorial called upon the legislature to fulfill its humanitarian and moral obligations. After a delay of over a year the legislature acted. At first some thought was given to the possibility of converting the old capitol at Tuscaloosa into a hospital. When this structure was destroyed by fire the legislature appropriated $100,000. The sum proved inadequate, and a supplemental grant met with both a gubernatorial veto and charges of mismanagement. The legislature ignored the governor's allegation and overrode his veto. Not until the summer of 1861, however, was the hospital ready for the reception of patients.[36]

Southern mental hospitals, then, lagged significantly behind

36. Mississippi State Lunatic Asylum, *AR*, 1870, 12–20; *An Appeal to the Legislature of Alabama, for the Establishment of a State Hospital for Lunatics and Idiots, Prepared by Order of the Alabama State Medical Association: Mobile, November, 1851* (Mobile, 1851); *New Orleans Medical and Surgical Journal*, VIII (January, 1852), 515–516 (March, 1852), 669–670; *American Journal of the Medical Sciences*, n.s. XXXIII (January, 1857), 164; *Report of the Trustees of the Alabama Insane Hospital, November 29, 1855* (n.p., n.d.), 1–5; Tiffany, *Life of Dorothea Lynde Dix*, 136–137; Katherine Vickery, "A History of Mental Health in Alabama 1803–1963" (ms. in possession of author), Chaps. I–II; James S. Tarwater, *The Alabama State Hospitals and the Parlow State School and Hospital: A Brief History* (New York, 1964), 8–9.

institutions in other sections. Lack of an adequate financial base of support, the weakness and isolation of the Southern medical profession, and an unwillingness to commit resources to the public sector all combined to inhibit severely the development of a comprehensive system of hospitals performing both therapeutic and custodial functions. The legacy of the antebellum South, moreover, proved enduring; the difficult problems faced by most of its hospitals persisted for decades.

VI

Since the founding of public mental hospitals had occurred on an incremental basis, little attention was paid to broader issues. Yet from the very inception of the drive to establish hospitals it was clear that a single institution within a given state could not possibly care for the total number of mentally ill persons. The surveys of incidence undertaken by promoters of hospitals, though superficial and often inaccurate, nevertheless regularly revealed that the number of cases far exceeded the total capacity of the proposed facility. So intent were reformers and physicians on securing legislative approval of a public facility, however, that they never considered the possibility that it might be inadequate even before it opened. Thus the need for multiple facilities never came up for debate or study when states were in the process of establishing their first hospitals.

The pressure on space was initially met in many states by expanding existing facilities. The 1830's and 1840's witnessed a steady rise in resident patient populations and the total admitted each year. By the late 1840's hospitals were being constructed with considerably larger physical plants than institutions founded before 1840. The Worcester hospital, to cite one example, was initially intended to care for 120 patients. In 1834 it admitted 130 patients and had an average daily population of 117. In 1846, as a result of two major additions to its physical plant, it admitted 293 individuals and had an average daily census of 359. This steady rise was by no means unique; it was paralleled at hospitals throughout the country. In 1840 eight institutions accepted 1,440 patients (an average of 180 each); a decade later twenty-two institutions admitted 7,227 persons (an average of 328.5 each).[37] Yet it was recognized that to keep increasing the size of mental hospitals was not a long-term solution to the problem. Consequently, a few states moved to establish additional public institutions within their borders. Once again the lead was taken by Massachusetts. By the 1840's the Worcester hospital was beginning to face all of the problems that have been endemic to mental institutions generally. Crowding, declining curability rates, an influx of lower-class and ethnic minority groups—to cite only a few examples—all combined to reduce sharply the effectiveness of that hospital as a therapeutic institution. By 1848 conditions at the institution had so deteriorated that the legislature established a committee to study the problems related to mental illness and to offer recommendations. Out of its work came a second state hospital at Taunton, which opened its doors in the spring of 1854.[38]

The opening of a second public institution, however, did little to improve conditions within the Bay State. The number of mentally ill persons seemed to increase faster than the general population. Moreover, the Worcester hospital, once a model institution, had deteriorated to the point where its trustees described it as "one of the poorest, if not the very poorest, in the country." The legislature's Committee on Public Charitable Institutions, when informed of substandard conditions at Worcester, decided that the problems growing out of mental illness were so complex that an impartial and exhaustive analysis was required that would provide the basis for a more intelligent and enlightened policy. The legislature concurred, and the result was the

37. Worcester State Lunatic Hospital, *AR*, XXIII (1855), 45; Illinois Board of State Commissioners of Public Charities, *BR*, I (1869/1870), Table II between 288 and 289.

38. See the *Report of the Joint Committee of the Legislature of Massachusetts, Appointed April 20, 1848, on the Subject of Insanity in the State, and Directed to Sit during the Recess of the Legislature, and to Report at the Early Part of the Session of 1849*, Massachusetts *Senate Document No. 9* (January 15, 1849). The growth of a system of public hospitals in Massachusetts is described and analyzed in Gerald N. Grob, *The State and the Mentally Ill: A History of Worcester State Hospital in Massachusetts, 1830–1920* (Chapel Hill, 1966), Chap. V.

famous *Report on Insanity and Idiocy in Massachusetts* by Edward Jarvis, probably the single most significant investigation of mental illness and public policy in mid-nineteenth-century America. One immediate result of Jarvis's study was the establishment of a third public hospital located in Northampton.[39]

The spread of public institutions in Massachusetts was but a portent of developments throughout the United States. Between 1850 and 1875 a number of states—including Ohio, Kentucky, New York, Pennsylvania, Virginia, Illinois, Iowa, Wisconsin, Missouri, and California—opened a second hospital and in some cases more. Although the process of founding institutions in the Bay State was far more systematic than elsewhere (nowhere else was a study comparable to the *Report on Insanity* by Jarvis undertaken), the differences were far outweighed by the similarities. Crowding, insufficient capacity, and a growing social acceptance of institutionalization made it impossible for a single hospital to meet the needs of most states. At the same time local welfare institutions were finding it increasingly difficult to provide adequate care for heterogeneous dependent groups, although many almshouses were conducted in an efficient and humane manner. Consequently, states moved to expand the number of institutions, locating them in different geographic areas adjacent to or in centers with high population densities. Each institution usually retained its autonomy; control was vested in the hands of a board of trustees. Although most institutions within a given state were similar in structure and function, separate governance often proved an impediment to the formulation of consistent and rational public policies. Mental hospitals also faced the same difficulties as welfare institutions, and the fact that their medical superintendents were neither knowledgeable nor equipped to deal with welfare and dependency simply compounded existing difficulties.

---

39. Massachusetts *Senate Document No. 60* (March 9, 1854), 1–8; *Report of the Committee on Public Charitable Institutions*, Massachusetts *Senate Document No. 83* (March, 1854); *Report on Insanity and Idiocy in Massachusetts, by the Commission on Lunacy, Under Resolve of the Legislature of 1854*, Massachusetts *House Document No. 144* (1855).

Appendix II

Average Annual Admissions to the American Mental Hospital, 1820-1870*

1820	31	1837	92	1854	157
1821	36	1838	100	1855	129
1822	40	1839	107	1856	130
1823	45	1840	89	1857	134
1824	42	1841	100	1858	141
1825	40	1842	87	1859	137
1826	35	1843	100	1860	142
1827	39	1844	100	1861	131
1828	42	1845	120	1862	131
1829	38	1846	119	1863	127
1830	38	1847	127	1864	140
1831	49	1848	141	1865	154
1832	48	1849	141	1866	151
1833	65	1850	140	1867	162
1834	69	1851	136	1868	172
1835	103	1852	139	1869	183
1836	92	1853	156	1870	182

* Average figures, of course, hide as much as they reveal. Newer hospitals pulled down the mean sharply, while hospitals with very small physical plants distorted the situation at other hospitals. In 1875, for example, the average annual admissions figure was 189 (as contrasted with 182 in 1870). Yet in 1875 the median was 320, and the mean for the upper half was 559.

Appendix III

Average Total Number of Patients Treated in the American Mental Hospital, 1820-1870

1820	57	1840	180	1860	369
1821	65	1841	192	1861	368
1822	68	1842	206	1862	378
1823	82	1843	191	1863	375
1824	78	1844	209	1864	399
1825	88	1845	248	1865	417
1826	81	1846	282	1866	416
1827	86	1847	301	1867	432
1828	75	1848	309	1868	449
1829	79	1849	335	1869	480
1830	77	1850	333	1870	473
1831	107	1851	323		
1832	93	1852	332		
1833	105	1853	354		
1834	126	1854	371		
1835	164	1855	313		
1836	168	1856	309		
1837	161	1857	337		
1838	189	1858	354		
1839	190	1859	351		

Appendix IV

Selected Statistics for American Mental Hospitals, 1820-1875, at Five-year Intervals[1]

Hospital and Date of Opening	Year											
	1820	1825	1830	1835	1840	1845	1850	1855	1860	1865	1870	1875
ALABAMA												
Alabama Insane Hospital (1861)												
Admissions										19	88	78
Total number of patients[2]											279	423
Average patient population[3]											211	356
Discharged as recovered[4]											11	33
Deaths											30	29
CALIFORNIA												
Insane Asylum of California (1851)												
Admissions								214	248	268	562	615
Total number of patients								348	615	849	1,482	1,839
Average patient population								162*	417*	632*	1,047*	1,302*
Discharged as recovered								168	123	93	221	259
Deaths								18	54	82	156	181
CONNECTICUT												
Connecticut General Hospital for the Insane (1868)												
Admissions											134	210
Total number of patients											343	605
Average patient population											225	426
Discharged as recovered											43	41
Deaths											21	36

Connecticut (Hartford) Retreat for the Insane (1824)

Admissions	44	51	72	84	105	135	169	168	155	123	78
Total number of patients					188	268	355	383	386	258	199
Average patient population	24*	20*	36	50	97	143	185	219	235	137	124
Discharged as recovered	10	28	6		45	64	73	70	57	41	31
Deaths	1	0		2	11	30	17	20	27	25	12

ILLINOIS

Illinois Southern Hospital for the Insane (1873)

Admissions	103
Total number of patients	236
Average patient population	149
Discharged as recovered	14
Deaths	7

Illinois State Hospital for the Insane (1851)[5]

Admissions	149	158	212	357	263
Total number of patients	315	552	513	757	737
Average patient population	214*	231*	318*	452*	290*
Discharged as recovered	59	77	67	105	55
Deaths	12	15	24	39	32

Northern Illinois Hospital for the Insane (1872)

Admissions	346
Total number of patients	560
Average patient population	314
Discharged as recovered	34
Deaths	26

Hospital and Date of Opening	Year											
	1820	1825	1830	1835	1840	1845	1850	1855	1860	1865	1870	1875
INDIANA												
Indiana Hospital for the Insane (1848)[5]												
Admissions							58	171	221	199	405	438
Total number of patients							134	331	524	473	792	920
Average patient population							80*	196*	288	277	479	556
Discharged as recovered							38	115	105	107	187	253
Deaths							1	20	19	18	51	47
IOWA												
Iowa Hospital for the Insane (1873)[5]												
Admissions												164
Total number of patients												221
Average patient population												251*
Discharged as recovered												28
Deaths												21
Iowa Hospital for the Insane at Mt. Pleasant (1861)[5]												
Admissions										133	260	261
Total number of patients										385*	441	506
Average patient population										284*	102	72
Discharged as recovered										25	56	52
Deaths										28		

Asylum for the Insane of the State of Kansas (1866)

Admissions	62	26
Total number of patients	93	136
Average patient population	41*	110
Discharged as recovered	38	18
Deaths	2	2

KENTUCKY

Central Kentucky Lunatic Asylum (1873)

Admissions	225
Total number of patients	453
Average patient population	337*
Discharged as recovered	48
Deaths	52

Kentucky Eastern Lunatic Asylum (1824)

Admissions	39	31	54	65	59	119	102	50	59	248	81
Total number of patients	72	125		201	213	342	294	278	300	678	617
Average patient population	54*	90*				203*	186*	232*	244	484	546
Discharged as recovered	17		21	5	22	41	36	23	26	70	49
Deaths	7	16		35	23	92	56	10	14	60	32

Kentucky Western Lunatic Asylum (1854)

Admissions	113	114	59	71	74
Total number of patients	113	318	182	372	398
Average patient population	81*	143*		325*	322*
Discharged as recovered	8	18		27	38
Deaths	17	19		14	30

Hospital and Date of Opening	Year											
	1820	1825	1830	1835	1840	1845	1850	1855	1860	1865	1870	1875
LOUISIANA												
Insane Asylum of Louisiana (1848)												
Admissions							37	88	81	84	42	39
Total number of patients							112	220	238	197	187	206
Average patient population							79*	162*	144*	172*	163*	162*
Discharged as recovered							15	23	48	7	9	12
Deaths							2	28	34	14	12	31
MAINE												
Maine Insane Hospital (1840)												
Admissions					129	99	110	128	136	142	130	188
Total number of patients					129	175	249	243	373	396	467	581
Average patient population					48	80	137	134	236	272	339	398
Discharged as recovered					36	39	66	41	63	47	48	68
Deaths					5	7	14	19	31	24	37	52
MARYLAND												
Maryland Hospital for the Insane (1798, 1834)												
Admissions				55	78	91	40	70	101	133	149	147
Total number of patients				73	145	178	173	189	208	253	263	295
Average patient population				40*	50*	107*	141*	121*	105*	122*	116*	171*
Discharged as recovered				5	30	40	14	26	51	86	123	24
Deaths				3	5	10	6	17	10	11	9	18

Mount Hope Institution (1840)												
Admissions						100	72	95	135	239	276	345
Total number of patients						146	218	242	346	597	471	613
Average patient population						57*	82*	122*	191*	228*	199*	304
Discharged as recovered						70	96	26	81	55	89	87
Deaths						2	8	14	18	19	24	22
MASSACHUSETTS												
Boston Lunatic Hospital (1839)												
Admissions					125	21	73	97	126	84	105	50
Total number of patients					125	136	276	353	265	251	317	248
Average patient population					96*	121*	204*	239*	167*	184*	227	207
Discharged as recovered					9	5	37	28	52	21	27	15
Deaths					6	7	25	38	29	26	42	20
McLean Asylum for the Insane (1818)[6]												
Admissions	102	59	82	83	155	119	173	123	121	82	79	85
Total number of patients	125	110	147	163	263	271	357	318	296	277	263	233
Average patient population	50*	54*	69*	77*	128	149	201	192	185	186	187	156
Discharged as recovered	22	21	34	45	75	74	78	56	39	35	33	16
Deaths	6	8	10	11	13	13	28	24	24	17	12	16
Northampton State Lunatic Hospital (1858)												
Admissions									167	134	202	153
Total number of patients									400	468	604	629
Average patient population									315*	342	409	475
Discharged as recovered									33	33	50	29
Deaths									27	41	33	41

Hospital and Date of Opening	Year											
	1820	1825	1830	1835	1840	1845	1850	1855	1860	1865	1870	1875
Taunton State Lunatic Hospital (1854)												
Admissions								167	245	197	375	477
Total number of patients								406	586	560	758	985
Average patient population								251	365	353	388	557
Discharged as recovered								70	101	89	112	114
Deaths								38	47	32	38	67
Massachusetts State Almshouse at Tewksbury (Insane Department) (1866)												
Admissions											163	92
Total number of patients											430	411
Average patient population											294*	286*
Discharged as recovered											0	0
Deaths											46	58
Worcester State Lunatic Hospital (1833)												
Admissions				113	162	293	241	199	215	221	384	362
Total number of patients				241	391	656	670	580	532	565	760	847
Average patient population				120	229	316	440	349	324	350	396	487
Discharged as recovered				52	82	122	125	109	129	105	158	90
Deaths				8	15	24	57	27	22	33	64	67
MICHIGAN												
Michigan Asylum for the Insane (1859)												
Admissions									141	67	144	268
Total number of patients									141	170	399	389
Average patient population									109*		110*	128*
Discharged as recovered									20		12	39
Deaths											21	

MINNESOTA

Minnesota Hospital for the Insane (1866)

Admissions	143	188
Total number of patients	304	569
Average patient population	206*	414
Discharged as recovered	49	66
Deaths	25	27

MISSISSIPPI

Mississippi State Lunatic Asylum (1855)

Admissions	70	28	31	86
Total number of patients	70	130	185	408
Average patient population	51*	107*	160*	324*
Discharged as recovered	7	4	18	30
Deaths	5	8	3	24

MISSOURI

Missouri State Lunatic Asylum No. 1 (1851)[5]

Admissions	25	53	73	89	144
Total number of patients	163	254	348	348	482
Average patient population	134*	191*	286*	303*	350*
Discharged as recovered	18	19	16	48	73
Deaths	3	39	19	36	35

Hospital and Date of Opening	Year											
	1820	1825	1830	1835	1840	1845	1850	1855	1860	1865	1870	1875
Missouri State Lunatic Asylum No. 2 (1875)[5]												
Admissions												169
Total number of patients												169
Average patient population												150*
Discharged as recovered												37
Deaths												14
St. Louis County Insane Asylum (1869)												
Admissions											294	110
Total number of patients												417
Average patient population												320*
Discharged as recovered												35
Deaths												23
St. Vincent's Institution for the Insane (1858)[5]												
Admissions										112		84	125
Total number of patients										180			
Average patient population										89*			
Discharged as recovered										27			
Deaths										5			

NEBRASKA

Nebraska Hospital for the Insane (1871)

Admissions	46
Total number of patients	92
Average patient population	61*
Discharged as recovered	20
Deaths	2

NEW HAMPSHIRE

New Hampshire Asylum for the Insane (1842)

Admissions	88	103	95	85	107	130	120
Total number of patients	158	217	246	267	324	367	401
Average patient population	76	121	155*	184*	223*	253*	261*
Discharged as recovered	37	45	50	38	42	37	53
Deaths	6	7	12	17	22	23	20

NEW JERSEY

Essex County Insane Asylum (1872)

Admissions	92
Total number of patients	203
Average patient population	150*
Discharged as recovered	22
Deaths	8

Hospital and Date of Opening	Year											
	1820	1825	1830	1835	1840	1845	1850	1855	1860	1865	1870	1875
New Jersey State Lunatic Asylum (1848)												
Admissions							110	139	174	196	247	218
Total number of patients							220	352	480	529	814	873
Average patient population							162*	233*	310*	367*	648*	704*
Discharged as recovered							32	67	73	72	68	60
Deaths							10	20	23	31	44	47
NEW YORK												
Brigham Hall (1855, incorporated 1859)												
Admissions									166		72	57
Total number of patients											135	124
Average patient population											70*	71*
Discharged as recovered											21	16
Deaths											6	5
Hudson River State Hospital (1871)												
Admissions												132
Total number of patients												353
Average patient population												186*
Discharged as recovered												47
Deaths												27

Kings County Lunatic Asylum (1839)

Admissions	160	180	263	314	318
Total number of patients	338	470	677	872	1,069
Average patient population	185*	308*	432*	602*	766*
Discharged as recovered		87	110	130	109
Deaths	40	26	75	58	81

New York City Asylum for the Insane, Ward's Island (1871)

Admissions	401
Total number of patients	1,074
Average patient population	593*
Discharged as recovered	106
Deaths	147

New York City Lunatic Asylum, Blackwell's Island (1839)

Admissions			391	371	525	780	412
Total number of patients		1,112	792	926	1,284	1,890	1,577
Average patient population	279*	367*	464*	573*	736*	1,252	1,233*
Discharged as recovered			77	100	127	212	127
Deaths						132	98

New York Hospital and Bloomingdale Asylum (1821)

Admissions	156	134	138	113	138	97	107	150	152	153	112
Total number of patients	270	217	241	269	242	200	234	302	323	314	287
Average patient population	119	89	136	130	119	110	127	159	176	166	182
Discharged as recovered	71	58	58	60	61	50	52	50	66	60	34
Deaths	3	7	13	14	12	18	19	29	28	27	23

Hospital and Date of Opening	Year											
	1820	1825	1830	1835	1840	1845	1850	1855	1860	1865	1870	1875
New York State Asylum for Insane Criminals (1859)												
Admissions									14	9	17	43
Total number of patients									65	80	96	138
Average patient population									55*		60*	115*
Discharged as recovered												
Deaths												
New York State Homeopathic Asylum for the Insane (1874)												
Admissions												99
Total number of patients												152
Average patient population												82*
Discharged as recovered												30
Deaths												11
Utica State Lunatic Asylum (1843)												
Admissions						293	367	275	337	356	481	432
Total number of patients						553	816	725	856	920	1,084	1,004
Average patient population						265	433	467	516	591	629	595
Discharged as recovered						135	171	128	105	113	153	132
Deaths						21	51	32	42	57	75	61

Willard Asylum for the Insane (1869)

Admissions	167	179
Total number of patients	309	1,084
Average patient population	226	938
Discharged as recovered	8	3
Deaths	14	49

NORTH CAROLINA

Insane Asylum of North Carolina (1856)

Admissions	41	76	29	42
Total number of patients		252	253	289
Average patient population	147*	179*	232	249
Discharged as recovered		22	6	16
Deaths		23	9	14

OHIO

[Central] Ohio Lunatic Asylum (1838)[7]

Admissions	188	101	150	193	174	208
Total number of patients	453	215	296	576	435	422
Average patient population	271	131	158	328	233	247
Discharged as recovered	77	53	44	99	110	101
Deaths	27	14	17	22	13	14

Hospital and Date of Opening	Year											
	1820	1825	1830	1835	1840	1845	1850	1855	1860	1865	1870	1875
Hamilton County Lunatic Asylum (1853–1859)												
Admissions								169				
Total number of patients								276				
Average patient population								161*				
Discharged as recovered								48				
Deaths								29				
Longview Asylum (1860)												
Admissions									422	163	273	195
Total number of patients									422	530	784	770
Average patient population									334	390	544*	590
Discharged as recovered									49	90	165	82
Deaths									14	30	62	44
Northern Ohio Lunatic Asylum (1855)												
Admissions								164	115	106	193	349
Total number of patients								164	253	240	509	640
Average patient population								112*	135*	138*	328	376
Discharged as recovered								42	54	56	103	86
Deaths								7	2	13	23	29

Southern Ohio Lunatic Asylum (1855)

Admissions	59	127	95	407	300
Total number of patients	59	283	257	753	826
Average patient population		157*	165	481	578
Discharged as recovered		64	53	160	138
Deaths		8	12	34	42

OREGON

Oregon Asylum for the Insane (186?)[5]

Admissions	
Total number of patients	
Average patient population	218*
Discharged as recovered	27
Deaths	17

PENNSYLVANIA

Friends' Asylum for the Insane (1817)

Admissions	20	31	18	45	54	48	27	42	25	25	33	44
Total number of patients	42	66	55	88	119	100	74	99	87	88	85	125
Average patient population	28*	37*	30	57*	59*	59	48*	59*	62	68	54	87
Discharged as recovered	4	8	10	7	25	25	14	17	10	7	14	14
Deaths	1	5	7	4	4	1	4	8	4	8	5	11

Hospital and Date of Opening	Year											
	1820	1825	1830	1835	1840	1845	1850	1855	1860	1865	1870	1875
Insane Department of the Philadelphia Almshouse (1859)												
Admissions										359	416	
Total number of patients										921	1,139	
Average patient population										574	755*	
Discharged as recovered										174	147	
Deaths										112	101	
Pennsylvania Hospital for the Insane (1841)												
Admissions						177	207	176	211	231	261	268
Total number of patients						328	428	399	465	510	574	684
Average patient population						162	219	233	273	298	344	430
Discharged as recovered						80	106	101	98	102	94	112
Deaths						20	27	21	26	38	35	43
Pennsylvania State Hospital for the Insane (1872)												
Admissions												125
Total number of patients												363
Average patient population												246
Discharged as recovered												28
Deaths												28

Admissions	164	144	153	168	178
Total number of patients	378	418	434	578	558
Average patient population	250*	291*	306*	434*	416*
Discharged as recovered	26	31	40	30	36
Deaths	29	8	35	39	35

Western Pennsylvania Hospital for the Insane (1853)[5]

Admissions	24	109	121	228	170
Total number of patients	26	209	279	562	682
Average patient population	5*	107	183	371	477
Discharged as recovered	17	46	34	60	64
Deaths	2	10	10	38	38

RHODE ISLAND

Butler Hospital for the Insane (1847)

Admissions	73	56	58	42	81	102
Total number of patients	180	187	193	174	235	229
Average patient population	113*	137*	127*	131*	95*	143*
Discharged as recovered	19	20	22	11	34	37
Deaths	16	11	15	16	12	14

Rhode Island State Asylum for the Incurable Insane (1870)

Admissions	59
Total number of patients	231
Average patient population	173*
Discharged as recovered	
Deaths	34

Hospital and Date of Opening	Year											
	1820	1825	1830	1835	1840	1845	1850	1855	1860	1865	1870	1875
SOUTH CAROLINA												
South Carolina Lunatic Asylum (1828)												
Admissions						23	54	62	69	34	90	136
Total number of patients						95	162	236	263	174	322	447
Average patient population						71*	120*	171*	192*	128*	245*	300*
Discharged as recovered						13	27	19	37	24	26	40
Deaths						6	15	31	26	19	31	52
TENNESSEE												
Tennessee Hospital for the Insane (1840)[5]												
Admissions						33	38	92	81	134	120	104
Total number of patients										338		
Average patient population							79*	192*	220*		352*	388*
Discharged as recovered							13	42	38		49	46
Deaths						7	13	12	18		29	25
TEXAS												
Texas State Lunatic Asylum (1861)												
Admissions										20	42	90
Total number of patients										61	122	271
Average patient population										47*	83*	152*
Discharged as recovered										12	25	33
Deaths										0	12	9

Vermont Asylum for the Insane (1836)[5]

Admissions	73	204	150	164	143	144	120	111
Total number of patients	142	362	468	553	574	602	631	
Average patient population	81*	263*	328*	394*	436*	480*	518*	489*
Discharged as recovered	33	59	79	79	58	55	35	28
Deaths	6	20	26	52	37	42	40	27

VIRGINIA

Virginia Central Lunatic Asylum (1869)

Admissions	80
Total number of patients	287
Average patient population	238
Discharged as recovered	30
Deaths	12

Virginia Eastern Lunatic Asylum (1773)[5]

Admissions	9	24				25	53	81	37	73	72
Total number of patients						157	234			273	366
Average patient population	43*	52*	58*	77*	101*	128*	193*	249*	284*	210*	302
Discharged as recovered											33
Deaths	4	9	4			12	22	36	26	7	19

Virginia Western Lunatic Asylum (1828)[5]

Admissions	7	22	92	132	77	42	67	59	68
Total number of patients	37	91	236	348	382	413	374	383	
Average patient population	41	70	163	246		376	319	335*	356*
Discharged as recovered	30	36						26	27
Deaths	0							13	13

Hospital and Date of Opening	Year											
	1820	1825	1830	1835	1840	1845	1850	1855	1860	1865	1870	1875
WEST VIRGINIA												
West Virginia Hospital for the Insane (1864)												
Admissions										36	42	52
Total number of patients										57	244	397
Average patient population										40*	205	350
Discharged as recovered										8	16	18
Deaths										3	14	21
WISCONSIN												
Northern Hospital for the Insane, Oshkosh, Wisconsin (1873)												
Admissions												101
Total number of patients												351
Average patient population												258
Discharged as recovered												2
Deaths												18
Wisconsin State Hospital for the Insane (1860)												
Admissions									89	87	168	160
Total number of patients									89	257	532	507
Average patient population									78*	177*	360*	364
Discharged as recovered									3	33	53	32
Deaths									3	13	32	20

DISTRICT OF COLUMBIA

Government Hospital for the Insane (1855)

Admissions	47	95	512	180	230
Total number of patients	107	262	866	549	912
Average patient population	93*	180*	281*	454*	718*
Discharged as recovered	5	48	112	41	78
Deaths	8	19	54	18	58

1 Statistics compiled from annual and biennial reports of American mental hospitals. In some cases these reports failed to provide all of the data; in other cases data were taken from the tables in Illinois Board of State Commissioners of Public Charities, *BR*, I (1869/1870), between 288 and 289.

2 This figure includes the total number of individual patients resident at any point in the hospital during the year.

3 Some hospitals did not list the average patient population. Instead they gave the number of patients resident at the time of the report. In the overwhelming majority of cases the two figures were nearly identical. An asterisk (*) at the end of a figure signifies that it represents the number of patients remaining in the hospital at the end of the report period; all other figures are for average populations.

4 This figure does not include patients who were discharged as improved or stationary.

5 Hospitals that reported biennially often did not break down the statistics by individual years. The figures listed in such cases represent the average for the two years.

6 The figures for 1820 for the McLean Asylum are from the time it opened in 1818 through 1820.

7 There are no figures for 1870 and 1875 for the Central Ohio Lunatic Asylum. During these years the hospital was being rebuilt after a fire destroyed it completely; its patients were sent elsewhere.

Bibliography

I. PRIMARY SOURCES

A. Manuscripts

American Freedmen's Inquiry Commission, Houghton Library, Harvard University, Cambridge, Mass.

John A. Andrew Papers, Massachusetts Historical Society, Boston, Mass.

Boston Insane Hospital Records, Countway Library of Medicine, Harvard Medical School, Boston, Mass.

Butler Hospital (letter collection) Library, Providence, R.I.

Butler Hospital Papers, John Carter Brown Library, Brown University, Providence, R.I.

George Chandler Papers, American Antiquarian Society, Worcester, Mass.

Dorothea L. Dix Papers, Houghton Library, Harvard University, Cambridge, Mass.

Pliny Earle Papers, American Antiquarian Society, Worcester, Mass.

Samuel Gridley Howe Papers, Houghton Library, Harvard University, Cambridge, Mass.

Institute of Living Collection, Library, Institute of Living, Hartford, Conn.

Edward Jarvis Ms. Autobiography, Houghton Library, Harvard University, Cambridge, Mass.

Edward Jarvis Papers, Concord Free Public Library, Concord, Mass.

Edward Jarvis Papers, Countway Library of Medicine, Harvard Medical School, Boston, Mass.

Thomas S. Kirkbride Papers, Institute of the Pennsylvania Hospital, Philadelphia, Pa.

Horace Mann Papers, Massachusetts Historical Society, Boston, Mass.

Original Papers Relating to Acts of the Massachusetts General Court, Massachusetts Archives, State House, Boston, Mass.

"Record Book of the Trustees, 1865–1868," Library of Osawatomie State Hospital, Osawatomie, Kans.

"Report of the Physicians of Massachusetts. Superintendents of Hospitals . . . and Others Describing the Insane & Idiotic persons in the State of Massachusetts in 1855. Made to the Commissioners in Lunacy," ms. volume in the Countway Library of Medicine, Harvard Medical School, Boston, Mass.

William F. Steuart, "History of the Maryland Hospital" (c. 1871), ms. bound in volume entitled *Report of the President and Board of Visitors of the Maryland Hospital*, in National Library of Medicine, Bethesda, Md.

Samuel B. Woodward, "Collected Writings," 3 vols., typescript, Library of Worcester State Hospital, Worcester, Mass.

Samuel B. Woodward Collection, Yale University, New Haven, Conn.

Samuel B. Woodward Papers, American Antiquarian Society, Worcester, Mass.

Worcester State Hospital Records, Worcester State Hospital, Worcester, Mass.

Jeffries Wyman Papers, Countway Library of Medicine, Harvard Medical School, Boston, Mass.

B. Published Hospital Records and State and Local Government Documents

Alabama

Alabama Insane Hospital, *AR*, I–II (1861–1862), VII (1867), IX–XV (1869–1875) (III–VI and VIII probably not published).

Dorothea L. Dix, *Memorial Soliciting a State Hospital for the Insane, Submitted to the Legislature of Alabama, November 15, 1849* (Montgomery: Advertiser and Gazette, 1849).

An Appeal to the Legislature of Alabama, for the Establishment of a State Hospital for Lunatics and Idiots, Prepared by Order of the

Alabama State Medical Association: Mobile, November, 1851 (Mobile: Dade, Thompson & Co., 1851).

Report of the Trustees of the Alabama Insane Hospital, November 29, 1855 (n.p.: n.p., n.d.).

California

Insane Asylum of California, *AR*, I–XIII (1853–1865), *BR*, 1865/1867–1873/1875.

Majority Report of Assembly Committee on State Hospitals in Relation to Assembly Bill No. 226 (n.p.: n.p., n.d. [c. 1863]).

Report of Senate Committee on Hospitals Relative to Senate Bill No. 309 (n.p.: n.p., n.d. [c. 1863]).

Report of the Joint Committee of Senate and Assembly to Investigate the Affairs of the Insane Asylum at Stockton (n.p.: O. M. Clayes, n.d. [c. 1865]).

Wilkins, E. T., *Insanity and Insane Asylums: Report of E. T. Wilkins, M.D., Commissioner in Lunacy for the State of California, Made to His Excellency H. H. Haight, Governor, December 2d, 1871* (Sacramento: T. A. Springer, n.d.).

Connecticut

Connecticut (Hartford) Retreat for the Insane, *AR*, I (1825), III (1827), VI–VII (1830–1831), X (1834), XVI–LI (1840–1875) (II not published; IV–V in VI; VIII–IX in X; and XI–XV not published).

Connecticut General Hospital for the Insane, *AR*, I–IX (1867–1875).

Report of a Committee of the Connecticut Medical Society, Respecting an Asylum for the Insane, With the Constitution of the Society for Their Relief. Accepted by the Medical Convention, October 3, 1821 (Hartford: Bowles and Francis, 1821).

Society for the Relief of the Insane. . . . Annual Meeting at Hartford, 2d Wednesday of May (Hartford: W. Hudson & L. Skinner, 1823).

Report of the Committee on the Insane Poor in Connecticut, to the General Assembly, May Session, 1838 (New Haven: Babcock & Galpin, 1838).

Report of the Committee Appointed in 1870, to Examine and Report De [sic] General Hospital for the Insane (Hartford: Case, Lockwood & Brainard Co., 1871).

Final Action on the Question of Government of the Retreat for the

Insane at Hartford, Conn. with Letters of Endorsement (Hartford: privately printed, 1873).

Letters on the Construction of the By-Laws of the Retreat for the Insane (Hartford: privately printed, 1873).

On the Revision of the By-Laws of the Retreat for the Insane with Letters on Hospital Organization and Government (Hartford: privately printed, 1873).

Reasons for Considering the Expediency of a Revision of the By-Laws of the Retreat for the Insane (Hartford: privately printed, 1873).

Service at the Dedication of the Elizabeth Chapel, at the Retreat for the Insane, Hartford, December 23, 1875 (Hartford: Case, Lockwood & Brainard Co., 1876).

Stearns, H. P., *Statistics of Insanity Relative to Re-Admissions to the Retreat* (Hartford: Case, Lockwood & Brainard Co., 1876).

Georgia

Georgia State Lunatic Asylum (Georgia Asylum for the Insane), *AR*, I (1842/1844), 1846/1847, 1858/1859, 1865/1866–1867/1868, 1873.

Reports of Jas. F. Bozeman, M.D., and Wm. Henry Cumming, M.D., on the State Lunatic Ayslum, Under Resolution of the General Assembly, Passed January, 1872 (Atlanta: W. A. Hemphill, 1872).

Illinois

Illinois State Hospital for the Insane, *BR*, I–VI (1847/1848–1857/1858), reprinted in *Reports of the Illinois State Hospital for the Insane 1847–1862* (Chicago: F. Fulton & Co., 1863), *BR*, VII–XV (1859/1860–1875/1876).

Northern Illinois Hospital for the Insane, *AR*, I (1870), *BR*, II–IV (1871/1872–1875/1876).

Illinois Southern Hospital for the Insane, *BR*, I–II (1873/1874–1875/1876).

Special Report of the Trustees of the Illinois State Hospital for the Insane, in Review of a Legislative Committee Appointed by the Twenty-Fifth General Assembly (Springfield: Baker, Bailhache & Co., 1868).

Report of the Investigating Committee on the Hospital for the Insane, Made to the Governor of Illinois, December 1, 1867, in Reports Made to the General Assembly of Illinois, at its Twenty-Sixth Session, Convened January 4, 1869 (Springfield: Illinois Journal Printing Office, 1869), vol. III.

Special Report of the Commissioners of Public Charities on the Financial Management and Condition of the State Institutions of Illinois (n.p.: n.p., 1874).

Indiana

Indiana Hospital for the Insane, *Annual Report of the Commissioners and Superintendent,* II–IV (1846–1848) (deals with construction of hospital).

Indiana Hospital for the Insane, *AR,* I–XXVII (1849–1875).

Iowa

Iowa Hospital for the Insane at Mt. Pleasant, *BR,* I–VIII (1860/1861–1874/1875).

Iowa Hospital for the Insane at Independence, *BR,* I–II (1872/1873–1874/1875).

Report of Commissioners for the Erection of Buildings for an Insane Asylum, at Independence, to the Governor of the State of Iowa. January, 1870 (Des Moines: F. M. Mills, 1870).

Kansas

Asylum for the Insane of the State of Kansas, *AR,* III–XI (1867–1875) (I–II probably not published; XI also contains the first annual report of the Commissioners of the State Insane Asylum at Topeka, which was established in 1875).

Kentucky

Kentucky Eastern Lunatic Asylum (in 1873 it became the First Kentucky Lunatic Asylum), *AR,* 1823–1837, XV–XXIX (1838–1851), *BR,* XXX/XXXI–XXXIV/XXXV (1852/1853–1858/1859), *AR,* XXXVI–LI (1860–1875) (*AR,* 1823–1838, in the *Kentucky Senate Journal,* 1823–1838).

Kentucky Western Lunatic Asylum, *BR,* 1854/1855–1858/1859, *AR,* 1861–1875.

Central Kentucky Lunatic Asylum (in 1873 it became the Fourth Kentucky Lunatic Asylum), *AR,* I–III (1873–1875).

Statement of the Board of Managers of the Western Lunatic Asylum, to the Governor of Kentucky, in Relation to the Burning of Said Institution, Accompanied by Estimate of Cost for Reconstruction, Kentucky *Legislative Document No. 6* (1861).

Louisiana

Insane Asylum of Louisiana, *BR*, II–III (1848/1849–1850/1851), *AR*, 1854–1860, 1865–1867, 1870–1875.

Memorial of the Late Board of Administrators of the Insane Asylum at Jackson; Together with the Reply of the Present Board of Administrators, and the Report of the Special Committee to Whom was Referred the Memorial of the Late Administrators (Baton Rouge: J. M. Taylor, 1858).

Minority Report of the Board of Administrators of the Insane Asylum at Jackson, of the State of Louisiana (Baton Rouge: J. M. Taylor, 1859).

Special Report of the Committee on Charitable Institutions, Relative to the Management of the Insane Asylum at Jackson, to the Legislature of the State of Louisiana (Baton Rouge: J. M. Taylor, 1859).

Maine

Maine Insane Hospital, *AR*, I–XXXV (1840–1875).

Maine *House Document No. 37* (August 28, 1850).

Report of the Commissioners of Investigation of the Insane Asylum, Made to the Governor and Council by Order of the Legislature. January, 1868 (Augusta: Stevens & Sayward, 1868).

Maryland

Maryland Hospital for the Insane, *AR*, 1843–1875.

Mount Hope Institution, *AR*, I–XXXIII (1843–1875) (first report issued under the name Mount Saint Vincent's Hospital).

Report on Pauper Insanity; Presented to the City Council of Baltimore, on March 28th, 1845: by Dr. Stephen Collins (Baltimore: James Lucas, 1845).

Dorothea L. Dix, *Memorial of Miss D. L. Dix to the Honorable The General Assembly in Behalf of the Insane of Maryland*, Maryland *Senate Document C* (February 25, 1852).

Report of the Trial of Dr. Wm. H. Stokes and Mary Blenkinsop, Physician and Sister Superior of Mount Hope Institution, before the Circuit Court for Baltimore Co., Md. Held at Towsontown, Tuesday, February 6, 1866. By Eugene L. Didier, Stenographic Reporter (Baltimore: Kelly and Piet, 1866).

Report on the Public Charities, Reformatories, Prisons and Almshouses, of the State of Maryland, by C. W. Chancellor, M.D., Secretary of the State Board of Health, Made to His Excellency, John

Lee Carroll, Governor. July, 1877 (Frederick: Baughman Brothers, 1877).

Massachusetts

McLean Asylum for the Insane, *AR*, 1823, 1828, XV–XVI (1832–1833), XVIII–LVIII (1835–1875), in Massachusetts General Hospital, *AR*, 1823, 1828, 1832–1833, 1835–1875.

Worcester State Lunatic Hospital, *AR*, I–XLIII (1833–1875).

Boston Lunatic Hospital, *AR*, I–XVI (1840–1855), 1857–1875, in Boston Board of Directors for Public Institutions, *AR*, I–XIX (1857–1875) (no report published for 1856).

Taunton State Lunatic Hospital, *AR*, I–XXII (1854–1875).

State Almshouse at Tewksbury, *AR*, I–XXII (1854–1875).

Northampton State Lunatic Hospital, *AR*, I–XX (1856–1875).

Rules and Regulations for the Government of the Asylum for the Insane, Adopted December 1, 1822, Additional to Those Adopted July 5, 1821 (Boston: Russell and Gardner, 1822).

Address of the Trustees of the Massachusetts General Hospital, to the Subscribers and to the Public (n.p.: n.p., n.d. [c. 1822]).

By-Laws of the Massachusetts General Hospital; With the Rules and Regulations Established by the Board of Trustees for the Government of the McLean Asylum for the Insane in Charlestown, and the Hospital in Boston (Boston: Daily Advertiser, 1830).

Testimony Given before the Committee of the City Government, in the Case of Charles Frost; Together with the Argument of C. M. Ellis, Esq., Touching the Management of the Lunatic Hospital; November 10, 1865 (Boston: Nation Press, 1866).

Howe, Samuel G., *Objections to the Proposed Plan for a City Hospital for Lunatics at Winthrop; With Answers to the Article of J. Putnam Bradlee, in the "Daily Advertiser," Nov. 6* (Boston: Wright & Potter, 1871).

(Massachusetts Government Publications)

The Colonial Laws of Massachusetts. Reprinted from the Edition of 1660, with the Supplements to 1672, Containing also, The Body of Liberties of 1641 (Boston: Rockwell & Churchill, 1889).

The Colonial Laws of Massachusetts, Reprinted from the Edition of 1671, with Supplements Through 1686 (Boston: Rockwell & Churchill, 1887).

The Acts and Resolves, Public and Private, of the Province of the Massachusetts Bay, 21 vols. (Boston: Wright & Potter Printing Co., 1869–1922).

Acts and Resolves, 1797–1875 (1797–1838 appeared in separate volumes; after that date they appeared in a single volume).

Report of Committee to Whom was Referred the Consideration of the Pauper Laws of the Commonwealth. Submitted to the Massachusetts Legislature, 1821 (Boston: n.p., 1821).

Massachusetts *House Report No. 50* (February 16, 1827).

Massachusetts *House Report No. 28* (1828).

Report of Commissioners Appointed Under a Resolve of the Legislature of Massachuetts, to Superintend the Erection of a Lunatic Hospital at Worcester . . . Made January 4th, 1832, Massachusetts *Senate Document No. 2* (January 4, 1832).

Report of the Commissioners Appointed by an Order of the House of Representatives, February 29, 1832, on the Subject of the Pauper System of the Commonwealth of Massachusetts, Massachusetts *House Document No. 6* (1833).

Reports and Other Documents Relating to the State Lunatic Hospital at Worcester, Mass. (Boston: Dutton and Wentworth, 1837).

Massachusetts *Senate Document No. 62* (March 14, 1838).

Massachusetts *House Document No. 39* (February 7, 1840).

Massachusetts *House Document No. 52* (March 12, 1845).

Massachusetts *House Document No. 139* (April 5, 1848).

Report of the Joint Committee of the Legislature of Massachusetts, Appointed April 20, 1848, on the Subject of Insanity in the State, and Directed to Sit During the Recess of the Legislature, and to Report at the Early Part of the Session of 1849, Massachusetts *Senate Document No. 9* (January 15, 1849).

Report on Insanity and Idiocy in Massachusetts, by the Commission on Lunacy, Under Resolve of the Legislature of 1854, Massachusetts *House Document No. 144* (1855) (reissued with a critical introduction by Gerald N. Grob under the title *Insanity and Idiocy in Massachusetts: Report of the Commission on Lunacy, 1855 by Edward Jarvis* [Cambridge: Harvard University Press, 1971]).

Commissioners of Alien Passengers and Foreign Paupers, *AR*, 1851–1863.

Report of the Special Joint Committee Appointed to Investigate the Whole System of the Public Charitable Institutions of the Commonwealth of Massachusetts, During the Recess of the Legislature in 1858, Massachusetts *Senate Document No. 2* (January, 1859).

Massachusetts *House Document No. 57* (February, 1862).

Massachusetts *House Document No. 269* (April 11, 1862).

Massachusetts *House Document No. 231* (April 8, 1863).

Massachusetts *Senate Document No. 10* (January, 1863).

Massachusetts *House Report No. 277* (April 20, 1863).

Massachusetts *Senate Document No. 72* (February 23, 1864).

Massachusetts *House Document No. 397* (May 13, 1869).

Massachusetts *House Document No. 496* (June, 1869).

(Boston City Publications)

Report of the Record Commissioners of the City of Boston, 39 vols. (Boston, 1876–1909). (Contains all of the records of colonial Boston.)

Report of the Board of Visitors of the Boston Lunatic Hospital, in the Matter of the Superintendent of that Institution. 1849, Boston City Document No. 10 (1849).

Report of Committee on the Subject of New Lunatic Hospital, Boston City Document No. 58 (1853).

Report of a Committee of the Board of Directors for Public Institutions in Relation to the Condition of the Lunatic Hospital, Made May 23, 1862 (Boston: J. E. Farwell and Co., 1862).

Report on the Lunatic Hospital. December, 1862, Boston City Document No. 90 (December 3, 1862).

Memorial of the Board of Directors for Public Institutions in Relation to the Lunatic Hospital. 1863, Boston City Document No. 11 (1863).

Report of the Committee on Institutions, on a Site for a New Lunatic Hospital. 1865, Boston City Document No. 97 (1865).

Plans, Descriptions and Estimates of the Boston Hospital for the Insane, at Winthrop. 1867, Boston City Document No. 94 (1867).

Report on Plans and Estimates for a New Hospital for the Insane. 1867, Boston City Document No. 105 (1867).

Modified Plans and Estimates of the Boston Hospital for the Insane, at Winthrop. 1868, Boston City Document No. 75 (1868).

Dissenting Opinion of Mr. Cobb, A Member of Board of Directors, for Public Institutions, Relative to a Site for a New Lunatic Hospital, Boston City Document No. 107 (1869).

Michigan

Michigan Asylum for the Insane, *BR*, 1857/1858–1865/1866, 1869/1870–1875/1876.

Minnesota

Minnesota Hospital for the Insane, *AR*, I–IX (1867–1875).

Mississippi

Mississippi State Lunatic Asylum, *AR*, I (1855), III–V (1857–1859), IX (1863), XI (1865), 1870–1875 (III, IX, XI are printed as appendices in the Mississippi *Senate Journal* for their respective years).

Report of the Commissioners of the Lunatic Asylum, to His Excellency Joseph W. Matthews, January 1, 1850 (Jackson: n.p., 1850).

Dorothea L. Dix, *Memorial Soliciting Adequate Appropriations for the Construction of a State Hospital for the Insane, in the State of Mississippi. February, 1850* (Jackson: Fall & Marshall, 1850).

Missouri

Missouri State Lunatic Hospital (Missouri State Lunatic Asylum No. 1), *BR*, I–XII (1851/1852–1875/1876) (no *BR* for 1861/1862 because of Civil War).

Missouri State Lunatic Asylum No. 2, *BR*, I (1875/1876).

St. Vincent's Institution for the Insane, *Report*, I–II (1859–1860), 1862/1863, 1864/1865, 1866/1868, 1869/1873, 1874/1875.

St. Louis County Insane Asylum, *AR*, I–VI (1869/1870–1874/1875) (VI included in the *Annual Report of the Public Institutions of St. Louis County . . . August 31, 1875*).

Annual Report of the Public Institutions of St. Louis County, for the Fiscal Year, Ending August 31, 1875 (St. Louis: R. & T. A. Ennis, 1875).

Nebraska

Nebraska Hospital for the Insane, *AR*, I–IV (1872–1875).

New Hampshire

New Hampshire Asylum for the Insane, *AR*, I–XXXIV (1840–1875).

Report Made to the Legislature of New Hampshire on the Subject of the Insane. June Session, 1836 (Concord: Cyrus Barton, 1836).

Report of the House Committee, in Relation to the Indigent Insane Persons Assisted By the State. June Session, 1849 (Concord: Butterfield and Hill, 1849).

New Jersey

New Jersey State Lunatic Asylum, *AR*, 1848–1875.

Essex County Lunatic Asylum, *AR*, 1875.

Report of the Commissioners Appointed by the Governor of New Jersey, to Ascertain the Number of Lunatics and Idiots in the State (Newark: M. S. Harrison & Co., 1840).

Dorothea L. Dix, *Memorial Soliciting a State Hospital for the Insane, Submitted to the Legislature of New Jersey: January 23, 1845,* 2nd ed. (Trenton: n.p., 1845).

By-Laws Adopted by the Managers of the New Jersey State Lunatic Asylum, at Trenton (Trenton: Brittain & Jones, 1848).

Report of the Joint Committee on Lunatic Asylums, in Regard to the Management of the Trenton Asylum. To the Legislature of New Jersey (Trenton: State Gazette Printing House, 1876).

New York

New York Hospital and Bloomingdale Asylum, *AR*, 1821–1875 (1821–1828 printed in the New York *Assembly Journal,* 1822–1829).

Utica State Lunatic Asylum, *AR*, I–XXXIII (1843–1875).

Kings County Lunatic Asylum, *AR*, 1855–1875 (1855–1857 in Superintendents of the Poor of the County of Kings, *AR*, 1855–1857).

New York City Lunatic Asylum, Blackwell's Island, *AR*, 1847–1875.

New York State Asylum for Insane Criminals, *AR*, I–XVII (1860–1876) (XIV–XV not published; other reports for the most part are included in Inspectors of State Prisons of the State of New York, *AR*).

Brigham Hall, *AR*, 1860, 1862, 1869–1875.

New York State Inebriate Asylum, *AR*, II–IV (1863–1865), 1867–1872, I–III (1873–1875).

Hudson River State Hospital for the Insane, *AR*, I–IX (1867–1875).

Willard Asylum for the Insane, *AR*, I–VII (1869–1875).

New York State Homeopathic Asylum for the Insane, *AR*, I–V (1871–1875).

Buffalo State Asylum for the Insane, *AR*, I–V (1871–1875).

New York City Asylum for the Insane, Ward's Island, *AR*, 1873–1875.

Rules and Regulations Adopted by the Managers of the New York State Lunatic Asylum, at Utica (Utica: R. W. Roberts, 1842).

Charter of the Society of the New-York Hospital, and the Laws Re-

lating Thereto . . . and Those of the Bloomingdale Asylum for the Insane (New York: Daniel Fanshaw, 1856).

Ceremonies, Etc. New York State Inebriate Asylum. Binghamton, New York (New York: Wynkoop, Hollenbeck, & Thomas, 1859).

Announcement of Brigham Hall, A Hospital for the Insane . . . January, 1860 (Canandaigua: N. J. Millken, 1860).

Laws and Regulations for the Admissions and Discharge of Patients. Utica, August, 1864 (Utica: Curtiss & White, 1864).

Wetmore, Edmund, *Statutory Law of New York Regarding the Insane* (Utica: Roberts, 1867).

The Buffalo State Asylum for the Insane. By-Laws and Acts Authorizing Location, Appointment of Commissioners, Organization, Etc. (Buffalo: Warren, Johnson & Co., 1871).

Proceedings in Connection with the Ceremony of Laying the Corner Stone of the Buffalo State Asylum for the Insane in the City of Buffalo. September 18th, 1872 (Buffalo: White & Brayley, 1872).

Rules and Regulations for the Government of Employees of the State Homoeopathic Asylum for the Insane, at Middletown, N.Y. (Middletown: Stivers & Slauson, 1874).

Report of the Superintending Builder of the Buffalo State Asylum for the Insane (Buffalo: White & Brayley, 1875).

Report of the Investigation of the Board of Supervisors of Kings County, in the Matter of Alleged Abuses at the Lunatic Asylum, Together with the Evidences Taken by the Committee, Presented April 19th, 1877 (New York: Charles M. Cromwell, 1877).

(New York State Government Publications)

Report by J. V. N. Yates on the subject of pauperism, New York State *Senate Journal*, 47th Sess., 1824, 95–108 and Appendix A.

New York *Assembly Document No. 263* (March 10, 1831).

Report of the Trustees of the State Lunatic Asylum, with the Documents Accompanying the Same, Pursuant to the Act of the Legislature Passed May 26th, 1841, New York *Senate Document No. 20* (January 12, 1842).

Dorothea L. Dix, *Memorial. To the Honorable the Legislature of the State of New-York*, New York *Assembly Document No. 21* (January 12, 1844).

Report and Memorial of the County Superintendents of the Poor of this State on Lunacy and its Relation to Pauperism, and for Relief of the Insane Poor, New York *Senate Document No. 17* (January 23, 1856).

Report of the Select Committee on Report and Memorial of County Superintendents of the Poor, on Lunacy and Its Relation to Pauperism, New York Senate Document No. 71 (March 5, 1856).

Report of Select Committee Appointed to Visit Charitable Institutions Supported by the State, and all City and County Poor and Work Houses and Jails, New York Senate Document No. 8 (January 9, 1857).

Willard, Sylvester D., *Report on the Condition of the Insane Poor in the County Poor Houses of New York,* New York Assembly Document No. 19 (January 13, 1865).

New York State Commissioner in Lunacy, *AR,* I–III (1873–1875).

(New York City Publications)
New York Board of Assistant Aldermen *Document No. 101* (March 10, 1834).

Report of the Commissioners of the Alms House, Bridewell and Penitentiary, New York Board of Aldermen *Document No. 32* (1837).

Report of the Superintendent of the Alms House, 1839/1840, New York Board of Aldermen *Document No. 9* (July 13, 1840).

Report of the Committee on Charity and Alms House, on the Communication of the Communication of the Commissioners of the Alms House, Relative to the Lunatic Asylum, New York Board of Aldermen *Document No. 30* (November 30, 1840).

Report of the Committee on Charity and Alms House on the Communication of the Commissioners of the Alms House, in Opposition to the Extension of the Lunatic Asylum on Blackwell's Island, New York Board of Aldermen *Document No. 87* (April 19, 1841).

Report of the Superintendent of the Almshouse, May 1840/May1841, New York Board of Aldermen *Document No. 15* (June 28, 1841).

Communication from the Commissioners of the Alms-House and Bridewell, New York Board of Aldermen *Document No. 28* (October 5, 1842).

Report of the Resident Physician of the Alms-House Establishment, New York Board of Aldermen *Document No. 119* (May 8, 1843).

Report of the Commissioners of the Alms House in Answer to Certain Resolutions of Enquiry, Adopted by the Board of Aldermen, New York Board of Aldermen *Document No. 23* (July 24, 1843).

New York Board of Aldermen *Document No. 11* (July 15, 1844).

New York Board of Aldermen *Document No. 40* (December 30, 1844).

New York Alms House Commissioner, *AR,* 1847, 1848.

New York Governors of the Almshouse, *AR*, I–XI (1849–1859).

New York Board of Governors of the Almshouse, *Minutes*, 1855–1857 (3 vols.).

New York Commissioners of Public Charities and Correction, *AR*, I–XII (1860–1871), XVI (1875) (XIII–XV not published).

North Carolina

Insane Asylum of North Carolina, *AR*, I–IX (1856/1857–1863/1864), X–XI (1865–1866), XIII/XX (1868–1875) (XII not published).

Dorothea L. Dix, *Memorial Soliciting a State Hospital for the Protection and Cure of the Insane, Submitted to the General Assembly of North Carolina. November, 1848* (Raleigh: Seaton Gales, 1848).

Report of Superintendent of Lunatic Asylum to the Board of Commissioners, November, 1854 (Raleigh: W. W. Holden, 1854).

Ohio

Ohio Lunatic Asylum (Central Ohio Lunatic Asylum), *Report of the Directors*, I (1835), III–IV (1837–1838), *AR*, I–XXXVII (1839–1875).

Commercial Hospital and Lunatic Asylum of Ohio, at Cincinnati, *AR*, 1845.

Hamilton County Lunatic Asylum, *AR*, I–II (1854–1855), VII (1859).

Northern Ohio Lunatic Asylum (Northern Ohio Hospital for the Insane), *AR*, I–XXI (1855–1875).

Southern Ohio Lunatic Asylum (Western Ohio Hospital for the Insane), *AR*, I–XXI (1855–1875).

Longview Asylum, *AR*, I–XVI (1860–1875).

An Act for the Government of the Ohio Lunatic Asylum, and the Care of Idiots and the Insane [March 19, 1850] (n.p.: n.p., n.d.).

Oregon

Oregon Hospital (Asylum) for the Insane, *BR*, I–VII (1863/1864–1875/1876).

Message of the Governor of Oregon, and Accompanying Documents. Delivered before the Legislative Assembly in Joint Convention, September 14, 1864 (Salem: Henry L. Pittock, 1864).

Pennsylvania

Friends' Asylum for the Insane, *AR*, I–LIX (1818–1876).

Pennsylvania Hospital for the Insane, *AR*, I–XXXV (1841–1875).

Western Pennsylvania Hospital, *AR*, 1848–1875.

Pennsylvania State Lunatic Hospital, *AR*, I–XXV (1851–1875).

Clifton Hall, *AR*, III–IV (1862–1863).

Insane Department of the Philadelphia Almshouse, *AR*, XIII–XV (1863–1865), 1868–1873.

New Brighton Retreat, *AR*, I (1864).

Pennsylvania State Hospital for the Insane at Danville, *AR*, 1873–1875.

Report of the Committee Appointed by the Board of Guardians of the Poor of the City and Districts of Philadelphia, to Visit the Cities of Baltimore, New–York, Providence, Boston and Salem (Philadelphia: Samuel Parker, 1827).

[Friends' Asylum] *Rules for the Management of the Asylum. Adopted by the Board of Managers, Ninth Month 8th, 1828* (Philadelphia: Solomon W. Conrad, 1828).

Report of a Committee Appointed by the Guardians for the Relief and Employment of the Poor of Philadelphia, &c. to Visit the Almshouses of Baltimore, New York, Boston and Salem, November, 1833 (Philadelphia: Wm. F. Geddes, 1834).

Report in Relation to an Asylum for the Insane Poor . . . March 11, 1839 (Harrisburg: Boas & Coplan, 1839).

A Second Appeal to the People of Pennsylvania on the Subject of an Asylum for the Insane Poor of the Commonwealth (Philadelphia: Brown, Bicking & Guilbert, 1840).

Dorothea L. Dix, *Memorial Soliciting a State Hospital for the Insane, Submitted to the Legislature of Pennsylvania, February 3, 1845* (Harrisburg: J. M. G. Lescure, 1845).

Code of Rules and Regulations for the Government of Those Employed in the Care of the Patients of the Pennsylvania Hospital for the Insane, Near Philadelphia, 2nd ed. (Philadelphia: T. K. and P. G. Collins, 1850).

By-Laws of the Penn'a State Lunatic Hospital, at Harrisburg; With the Acts of the Legislature Establishing the Same (Harrisburg: M'Kinley and Lescure, 1851).

Rules and Regulations of the Penn'a State Lunatic Hospital, Harrisburg, Pa.; Prepared by Order of the Board of Trustees (Harrisburg: M'Kinley and Lescure, 1851).

[Board of Managers of the Pennsylvania Hospital] *An Appeal to the Citizens of Pennsylvania for Means to Provide Additional Accom-*

modations for the Insane (Philadelphia: T. K. and P. G. Collins, 1854).

Smith, Edward A., *A Lecture Introductory to the Thirteenth Annual Course of Lectures and Evening Entertainments at the Pennsylvania Hospital for the Insane, at Philadelphia* (Philadelphia: Collins, 1857).

Proceedings on the Occasion of Opening the New Pennsylvania Hospital for the Insane, at Philadelphia (Philadelphia: Collins, 1859).

Acts of Assembly Relative to the Western Pennsylvania Hospital, and Regulating the Admission of Insane Patients Therein (Pittsburgh: W. S. Haven, 1863).

Commissioners for the Erection of the Hospital for the Insane for the Northern District of Pennsylvania, at Danville, *Report*, I–V (1868–1872).

Pennsylvania Board of Public Charities, *A Plea for the Insane in the Prisons and Poor-Houses of Pennsylvania* (Philadelphia: A. C. Bryson & Co., 1873).

Pennsylvania Board of Public Charities, *Addenda to A Plea for the Insane in the Prisons and Poor-Houses of Pennsylvania* (Philadelphia: A. C. Bryson & Co., 1873).

Statement of the Trustees of the Penna State Lunatic Hospital, in Regard to Certain Charges of the Board of Public Charities of the State of Pennsylvania, with an Appendix (Harrisburg: George Bergner, 1874).

Committee on Lunacy of Board of Public Charities, *AR*, II (1884), in Pennsylvania Board of Commissioners of Public Charities, *AR*, XV (1884).

[Committee of the Medical Society of the State of Pennsylvania] *Memorial* ["to the State Legislature in Reference to the Proper Care and Treatment of Insane Criminals"] (n.p.: n.p., n.d.).

Rhode Island

Butler Hospital for the Insane, *AR*, 1847–1875.

Charter of the Butler Hospital for the Insane; Proceedings Under the Same, Reports of Trustees, &C., &C. (Providence: John F. Moore, 1847).

Circular of the Trustees of the Butler Hospital for the Insane, in Providence, R.I. (n.p.: n.p., 1847).

Hazard, Thomas R., *Report on the Poor and Insane in Rhode Island;*

Made to the General Assembly at its January Session, 1851 (Providence: Joseph Knowles, 1851).

South Carolina

South Carolina Lunatic Asylum, *AR*, 1841–1842, 1844–1875.

Acts Concerning the Lunatic Asylum of South Carolina; and By-Laws for its Government, Revised and Passed by the Board of Regents . . . 1850 (Columbia: A. S. Johnston, 1851).

Trezevant, Daniel H., *Letters to His Excellency Governor Manning on the Lunatic Asylum* (Columbia: R. W. Gibbes & Co., 1854).

Tennessee

Tennessee Hospital for the Insane (Lunatic Asylum of Tennessee), *AR* and *BR*, 1840–1843, 1844/1845–1850/1851, I–V (1852/1853–1860/1861), 1862/1865, 1866, 1865/1867, 1867/1869, 1869/1870, VIII (1869/1871), 1871/1872, 1873/1874, XI (1875/1876).

Remarks and Facts in Relation to Insanity and the Insane Asylum. Directed to the Members of the General Assembly of the State of Tennessee (Nashville?: n.p., 1841?).

Jones, W. P., *The Necessities of the Insane in Tennessee* (n.p.: n.p., n.d. [c. 1875]).

Texas

Lunatic Asylum of the State of Texas (Texas State Lunatic Asylum), *Semi-Annual Report*, I (1857), *AR*, 1866, 1869–1875, *Semi-Annual Report*, I (August, 1866/March, 1867), August, 1867/September, 1868.

Vermont

Vermont Asylum for the Insane, *AR*, I–XXXIV (1837–1870), *BR*, 1871/1872–1875/1876.

Rules for the Government of the Attendants and Employees of the Vermont Asylum for the Insane (Brattleboro: F. D. Cobleigh, 1873).

Review of the Report of the Commissioners of the Insane, By the Officers of the Vermont Asylum for the Insane. 1876 (Brattleboro: O. Leonard, 1876).

Virginia

Virginia Eastern Lunatic Asylum, *AR*, 1845–1851, *BR*, 1852/1853–1856/1857, *AR*, 1868, 1870–1875.

Virginia Western Lunatic Asylum, *AR*, IX–XIII (1836–1840), XV (1842), XIX–XXVI (1846–1853), *BR*, 1854/1855–1871/1872 and 1872/1873, *AR*, 1861/1862, 1869/1870, 1871/1872–1874/1875.

Virginia Central Lunatic Asylum, *AR*, I–V (1870–1874/1875).

Hening, William W., ed., *The Statutes at Large: Being a Collection of All the Laws of Virginia from the First Session of the Legislature in the Year 1619*, 13 vols. (Richmond: various publishers, 1809–1823).

Report of the Board of Directors of the Western Lunatic Asylum, 1852–3 (n.p.: n.p., 1853).

Washington

Asylum for the Insane of Washington Territory, *AR*, 1871, *BR*, October 1, 1871/September 30, 1873.

Report of the Committee of Ways and Means, of the Legislative Council of the Territory of Washington Recommending an Appropriation of Five Thousand Five Hundred and Forty-One Dollars and Eighty Cents, to Compensate the Sisters of Charity for Keeping the Insane and Idiotic of the Territory (Olympia: Charles Prosch, 1867).

West Virginia

West Virginia Hospital for the Insane, *AR*, I–XI (1864–1874), *BR*, XII (1875/1876).

Wisconsin

Wisconsin State Hospital for the Insane, *AR*, I–XVI (1860–1875).

Northern Hospital for the Insane, Oshkosh, Wisconsin, *AR*, I–III (1873–1875).

Majority and Minority Reports of the Joint Committee of the Two Houses, to Investigate the Matters of the Lunatic Asylum, with the Evidence Taken Before Them (Madison: Beriah Brown, 1855).

Wisconsin State Lunatic Asylum, *Annual Report of the Commissioners*, I (1854), I–II (1857–1858) (construction).

Reports of the Trustees and Building Commissioners of the Wisconsin State Hospital for the Insane. December, 1859 (Madison: James Ross, 1859).

An Act to Provide for the Government of the Wisconsin State Hospital for the Insane, Approved March 30, 1860 (Madison: Atwood, Rubles & Reed, 1860).

The Acts to Provide for the Government of the Wisconsin State Hospital for the Insane (Madison: Atwood & Rubles, 1866).

Remarks of Hon. S. D. Hastings, Chairman of the Committee Appointed to Investigate the Affairs of the State Hospital for the Insane, before the Board of Trustees at Madison, June 4th, 1868 (n.p.: n.p., n.d.).

Report of the Committee on Behalf of the Northern Hospital for the Insane, Located at Oshkosh, Wisconsin, to Investigate Methods of Heating Similar Institutions in Other States (n.p.: n.p., n.d.).

District of Columbia

Government Hospital for the Insane, *AR*, I–XX (1856–1874/1875).

Government Hospital for the Insane, *Report of the Superintendent,* 1855.

By-Laws of the Government Hospital for the Insane, Etc. September, 1855 (Washington, D.C.: G. S. Gideon, 1855).

Report and Correspondence Relating to the Release from the Government Hospital for the Insane of Certain Persons Admitted Thereto Upon the Order of the Authorities of the District of Columbia (Washington, D.C.: Government Printing Office, 1875).

C. Reports of State Charity Boards

Connecticut State Board of Charities, *AR*, I–III (1881–1883).

Illinois Board of State Commissioners of Public Charities, *BR*, I–IV (1869/1870–1875/1876).

Massachusetts Board of State Charities, *AR*, I–XII (1864–1875).

Michigan Board of State Commissioners for the General Supervision of Charitable, Penal, Pauper, and Reformatory Institutions, *BR*, I–III (1871/1872–1875/1876).

New York Board of State Commissioners of Public Charities, *AR*, I–VI (1867–1872); New York State Board of Charities, *AR*, VII–X (1873–1876).

North Carolina Board of Public Charities, *AR*, I–IV (1869–1872).

Ohio Board of State Charities, *AR*, I–V (1867–1871), I (1876).

Pennsylvania Board of Commissioners of Public Charities, *AR*, I–VI (1870–1875).

Rhode Island Board of State Charities and Corrections, *AR*, I–VII (1869–1875).

Wisconsin State Board of Charities and Reform, *AR*, I–V (1871–1875).

D. Federal Documents

Compendium of the Enumeration of the Inhabitants and Statistics of the United States, as Obtained at the Department of State, from the Returns of the Sixth Census (Washington, D.C.: Thomas Allen, 1841).

Memorial of the American Statistical Association, Praying the Adoption of Measures for the Correction of Errors in the Returns of the Sixth Census, 28th Cong., 2d Sess., *Senate Document No. 5* (December 11, 1844).

Errors in the Sixth Census: Letter from the Secretary of State Relative to Alleged Errors of the Sixth Census, 28th Cong., 2d Sess., *House Document No. 116* (February 12, 1845).

28th Cong., 2d Sess., *Senate Document No. 146* (February 27, 1845).

Congressional Globe, 1848–1854.

Memorial of D. L. Dix, Praying a Grant of Land for the Relief and Support of the Indigent, Curable and Incurable Insane in the United States June 27, 1848, 30th Cong., 1st Sess., *Senate Miscellaneous Document No. 150.*

Memorial of D. L. Dix, Praying an Appropriation of Land for the Relief of the Insane, June 25, 1850, 31st Cong., 1st Sess., *Senate Miscellaneous Document No. 118.*

31st Cong., 1st Sess., *House Report No. 487* (August 8, 1850).

33d Cong., 1st Sess., *Senate Report No. 57* (January 23, 1854).

33d Cong., 1st Sess., *House Report No. 125* (March 29, 1854).

E. Journals and Proceedings

American Journal of Insanity, I–XXXVI (1844–1880).

American Journal of the Medical Sciences, I–XXVI (1828–1840), n.s. I–LXXX (1841–1880).

American Medical Association, *Transactions,* I–XXXI (1848–1880).

American Medical and Philosophical Register: or, Annals of Medicine, Natural History, Agriculture, and the Arts, I–IV (1811–1814).

American Medical Recorder, I–XIII (1818–1828).

American Phrenological Journal, I–XLIX (1838–1869).

Boston Medical and Surgical Journal, I–CIII (1828–1880).

Boston Prison Discipline Society, *AR,* I–XXIX (1826–1854). (The edition used was the 3-volume collection published in Boston by T. R. Marvin in 1855.)

Conference of Charities and Correction, *Proceedings*, I–VI (1874–1880).

Journal of Prison Discipline and Philanthropy, I–XVI (1845–1861), n.s. I–XV (1862–1876).

Journal of Social Science, I–XI (1869–1880).

The Lancet, 1875–1876.

Medical Communications of the Massachusetts Medical Society, VII (1842–1848).

Medical Repository, I–VI (1798–1803), n.s. I–VI (1804–1809), 3rd ser. I–III (1810–1812), n.s. VI–VIII (1821–1824).

New England Journal of Medicine and Surgery, I–XIV (1812–1825).

New Orleans Medical and Surgical Journal, I–XXIII (1844–1870) (not published May, 1861–July, 1866), n.s. I–IV (1873–1877).

New York Journal of Medicine and the Collateral Sciences, I–X (1843–1848), n.s. I–XVI (1848–1856).

New York Medical Journal, I–XXII (1865–1875).

Reprint of the Proceedings of the Connecticut Medical Society from 1792 to 1829 Inclusive (Hartford: Lockwood & Brainard Co., 1884).

F. Books and Pamphlets

Abdy, E. S., *Journal of a Residence and Tour in the United States of North America, from April, 1833, to October, 1834*, 3 vols. (London: John Murray, 1835).

Account of the Rise and Progress of The Asylum, Proposed to be Established, near Philadelphia, for the Relief of Persons Deprived of the Use of Their Reason, With an Abridged Account of the Retreat, A Similar Institution near York, in England (Philadelphia: Kimber and Conrad, 1814).

Allen, Nathan, *The Treatment of the Insane* (Albany: Joel Munsell, 1876).

Bard, Samuel, *A Discourse Upon the Duties of a Physician, with Some Sentiments, on the Usefulness and Necessity of a Public Hospital* (New York: A. & J. Robertson, 1769).

Beck, Theodric Romeyn, *An Inaugural Dissertation on Insanity* (New York: J. Seymour, 1811).

Bowditch, Nathaniel I., *A History of the Massachusetts General Hospital*, 2d ed. (Boston: privately printed, 1872).

Bremer, Fredrika, *The Homes of the New World: Impressions of America*, 2 vols. (New York: Harper & Brothers, 1854).

A Brief Account of the New-York Hospital (New York: Isaac Collins and Son, 1804).

Brigham, Amariah, *Remarks on the Influence of Mental Cultivation and Mental Excitement Upon Health*, 2d ed. (Boston: March, Capen and Lyon, 1833; 1st ed. 1832).

Bucknill, John C., *Notes on Asylums for the Insane in America* (London: J. & A. Churchill, 1876).

Calhoun, John C., *The Works of John C. Calhoun*, ed. by Richard K. Crallé, 6 vols. (New York: D. Appleton & Co., 1870–1876).

Chaillé, Stanford, *A Memoir of the Insane Asylum of the State of Louisiana, at Jackson* (New Orleans: Delta Book and Job Printing Office, 1858; reprinted from the January, 1858, issue of the *New Orleans Medical and Surgical Journal*).

Chambers, Julius, *A Mad World and Its Inhabitants* (New York: D. Appleton and Co., 1877).

Combe, George, *Notes on the United States of North America during a Phrenological Visit in 1838–9–40*, 2 vols. (Philadelphia: Carey & Hart, 1841).

Conolly, John, *The Treatment of the Insane Without Mechanical Restraints* (London: Smith, Elder & Co., 1856).

Correspondence with Officers Connected with the Retreat for the Insane, at Hartford . . . and Comments . . . in Withholding the Fact of the Removal from the Friends of the Patient. . . . By a Patron of the Retreat (Middletown, Conn.: C. H. Pelton, 1862).

Curwen, John, *History of the Association of Medical Superintendents of American Institutions for the Insane, from 1844 to 1874, Inclusive* (Harrisburg: Theo. T. Scheffer, 1875).

Davis, Phebe B., *Two Years and Three Months in the Lunatic Asylum, at Utica; Together with the Outlines of Twenty Years' Peregrinations in Syracuse* (Syracuse: published by the author, 1855).

Dewey, Richard, *Recollections of Richard Dewey: Pioneer in American Psychiatry* (Chicago: University of Chicago Press, 1936).

Dickens, Charles, *American Notes and Pictures from Italy* (London: Oxford University Press, 1957; *American Notes* first published in 1842).

Dix, Dorothea L., *Remarks on Prisons and Prison Discipline in the United States* (Boston: Munroe and Francis, 1845).

Earle, Pliny, *The Curability of Insanity: A Series of Studies* (Philadelphia: J. B. Lippincott, 1887).

————, *History, Description, and Statistics of the Bloomingdale Asylum for the Insane* (New York: Egbert, Hovey & King, 1848).

————, *Institutions for the Insane, in Prussia, Austria and Germany* (New York: Samuel S. & William Wood, 1854).

————, *Memoirs of Pliny Earle, M.D.*, ed. by F. B. Sanborn (Boston: Damrell & Upham, 1898).

Eddy, Thomas, *Hints for Introducing an Improved Mode of Treating the Insane in the Asylum; Read before the Governors of the New-York Hospital, on the 4th of Fourth-month, 1815* (New York: Samuel Wood & Sons, 1815).

Extracts from Newspapers and Periodicals in Relation to the Condition of the Insane in New Hampshire, Previous to the Erection of the N. H. Asylum for the Insane (Concord: Asylum Press, 1890).

Franklin, Benjamin, *Some Account of the Pennsylvania Hospital; From Its First Rise, to the Beginning of the Fifth Month, called May, 1754* (Philadelphia: B. Franklin and D. Hall, 1754).

————, *The Writings of Benjamin Franklin*, ed. by Albert H. Smyth, 10 vols. (New York: The Macmillan Co., 1910).

Fuller, Robert, *An Account of the Imprisonment and Sufferings of Robert Fuller, of Cambridge* (Boston: printed for the author, 1833).

Galt, John M., *Essays on Asylums for Persons of Unsound Mind* (Richmond: H. K. Ellyson's Power Press, 1850).

————, *Essays on Asylums for Persons of Unsound Mind. Second Series* (Richmond: Ritchies & Dunnavant, 1853).

————, *The Treament of Insanity* (New York: Harper & Brothers, 1846).

Grimes, G., *The Lily of the West. On Human Nature, Education, The Mind, Insanity. . . .* (Nashville: n.p., 1846).

————, *A Treatise on the Most Important Subject of the World: Simply to Say, Insanity. . . .* (Nashville: n.p., 1846).

Gundry, Richard, *Report on Insanity* (Columbus: Follett, Foster, & Co., 1860).

Hamilton, Frank H., *Eulogy on the Life and Character of Theodric Romeyn Beck, M.D., LL.D., Delivered before the Medical Society of the State of New York* (Albany: Charles van Benthuysen, 1856).

Holmes, Oliver Wendell, *Medical Essays 1842–1882* (Boston: Houghton Mifflin & Co., 1891).

Howe, Samuel Gridley, *An Essay on Separate and Congregate Systems of Prison Discipline; Being a Report Made to the Boston Prison Discipline Society* (Boston: William D. Ticknor & Co., 1846).

————, *Letters and Journals of Samuel Gridley Howe*, ed. by Laura E. Richardson, 2 vols. (Boston: Dana Estes & Co., 1906–1909).

[Hunt, E. K.] *Biographical Sketch of Amariah Brigham, M.D.* (Utica: W. O. McClure, 1858).

Hunt, Isaac H., *Astounding Disclosures! Three Years in a Madhouse by a Victim. . . .* , 2d ed. (n.p.: printed for the author, 1852).

Hunter, Richard, and Macalpine, Ida, eds., *Three Hundred Years of Psychiatry 1535–1860: A History Presented in Selected English Texts* (London: Oxford University Press, 1963).

Jarvis, Edward, *Address Delivered at the Laying of the Corner Stone of the Insane Hospital, at Northampton, Massachusetts* (Northampton: J. & L. Metcalf, 1856).

————, *Lecture on the Necessity of the Study of Physiology, Delivered before the American Institute of Instruction, at Hartford, August 22, 1845* (Boston: William D. Ticknor & Co., 1845).

————, *On the Causes of Insanity* (n.p.: n.p., 1851).

————, *Relation of Education to Insanity* (Washington, D.C.: Government Printing Office, 1872).

Kennard, Caroline A., *Miss Dorothea L. Dix and Her Life-Work* (n.p.: n.p., n.d. [c. 1887]).

Kirkbride, Thomas S., *Autobiographical Sketch Dictated by Thomas S. Kirkbride, M.D., in 1882* (n.p.: n.p., n.d.).

————, *Memoir of Isaac Ray, M.D., LL.D. Read before the College of Physicians of Philadelphia, July 6, 1881* (Philadelphia: n.p., 1881).

————, *On the Construction, Organization, and General Arrangements of Hospitals for the Insane* (Philadelphia: Lindsay & Blakiston, 1854; 2d ed., Philadelphia: J. B. Lippincott & Co., 1880).

Knapp, Samuel L., *The Life of Thomas Eddy* (New York: Conner & Cooke, 1834).

Lawrence, Amos, *Extracts from the Diary and Correspondence of the Late Amos Lawrence; With a Brief Account of Some Incidents in His Life* (Boston: Gould and Lincoln, 1855).

[Lunt, Adeline T. P.] *Behind the Bars* (Boston: Lee and Shepard, 1871).

Mann, Mary, *Life of Horace Mann By His Wife* (Boston: Lee and Shepard, 1888).

Manning, Fredc. Norton, *Report on Lunatic Asylums* (Sydney, Australia: Thomas Richards, 1868).

Millingen, J. G., *Aphorisms on the Treatment and Management of the Insane* (Philadelphia: Ed. Barrington & George D. Haswell, 1842; first published in England).

Mills, Charles K., ed., *Philadelphia Hospital Reports*. Vol. I (1890) (Philadelphia: Detre & Blackburn, 1890).

National Association for the Protection of the Insane and the Prevention of Insanity (Boston: Tolman & White, 1880).

Nott, J. C., and Gliddon, George R., *Types of Mankind* (Philadelphia: Lippincott, Grambo & Co., 1854).

Packard, E. P. W., *Great Disclosures of Spiritual Wickedness!! In High Places. With an Appeal to the Government to Protect the Inalienable Rights of Married Women*, 4th ed. (Boston: published by the author, 1865; 1st ed. 1864).

———, *Modern Persecution, or Insane Asylums Unveiled, as Demonstrated by the Report of the Investigating Committee of the Legislature of Illinois*, 2 vols. (Hartford: Case, Lockwood & Brainard Co., 1873).

———, *Mrs. Packard's Reproof to Dr. McFarland, for His Abuse of His Patients . . . Nov. 12th, 1860* (Chicago: Times Steam Job Printing House, 1864).

Parkman, George, *Management of Lunatics, with Illustrations of Insanity* (Boston: John Eliot, 1817).

———, *Proposals for Establishing a Retreat for the Insane, to be Conducted by George Parkman, M.D.* (Boston: John Eliot, 1814).

Pinel, Philippe, *A Treatise on Insanity*, transl. by D. D. Davis (Sheffield, England: W. Todd, 1806).

Prichard, James C., *A Treatise on Insanity and Other Disorders Affecting the Mind* (London: Sherwood, Gilbert, and Piper, 1835).

Quincy, Josiah, *Remarks on Some of the Provisions of the Laws of Massachusetts Affecting Poverty, Vice, and Crime* (Cambridge: Hilliard & Metcalf, 1822).

Ray, Isaac, *Address Delivered by Isaac Ray, M.D., of Philadelphia, on the Occasion of Laying the Corner Stone of the State Hospital for the Insane, at Danville, Pa. August 26, 1869* (Harrisburg: Theodore F. Scheffer, 1869).

———, *Contributions to Mental Pathology* (Boston: Little Brown & Co., 1873).

———, *Mental Hygiene* (Boston: Ticknor and Fields, 1863).

————, *A Treatise on the Medical Jurisprudence of Insanity* (Boston: Charles C. Little and James Brown, 1838).

Remarks by Elizabeth T. Stone, Upon the Statements Made by H. B. Skinner . . . June 1843 (n.p.: printed for the author, 1843).

Report of a Committee of the Connecticut Medical Society, Respecting an Asylum for Inebriates, with the Resolutions of the Society, Adopted at their Annual Meeting, May, 1830 (New Haven: Hezekiah Howe, 1830).

Robbins, Thomas, *An Address Delivered at the Retreat for the Insane, in Hartford, at the Dedication of that Institution . . . April 1, 1824* (Hartford: Goodwin and Co., 1824).

Rush, Benjamin, *Letters of Benjamin Rush,* ed. by Lyman H. Butterfield, 2 vols. (Princeton: Princeton University Press, 1951).

————, *Medical Inquiries and Observations Upon the Diseases of the Mind* (Philadelphia: Kimber & Richardson, 1812).

Scattergood, Thomas, *Journal of the Life and Religious Labors of Thomas Scattergood, A Minister of the Gospel, in the Society of Friends* (Philadelphia: n.p., n.d.).

————, *Memoirs of Thomas Scattergood, Late of Philadelphia, A Minister of the Gospel of Christ,* compiled by William and Thomas Evans (London: Charles Gilpin, 1845).

Stone, Elizabeth T., *A Sketch of the Life of Elizabeth T. Stone, and of her Persecutions, With an Appendix of her Treatment and Sufferings While in the Charlestown McLean Asylum, Where She was Confined Under the Pretence of Insanity* (n.p.: printed by the author, 1842).

Swett, John A., *Eulogy on James Macdonald, M.D.* (New York: D. Fanshaw, 1849).

Tiffany, Francis, *Life of Dorothea Lynde Dix* (Boston: Houghton Mifflin & Co., 1890).

Tuke, Daniel Hack, *Chapters in the History of the Insane in the British Isles* (London: Kegan Paul, Trench & Co., 1882).

————, *The Insane in the United States and Canada* (London: H. K. Lewis, 1885).

Tuke, Samuel, *Description of the Retreat, an Institution Near York for Insane Persons of the Society of Friends* (York, England: W. Alexander, 1813).

————, *A Letter on Pauper Lunatic Asylums* (New York: Samuel Wood & Sons, 1815).

Turner, Jonathan E., *The History of the First Inebriate Asylum in the World: By Its Founder: An Account of His Indictment* (New York: published by the author, 1888).

Van Voorhis, John S., *Management of the Insane: A Paper Read before the Fayette County Medical Society . . . 1870* (Pittsburgh: Bakewell & Marthens, 1870).

Wines, Frederick H., *Punishment and Reformation: A Study of the Penitentiary System*, new ed. (New York: Thomas Y. Crowell Co., 1919).

Wood, Robert W., *Memorial of Edward Jarvis, M.D.* (Boston: T. R. Marvin & Son, 1885).

Woodward, Samuel B., *Hints for the Young in Relation to the Health of Body and Mind* (Boston: George W. Light, 1840).

Wyman, Morrill, Jr., *A Brief Record of the Lives and Writings of Dr. Rufus Wyman* [1778–1842] *and His Son Dr. Morrill Wyman* [1812–1903] (Cambridge: privately printed, 1913).

G. Articles*

Bell, Luther V., "On the Practical Methods of Ventilating Buildings," *Medical Communications of the Massachusetts Medical Society,* VII (1842–1848), 297–400.

"Blackwell's Island Lunatic Asylum," *Harper's*, XXXII (February, 1866), 273–294.

Brigham, Amariah, "Insanity and Insane Hospitals," *North American Review*, XLIV (January, 1837), 91–121.

"Dr. Burrows and Others on Insanity," *Monthly Review*, reprinted in *Museum of Foreign Literature and Science*, XIV (April, 1829), 359–367.

Earle, Pliny, "Historical Sketch of the Institutions for the Insane in the United States of America," in New York Academy of Medicine, *Transactions*, I, part I, 9–30 [published 1851].

——, "Insanity and Hospitals for the Insane," in *National Almanac and Annual Record for the Year 1863* (Philadelphia: George W. Childs, 1863), 54–60.

Eaton, Dorman B., "Despotism in Lunatic Asylums," *North American Review*, CXXXII (March, 1881), 263–275.

Hammond, William A., "The Treatment of the Insane," *International Review*, VIII (March, 1880), 225–241.

* I have in general not listed individual articles from the journals cited in Section E above, for the list would be too long.

Hayden, C. B., "On the Distribution of Insanity in the U. States," *Southern Literary Messenger*, X (March, 1844), 179–181.

Henry, John, "The Memoirs of John Henry," ed. by C. H. Rammelkamp, *Journal of the Illinois State Historical Society*, XVIII (April, 1925), 39–75.

Howe, Samuel Gridley, "The Insane and their Treatment Past and Present," *National Quarterly Review*, VII (September, 1863), 207–232.

————, "Insanity in Massachusetts," *North American Review*, LVI (January, 1843), 171–191.

Jarvis, Edward, "Insanity and Asylums for the Insane," *Western Journal of Medicine and Surgery*, IV (December, 1841), 443–482 (also issued in pamphlet form under the title *Insanity and Insane Asylums* [Louisville: Prentice and Weissinger, 1841]).

————, "Law of Physical Life," *Christian Examiner*, XXXV (September, 1843), 1–31.

————, "The Production of Vital Force," *Medical Communications of the Massachusetts Medical Society*, 2nd ser., IV (1854), 1–40.

————, Review article on the *Report of the Sanitary Commission of Massachusetts, Made by the Legislature in 1850* [Shattuck Report], *American Journal of the Medical Sciences*, XXI (April, 1851), 391–409.

————, "Tendency of Misdirected Education and the Unbalanced Mind to Produce Insanity," *American Journal of Education*, IV (March, 1858), 591–612.

————, "What Shall We Do with the Insane of the Western Country?," *Western Journal of Medicine and Surgery*, V (February, 1842), 81–125 (issued as a pamphlet under the same title).

————, Thornton, J. Wingate, and Brigham, William, "The Sixth Census of the United States," *Hunt's Merchants' Magzine*, XII (February, 1845), 131–139.

"Edward Jarvis, M.D.," in American Antiquarian Society, *Proceedings*, n.s. III (October, 1883–April, 1885), 484–487.

Jones, Robert E., ed., "Correspondence of the A.P.A. Founders," *American Journal of Psychiatry*, CXIX (June, 1963), 1121–1134.

"Lunatic Hospital at Worcester," *Christian Examiner*, XXVI (May, 1839), 247–259.

"A Modern Lettre de Cachet," *Atlantic Monthly*, XXI (May, 1868), 588–602.

"'A Modern Lettre de Cachet' Reviewed," *Atlantic Monthly,* XXII (August, 1868), 227–243.

"Notes on the Nature of Insanity," *United States Magazine, and Democratic Review,* n.s. XXVII (November, 1850), 447–451.

Peabody, Andrew P., "Memoir of Edward Jarvis, M.D.," *New England Historical and Genealogical Register,* XXXIX (July, 1885), 217–224.

Ray, Isaac, "American Hospitals for the Insane," *North American Review,* LXXIX (July, 1854), 66–90.

———, "Statistics of Insanity in Massachusetts," *North American Review,* LXXXII (January, 1856), 78–100.

———, "What Shall Philadelphia Do for Its Paupers?", *Penn Monthly,* IV (April, 1873), 226–238.

"Reflections on the Census of 1840," *Southern Literary Messenger,* IX (June, 1843), 340–352.

Sanborn, Franklin B., "Work Accomplished by the State Boards," in National Conference of Charities and Correction, *Proceedings,* XIV (1887), 75–105.

Seguin, E. C., "Lunacy Reform.—Historical Considerations," *Archives of Medicine,* II (October, 1879), 184–198.

———, "Lunacy Reform. II. Insufficiency of the Medical Staff of Asylums," *Archives of Medicine,* II (December, 1879), 310–318.

"Statistics of Population. Table of Lunacy in the United States," *Hunt's Merchants' Magazine,* VIII (March, 1843), 290.

"Table of Lunacy in the United States," *Hunt's Merchants' Magazine,* VIII (May, 1843), 460–461.

Theobold, Samuel, "Some Account of the Lunatic Asylum of Kentucky, with Remarks, &c.," *Transylvania Journal of Medicine and the Associate Sciences,* II (November, 1829), 500–511, III (February, 1830), 79–94.

R. C. W. [Waterston, Robert C.], "The Insane of Massachusetts," *Christian Examiner,* XXXIII (January, 1843), 338–352.

Wyman, Rufus, "A Discourse on Mental Philosophy as Connected with Mental Disease, Delivered before the Massachusetts Medical Society, in June, 1830," *Medical Communicaitons of the Massachusetts Medical Society,* V, part I (1830), 1–24.

II. SECONDARY SOURCES*

A. Unpublished Manuscripts

"A Brief History of the Care of the Insane in Essex County, New Jersey" (anonymous typescript copy in Essex County Overbrook Hospital, Cedar Grove, N.J.).

Blackmon, Dora M. E., "The Care of the Mentally Ill in America, 1604–1812 in the Thirteen Original Colonies" (unpubl. Ph.D. dissertation, University of Washington, 1964).

Burke, William W., "The Supervision of the Care of the Mentally Diseased by the Illinois State Board of Charities (1869–1909)" (unpubl. Ph.D. dissertation, University of Chicago, 1934).

Cahow, Clark R., "The History of the North Carolina Mental Hospitals 1848–1960" (unpubl. Ph.D. dissertation, Duke University, 1967).

Cooley, Clara, "The Western State Hospital: Fort Steilacoom, Washington (History 1871–1950)" (unpubl. ms., Western State Hospital Library, Fort Steilacoom Branch, Tacoma, Wash., 1964).

King, Malvena G. S., "The South Carolina State Hospital and It's Treatment of Mental Disease" (unpubl. M.A. thesis, University of South Carolina, 1930).

Klebaner, Benjamin J., "Public Poor Relief in America 1790–1860" (unpubl. Ph.D. dissertation, Columbia University, 1952).

Klein, Stanley B., "A Study of Social Legislation Affecting Prisons and Institutions for the Mentally Ill in New York State, 1822–1846" (unpubl. Ph.D. dissertation, New York University, 1956).

Vickery, Katherine, "A History of Mental Health in Alabama 1803–1963" (unpubl. ms. in possession of author).

B. Books

Ackerknecht, Erwin H., *Medicine at the Paris Hospital 1794–1848* (Baltimore: The Johns Hopkins Press, 1967).

——, *A Short History of Psychiatry* (New York: Hafner Publishing Co., 1959).

* My listing of secondary sources is a selective one; I have not attempted to include all relevant secondary sources. For a more complete listing see Gerald N. Grob, *American Social History before 1860* (New York: Appleton-Century-Crofts, 1970).

Benton, Josiah H., *Warning Out in New England* (Boston: W. B. Clarke Co., 1911).

Billington, Ray A., *The Protestant Crusade 1800–1860: A Study of the Origins of American Nativism* (New York: The Macmillan Co., 1938).

Blanton, Wyndham B., *Medicine in Virginia during the Eighteenth Century* (Richmond: Garrett & Massie, 1931).

———, *Medicine in Virginia in the Nineteenth Century* (Richmond: Garrett & Massie, 1933).

———, *Medicine in Virginia in the Seventeenth Century* (Richmond: William Byrd Press, 1930).

Bond, Earl D., *Dr. Kirkbride and His Mental Hospital* (Philadelphia: J. B. Lippincott Co., 1947).

Bremner, Robert H., *American Philanthropy* (Chicago: University of Chicago Press, 1960).

———, *From the Depths: The Discovery of Poverty in the United States* (New York: New York University Press, 1956).

Bridenbaugh, Carl, *Cities in Revolt: Urban Life in America, 1743–1776* (New York: Alfred A. Knopf, 1955).

———, *Cities in the Wilderness: The First Century of Urban Life in America 1625–1742* (New York: The Ronald Press, 1938).

Briggs, John E., *History of Social Legislation in Iowa* (Iowa City: n.p., 1915).

Brown, Roy M., *Public Poor Relief in North Carolina* (Chapel Hill: University of North Carolina Press, 1928).

Browning, Grace A., *The Development of Poor Relief Legislation in Kansas* (Chicago: University of Chicago Press, 1935).

Bruce, Isabel C., Eickhoff, Edith, and Breckinridge, Sophonisba P., *The Michigan Poor Law: Its Development and Administration with Special Reference to State Provision for Medical Care of the Indigent* (Chicago: University of Chicago Press, 1936).

Burrage, Walter L., *A History of the Massachusetts Medical Society . . . 1781–1922* (n.p.: privately printed, 1923).

Callow, Alexander B., Jr., *The Tweed Ring* (New York: Oxford University Press, 1965).

Capen, Edward W., *The Historical Development of the Poor Law of Connecticut* (New York: n.p., 1905).

Coll, Blanche D., *Perspectives in Public Welfare: A History* (Washington, D.C.: Government Printing Office, 1969).

Cowen, David, *Medicine and Health in New Jersey: A History* (Princeton: D. Van Nostrand Co., Inc., 1964).

Creech, Margaret, *Three Centuries of Poor Law Administration: A Study of Legislation in Rhode Island* (Chicago: University of Chicago Press, 1936).

Croskey, John W., comp., *History of Blockley: A History of the Philadelphia General Hospital from Its Inception, 1731–1928* (Philadelphia: F. A. Davis, 1929).

Cummings, John, *Poor-Laws of Massachusetts and New York* (New York: Macmillan & Co., 1895).

D'Agostino, Lorenzo, *The History of Public Welfare in Vermont* (Washington, D.C.: Catholic University of America Press, 1948).

Dain, Norman, *Concepts of Insanity in the United States, 1789–1865* (New Brunswick: Rutgers University Press, 1964).

———, *Disordered Minds: The First Century of Eastern State Hospital in Williamsburg, Virginia 1766–1866* (Williamsburg: Colonial Williamsburg Foundation, 1971).

Davies, John D., *Phrenology: Fad and Science: A 19th-Century American Crusade* (New Haven: Yale University Press, 1955).

Deutsch, Albert, *The Mentally Ill in America: A History of Their Care and Treatment from Colonial Times* (Garden City, New York: Doubleday, Doran & Co., 1937).

Duffy, John, *Epidemics in Colonial America* (Baton Rouge: Louisiana State University Press, 1953).

———, *A History of Public Health in New York City 1625–1866* (New York: Russell Sage Foundation, 1968).

Eaton, Leonard K., *New England Hospitals 1790–1833* (Ann Arbor: University of Michigan Press, 1957).

Ernst, Robert, *Immigrant Life in New York City 1825–1863* (New York: Columbia University Press, 1949).

Foucault, Michel, *Madness and Civilization: A History of Insanity in the Age of Reason* (New York: Pantheon Books, 1965).

Frederickson, George M., *The Inner Civil War: Northern Intellectuals and the Crisis of the Union* (New York: Harper & Row, 1965).

Friends' Asylum for the Insane 1813–1913: A Description Account from Its Foundation, List of Managers and Officers from the Beginning, Facts and Events in Its History with Appendix (Philadelphia: John C. Winston, n.d.).

Frothingham, Octavius B., *Boston Unitarianism 1820–1850: A Study of the Life and Work of Nathaniel Langdon Frothingham* (New York: G. P. Putnam's Sons, 1890).

Gay, Peter, *The Enlightenment: An Interpretation*, 2 vols. (New York: Alfred A. Knopf, 1966–1969).

Gish, Lowell, *The First Hundred Years: A History of Osawatomie State Hospital, Osawatomie, Kansas* (Topeka: Vocational Printing Classes, 1966).

Goffman, Erving, *Asylums: Essays on the Social Situation of Mental Patients and other Inmates* (Garden City, New York: Doubleday & Co., 1961).

Goldhamer, Herbert, and Marshall, Andrew W., *Psychosis and Civilization: Two Studies in the Frequency of Mental Disease* (Glencoe, Illinois: The Free Press, 1953).

Greenblatt, Milton, York, Richard H., Brown, Esther L., and Hyde, Robert W., *From Custodial to Therapeutic Patient Care in Mental Hospitals* (New York: Russell Sage Foundation, 1955).

Griffin, Clifford S., *Their Brothers' Keepers: Moral Stewardship in the United States, 1800–1865* (New Brunswick: Rutgers University Press, 1960).

Grob, Gerald N., *The State and the Mentally Ill: A History of Worcester State Hospital in Massachusetts, 1830–1920* (Chapel Hill: University of North Carolina Press, 1966).

Hall, J. K., et al., eds., *One Hundred Years of American Psychiatry* (New York: Columbia University Press, 1944).

Haller, John S., Jr., *Outcasts from Evolution: Scientific Attitudes of Racial Inferiority, 1859–1900* (Urbana: University of Illinois Press, 1971).

Handlin, Oscar, *Boston's Immigrants: A Study in Acculturation*, rev. ed. (Cambridge: Harvard University Press, 1959).

Handlin, Oscar and Mary F., *Commonwealth: A Study of the Role of Government in the American Economy: Massachusetts, 1774–1861*, rev. ed. (Cambridge: Harvard University Press, 1969).

Hartz, Louis, *Economic Policy and Democratic Thought: Pennsylvania, 1776–1860* (Cambridge: Harvard University Press, 1948).

Hathway, Marion, and Rademaker, John A., *Public Relief in Washington 1853–1933* (Olympia: n.p., 1934).

Heath, Milton S., *Constructive Liberalism: The Role of the State in Economic Development in Georgia to 1860* (Cambridge: Harvard University Press, 1954).

Heffner, William C., *History of Poor Relief Legislation in Pennsylvania 1682–1913* (Cleona, Pa.: Holzapfel Publishing Co., 1913).

Hollingshead, August B., and Redlich, Fredrick C., *Social Class and Mental Illness: A Community Study* (New York: John Wiley & Sons, Inc., 1958).

Howe, Mark A. DeWolfe, *The Humane Society of the Commonwealth of Massachusetts: An Historical Review 1785–1916* (Boston: printed for The Humane Society by the Riverside Press, 1918).

Hurd, Henry M., ed., *The Institutional Care of the Insane in the United States and Canada*, 4 vols. (Baltimore: The Johns Hopkins Press, 1916–1917).

Jaffary, Stuart K., *The Mentally Ill and Public Provision for Their Care in Illinois* (Chicago: University of Chicago Press, 1942).

James, Sydney V., *A People among Peoples: Quaker Benevolence in Eighteenth-Century America* (Cambridge: Harvard University Press, 1963).

Jenkins, William S., and Hamrick, Lillian A., *A Guide to the Microfilm Collection of Early State Records* (Washington, D.C.: Library of Congress, 1950).

Jernegan, Marcus W., *Laboring and Dependent Classes in Colonial America 1607–1783* (Chicago: University of Chicago Press, 1931).

Johnson, Allen, et al., eds., *Dictionary of American Biography*, 22 vols. (New York: Charles Scribner's Sons, 1928–1958).

Jordan, W. K., *Philanthropy in England 1480–1660: A Study of the Changing Pattern of English Social Aspirations* (London: George Allen & Unwin Ltd., 1959).

Keller, Charles R., *The Second Great Awakening in Connecticut* (New Haven: Yale University Press, 1942).

Kelso, Robert W., *The History of Public Poor Relief in Massachusetts 1620–1920* (Boston: Houghton Mifflin Co., 1922).

Kennedy, Aileen E., *The Ohio Poor Law and Its Administration* (Chicago: University of Chicago Press, 1934).

Kett, Joseph F., *The Formation of the American Medical Profession: The Role of Institutions, 1780–1860* (New Haven: Yale University Press, 1968).

Knights, Peter R., *The Plain People of Boston, 1830–1860: A Study in City Growth* (New York: Oxford University Press, 1971).

Kraditor, Aileen S., *Means and Ends in American Abolitionism: Garrison and His Critics on Strategy and Tactics, 1834–1850* (New York: Pantheon Books, 1969).

Langstaff, John B., *Doctor Bard of Hyde Park: The Famous Physician of Revolutionary Times, the Man Who Saved Washington's Life* (New York: E. P. Dutton & Co., 1942).

Lawrence, Charles, comp., *History of the Philadelphia Almshouses and Hospitals from the Beginning of the Eighteenth to the Ending of the Nineteenth Centuries* (n.p.: Charles Lawrence, 1905).

Leiby, James, *Charity and Correction in New Jersey: A History of State Welfare Institutions* (New Brunswick: Rutgers University Press, 1967).

Leonard, E. M., *The Early History of English Poor Relief* (Cambridge, England: Cambridge University Press, 1900).

Lewis, W. David, *From Newgate to Dannemora: The Rise of the Penitentiary in New York, 1796–1848* (Ithaca: Cornell University Press, 1965).

Little, Nina F., *Early Years of the McLean Hospital* (Boston: Francis A. Countway Library of Medicine, 1972).

Litwack, Leon, *North of Slavery: The Negro in the Free States, 1790–1860* (Chicago: University of Chicago Press, 1961).

Lubove, Roy, *The Professional Altruist: The Emergence of Social Work as a Career 1880–1930* (Cambridge: Harvard University Press, 1965).

McCloy, Shelby T., *Government Assistance in Eighteenth-Century France* (Durham: Duke University Press, 1946).

McKelvey, Blake, *American Prisons: A Study in American Social History Prior to 1915* (Chicago: University of Chicago Press, 1936).

Mandelbaum, Seymour J., *Boss Tweed's New York* (New York: John Wiley & Sons, Inc., 1965).

Marshall, Helen E., *Dorothea Dix: Forgotten Samaritan* (Chapel Hill: University of North Carolina Press, 1937).

Matas, Rudolph, *The Rudolph Matas History of Medicine in Louisiana*, ed. by John Duffy, 2 vols. (Baton Rouge: Louisiana State University Press, 1958).

Mencher, Samuel, *Poor Law to Poverty Program: Economic Security Policy in Britain and the United States* (Pittsburgh: University of Pittsburgh Press, 1967).

Morton, Thomas G., *The History of the Pennsylvania Hospital 1751–1895* (Philadelphia: Times Printing House, 1895).

Odegard, Bernett O., and Keith, George M., *A History of the State Board of Control of Wisconsin and the State Institutions 1849–1939* (Madison: State Board of Control, n.d.).

Owen, David, *English Philanthropy 1660–1960* (Cambridge: Harvard University Press, 1964).

Packard, Francis R., *History of Medicine in the United States*, 2 vols. (New York: Paul B. Hoeber, Inc., 1931).

———, *Some Account of the Pennsylvania Hospital from Its First Rise to the Beginning of the Year 1938* (Philadelphia: Engle Press, 1938).

Pickett, Robert S., *House of Refuge: Origins of Juvenile Reform in New York State, 1815–1857* (Syracuse: Syracuse University Press, 1969).

Primm, James N., *Economic Policy in the Development of a Western State: Missouri, 1820–1860* (Cambridge: Harvard University Press, 1954).

Quincy, Edmund, *Life of Josiah Quincy of Massachusetts* (Boston: Ticknor and Fields, 1868).

Riese, Walther, *The Legacy of Philippe Pinel: An Inquiry into Thought on Mental Alienation* (New York: Springer Publishing Co., 1969).

Rosen, George, *Madness in Society: Chapters in the Historical Sociology of Mental Illness* (Chicago: University of Chicago Press, 1968).

Rosenberg, Charles E., *The Cholera Years: The United States in 1832, 1849, and 1866* (Chicago: University of Chicago Press, 1962).

Rosenkrantz, Barbara G., *Public Health and the State: Changing Views in Massachusetts, 1842–1936* (Cambridge: Harvard University Press, 1972).

Rothman, David J., *The Discovery of the Asylum: Social Order and Disorder in the New Republic* (Boston: Little, Brown and Co., 1971).

Russell, William L., *The New York Hospital: A History of the Psychiatric Service 1771–1936* (New York: Columbia University Press, 1945).

Sanborn, Franklin B., *Dr. S. G. Howe: The Philanthropist* (New York: Funk & Wagnalls, 1891).

———, "The Public Charities of Massachusetts during the Century Ending Jan. 1, 1876," in Massachusetts State Board of Charities, Supplement to *AR*, XII (1875).

Schneider, David M., *The History of Public Welfare in New York State 1609–1866* (Chicago: University of Chicago Press, 1938).

———, and Deutsch, Albert, *The History of Public Welfare in New York State 1867–1940* (Chicago: University of Chicago Press, 1941).

Schwartz, Harold, *Samuel Gridley Howe: Social Reformer 1801–1876* (Cambridge: Harvard University Press, 1956).

Shafer, Henry B., *The American Medical Profession, 1783–1850* (New York: Columbia University Press, 1936).

Shaffer, Alice, Keefer, Mary W., and Breckinridge, Sophonisba P., *The Indiana Poor Law: Its Development and Administration with Special Reference to the Provision of State Care for the Sick Poor* (Chicago: University of Chicago Press, 1936).

Shryock, Richard H., *The Development of Modern Medicine: An Interpretation of the Social and Scientific Factors Involved*, rev. ed. (New York: Alfred A. Knopf, 1947).

———, *Medicine and Society in America 1660–1860* (New York: New York University Press, 1960).

Stanton, William, *The Leopard's Spots: Scientific Attitudes toward Race in America 1815–59* (Chicago: University of Chicago Press, 1960).

Tarwater, James S., *The Alabama State Hospitals and the Partlow State School and Hospital: A Brief History* (New York: Newcomen Society in North America, 1964).

Tolles, Frederick B., *Meeting House and Counting House: The Quaker Merchants of Colonial Philadelphia 1682–1763* (Chapel Hill: University of North Carolina Press, 1948).

U.S. Bureau of the Census, *Historical Statistics of the United States: Colonial Times to 1957* (Washington, D.C.: Government Printing Office, 1960).

———, *Negro Population 1790–1915* (Washington, D.C.: Government Printing Office, 1918).

Viets, Henry R., *A Brief History of Medicine in Massachusetts* (Boston: Houghton Mifflin Co., 1930).

Wade, Richard C., *The Urban Frontier: The Rise of Western Cities, 1790–1830* (Cambridge: Harvard University Press, 1959).

Webb, Sidney and Beatrice, *English Poor Law History: Part I. The Old Poor Law* (London: Longmans Green & Co., 1927).

Weber, Adna F., *The Growth of Cities in the Nineteenth Century* (New York: The Macmillan Co., 1899).

Wiebe, Robert H., *The Search for Order, 1877–1920* (New York: Hill and Wang, 1967).

Wilson, Helen, *The Treatment of the Misdemeanant in Indiana 1816–1936* (Chicago: University of Chicago Press, 1938).

Wisner, Elizabeth, *Public Welfare Administration in Louisiana* (Chicago: University of Chicago Press, 1930).

———, *Social Welfare in the South: From Colonial Times to World War I* (Baton Rouge: Louisiana State University Press, 1970).

Zilboorg, Gregory, *A History of Medical Psychology* (New York: (W. W. Norton & Co., Inc., 1941).

C. Articles

Adams, Evelyn C., "The Growing Concept of Social Responsibility Illustrated by a Study of the State's Care of the Insane in Indiana," *Indiana Magazine of History*, XXXII (March, 1936), 1–22.

Allen, Phyllis, "Etiological Theory in America Prior to the Civil War," *Journal of the History of Medicine and Allied Sciences*, II (Autumn, 1947), 489–520.

Bockoven, J. Sanbourne, "Moral Treatment in American Psychiatry," *Journal of Nervous and Mental Disease*, CXXIV (August–September, 1956), 167–194, 292–321.

Bremner, Robert H., "The Impact of the Civil War on Philanthropy and Social Welfare," *Civil War History*, XII (December, 1966), 293–303.

Brenner, M. Harvey, "Economic Change and Mental Hospitalization: New York State, 1910–1960," *Social Psychiatry*, II (November, 1967), 180–188.

———, "Patterns of Psychiatric Hospitalization among Different Socioeconomic Groups in Response to Economic Stress," *Journal of Nervous and Mental Disease*, CXLVIII (January, 1969), 31–38.

———, Mandell, Wallace, Blackman, Sheldon, and Silberstein, Richard M., "Economic Conditions and Mental Hospitalization for Functional Psychosis," *Journal of Nervous and Mental Disease*, CXLV (November, 1967), 371–384.

Carlson, Eric T., and Dain, Norman, "The Psychotherapy That Was Moral Treatment," *American Journal of Psychiatry*, CXVII (December, 1960), 519–524.

Cochrane, Hortense S., "Early Treatment of the Mentally Ill in Georgia," *Georgia Historical Quarterly*, XXXII (June, 1948), 105–118.

Craig, Oscar, et al., "History of State Boards," in National Conference of Charities and Correction, *Proceedings*, XX (1893), 33–51.

Dain, Norman, "Social Class and Psychological Medicine in the United States, 1789–1824," *Bulletin of the History of Medicine*, XXXIII (September–October, 1959), 454–465.

———, and Carlson, Eric T., "Milieu Therapy in the Nineteenth Century: Patient Care at the Friends' Asylum, Frankford, Pennsylvania, 1817–1861," *Journal of Nervous and Mental Disease*, CXXXI (October, 1960), 277–290.

Davis, David Brion, "Some Themes of Counter-Subversion: An Analysis of Anti-Masonic, Anti-Catholic, and Anti-Mormon Literature," *Mississippi Valley Historical Review*, XLVII (September, 1960), 205–224.

Deutsch, Albert, "The First U.S. Census of the Insane (1840) and Its Use as Pro-Slavery Propaganda," *Bulletin of the History of Medicine*, XV (May, 1944), 469–482.

———, "The Sick Poor in Colonial Times," *American Historical Review*, XLVI (April, 1941), 560–579.

Goodman, Paul, "Ethics and Enterprise: The Values of a Boston Elite, 1800–1860," *American Quarterly*, XVIII (Fall, 1966), 437–451.

Hathway, Marion, "Dorothea Dix and Social Reform in Western Pennsylvania, 1845–1875," *Western Pennsylvania Historical Magazine*, XVII (December, 1934), 247–258.

Heale, M. J., "Humanitarianism in the Early Republic: The Moral Reformers of New York, 1776–1825," *Journal of American Studies*, II (October, 1968), 161–175.

Higham, John, "Another Look at Nativism," *Catholic Historical Review*, XLIV (July, 1958), 147–158.

"Historical. Longview Asylum," in Longview Asylum, *AR*, XXXIII (1892), 59–69.

"Historical Sketch of the First Hospital in Maryland for the Insane," in Maryland Lunacy Commission, *AR*, XXIV (1909), 45–54.

Jones, Kathleen, "Moral Management and the Therapeutic Community," in Society for the Social History of Medicine, *Bulletin No. 5* (October, 1971), 6–10 (mimeographed).

Klebaner, Benjamin J., "Employment of Paupers at Philadelphia's Almshouse before 1861," *Pennsylvania History*, XXIV (April, 1957), 137–147.

———, "The Home Relief Controversy in Philadelphia, 1782–1861," *Pennsylvania Magazine of History and Biography*, LXXVIII (October, 1954), 413–423.

———, "Pauper Auctions: The 'New England Method' of Public Poor Relief," *Essex Institute Historical Collections*, XCI (July, 1955), 195–210.

———, "Poverty and Its Relief in American Thought, 1815–61," *Social Service Review*, XXXVIII (December, 1964), 382–399.

———, "Public Poor Relief in Charleston, 1800–1860," *South Carolina Historical Magazine*, LV (October, 1954), 210–220.

————, "Some Aspects of North Carolina Public Poor Relief, 1700–1860," *North Carolina Historical Review*, XXXI (October, 1954), 479–492.

Lewis, Temple B., "The Michigan Board of Corrections and Charities," *Michigan History*, XXXVI (September, 1952), 279–286.

McCamic, Charles, "Administration of Poor Relief in the Virginias," *West Virginia History*, I (April, 1940), 171–191.

McClure, A. W., "The State Hospital at Mt. Pleasant," *Bulletin of Iowa Institutions*, III (1901), 305–316.

McCulloch, Margaret C., "Founding the North Carolina Asylum for the Insane," *North Carolina Historical Review*, XIII (July, 1936), 185–201.

Mackey, Howard, "The Operation of the English Old Poor Law in Colonial Virginia," *Virginia Magazine of History and Biography*, LXXIII (January, 1965), 29–40.

————, "Social Welfare in Colonial Virginia: The Importance of the English Old Poor Law," *Historical Magazine of the Protestant Episcopal Church*, XXXVI (December, 1967), 357–382.

Parkhurst, Eleanor, "Poor Relief in a Massachusetts Village in the Eighteenth Century," *Social Service Review*, XI (September, 1937), 446–464.

Pendleton, O. A., "Poor Relief in Philadelphia, 1790–1840," *Pennsylvania Magazine of History and Biography*, LXX (April, 1946), 161–172.

Powell, T. O., "A Sketch of Psychiatry in the Southern States," in American Medico-Psychological Association, *Proceedings*, LIII (1897), 74–131.

Riese, Walther, "The Impact of Nineteenth-Century Thought on Psychiatry," *International Record of Medicine*, CLXXIII (January, 1960), 7–19.

Rosen, George, "The Hospital: Historical Sociology of a Community Institution," in *The Hospital in Modern Society*, ed. by Eliot Freidson (New York: The Free Press, 1963), 1–36.

————, "The Philosophy of Ideology and the Emergence of Modern Medicine in France," *Bulletin of the History of Medicine*, XX (July, 1946), 328–339.

————, "Political Order and Human Health in Jeffersonian Thought," *Bulletin of the History of Medicine*, XXVI (January–February, 1952), 32–44.

————, "Problems in the Application of Statistical Analysis to Questions of Health: 1700–1880," *Bulletin of the History of Medicine*, XXIX (January–February, 1955), 27–45.

———, "Social Stress and Mental Disease from the Eighteenth Century to the Present: Some Origins of Social Psychiatry," *Milbank Memorial Fund Quarterly*, XXXVII (January, 1959), 5–32.

Sparling, Samuel E., "State Boards of Control with Special Reference to the Experience of Wisconsin," in American Academy of Political and Social Science, *Annals*, XVII (January, 1901), 74–91.

Teeters, Negley K., "The Early Days of the Philadelphia House of Refuge," *Pennsylvania History*, XXVII (April, 1960), 165–187.

Thompson, E. Bruce, "Reforms in the Care of the Insane in Tennessee, 1830–1850," *Tennessee Historical Quarterly*, III (December, 1944), 319–334.

Viets, Henry, "Some Features of the History of Medicine in Massachusetts during the Colonial Period (1620–1770)," *Isis*, XXIII (September, 1935), 389–405.

Wisner, Elizabeth, "The Puritan Background of the New England Poor Laws," *Social Service Review*, XIX (September, 1945), 381–390.

Woods, Evelyn A., and Carlson, Eric T., "The Psychiatry of Philippe Pinel," *Bulletin of the History of Medicine*, XXXV (January–February, 1961), 14–25.

Index